The Nature
of Expertise

The Nature of Expertise

MICHELENE T.H. CHI
University of Pittsburgh

ROBERT GLASER
University of Pittsburgh

M.J. FARR
Office of Naval Research

LEA

LAWRENCE ERLBAUM ASSOCIATES, PUBLISHERS
1988   Hillsdale, New Jersey   Hove and London

Lawrence Erlbaum Associates, Inc., Publishers
365 Broadway
Hillsdale, New Jersey 07642

Library of Congress Cataloging-in-Publication Data

The nature of expertise.

   Bibliography: p.
   Includes index.
   1. Performance — Psychological aspects — Congresses.
2. Apperception — Congresses.   3. Human information
processing — Congresses.   I. Chi, Michelene T. H.
II. Glaser, Robert, 1921ffl   .   III. Farr, Marshall J.
BF323.E2N37   1988   153   87ffl33071
ISBN 0-89859-711-0

Printed in the United States of America
10   9   8   7   6   5   4   3

In loving remembrance of
William G. Chase
1940–1983

Contents

In Memoriam

This volume is a tribute to the late William G. Chase. He died suddenly and unexpectedly three weeks after the conference from which the majority of the chapters in this volume are drawn. Although his career was short (15 years), the impact of his work is profound. In that short span he made several major contributions to the field of psychology. His dissertation, *Parameters of Visual and Memory Search*, would have been his first major piece of work. It had earned recognition from the American Institute of Research Creative Talents Award Program, but Bill's high standard of excellence prevented him from publishing it. He felt that the dissertation work was not deserving of publication because it did not answer to his satisfaction the question he asked.

Bill's subsequent contributions are well known. They consist of his work with Herbert Clark on the mental operations involved in the comparison of sentences and pictures (Chase & Clark, 1972); the work with Herbert Simon on the skills underlying chess playing (Chase & Simon, 1973); and the work with Anders Ericsson on skilled memory (Chase & Ericsson, 1981, 1982). In fact, his research on the nature of expertise is a primary source which shapes our current understanding. Numerous citations across the chapters in this volume describe his work, and attest to the significance and lasting contribution of his research. At the time of his death, he was on the verge of completing the most comprehensive theory of skilled memory to date, based on the extensive evidence he collected on the digit-span task. He was also pursuing the application of his theory to other domains, such as mental calculation (see Staszewski, this volume) and the memory of waiters (see Ericsson & Polson, this volume). Bill also began working on the

fascinating new topic of cognitive maps (see Chase & Chi, 1981). Preliminary findings on the spatial representation of taxi drivers have been published (see Chase, 1983), but unfortunately the voluminous amount of data
in the form of video tapes remain unanalyzed.

Bill had a unique research style: He used methodologically creative and
rigorous ways to uncover mental processes and then developed stringent
theories to explain and test his findings. His knack for reducing a complex
task to a simple and elegant empirical investigation inspired all of us who
were his students and colleagues.

Bill also became a superb teacher. His first teaching experience in the
fall of 1968, at Carnegie–Mellon University, a course on Human Learning and Complex Behavior, presented him as a shy, soft-spoken, and in-
comprehensible lecturer. He would often mutter to the blackboard rather
than to the students, and would present what seemed to the students to be
a perpetual sequence of experimental evidence that was too complicated
to understand. A decade later, his teaching became so enlightening that
students would applaud him in a standing ovation at the last lectures of
his classes.

Bill was a man of integrity. He spoke of what he believed to be right,
and ignored any consequences that might have been damaging to himself.
He was unpretentious and down-to-earth. Yet he had a fierce but good-
natured competitiveness that seemed contradictory to his personality. This
was manifested both in the way he conducted his research and the way he
liked to excel in other accomplishments. For example, he took up badmin-
ton in his late thirties. He pursued it with such tenacity that within five
years he won the championship for Pittsburgh Men's Singles. Everyone —
students, colleagues, and friends — loved Bill. They loved him for his modes-
ty, his gentleness, his sense of humor, and his accessibility. He was always
available to listen to people's research problems as well as their personal
problems, and offered genuine help, understanding, and suggestions.

Those of us who had the privilege of knowing Bill know how fortunate
we are in having met such a special person. He will be missed by his family, friends, and colleagues for many years to come.

Micki Chi

REFERENCES

Chase, W. G. (1983). Spatial representations of taxi drivers. In D. R. Rogers & J. A. Sloboda
    (Eds.), *The acquisition of symbolic skills* (pp. 391–411). New York: Plenum Press.
Chase, W. G., & Chi, M. T. H. (1981). Cognitive skill: Implications for spatial skill in large-
    scale environments. In J. Harvey (Ed.), *Cognition, social behavior, and the environment*
    (pp. 111–136). Hillsdale, NJ: Lawrence Erlbaum Associates.

Chase, W. G., & Clark, H. H. (1972). Mental operations in the comparison of sentences and pictures. In L. W. Gregg (Ed.), *Cognition in learning and memory* (pp. 205–252). New York: Wiley.

Chase, W. G., & Ericsson, K. A. (1982). Skill and working memory. In G. Bower (Ed.), *The psychology of learning and motivation: Vol. 16* (pp. 2–58). New York: Academic Press.

Chase, W. G., & Ericsson, K. A. (1981). Skilled memory. In J. R. Anderson (Ed.), *Cognitive skills and their acquisition* (pp. 141–189). Hillsdale, NJ: Lawrence Erlbaum Associates.

Chase, W. G., & Simon, H. A. (1973). Perception in chess. *Cognitive Psychology, 4*, 55–81.

Overview

Robert Glaser
Michelene T. H. Chi
University of Pittsburgh

Expertise became an intriguing subject for investigation as a result of work in the mid- to late sixties, largely due to developments in artificial intelligence (AI) and cognitive psychology. Research in AI and attempts to simulate human capabilities had failed to construct programs that could outperform humans, even though computers were by then equipped with powerful search heuristics and essentially limitless search capabilities. Even in programs using selective search, such as Greenblatt's (Greenblatt, Eastlake, & Crocker, 1967) chess program, the best "plausible" move was still selected on the basis of an extensive evaluation, whereas human experts do not engage in particularly extensive searches or elaborate analyses, as shown by findings in cognitive psychology. Investigations of chess playing, for example, the early work of deGroot (1966) and the later extended work of Chase and Simon (1973), demonstrated that what distinguishes strong from weak players are their abilities to correctly reproduce large patterns of chess positions after a few seconds of viewing, rather than their searching more deeply or broadly than weaker players. Clearly, specialized structures of knowledge were strongly implicated, but the nature of this knowledge and of its interactions with general heuristic processes required further analysis.

Newell and Simon (1972) described the chess master's "perceptual" ability as follows:

> Clusters of related pieces in a position are recognized as familiar constellations; hence, each cluster is stored as a single symbol. Less skilled players have to describe the board as a larger number of simpler chunks — hence cannot

hold all of the information required to reproduce the board in short-term memory. When the same number of pieces is arranged on the board at random, few of the resulting configurations are familiar even to grandmasters. They then need more symbols to describe the position that can be held simultaneously in short-term memory, hence, they perform as poorly as weaker players. (p. 781)

By using the concept of chunks to explain the chess master's pattern recognition superiority, it became necessary to identify experimentally the structure and size of chunks in the knowledge base, because a chunk appeared to be a defining unit of knowledge structure. Hence, early in its history, the study of expertise provided evidence of a knowledge-competence dimension as a primary focus.

In AI research, it became widely acknowledged that the creation of intelligent programs did not simply require the identification of domain-independent heuristics to guide search through a problem space; rather, that the search processes must engage a highly organized structure of specific knowledge for problem solving in complex knowledge domains. This shift in AI was characterized by Minsky and Papert (1974) as a change from a power-based strategy for achieving intelligence to a knowledge-based one. They wrote:

> The *Power* [italics added] strategy seeks a generalized increase in computational power. It may look toward new kinds of computers ("parallel" or "fuzzy" or "associative" or whatever) or it may look toward extensions of deductive generality, or information retrieval, or search algorithms. . . . In each case, the improvement sought is intended to be "uniform" — independent of the particular data base. The *Knowledge* strategy sees progress as coming from better ways to express, recognize, and use diverse and particular forms of knowledge. (p. 59)

This point of view has since been reiterated in the textbooks and handbooks on building expert systems (e.g., Hayes-Roth, Waterman, & Lenat, 1983). These texts point out that the principal developments in AI fostered the current emphasis on knowledge-based expert systems and the related field of knowledge engineering. Machines that lack knowledge can perform only intellectually trivial tasks. Those that embody knowledge and apply it can approximate the performance of human experts. As a consequence, expert-system building has concentrated on the knowledge that underlies human expertise and given less emphasis to the significance of domain-independent problem-solving heuristics.

Thus, the seeds of the study of the characteristics of highly competent expert performance were sown in the fertile ground of Newell and Simon's 1972 book, *Human Problem Solving*, although the topic *expertise* was not listed. In the ensuing years, the need for research in expertise has been recognized, and much research in cognitive psychology has been devoted to this topic.[1] In the following pages, we briefly summarize some key characteristics of experts' performances that this research has uncovered. These findings are robust and generalizable across the various domains that have been studied (Glaser, 1988). We also highlight other relevant findings, and speculate briefly on the nature of the organization of the knowledge base that generates each characteristic.

1. Experts Excel Mainly in Their Own Domains.   There is little evidence that a person highly skilled in one domain can transfer the skill to another. As Minsky and Papert (1974) noted: "A very intelligent person might be that way because of specific local features of his knowledge-organizing knowledge rather than because of global qualities of his 'thinking' "(p. 59). Evidence for such a conclusion can be drawn from the work of Voss and Post (this volume) on problem solving in political science. In that work, nondomain experts (chemists) solved political science problems much like novices, describing the causes for the problem at a very concrete and specific level, whereas domain experts described more abstract causal categories.

The obvious reason for the excellence of experts is that they have a good deal of domain knowledge. This is easily demonstrated; for example, in medical diagnosis, expert physicians have more differentiations of common diseases into disease variants (Johnson et al., 1981). Likewise, in examining taxi drivers' knowledge of routes, Chase (1983) found that expert drivers can generate a far greater number of secondary routes (i.e., lesser known streets) than novice drivers.

2. Experts Perceive Large Meaningful Patterns in Their Domain.   As mentioned, this is apparent in chess, where it is well known that chess masters excel in their recall of the clusters of pieces that they see. This perceptual superiority has been replicated in several other domains, such as in the game of GO (Reitman, 1976), in reading circuit diagrams (Egan & Schwartz, 1979), in reading architectural plans (Akin, 1980), and in interpreting x-ray plates (Lesgold et al., this volume). It should be pointed out, however, that this ability to see meaningful patterns does not reflect a generally superior perceptual ability; rather, it reflects an organization of the knowledge base. Programmers, for example, can recall key programming language words in meaningful clusters (McKeithen, Reitman, Reuter, & Hirtle, 1981), and expert programmers can also recognize and recall familiar subroutines (see Soloway, Adelson, & Ehrlich, this volume).

---

[1]The topic of expertise first appears in major textbooks in cognitive psychology in 1985, in John Anderson's second edition of *Cognitive Psychology and Its Implications.*

3. Experts are Fast; They Are Faster than Novices at Performing the Skills of Their Domain, and They Quickly Solve Problems with Little Error. An easy way to observe the skill of master chess players is to watch them play "lightning chess," where they have only a few seconds to decide on a move. Although studies in the literature actually find experts slower than novices in the initial phases of problem solving, experts solve problems faster overall.

There are at least two ways to explain experts' speed. For simple tasks, such as typing, the speed that experts have acquired comes with many hours of practice, which makes the skill more automatic and frees up memory capacity for processing other aspects of the task (see Gentner, this volume). Thus, they can be fast because they are actually faster at the skill itself or because they have more capacity to perform the total task. The expert typists in Gentner's study were fast because their fingers moved quickly (there were more overlapping movements), as well as because they could free up resources to perform related tasks such as typing degraded pseudowords, whereas novices had few resources available for attending to pseudowords.

A further possible explanation for experts' speed in solving problems rests on the idea emphasized earlier that experts can often arrive at a solution without conducting extensive search. The patterns that chess experts see on the board suggest reasonable moves directly, presumably because, through many hours of playing, they have stored straightforward condition-action rules in which a specific pattern (the condition) will trigger a stereotypic sequence of moves. Cab drivers, for instance, will recognize a shorter route while traveling to their destination, even though they may not have generated this shorter route in the laboratory (Chase, 1983).

4. Experts Have Superior Short-Term and Long-Term Memory. With recently presented materials, experts' recall seems to exceed the limits of short-term memory. This is not because their short-term memory is larger than other humans', but because the automaticity of many portions of their skills frees up resources for greater storage. Experts seem to excel in long-term recall as well. For example, in chess, it is not uncommon for chess masters to recognize plays from certain well-known games.

Chase and Ericsson's (1982) study demonstrated experts' superiority in both short-term and long-term recall. They found that their trained memory expert could remember more than 80 digits in a short-term memory serial recall task. They also found, however, that he could recognize over 80–90% of the digit groups that had been presented to him for recall a week earlier.

5. Experts See and Represent a Problem in Their Domain at a Deeper (More Principled) Level than Novices; Novices Tend to Represent a Problem at a Superficial Level. An easy and robust way to demonstrate this is to ask experts and novices to sort problems and analyze the nature of their groupings. Using physics problems, Chi, Feltovich, and Glaser (1981) found that experts used principles of mechanics to organize categories, whereas novices built their problem categories around literal objects stated in the problem description. Similar results have been found in the domain of programming (Weiser & Shertz, 1983); when expert and novice programmers were asked to sort programming problems, the experts sorted them according to solution algorithms, whereas the novices sorted them according to areas of application (e.g., whether the program was supposed to create a list of employees' salaries or whether it was supposed to keep a file of current user identifications). These results indicate that both experts and novices have conceptual categories, but that the experts' categories are semantically or principle-based, whereas the categories of the novices are syntactically or surface-feature oriented.

6. Experts Spend a Great Deal of Time Analyzing a Problem Qualitatively. Protocols show that, at the beginning of a problem-solving episode, experts typically try to "understand" a problem, whereas novices plunge immediately into attempting to apply equations and to solve for an unknown. What do the experts do when they qualitatively analyze a problem? Basically they build a mental representation from which they can infer relations that can define the situation, and they add constraints to the problem. Paige and Simon's (1966) well-known example illustrates this by asking students to solve simple algebra word problems, such as: A board was sawed into two pieces. One piece was two thirds as long as the whole board and was exceeded in length by the second piece by four feet. How long was the board before it was cut? Paige and Simon found that some students immediately applied equations, which then resulted in their coming up with a negative length; others, however, remarked that the problem was meaningless because one cannot have a board with a negative length. One can conclude that those students who paused had formed a mental model of the situation and made some inferences about the relation between the boards.

The utility of qualitative analysis for adding constraints to a problem can be seen most clearly in ill-defined problems. Voss and Post (this volume) presented economic problems, such as: Imagine you are the Minister of Agriculture for the Soviet Union. Crop productivity has been too low for the past several years. What would you do to increase crop production? About 24% of the experts' solution protocols (those of political scientists specializing in the Soviet Union) were elaborations on the initial state of the problem, as opposed to 1% of the novices' protocols. By elaborating the initial state, the experts identified possible constraints, such as Soviet ideology and the amount of arable land. (Adding constraints, in effect, reduced the search space. For example, introducing the constraint of the amount of arable land eliminated the solution of increasing planting, and considering the constraint of the Soviet ideology precluded the solution of fostering private competition — a capitalistic solution.) Other examples of adding constraints can be seen in the work of Lawrence (this volume) on magistrates' decision-making processes.

7. Experts Have Strong Self-Monitoring Skills.   Experts seem to be more aware than novices of when they make errors, why they fail to comprehend, and when they need to check their solutions. For example, the expert physics-problem solver in Simon and Simon's study (1978) would often check his answer, and the expert physics-problem solver in Larkin's study (1983) would often abandon solution attempts before carrying out the mathematical details. Experts' self-knowledge is also manifested in their being more accurate than novices in judging the difficulty of a physics problem (Chi, Glaser, & Rees, 1982). Expert chess players are more accurate than novice players at predicting how many times they will need to see a given board position before they can reproduce it correctly (Chi, 1978). Experts ask more questions, particularly when the texts from which they have to learn are difficult (Miyake & Norman, 1979). Novice learners, on the other hand, ask more questions on the easier materials.

We can argue that, in each of the above examples, the superior monitoring skills and self-knowledge of experts reflect their greater domain knowledge as well as a different representation of that knowledge. We illustrate this dependence on domain knowledge with an example from our own work on physics. As stated, we found that expert physicists were more accurate than novices in predicting which physics problems will prove more difficult to solve. If we probe further and look at the bases on which they made such judgments, we see that they relied on the same knowledge of principles in this task as they used to sort problems into categories. Although about a third of both experts' and novices' decisions about problem difficulties were based on the problems' characteristics (such as "the problem is simplified because it is frictionless"), another third of the experts' judgments were based on the underlying physics principle governing the solution (such as "it's a straightforward application of Newton's second Law"). Only 9% of the novices' judgments were based on the underlying principle. In addition, novices used nonproblem related characteristics (such as, "I've never done problems like this before") about 18% of the time as compared to 7% for the experts (Chi, 1987). The ability of experts to predict accurately which problems were difficult and which were easy enabled them to monitor accurately how they should allocate their time for solving problems. Thus, the monitoring skills of experts appear to reflect their greater underlying knowledge of the domain, which allowed them to predict problem difficulty on the basis of the physics principles rather than less relevant surface features.

Summary

The short history of research on expertise might be written as follows: Information-processing studies of problem solving in the 1960s and 1970s and early work in AI and expert systems accepted a tradition of concentrating primarily on basic information-processing capabilities that humans employ when they behave more and less intelligently in situations in which they lack any specialized knowledge and skill. The pioneering work of Newell and Simon and others richly described these general heuristic processes, but they also offered crucial beginning insight on the learning and thinking of experts, processes that require a rich structure of domain-specific knowledge. In recent years, research has examined knowledge-rich tasks — tasks that require hundreds and thousands of hours of learning and experience. These studies of expertise, together with theories of competent performance and attempts at the design of expert systems, have sharpened this focus by contrasting novice and expert performances. These investigations into knowledge-rich domains show strong interactions between structures of knowledge and processes of reasoning and problem solving. The results force us to think about high levels of competence in terms of the interplay between knowledge structure and processing abilities. They illuminate the set of critical differences highlighted in this overview between individuals who display more and less ability in particular domains of knowledge and skill. We interpret these differences as primarily reflecting the expert's possession of an organized body of conceptual and procedural knowledge that can be readily accessed and used with superior monitoring and self-regulation skills.

Now research needs to go beyond this stage of analysis. We must better understand the properties of domain structure and integrated knowledge; the mechanisms of problem-space definition with minimal search through rapid pattern recognition; and the processes involved in redefining the space of ill-structured and difficult problems. To do so, we should investigate the forms of reasoning and problem-solving strategies that structured knowledge facilitates. We also need to understand how expertise is acquired, how it can be taught, and how beginning learners can be presented with appropriate experience. The papers in this volume consider these themes and represent the type of research that is presently being carried out that investigates both human and artificial expertise.

The Contents of This Volume

The majority of the chapters in this volume were presented at a conference held at the Learning Research and Development Center at the University of Pittsburgh, sponsored by the Personnel and Training Research Program,

Office of Naval Research. The conference focused on four areas: practical skills, programming skills, medical diagnosis, and ill-defined problems. In each domain, we selected work that is representative and we sought a diversity of approaches.

Michael I. Posner, in his introduction to this volume, briefly reviews some key readings on expertise. He indicates that the impressive coding and chunking feats of experts are also present more generally in people who have been exposed to a sufficiently large number of experiences to allow performance to become truly automated, and he emphasizes the importance of memory representation for understanding expert performance. He speculates on the role of individual differences in learning abilities that could influence the development of expertise and suggests that the problem of producing an expert may be, to a large extent, that of creating and maintaining the motivation for the long training that is necessary.

Practical Skills

The chapters in the section on practical skills discuss expertise in three areas: typing, memorizing restaurant orders, and mental calculation. Gentner (Expertise in Typewriting) is impressed with the resiliency of expertise in motor skills, and minutely examines the details of the typist's skill. He considers an overlapped processing model of skilled performance that suggests critical roles for parallel mental processes that underlie the typing of successive letters, and the importance of the substantial amount of unused cognitive resources that the automated performance of experts makes available for planning, handling texts that are difficult to read, concurrent phone conversations, and easy response to varied contextual and task demands.

As another example of a practical skill, Ericsson and Polson (A Cognitive Analysis of Exceptional Memory for Restaurant Orders) analyzed the exceptional memory of a headwaiter who was able to remember dinner orders from over 20 people at different tables without extensive aids. Their theoretical framework is the model of skilled memory proposed by Chase and Ericsson (1982). According to this framework, skilled memory requires efficient encoding of presented information using existing semantic knowledge and patterns; the stored information is then rapidly accessed through retrieval cues associated with the encoding during initial storage. In the work reported in this chapter, naive subjects used very different encoding processes that could be described by standard models for free recall, developed to describe memory for unrelated material in laboratory tasks. Of significant interest was the ability of skilled subjects to generalize their skills to other kinds of information. This latter unusual finding suggests the possibility of the existence of transferrable acquired general cognitive processes that can improve memory in a range of situations.

Staszewski's chapter (Skilled Memory and Expert Calculation) examined the extent to which skills in mental calculation, as exercised by people who are proficient at it, are trainable to an average person. Through tracking the learning acquired by two subjects through training, Staszewski found that the principles of skilled memory adequately characterize the way in which mental calculation experts manage the heavy memory demands that arise in mental arithmetic. However, expert-level performance in mental calculation also requires that experts devise strategies to use content information from long-term memory efficiently. Thus, although a mental calculation task does not have the explicit goal of information retention for its own sake, successful performance in that task does require access to more information than short-term memory can hold. The memory skill that underlies a critical component of mental calculation is the proficiency with which individuals can learn to represent and maintain large amounts of task-related information in an easily accessible state — in effect, expand their working memory capacity.

Programming

Three different tasks are examined in the section on programming: understanding, learning, and software design. Soloway, Adelson, and Ehrlich (Knowledge and Processes in the Comprehension of Computer Programs) report on efforts to investigate the knowledge and processing strategies programmers employ in attempting to understand computer programs. They ask: What is it that expert programmers know that novice programmers do not? They focus on two types of knowledge: The first type, programming plans, consists of program fragments that represent stereotypic action sequences; and the second type, rules of programming discourse, consists of rules that specify conventions in programming. These two types of knowledge correspond to the notion of schema and to chunks or patterns that represent functional units in a domain of knowledge. Modeling an experiment after the Chase and Simon chess study, Soloway and his colleagues presented both plan-like programs that conformed to programming conventions and runnable unplan-like programs to experts and novices. The data replicated the chess experiments in that the performance of advanced programmers was reduced to that of novices on the unplan-like material. This finding and others are considered with respect to the development of a measure of program complexity, a model of the processes used in reading and writing programs, and program design.

Anderson, Pirolli, and Farrell (Learning to Program Recursive Functions) discuss work that investigates learning to write recursive functions in LISP. As a framework for their discussion, they describe a model of the programming behavior of an expert. They explain why recursive programming is difficult and propose how it is learned. It appears that recursive programming is difficult because it is a highly unfamiliar mental activity and because it depends on acquiring a great deal of knowledge about specific program patterns. In the instructional context provided, students first studied worked-out examples and then solved similar problems. It was found that students solved problems by mapping analogically the solution of examples to their current problem. They generalized their solutions to a problem by developing new problem-solving operators that could be applied to another problem. Protocols and simulations are presented to give evidence for the conclusions that were made about learning.

Adelson and Soloway (A Model of Software Design) report an analysis of the problem-solving skills of expert software designers and present a model of the process of software design. Their model unites a number of recurrent behaviors found in protocol analysis. These behaviors include the use of mental models that begin as abstract versions of the task and become more concrete as the design progresses, as well as "balanced development" in which the modules or elements of design are defined at the same level of detail. In addition, the model accommodates the finding that expert designers make *memory notes* of constraints, partial solutions, or potential inconsistencies, which eventually they will need to handle. The experts also repeatedly conducted mental simulation runs of partially completed designs. Adelson and Soloway comment on the findings by raising such questions as: Why is balanced development found so frequently in expert behavior? What role does it play and how is it acquired? They see as an unresolved major issue the specification of mechanisms that facilitate the interactions between the domain-independent design model they propose and domain-specific knowledge in particular applications.

Ill-Defined Problems

Three chapters in this section focus on ill-defined problems from very different perspectives. Johnson (Expertise and Decision Under Uncertainty: Performance and Process) considers expertise in an ill-defined problem from the point of view of research in behavioral decision theory. In contrast to the task domains studied in the previous chapters, the tasks he considers require decision under uncertainty, such as when some uncontrolled intervening event occurs between the choice and the outcome. In these tasks, experts are not consistently better than novices, and linear regression models are more accurate than experts most of the time. Two different domains are studied here — the evaluation of applicants for medical internships and the prediction of changes in stock prices. In these tasks, no single or optimally correct procedure exists, only rules that are relatively more accurate under varying circumstances. In general, in these tasks, experts focus on fewer cues than novices, and they use different information and different patterns of search that take advantage of usual, opportunistic information. In his discussion, Johnson considers why expert performance may be inferior to the predictions made by simple linear models.

Lawrence (Expertise on the Bench: Modeling Magistrates' Judicial Decision-Making) describes studies of the judicial decisions of magistrates on the bench. She points out that legal judging is a problem-solving domain where problems are always ill-structured, solutions are inconclusive, and important features of the problem space become apparent from different sources at different times only after initial processing has begun. She describes a technique for analyzing verbal protocols by identifying information selection propositions connected to consequent inferences and decisions in an *if–then condition–action* form. Her model of the judging process involves the magistrates' (a) frames of reference, which include penal philosophies, sentencing objectives, and views of the severity of particular crimes; and (b) external, environmental constraints, such as interpretation of statutory forces, laws of evidence, parliamentary ranges of penalties, and case load. According to her findings, the experts' performance was different from the novices' in terms of the amount and kind of information and goals that influenced the inferences made, based on case details. Although novices knew and responded to ritualized evidence-gathering procedures, they seemed to work with single details, as compared with the more patterned approach of experts. These patterns enabled experts to reduce their work loads.

Voss and Post (On the Solving of Ill-Structured Problems) extend the analysis of previous accounts of the nature of ill-structured problems and comment on Johnson's and Lawrence's work and their own research on problems in social science. Ill-structured problems are described as problems in which there is little consensus regarding the appropriate solutions; they include open constraints that are resolved in the course of solution; and as solution proceeds they may become at some point well-defined. As experts proceed, structure is obtained by decomposing the ill-structured problem into a set of well-structured problems which are then solved. To be able to do this, it is asserted here, the expert must have a relatively larger amount of information in memory so that they can utilize appropriate components of knowledge to organize the problem solution. In their own work on political science problems, such as domestic policy in a foreign country, Voss and Post contrast specialists and novices. Experts develop a problem representation by using the general strategy of decomposition to delineate major factors causing the problem; these factors then are used to convert the problem into one that can be solved. In utilizing this general strategy, experts draw on their knowledge to state a history of previous attempts at solution, and to build a case by enumerating reasons why their solution might work.

Medical Diagnosis

Finally, the chapters on medical diagnosis introduce three very distinct analyses and approaches. Groen and Patel (Relationship Between Comprehension and The Reasoning in Medical Expertise) approach the study of diagnostic expertise in the context of research on comprehension. Theories of comprehension, they claim, have been primarily concerned with structural issues and propositional analyses, whereas theories in the area of problem-solving have been concerned with the explication of processes. The connection between the two needs to be considered in the study of expertise. Groen and Patel conducted a series of studies that used propositional analysis of the recall of textually presented clinical cases to assess differences between experts and novices. Their results indicate that experts make inferences from relevant information, whereas novices infer from less relevant material. With texts scrambled on the basis of propositional structure, the differences between experts and novices disappeared; experts recalled as much irrelevant material as novices. A major conclusion is that the selectivity of experts with respect to relevant information can be explained by the development of a problem representation that filters out irrelevant information.

Lesgold, Rubinson, Feltovich, Glaser, Klopfer, and Wang (Expertise in a Complex Skill: Diagnosing X-ray Pictures) report on expertise in radiological diagnosis, the interpretation of x-ray pictures, which is a skill that involves the integration of knowledge from physiology, anatomy, medical theories of disease, and the projective geometry of radiography. In a series of studies, they observed radiologists in their offices and then moved to more controlled experiments using radiologists with 10 years of experience and residents with 1 to 4 years of training. Their quantitative analysis involved both *findings* — in particular, identification of specific properties of the film or patient, and *relationships* — especially the reasoning paths between findings. As contrasted with the residents, the experienced radiologists showed a greater number of findings, more clustered findings, and larger reasoning chains. Qualitative analysis of protocols led to a general account of the behavior of an expert radiologist. During the initial phase of building a mental representation, a schema entails a set of criteria it must satisfy before it can control viewing and diagnosis. The expert works efficiently toward the stage where an appropriate schema is in control. This schema then contains a set of procedures that allows a diagnosis to be made and confirmed. Novice performance involves incompleteness in each of these three aspects, and novices are less able to modify a schema in response to new information. Lesgold and his colleagues conclude with discussion of the course of acquisition of this complex skill.

Clancey (Acquiring, Representing, and Evaluating a Competence Model of Diagnostic Strategy) discusses NEOMYCIN, a computer program that models a physician's diagnostic reasoning in a limited area of medicine. The diagnostic procedure is represented in a well-structured way, separately from the domain knowledge it operates on. His general objectives are to articulate a design that will enable an expert system to acquire knowledge interactively from human experts, to explain reasoning to people seeking advice, and to teach students. His premise is that these applications, particularly explanation and teaching, necessitate closer adherence to human problem-solving methods and more explicit knowledge representation than systems that are not required to be comprehensible to people. The major section of the chapter considers (a) how the model is acquired — what a representation methodology is for replicating what people know and what they do; (b) a description of the flow of information in the diagnostic model — how, in the course of reasoning, knowledge is activated, problems are formulated, and hypotheses confirmed; and (c) evaluating the model — how well the model matches expert performance and reasoning and the detail of explanation to students. Clancey's chapter clearly describes his search for a design of a knowledge representation that can be used to model human diagnostic reasoning and human explanation capability. In general, he sees such a model as requiring relatively stereotypical patterns that encompass richly structured knowledge about possible solutions and problem features that greatly facilitate search and classification. In addition, the model requires *metacognition* (knowledge for organizing knowledge) that orients the problem solver toward constructing and refining an appropriate problem space.

The chapters in the book display the variety of domains and human performances to which the study of expertise has been carried. The different approaches employed show the influence of methodologies from cognitive psychology, artificial intelligence, and cognitive science in general. The chapters also make a case for increased attention to learning — to how expertise is acquired and to the conditions that enhance and limit the development of high levels of cognitive skill.

ACKNOWLEDGMENTS

Funding for the publication of this volume and the organization of the conference was provided by the Office of Naval Research, Psychological Sciences Division, Personnel and Training Research Program on Cognitive Processes. We greatly appreciate the help of Joyce Holl in typing and organizing all the manuscripts, Shoulamit Milch-Reich for preparing the subject index, and Anne Robin for editing and proofreading.

REFERENCES

Akin, O. (1980). *Models of architectural knowledge*. London: Pion.

Chase, W. G. (1983). Spatial representations of taxi drivers. In D. R. Rogers & J. H. Slobada (Eds.), *Acquisition of symbolic skills* (pp. 391–405). New York: Plenum.

Chase, W. G., & Ericsson, K. A. (1982). Skill and working memory. In G. Bower (Ed.), *The psychology of learning and motivation* (Vol. 16, pp. 2–58). New York: Academic Press.

Chase, W. G., & Simon, H. A. (1973). Perception in chess. *Cognitive Psychology, 4*, 55–81.

Chi, M. T. H. (1987). Representing knowledge and metaknowledge: Implications for interpreting metamemory research. In F. E. Weinert & R. H. Kluwe (Eds.). *Metacognition, motivation and understanding* (pp. 239–266). Hillsdale, NJ: Lawrence Erlbaum Associates.

Chi, M. T. H. (1978). Knowledge structures and memory development. In R. Siegler (Ed.), *Children's thinking: What develops?* (pp. 73–96). Hillsdale, NJ: Lawrence Erlbaum Associates.

Chi, M. T. H., Feltovich, P. J., & Glaser, R. (1981). Categorization and representation of physics problems by experts and novices. *Cognitive Science, 5*, 121–125.

Chi, M. T. H., Glaser, R., & Rees, E. (1982). Expertise in problem solving. In R. Sternberg (Ed.), *Advances in the psychology of human intelligence* (Vol. 1, pp. 17–76). Hillsdale, NJ: Lawrence Erlbaum Associates.

deGroot, A. (1966). Perception and memory versus thought: Some old ideas and recent findings. In B. Kleinmuntz (Ed.), *Problem solving* (pp. 19–50). New York: Wiley.

Egan, D. E., & Schwartz, B. J. (1979). Chunking in recall of symbolic drawings. *Memory and Cognition, 7*, 149–158.

Glaser, R. (1987). Thoughts on expertise. In C. Schooler & W. Schaie (Eds.), *Cognitive functioning and social structure over the life course* (pp. 81–94). Norwood, NJ: Ablex.

Greenblatt, R. D., Eastlake, D. E., & Crocker, S. D. (1967). The Greenblatt chess program. *Proceedings of the Fall Joint Computer Conference, 31*, 801–810.

Hayes-Roth, F., Waterman, D. A., & Lenat, D. P. (Eds.). (1983). *Building expert systems.* Reading, MA: Addison-Wesley.

Johnson, P. E., Duran, A. S., Hassebrock, F., Moller, J. H., Prietula, M., Feltovich, P. J., & Swanson, D. B. (1981). Expertise and error in diagnostic reasoning. *Cognitive Science, 5*, 135–283.

Larkin, J. H. (1983). The role of problem representation in physics. In D. Gentner & A. L. Stevens (Eds.), *Mental models* (pp. 75–100). Hillsdale, NJ: Lawrence Erlbaum Associates.

McKeithen, K. B., Reitman, J. S., Rueter, H. H., & Hirtle, S. C. (1981). Knowledge organization and skill differences in computer programmers. *Cognitive Psychology, 13*, 307–325.

Minsky, M., & Papert, S. (1974). *Artificial intelligence.* Condensed lectures, Oregon State System of Higher Education, Eugene.

Miyake, N., & Norman, D. A. (1979). *To ask a question one must know enough to know what is not known. Journal of Verbal Learning and Verbal Behavior, 18*, 357–364.

Newell, A., & Simon, H. A. (1972). *Human problem solving.* Englewood Cliffs, NJ: Prentice-Hall.

Paige, J. M., & Simon, H. A. (1966). Cognition processes in solving algebra word problems. In B. Kleinmuntz (Ed.), *Problem solving* (pp. 119–151). New York: Wiley.

Reitman, J. S. (1976). Skilled perception in GO: Deducing memory structures from interresponse times. *Cognitive Psychology, 8*, 336–356.

Simon, D. P., & Simon, H. A. (1978). Individual differences in solving physics problems. In R. Siegler (Ed.), *Children's thinking: What develops?* (pp. 325–348). Hillsdale, NJ: Lawrence Erlbaum Associates.

Weiser, M., & Shertz, J. (1983). Programming problem representation in novice and expert programmers. *Instructional Journal of Man-Machine Studies, 14*, 391–396.

Introduction:
What Is It to Be an Expert?

Michael I. Posner
University of Oregon

How do we identify a person as exceptional or gifted? One aspect is truly expert performance in some domain. An adult or child who composes exceptional music, runs extremely fast, or receives particularly high scores on academic achievement tests, may be said to be gifted or exceptional. Only in the last dozen years or so has experimental research in cognitive psychology and related disciplines begun to discover what is required to be expert in some domain.

EXPERT PERFORMANCE

How did we arrive at this understanding of expertise, and what implications might it have for understanding the nature of giftedness or exceptionality in children?

One of the most striking examples of experimental research into exceptional performance attempts to explain the ability of people to perform exceptional feats of memory. A very simple traditional memory test is to repeat, as accurately as possible, a series of digits that you have just heard. The average college student is capable of repeating about eight of these digits. Memory experts, however, often repeat twenty or more. What is the basis of this exceptional memory? Several years ago, William Chase at Carnegie–Mellon University (Ericsson & Chase, 1982) trained two normal people to remember a sequence of random numbers, so they could repeat it back immediately after presentation. The best subject, after 250 days of practice, could repeat random digit strings as long as 80 items. He did so by a relatively simple technique. He grouped the digits into chunks of three or four digits based on what he thought was a codable running time. Or, as Chase put it, "What S.F. did was begin mentally to encode three- and four-digit groups as running times for various races. For example, he'd remember 3, 4, 9, 2, as 3 minutes, 49.2 seconds, near the world record time for running a mile." These chunks, then, could be grouped into higher level chunks; and finally, when asked to recall, he was able to organize a recall of a very large number of digits where each chunk had only 3 to 4 digits in it. Chase was able to train other expert memorizers in very much the same way. These experts showed normal spans if the items were shifted from digits to letters. In other words, Chase found that what appears to be a very exceptional, perhaps a photographic memory, could be obtained presumably by any normal person whose practice was sustained over many days and who applied a systematic method of coding information in memory.

There is some evidence that even the increase in memory span between the ages of five and adulthood, from about 2 or 3 items to 8 items, also depends on specific learning. Most people believe that the memory span increases because the capability of storing information changes from childhood to adulthood. Chi (1976) reasoned that the change in memory span might result from the child simply learning more about how to code and recognize letters and digits. Compare a brief exposure to a list of 8 arabic digits with a list of 8 roman numerals. The roman numerals are certainly familiar but they take time to name, and thus the number coded in a fixed exposure time is reduced. The studies of Chase and Chi indicate how important specific long continued experience is for expert skill.

Striking evidence on the nature of expertise arose from studies of chess which began nearly 25 years ago, when a famous Dutch chess master, Adrian deGroot (1966), began to study the intellectual capabilities and coding processes of chess masters compared to less expert chess players. He began his study of expertise by the use of protocol analysis. That is, he attempted to have chess masters, experts, and novices speak aloud as they selected a chess move. He then analyzed in detail the depth to which they searched the board, their use of various heuristics (e.g., to control the center of the board), and other aspects of their thought processes. He found relatively little difference between people who were only fair chess players and people who were chess masters. A striking thing was that, although the chess masters picked the right moves, there was nothing in the protocol of their thought processes that seemed to indicate why it was that they were so much better than lesser experts.

Next de Groot did an interesting thing. He asked each of the players to reproduce a chess position after a 5-second exposure to a slide of the 20th move of a chess master's game. These were games with which all the players were equally unfamiliar, but they were the type of game that might be played by masters. He found striking differences in memory. Chess masters could reproduce nearly all the pieces on the board with few errors, while chess experts and novice players had much poorer performance. This work has been replicated many times with chess players and has also been found in other forms of expert performance.

Chase and Simon (1973) studied in detail some of the mental processes involved in this memory performance, and, unsurprisingly, they found much the same result as in the study of expert memory. The reproduction consists of chunks of information which represent units on the chess board. When either the chess masters or the expert players were required to produce a meaningless chess position — that is, one where the pieces had been scrambled — their performances were very much reduced and about equivalent to each other's. Chess masters, like the memory experts, were good in the specific domain of meaningful chess positions. They did not show a greater memory in general, but only in this specific domain.

Cognitive psychologists suppose there are some domains where nearly everyone becomes an expert much like the chess master. Consider reading English words. We all have many hundreds of hours' experience with reading. We can do so effortlessly, essentially automatically. Yet reading is a formidable achievement. A very brief exposure to a set of letters produces a representation of the particular word which was seen. In the expert reader, words are handled so well that letters seen within a word are often more visible than the letter is by itself. Reicher (1969) exposed subjects to either four-letter words (e.g., WORD) or individual letters (D). These were followed by a mask so it became very difficult to see the words or letters. He then gave each subject a forced choice between two letters (D or K) that both made perfectly acceptable English words. Thus, they could not guess based on their knowledge of the English language, but they still did better when the letter was in a word than in isolation. Thus, some of the same impressive coding and chunking feats that are features of expert chess players are also present in those of us who may be less generally gifted, when we have been exposed to a sufficiently large number of trials to allow the performance to become truly automated.

SKILL ACQUISITION

Herbert Simon (Chase & Simon, 1973) has reasoned that masters level chess players have spent 10,000 to 20,000 hours staring at chess positions. To put this in perspective, the student who spends 40 hours a week for 33 weeks spends 1320 hours a year studying. Imagine spending more than 10 years in college studying one subject, chess, and you get some appreciation of the time commitment of master level players. As a result of such extensive study, they are believed to store from 10,000 to 100,000 different chess patterns. Simon concluded that it is reasonable to assume a chess master can recognize 50,000 different configurations of chess, not too far different from the number of different words an English reader may be able to recognize.

Fortunately, we now know something about how information is represented in the memory system during learning (Anderson, 1983). Consider learning a set of statements such as "a doctor is in the bank," "a fireman is in the park," "a lawyer is in the church," "a lawyer is in the park." This set of sentences can be represented in terms of a propositional network. What is important is that the concept "lawyer" is related both to its location in the church and its location in the park. There are two relationships stemming from the same concept.

How do we know the structure of the memory? One clue is that the more ideas associated, the longer the time it takes to retrieve any particular item. Thus, experimental studies having subjects learn relationships of this sort, and asking them then to answer as quickly as possible such questions as "is there a doctor in the park?" show that the time needed to answer any question is a function of the number of relationships associated to the idea — in this case, *"doctor."*

This finding suggests that propositions about lawyers are tied to a single concept in memory. Clearly there is a paradox — the more items attached to any one concept, the longer the retrieval time, and yet experts do not necessarily take longer to retrieve information. In part, this paradox is overcome by the long practice which is associated with becoming an expert. The reaction time for retrieving information improves with practice, and comes to be independent of the number of propositions attached to a node. The expert must also unify the stored information into a meaningful whole that allows it to be retrieved more rapidly. Usually we are not asked to retrieve exact information, but instead are asked questions which might be inferred or thought to be consistent with what we know.

Experimental studies suggest that when subjects are required only to say whether information is consistent with what has been learned, the more information they have, the more quickly such information can be retrieved. This may also be a way in which the expert can quickly answer questions which would require a study of the individually stored propositions on the part of nonexperts. These studies of memory representation after long training may begin to give us methods to assess and guide the training of expertise.

EXPERT SYSTEMS

Our understanding of the specific nature of human expertness has progressed far enough so that we are beginning to see the development of artificial computer-based systems able to achieve some of the same performance as the expert. These systems take advantage of the fact that digital computers are general-purpose processors of symbols (Duda & Shortliffe, 1983). Some of these expert systems are being put to use in tasks like deciding which antibiotic to prescribe, testing pulmonary functions, or guiding geological exploration.

These findings about the importance of representing information in memory for understanding expert performance have been embodied in these computer systems. In the article just cited, Duda and Shortliffe say:

> The early hope that a relatively small number of powerful general mechanisms would be sufficient to generate intelligent behavior gradually waned. When significant problems were addressed, it was often discovered that problem independent, heuristic methods alone were incapable of handling the sheer, combinatorial complexity that was encountered. Similarly, general problem solving techniques confronted in precisely stated "problems," uncertain "facts," and unreliable "axioms" were found to be inadequate to the task.
>
> When it was asked how people were able to devise solutions to these problems a frequent answer was that people possess knowledge of which the programs were wholly innocent. This knowledge is employed in a variety of ways. . .in clarifying the problem, suggesting the kinds of procedure to use, judging the reliability of facts and deciding whether a solution is reasonable. (p. 261)

The growing recognition of the many kinds of knowledge required for high performance reasoning systems changed the shape of AI research. In the words of Goldstein and Pappert, as quoted by Duda and Shortliffe:

> Today there has been a shift in paradigm. The fundamental problem of understanding intelligent behavior is not the identification of a few powerful techniques, but rather the question of how to represent large amounts of knowledge in a fashion that permits their effective use and interaction. The current point of view is that the problem solver, whether man or machine, must know explicitly how to use its knowledge with general techniques supplemented by a domain specific pragmatic knowhow. Thus, we see AI as having shifted from a power based strategy for achieving intelligence to a knowledge-based approach. (p. 262)

INDIVIDUAL ABILITY

The burden of this work on expertness is a hopeful one. Ordinary people seem to have within them the potentiality for expertise, should they be able to acquire the large technical vocabulary and make the long commitment of study that such expertise requires. But this can hardly be the whole story. When we have the insight that children are gifted or exceptional we suppose not just that they are experts in some domain, but that they have the capacity to acquire expertise in many domains more quickly than others who may not be able to acquire it at all. The studies that I have presented so far do not support this insight, but there are other studies which do.

Lyon (1977) studied the very same memory span tests I referred to in the work of Chi and Chase. Lyon studied normal adults who differ widely in their memory span. Memory span is a skill which is correlated with the overall scores that people obtain in intelligence tests. Lyon wished to know what is the basis of these individual differences. The burden of the studies of Chi and Chase would suppose that it must lie in either overall experience or some specific strategy such as chunking or grouping material. Lyon induced several specific strategies in his subjects, and their performance greatly increased. However, the individual differences remained pretty much the same. The strategies, although important, did not erase the seemingly more basic differences among individuals.

Most of us maintain an intuition that there are important underlying differences among people in how well they could develop expertise. Even within individuals, it's hard to believe that there is not more potential for the development of some capabilities than of others. Some people seem to learn music easily, but have trouble with languages, while others acquire mathematics effortlessly, but do poorly in mechanical ability. A hundred years of testing of intelligence by psychometricians is based on an effort to build a measurement technology based upon this intuition.

Although the psychometric approach to intelligence testing was not related to any theory of intelligence, more recent efforts by cognitive psychologists (Hunt, 1983) are based upon the theory of symbolic representations that I have been discussing. They seek to measure cognitive processes in various domains. It seems clear that some people are systematically faster than others in retrieving the names of letters or words, in performing mental operations on visual images, and in comprehending written and oral words. Correlations are often found between processing speed and psychometrically measured intelligence (Jensen, 1979). This has led some to argue that we now have clear measures of fundamental mental operations that are culture-free and that give us a more direct approach to the efficiency of the neural systems underlying cognition. Indeed, there are some impressive results tieing studies of speeded processing in normal and brain injured humans that suggest deep ties between the performance of elementary mental operations and brain function, particularly in reading (Coltheart, 1981).

Yet I remain skeptical that the measurement so far achieved can be thought to be free of past learning in any fundamental sense. Remember that Chi found the improvements over 15 years in the speed of recognizing digits could influence even the basic memory span. It can be argued that many of the tests employed to study elementary operations similarly reflect past experience with symbols, training in maintenance of alertness, and conforming to the experimenter's goals.

The problem of producing an expert may be not so much in selecting someone who has special capability, but to create and maintain the motivation needed for long-continued training. Whether someone will work hard is itself a possible basis of individual differences. Only motivated people are likely to undergo the long training necessary to become a chess master. Perhaps we should be using these new cognitive tests of mental operations to determine which domains of material seem to be the most promising for a given individual — understanding that these may be properties not only of innate abilities, but of interest in the field. From this perspective, it will be important to assess motivation, as well as capability of learning, within any domain. Tests of speed of mental operations may also help us assess the structure obtained at any level of practice, and guide the exercises needed to aid in the development of expertise.

SUMMARY

I begin this chapter by noting that there is now a cognitive science related to the representation and execution of expert performance. This science has developed a technology in the form of programs for performing tasks formerly done only by experts. Although this technology is still primitive, it represents an important contribution of fundamental research on the nature of representation of information in memory. Behind this technology is a better understanding of what it means to be an expert. Expertness lies more in an elaborated semantic memory than in a general reasoning process. Such knowledge is present not only in the performance of unusual people, but in a skill like reading which is widely distributed in most of us. We are beginning to understand the nature of the propositional network underlying such representation. The expert has available access to a complex network without any conscious representation of the search processes that go on in its retrieval.

Despite the overwhelming emphasis in the recent cognitive literature on the ability of any person to achieve expert performance with practice, there is still considerable evidence in the literature that individuals may differ in overall ability or particular abilities. Our new knowledge about the nature of expertness should suggest ways in which these basic capabilities and interests may interact with the acquisition of information in the production of expert performance. Perhaps they will also give us a method for sustaining the necessary motivation to achieve truly expert performance.

ACKNOWLEDGMENTS

This chapter was written for a conference of teachers of gifted children held at the University of Oregon in the summer of 1983. The general conference stressed methods of locating children with extraordinary abilities. In this paper I tried to show that psychologists were also trying to understand how expertise might be acquired by people who were otherwise average in their ability. It is not based on original research of my own but was based upon relevant literature.

I am grateful to Dr. Mary K. Rothbart for her help with the manuscript and to Dr. M. T. H. Chi for suggesting that it might be of interest to a wider audience.

REFERENCES

Anderson, J. R. (April 1983). Retrieval of information from long-term memory. *Science, 220,* 25–30.

Chase, W. G., & Simon, H. A. (1973). Perception in chess. *Cognitive Psychology, 4,* 55–81.

Chi, M. T. H. (1976). Short-term memory limitations in children: Capacity or processing deficits? *Memory & Cognition, 4,* 559–572.

Coltheart, M. (1981). Disorders of reading and their implications for models of normal reading. *Visible Language, 15,* 245–286.

deGroot, A. D. (1966). Perception and memory versus thought. In B. Kleinmuntz (Ed.), *Problem Solving Research, Methods and Theory* (pp. 19–50). New York: Wiley.

Duda, R. O., & Shortliffe, E. H. (1983). Expert systems research. *Science, 220,* 261–268.

Ericsson, K. A., & Chase, W. G. (1982). Exceptional memory. *American Scientist, 6,* 607–612.

Hunt, E. B. (1983). On the nature of intelligence. *Science, 219,* 141–146.

Jensen, A. R. (1979). *Bias in Mental Testing.* Riverside, NJ: Free Press.

Lyon, D. R. (1977). Individual differences in immediate serial recall: A matter of mnemonics. *Cognitive Psychology, 9,* 403–411.

Reicher, G. M. (1969). Perceptual recognition as a function of meaningfulness of stimulus material. *Journal of Experimental Psychology, 81,* 275–280.

1 Expertise in Typewriting

Donald R. Gentner
University of California, San Diego

INTRODUCTION

The other chapters in this book are concerned primarily with expertise in mental tasks. Even though an expert waiter or radiologist may use motor skills, such as speech and handwriting, the motor skills themselves are not of direct interest to most investigators. This chapter, on the other hand, is concerned with the acquisition and performance of the motor skill of typewriting. Motor skills provide a unique psychological insight, because they are the direct, concrete product of the large amount of mental processing required for the planning, coordination, and control of actions. From a practical standpoint, motor skills offer a unique advantage to the scientist studying expertise. Most of the interesting events in mental skills go on inside the head, and are hidden from our view. The scientist must make indirect inferences about these mental events from such data as reaction times and verbal protocols. In contrast, the normal performance of a motor skill produces an externally observable sequence of events that are directly related to the task.

It is clear from anatomical studies of the brain, and observation of patients with brain injury, that even in humans a large portion of the brain is involved in the performance of motor skills. Some motor skills, such as walking and speech, develop in childhood as the motor system itself develops, and are normally acquired without special effort. Other motor skills, such as juggling, playing piano, or flying an airplane, although based on existing perceptual and motor skills, require special instruction to acquire and gain expertise. Expertise in typewriting belongs in the latter class.

Prospective typists spend hundreds of hours in classes and at practice before they are expert enough to be employed. In fact, when typewriters were first manufactured, they were operated by the hunt-and-peck method. It took at least another 20 years before it was generally realized that it was even possible to type using all ten fingers and without looking at the keyboard.

A typical professional typist has accumulated an incredible amount of practice. A conservative assumption would be that a typist averages 50 words per minute (wpm) for 20 hours per week. Over the course of 10 years, that would amount to 150 million keystrokes or 25 million words. In those 10 years, this hypothetical typist would have typed the word *the* 2 million times, and typed a common word like *system* 10,000 times. The speed of professional typists is also quite remarkable. A typing rate of 60 wpm corresponds to an average of five keystrokes per second. The fastest typists I have studied maintain an average of more than nine keystrokes per second over the period of an hour.

ACQUISITION OF TYPEWRITING

In common with the other tasks described in this book, it takes people a surprisingly long time to become expert typists. The performance norms listed by West (1983, p. 346) give the following median typing speeds for students: 38 wpm for students completing the first year of high school typing, 44 wpm for students completing the second year of high school typing, and 56 wpm for students at the end of business school training. (These scores are gross words per minute, with no correction for errors.) The surprising finding is that after 3 years of practice, the median graduate of business school is just barely meeting minimal employment standards. Estimating 5 hours of practice per week and 40 weeks per year, in 3 years a student would have accumulated about 600 hours of practice on the typewriter.

It's instructive to contrast the time required to become an expert typist with the time required to learn to fly an airplane, which is generally acknowledged to be a reasonably difficult motor skill. A private pilot's license requires only 35 hours of flight time. Even combat pilots in the U.S. Air Force have only 300 to 350 hours flying time plus another 75 hours of simulator training when they report to their operational squadron (D. Lyon, personal communication, August, 1983). Of course there are probably motivational and aptitude differences between pilot trainees and typing students, but the similarity in acquisition times makes clear that learning to type at the professional level is not an easy task.

Like other motor skills, typewriting, once acquired, is remarkably resilient. In a classic series of motor learning studies, Hill (1934, 1957; Hill,

Rejall, & Thorndike, 1913) recorded data from three month-long efforts to learn typewriting that were separated by lapses of 25 years. Hill found significant savings of skill at the beginning of the second and third learning efforts, despite the intervening 25 years between efforts. Salthouse (1984) studied the performance of professional typists ranging in age from 19 to 68 years. He measured performance of the typists on a battery of tasks, including a forced-choice reaction time task on the typewriter keyboard and a normal transcription typing task. Salthouse found that performance in the transcription typing task was not correlated with age, even though performance on supposedly similar motor tasks, such as tapping speed and forced-choice reaction time, showed the usual decline with age.

COMPARISONS OF EXPERT AND NOVICE TYPISTS

How do expert typists differ from novices? I've examined this question by comparing the performance of student typists and professional typists. For most of the studies reported here, the typists were asked to transcribe normal prose texts for about an hour. They typed on an electronic keyboard with a layout and "feel" similar to the IBM Selectric keyboard (Figure 1.1). Keystrokes and the corresponding times were recorded by a microcomputer with a resolution of 1 msec. The typists' finger movements were recorded on videotape.

The student typists were volunteers from the first semester typing class at a local high school. They came to the laboratory once a week between the fourth and eighth weeks of class. The expert typists were professional typists recruited from the university and from local businesses. Most of the experts were typical office secretaries, but a special effort was made to recruit a few very fast typists.

Faster Interstroke Intervals

The first measure of keystroke timing examined was the distribution of interstroke intervals. Figure 1.2 illustrates the range of distributions found among typists, showing the distribution of interstroke intervals for a student (Typist 21) at two points in time, a typical office typist (Typist 2), and an unusually fast typist (Typist 8). This figure also demonstrates the most obvious difference between novice and expert typists: experts type faster than novices. The typing speed of the students participating in this study ranged from 13 wpm for one student in the fourth week of class to 41 wpm for another student in the eighth week of class. (The typing speeds reported in this chapter are gross words per minute, with no correction for errors. A word was taken to be five characters, including spaces.) The typing

STANDARD QWERTY KEYBOARD

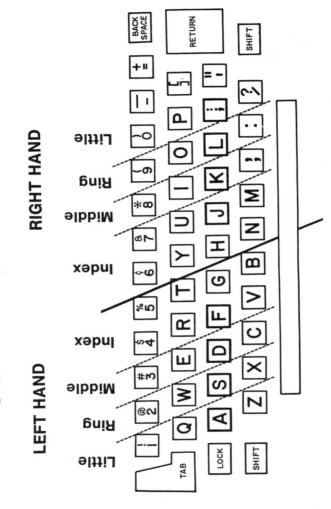

FIGURE 1.1 The layout of the keyboard used in these studies. This is the standard American "qwerty" keyboard and is identical to the layout of the IBM Selectric typewriter.

4

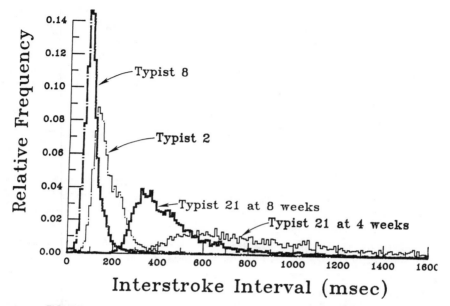

FIGURE 1.2   The distribution of all interstroke intervals for Typist 21 after 4 weeks (13 wpm) and 8 weeks (25wpm) of typing class, Typist 2 (66 wpm), and Typist 8 (112 wpm).

speed of the expert typists ranged from 61 to 112 wpm. In addition to being faster, the expert typists generally had a much lower error rate than the student typists.

How does the performance of the expert typists compare in detail with the performance of the student typists? Is expert performance simply a speeded-up version of student performance, or do qualitative changes in performance occur during acquisition of typing skill? As one approach to these questions, consider the simple movement required to type two letters in sequence with the same finger, such as *de*. The *de* interstroke intervals of experts were more than twice as fast as the *de* interstroke intervals of students. There are only three basic ways that an expert could type the *e* more quickly: (a) the finger movement to type the *e* could start earlier; (b) the finger could travel a shorter path; (c) the finger could move faster.

To investigate this issue, I have examined the videotape records of the expert and student typists when typing the digraph *de*. The study included eleven expert typists ranging in speed from 61 to 112 wpm, and eight student typists in the seventh week of their typing class, ranging in speed from 17 to 40 wpm. For each typist, the 10 instances of *de* (5 instances in the case of student typists) with interstroke intervals closest to that typist's median *de* interstroke interval were selected for study. For each instance, the

position of the left-middle fingertip was digitized on the videotape recording and the trajectory was calculated in three-dimensional space. The time
of the first visible movement toward the e key was determined from a plot
of the finger trajectory. Three measures were calculated for each trajectory: (a) the lag time—the time from the initial depression of the d key until
the first visible movement toward the e on the top row; (b) the path
length—the distance moved by the fingertip from the beginning of the movement until the e keypress; (c) the average speed of movement—the path
length divided by the movement time. The results are shown in Table 1.1.
Surprisingly, the mean path length of the students was slightly shorter than
that of the experts, so the experts were not typing the e more quickly because of a shorter path. Instead, the experts started their finger movements
with a shorter lag time after pressing the d (accounting for about 60 msec)
of the difference in interstroke intervals), and moved their fingers about
twice as fast (accounting for the remaining 150 msec).

This picture develops an interesting twist when the data are examined
for each group separately. An analysis of the correlations between the interstroke interval and the three measures (See Table 1.2) showed that the
speed of finger movement was the primary determinant of the interstroke
interval for the students ($r = -.92$). For the expert typists, however, speed
was not correlated ($r = .06$) with the interstroke interval. Although there
was considerable variation in speed among the experts (mean speeds ranged
from 231 to 524 mm/sec), the typists with higher speeds also had longer
path lengths, and the two factors cancelled out. Instead, the primary determinant of the interstroke intervals among experts was the lag times. The
fastest experts had very short lag times between pressing the d key and starting the movement toward the e key.

Differential Speedup of Digraph Classes

The results described for the digraph de are consistent with the view that
expert performance is simply a speeded-up version of student performance.
Recall that the experts and students had similar path lengths, but the experts had shorter lag times and moved their fingers faster than the students.
When other types of digraphs are examined, however, this simple picture

TABLE 1.1
Mean Characteristics of "de" Finger Movements

	Interstroke Interval (msec)	Lag Time (msec)	Path Length (mm)	Average Speed (mm/sec)
Students	384	104	38	152
Experts	178	46	45	353

TABLE 1.2
Correlations with Interstroke Inverval (Within-Group)

	Lag Time	Path Length	Speed
Students	− .18	+ .51	− .92
Experts	+ .74	+ .41	+ .06

of expert performance is no longer adequate. Although experts typed all sequences faster than students, the increase in speed was not equal for all interstroke intervals.

For this analysis, it is useful to divide the digraphs into classes according to the fingers used to type them (the keyboard is shown in Figure 1.1). Repeated letters, such as *dd*, are called doubles. The remaining (nondouble) digraphs typed by one finger, such as *de*, are called one-finger digraphs. Digraphs typed by two fingers on the same hand, such as *dr*, are called two-finger digraphs. And finally, digraphs typed by fingers on opposite hands such as *do*, are called two-hand digraphs.

Figure 1.3 shows the median interstroke intervals for the various digraph classes as a function of the typist's overall speed. Doubles were the fastest digraph class typed by students, but were among the slowest digraphs typed by experts. The other digraph classes were all typed at about the same speed by the slowest students, but were typed at significantly different speeds by experts. One-finger digraphs were typed the slowest by expert typists, and two-hand digraphs were typed the fastest. As overall typing speed increases, the median interstroke intervals get shorter for all digraph classes, but the amount of reduction in the interstroke interval varies, depending on the digraph class. Across this group of typists, the interstroke intervals for doubles decreased by a factor of 3 from the slowest to the fastest typists. By contrast, the interstroke intervals of two-hand digraphs decreased by a factor of 12. The interstroke intervals of one-finger and two-finger digraphs showed intermediate improvement, decreasing by factors of 6 and 10, respectively.

Consideration of the finger movements required to type these digraphs suggests a mechanism for the differential improvement in interstroke intervals. With two-hand digraphs, which showed the greatest improvement, it would be possible to overlap finger movements, so that the finger movement for the second letter could be started before the first letter was typed. Alternatively, at least the movement to type the first letter with one hand should not interfere with the movement to type the second letter with the other hand. In contrast, doubles and one-finger digraphs, which showed the least speed improvement, are typed by a single finger and thus no overlapped movements are possible.

The possibility of overlapped movements for two-finger and two-hand

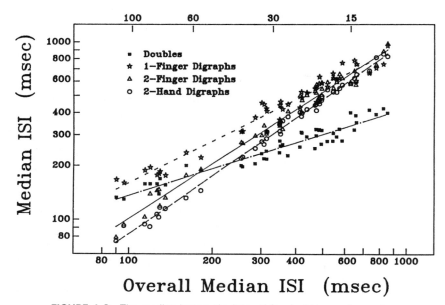

Approximate Words per Minute

Overall Median ISI (msec)

FIGURE 1.3   The median interstroke interval for double, one-finger, two-finger, and two-hand digraphs plotted as a function of the typists' overall median interval. The fastest typist (112 wpm) is on the left; the slowest typist (13 wpm) is on the right. The data on the left are from 10 skilled typists; the data at center and right are from 37 sessions with 8 student typists in the fourth through eighth week of a beginning typing class. The typists were copying normal prose. The data plotted are based on approximately 12,000 keystrokes per typist for the skilled typists, and from 3,000 to 6,000 keystrokes per typist for the student typists. Note that one-finger doubles were among the slowest for skilled typists but fastest for the students.

digraphs was confirmed by analysis of videotape and high-speed film records of typists' finger movements (Gentner, 1981; Gentner, Grudin, & Conway, 1980). Numerous instances were found in the videotapes of expert typists when two, or occasionally three, keystrokes were in progress at one time. The overlapping of finger movements in time is not the only way a typist can take advantage of the ability to move fingers independently. When successive letters are typed on different rows of the keyboard, moving the whole hand to type the first letter can carry the other finger out of position for the second letter. There were many cases on the videotape records where no overlapped movement was seen, but digraphs typed by different fingers on the same hand were faster because the second finger was not pulled out of position by the keystroke of the first finger (Gentner, 1983).

Increase in Overlapped Movements

The extent of overlapped finger movements varied considerably from one expert typist to another, and was moderately correlated with typing speed. Unfortunately, the direct determination of the extent of overlapping finger movements from the videotape records is very time consuming. I have, therefore, tried to estimate the extent of overlapped movements from the interstroke intervals. Although this is an indirect measure, it at least has the virtues of ease and objectivity. The basic assumption, in this measure of the extent of overlapped finger movement, is that the interstroke interval for a normal one-finger digraph represents the time for a keystroke with no overlap. Interstroke intervals for two-finger and two-hand digraphs are normally shorter than for one-finger digraphs, and this estimate assumes that these shorter intervals are the result of overlapped movements. Thus, for each typist, I calculated a "cross-hand overlap index" by taking the difference between the median interstroke intervals for one-finger digraphs and for two-hand digraphs, and dividing by the median one-finger interstroke interval. I also calculated a "within-hand overlap index" in an analogous fashion, as a measure of the amount of overlapping movement between two fingers on the same hand, by comparing the median two-finger and one-finger interstroke intervals. Figure 1.4 shows these cross-hand and within-

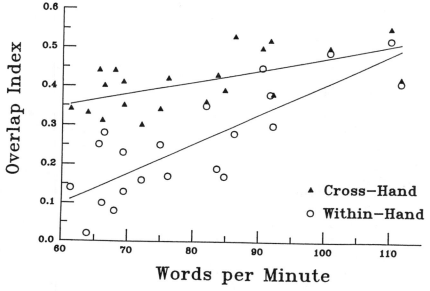

FIGURE 1.4   Cross-hand and within-hand overlap indices for expert typists, as a function of typing speed. The overlap index, plotted on the vertical axis, is a rough estimate of the fraction of a keystroke that overlaps the previous keystroke. Although the amount of cross-hand overlap increases with increasing speed, the increase in within-hand overlap is much greater.

hand overlap indices for a group of 21 expert typists with varying typing speeds. Although the absolute values of these overlap indices should not be taken too seriously, they appear to be a reliable measure of the relative extent of overlapped movements exhibited by different typists for cross-hand and within-hand movements. Figure 1.4 indicates that there was a modest increase in cross-hand overlapped movements as expert typists increased in speed from 60 to 112 wpm ($r = +.63$). The increase in within-hand overlapped movements with typing speed ($r = +.82$) was much greater, however, and appears to be a major contributor to the high speed of the fastest experts. Within-hand overlapped movements are negligible for the typists in the range of 60 wpm, but the fastest typists show as much overlapped movement within-hand as across-hand. This trend is also evident on close examination of Figure 1.3: The fastest typists have almost identical interstroke intervals for two-finger and two-hand digraphs.

The large differences in within-hand overlap among expert typists is related to another finding. The median interstroke intervals for two-finger digraphs were more variable among expert typists than any other digraph class. This variability was based on differences in the degree to which the fingers within a hand were moved independently. Analysis of the videotape records showed that typists with rapid interstroke intervals for two-finger digraphs moved their fingers independently or actually overlapped finger movements within a hand. Typists who had slow interstroke intervals for two-finger digraphs tended to move all the fingers on a hand together and thus their other finger was often out of position to easily type the second letter of a two-finger digraph (Gentner, 1981).

Simulation of Acquisition

This view, that the differential speedup of digraph types is based on the possibility of overlapped movements, is supported by results from the computer simulation of a typist developed by Rumelhart and Norman (1982). Their typing simulation model is based on a parallel, distributed view of cognitive processes, and does not have any central planning or timing control. Instead, their simulation model attempts to type several characters at once, and the interstroke intervals are a result of competition and collaboration among concurrent goals to move the fingers to the different keyboard locations.

Producing a sequence of events in the proper serial order has always been a problem for theories of action (Lashley, 1951). In the Rumelhart and Norman simulation model, the proper serial order is obtained by having each letter inhibit all following letters. Thus the first letter in a sequence, because it is not inhibited by any other letters, will normally be the most highly activated letter and will be typed first. The second letter will be inhibited

by only one letter to the left and will normally have the next highest activation, and so fourth.

D. Rumelhart (personal communication, 1982) found that, if the amount
by which a given letter inhibited the following letters was varied, the simulation model showed a pattern of changes similar to the pattern of changes
found in going from student to expert typists (see Figure 1.5). Decreasing
the amount of inhibition between successive letters in the model has the
effect of increasing the degree to which several letters tend to be typed at
once. When the simulation model had a high level of inhibition between
successive letters, and thus tended to type one letter at a time, the pattern
of interstroke intervals was similar to the pattern observed with student
typists. Whereas when the level of inhibition between successive letters was
low, causing the simulation model to attempt to type several letters simultaneously, the pattern of interstroke intervals was similar to the pattern observed with expert typists. Thus, this simulation result suggests that an
important component of the acquisition of typewriting skill is the change
toward a less sequential and more overlapped mode of performance.

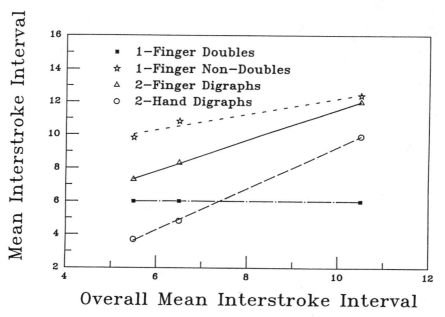

FIGURE 1.5 The effect of changing the amount of inhibition between successive letters in the Rumelhart and Norman (1982) simulation model of a
typist. Points on the right have the most inhibition; points on the left have
the least inhibition. Decreasing the amount of inhibition decreases the average interstroke intervals and also changes the pattern interstroke intervals
for the different digraph classes. Compare this figure with Figure 1.3.

Overlapped Processing

The observation that finger movements of expert typists overlap in time suggests that the mental processes underlying the typing of successive letters also overlap in time. Figure 1.6 is a very schematic representation of the mental processes involved in typing three letters. It proposes that several letters are in different stages of parallel mental processing at any one time. While the finger movement is in progress for one letter, the movement is being planned for another letter, and still other letters are being read from the original text. No doubt this view of typing is much too simpleminded. For example, letters are presumably perceived as parts of words, and not as completely independent symbols, as Figure 1.6 would suggest. The point of this figure is just to propose that the mental processing relevant to successive letters is carried out in parallel, and that it overlaps in time. This picture of overlapped mental processing in transcription typing is supported and elaborated by a number of other studies.

A simpler model of typing would be that each letter is perceived and typed before starting mental processing for the next letter. In this model, typing is like a series of choice reaction time tasks. But a typical reaction time to perceive and type a letter is between 500 and 600 msec (Salthouse, 1984). This reaction time is in reasonable accord with the interstroke intervals of beginning student typists; but the interstroke intervals of expert typists were in the range of 100 to 200 msec, much too fast for this completely sequential model. Therefore, in order to explain the short interstroke inter-

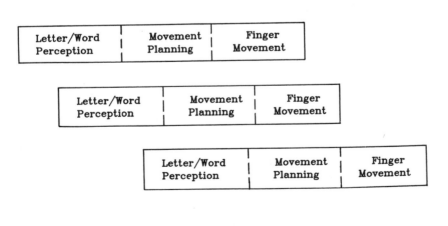

➡ TIME ➡➡

FIGURE 1.6 A schematic representation of the mental processes involved in typing three successive letters. The mental processes, and often the finger movements, overlap in time.

vals of expert typists, we must postulate that the mental processing and execution of successive keystrokes overlap in time.

Another line of support for the overlapped processing model comes from experiments that vary the amount of preview that typists are allowed. For example, Shaffer (1973) presented text to an expert typist on a CRT screen, and varied the number of characters the typist could see ahead of the character being typed. When the typist could see only two characters (the character being typed and the next character) her typing speed was reduced to one-fourth her normal rate. Shaffer found that the typist had to have eight characters of preview in order to attain her normal, unlimited-preview typing rate. Salthouse (1984) has reported similar studies of transcription typing with variable preview, and found that a preview of about seven characters was required for typists to attain their normal typing rate.

A closely related line of evidence supporting the overlapped processing model of typing comes from studies of eye movements. James Hollan and I recorded eye fixations during transcription typing. We found that typists were typically reading about five characters ahead of where they were typing. Butsch (1932) reported similar results in an early study of eye movements during typing. Butsch studied 19 typists and found that the faster typists tended to look further ahead in the text. The two factors compensated, so that typists of all speeds were fixating characters about one second before the character was typed.

One might ask whether, in reading ahead, typists are utilizing the larger structure of English prose to speed up their processing and performance. Several experimenters (Fendrick, 1937; Shaffer, 1973; West & Sabban, 1982) have varied the regularity in text to determine if typists are sensitive to structures larger than letters. These studies found that typing speed increases with structure up to the word level. That is, good pseudowords were typed faster than random letters, and real words were typed faster still, but prose is not typed faster than random words. In a study of short-range structure in the text, Grudin and Larochelle (1982) have found small effects of digraph frequency on typing speed: high-frequency digraphs are typed slightly faster than matched low-frequency digraphs.

I have found similar effects of word frequency. I had experts type a text containing pairs of words that differed in frequency, but that shared identical four-letter sequences. For example, one pair of words was *system* and *oyster*, which share the sequence *yste*. On average, the interstroke interval in the middle of the shared sequence was typed about 10 msec faster when it was embedded in the high-frequency word than when it was embedded in the low-frequency word. The common thread running through the results from all these studies is that typing performance is sensitive to higher level units in the text, such as digraph and word frequency. It should be kept in mind that these higher level effects are small compared with the predominant effects of the letter sequence, as reflected in the keyboard lay-out and hand constraints. Nonetheless, these studies clearly demonstrate that expert typing is not merely a sequential, letter-by-letter process.

Cognitive Resources Available

Expert typists appear to normally have substantial amounts of unused cog-nitive resources. There are numerous stories of typists who can hold con-versations or answer telephones while typing. Some typists commonly check the original text for grammatical and spelling errors while typing. Other typists report that they usually daydream while typing or read the manuscript for content, and have little conscious awareness of typing. In addition to these anecdotes, there is some experimental data relevant to the issue of available cognitive resources.

Transcription typing involves perception (reading the original text), men-tal processing (translating the letters into the corresponding finger move-ments and planning the movements), and action (performing the keystrokes). In the experiments to be described, I looked at how increasing the difficulty of the perceptual part of the task affected overall performance. If typists normally have extra cognitive resources available, they might be able to utilize those resources to cope with the increased perceptual difficulty, with little effect on overall task performance. On the other hand, if typists do not have extra cognitive resources available, increasing the perceptual part of the task should degrade overall performance. In this experiment, I had expert typists transcribe prose from original texts that were obscured by dot screens of varying density. To determine if the dot screens in fact increased the perceptual difficulty, there was also a second task, in which the typists read aloud from the obscured texts. The results are shown in Figure 1.7. Performance on the reading-aloud task indicated that the obscured texts were more difficult to read; the speaking rate decreased by a factor of more than two for the highest dot density. However, the typing rate was not sig-nificantly affected by the obscuring dot screens. Apparently, the typists had excess cognitive resources available to read the obscured texts without af-fecting their performance.

Larochelle (1983) studied the performance of novice and expert typists in a discontinuous typing task similar to the task used by Sternberg, Mon-sell, Knoll, and Wright (1978). In this task, typists were presented short letter strings, which might be either words, pseudowords containing simi-lar English digraphs, or nonwords containing few common English di-graphs. After warning and start signals, they typed the letters as rapidly as possible. Larochelle measured the latency between the starting signal and the first keystroke, and the interstroke interval between successive key-

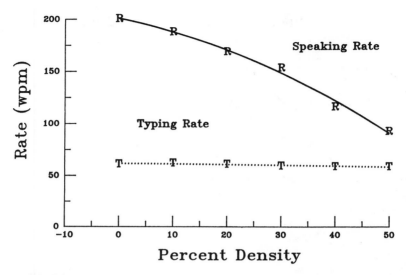

FIGURE 1.7 Speaking-aloud rate and typing rate by expert typists from a series of texts obscured by dot screens of varying densities. Although the speaking-aloud rates indicate that the obscured texts were more difficult to read, the typing rates were unaffected. These data are the means of three typists.

strokes. The results are shown in Figure 1.8. Novice performance, particularly the latency until first keystroke, was degraded with pseudowords and nonwords. If expert typing is based on higher level units such as letter sequences or words, we would expect that the effect of the type of letter string would be even greater on expert performance. Instead, expert performance on pseudowords was identical to expert performance on words, and on nonwords it was only slightly slower. This result suggests that word-level units are not a major factor in expert typing when typing single words in a discontinuous typing task; instead, the automated performance of experts frees their cognitive resources for the extra memory and planning required to type pseudowords and nonwords.

Performance Variability

Finally, a brief discussion follows of the variability of novice and expert performance. Quantitative measures of the nature and sources of performance variability can illuminate the mechanisms that determine motor skills. Performance variability can be decomposed into two parts. The first is *task-based* variability resulting from the performance of differing tasks

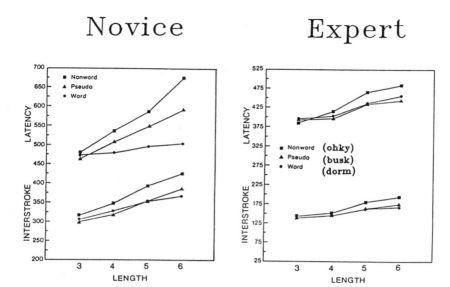

FIGURE 1.8   Performance of novice and expert typists on a discontinuous typing task. The data plotted are the latency from the start signal to the first keystroke, and the mean interstroke interval between successive keystrokes. Example letter strings are shown in parentheses. *Note.* From Larochelle, S. (1983). A comparison of skilled and novice performance in discontinuous typing, in W. E. Cooper (Ed.), *Cognitive Aspects of Skilled Typewriting* (pp. 71 and 75), New York: Springer-Verlag. Copyright 1983 by Springer-Verlag. Adapted by permission.

(for example, the difference in interstroke intervals for the digraphs *ed* and *ec*). The second is *repetition* variability: the variability found when the task is maintained constant. This decomposition is illustrated in Figure 1.9.

The distribution of all interstroke intervals for a given typist is composed of a set of much narrower distributions, one for each digraph in a given letter context. I have shown (Gentner, 1982) that the main determinants of the interstroke interval are the four characters surrounding the interval. Therefore, the widths of the narrower distributions in Figure 1.9 represent examples of repetition variability, whereas the distance between the centers of the two distributions represents an example of task-based variability.

Because the interstroke interval distributions are highly skewed, I have used two nonparametric measures of variability. The absolute variability of a distribution is measured by its half-width — the difference between the third and first quartiles. The relative variability of a distribution is the half-width divided by the median. Not surprisingly, both the absolute task-based variability and the absolute repetition variability decrease dramatically with greater expertise, as the interstroke intervals decrease by an order of magnitude.

The relative variability is a more meaningful measure when performance differs by such large factors. The relative task-based variability is roughly indicated in Figure 1.3. The points falling on a vertical line in Figure 1.3 represent the median interstroke intervals of a given typist for the different digraph classes. Because the median interstroke intervals for the different digraph classes are plotted on a log scale, the vertical scatter of the medians for each typist is a measure of the relative task-based variability. If doubles are ignored for the moment, Figure 1.3 shows that beginning students typed the remaining three digraph classes at roughly the same speed, showing very little task-based variability. The relative task-based variability increased with skill, with the fastest experts showing the greatest variability for the three digraph classes. Inclusion of doubles complicates the picture, because beginners type doubles twice as fast as other digraphs, whereas doubles fall between one-finger and two-finger digraphs for the experts. Considering all four digraph classes, then, there is no major change in task-based variability with skill, although typists at the lowest and highest skill levels have greater relative task-based variability than typists of intermediate skill.

In contrast with task-based variability, students and experts showed clear

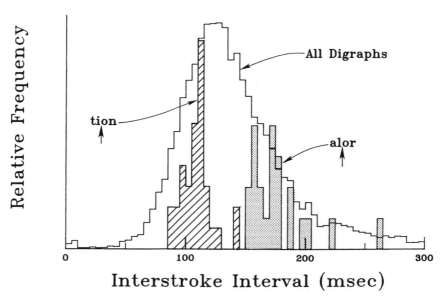

FIGURE 1.9 The distribution of all interstroke intervals is composed of many narrower distributions of interstroke intervals in specific contexts. This is illustrated with data from Typist 4, showing the distribution of all interstroke intervals, the distribution of *lo* intervals in the sequence *alor*, and the distribution of *io* intervals in the sequence *tion*. For Typist 4, the half-width of the overall distribution was 51 msec, whereas the median half-width of distributions of interval in a fixed four-character sequence was 19 msec.

differences in repetition variability. Table 1.3 lists the mean value of the relative repetition variability for student and expert typists. Because an interstroke interval is affected by the surrounding four-character context, repetition variability is best measured by the variability of the middle interstroke interval in a four-letter sequence. Unfortunately, many of the students did not produce enough repetitions of four-letter sequences for this type of analysis. Instead, Table 1.3 lists the relative variability of the second interstroke interval in a three-letter sequence (for example, the *os* interstroke interval in *most*), which should be almost as good a measure of repetition variability. The relative repetition variability is lower for expert typists than for students. The largest difference was for one-finger digraphs, where the relative variability of experts was only a third that of students. One-finger digraphs had the highest relative variability for students, but were very regular and similar to doubles for the expert typists.

In summary, both the absolute and relative variability of expert performance is lower, compared with the variability of student performance. The difference between the relative repetition variability of expert and student typists, however, depends on the task. For example, the relative repetition variability of one-finger digraphs is dramatically lower for experts than for students, but the relative variability of two-finger and two-hand interstrokes intervals is only moderately lower for experts.

CHARACTERISTICS OF EXPERT PERFORMANCE

Cognitive versus Motoric Constraints

When the performance of student typists is compared with the performance of expert typists, by far the largest change we see is that experts are much faster than students. Interstroke intervals decrease by factors of three to ten. This increase in speed is accompanied by a shift in the underlying determinants of performance. The performance of student typists is limited primarily by cognitive constraints, whereas the performance of expert typists is limited primarily by motoric constraints. Students type all digraph class-

TABLE 1.3
Mean Relative Repetition Variability for the Second Interstroke
Interval in a Three-Letter Sequence

Digraph Type	Student	Expert
Double	.256	.149
One-finger	.450	.154
Two-finger	.329	.255
Two-hand	.382	.324

es at approximately the same speed, regardless of the letter locations on the keyboard. The only exception is doubles, which are typed twice as fast, either because they are typed as a single unit or because movement planning is simplified for the second letter of a double. For experts, however, inter-stroke intervals can vary by factors of two or more depending on the keyboard location of the letters and fingers used to type them. In general, digraphs that allow independent or overlapping finger movements are typed much faster by experts than digraphs that do not. All expert typists appear to take at least some advantage of these possibilities when typing sequences on opposite hands. The fastest typists are also able to move fingers on the same hand independently, and thus can rapidly type letter sequences involving different fingers on the same hand. Doubles and one-finger digraphs, where no overlapped movements are possible, are typed most slowly by all expert typists.

The differences in repetition variability mirror the differences in the interstroke intervals. Absolute and relative variability decrease with increasing skill. Among student typists, the relative variability of one-finger digraphs is similar to that of two-finger and two-hand digraphs. Among experts, however, performance on doubles and one-finger digraphs is limited by motoric constraints. Experts, therefore, type doubles and one-finger digraphs more slowly and with lower relative variability than the other digraph classes.

Although motoric constraints are the main determinants of expert performance, small effects of cognitive constraints can be found. For example, experts type high-frequency digraphs and words slightly faster than matched low-frequency digraphs and words.

Adaptable, Context-Sensitive Performance

When we first started to study typists, we expected that such a highly practiced motor skill would be performed in a rigid fashion. Instead, typing has turned out to be a very flexible skill that responds easily to the varied demands of the task. Although expert typists practice primarily with prose texts, they are able to adapt their skill to novel tasks with little or no decrement in performance. For example, typists can transcribe random words or obscured texts at the same speed as normal prose. In another experiment, I asked expert typists (who did not know Dutch) to transcribe magazine articles written in Dutch. Surprisingly, they were able to do this task at a rate only about 20% lower than their normal typing rates. We have also seen that expert performance is routinely sensitive to the opportunities and limitations of the task. For example, interstroke intervals are shorter for sequences which allow movement overlap; and when typists increase their overall rate, the sequences permitting overlapped movements speed up the most.

Overlapped Processing

Expert typists achieve their high speeds by overlapped, parallel processing of successive letters. This overlap is evident throughout the perceptual, the planning, and often the execution phases of performance. The evidence that mental processing of successive letters overlaps in time comes from a number of studies showing that (a) there is insufficient time for serial processing of the letters; (b) the eye fixations of typists are about one second ahead of their typing; and (c) typists are responsive to text structure above the letter level.

The Expert–Novice Continuum

Expertise in typing, ranging from student typist to normal office typist to champion typist, does not lie along a single continuum. Even in the simple case of the finger movement from d to e, student progress is marked primarily by increasing speed of finger movement, whereas experts differ primarily in the amount of lag time between the first keystroke and the initiation of movement to the second key. As another example, the overlap of finger movements on opposite hands is acquired first in the development of expertise, but the fastest typists achieve their speed by also overlapping finger movements within a hand.

Large Individual Differences

Finally, one major characteristic of expert performance in typing that has not been discussed here is individual differences. In most experimental psychology studies, it is not possible to tell whether the differences observed among subjects are significant or merely the result of random variation. The situation is different with studies of typing, however, because it is easy to record more than ten thousand keystrokes in the course of an hour, and thus to obtain very high reliability for an individual subject.

Although there are many findings, such as those reported in this paper, that hold for typists in general, I often find large individual differences among expert typists. Differences in typing speed among professional typists are well known. I have also found large differences in the finger trajectories for a given keystroke. Typists differ in their sensitivity to the effects of word frequency and digraph frequency. They also exhibit major differences in error rates, the pattern of errors made, and the error mechanisms. It's clear that there are many ways to be an expert typist.

ACKNOWLEDGMENTS

This research was supported by Contract N00014-79-C-0323,NR 667-437 with the Personnel and Training Research Programs of the Office of Naval Research. Judith Stewart made many helpful comments on the manuscript.

REFERENCES

Butsch, R. L. C. (1932). Eye movements and the eye-hand span in typewriting. *Journal of Educational Psychology, 23,* 104–121.

Fendrick, P. (1937). Hierarchical skills in typewriting. *Journal of Educational Psychology, 28,* 609–620.

Gentner, D. R. (1981). *Skilled finger movements in typing* (Tech. Rep., CHIP 104). La Jolla: University of California, San Diego, Center for Human Information Processing.

Gentner, D. R. (1982). Evidence against a central control model of timing in typing. *Journal of Experimental Psychology: Human Perception and Performance, 8,* 793–810.

Gentner, D. R. (1983). Keystroke timing in transcription typing. In W. E. Cooper (Ed.), *Cognitive aspects of skilled typewriting* (pp. 95–120). New York: Springer-Verlag.

Gentner, D. R., Grudin, J., & Conway, E. (1980). *Finger movements in transcription typing* (Tech. Rep. 8001). La Jolla: University of California, San Diego, Center for Human Information Processing.

Grudin, J. T., & Larochelle, S. (1982). *Digraph frequency effects in skilled typing* (Tech. Rep., CHIP 110). La Jolla: University of California, San Diego, Center for Human Information Processing.

Hill, L. B. (1934). A quarter century of delayed recall. *Pedagogical Seminary and Journal of Genetic Psychology, 44,* 231–238.

Hill, L. B. (1957). A second quarter century of delayed recall or relearning at 80. *Journal of Educational Psychology, 48,* 65–68.

Hill, L. B., Rejall, A. E., & Thorndike, E. L. (1913). Practice in the case of typewriting. *Pedagogical Seminary, 20,* 516–529.

Larochelle, S. (1983). A comparison of skilled and novice performance in discontinuous typing. In William E. Cooper (Ed.), *Cognitive aspects of skilled typewriting,* (pp. 67–94). New York: Springer-Verlag.

Lashley, K. S. (1951). The problem of serial order in behavior. In L. A. Jeffress (Ed.), *Cerebral mechanisms in behavior* (pp. 112–136). New York: Wiley.

Rumelhart, D., & Norman, D. E. (1982). Simulating a skilled typist: A study of skilled cognitive-motor performance. *Cognitive Science, 6,* 1–36.

Salthouse, T. A. (1984). Effects of age and skill in typing. *Journal of Experimental Psychology, General, 113,* 345–371.

Shaffer, L. H. (1973). Latency mechanisms in transcription. In S. Kornblum (Ed.), *Attention and performance* (Vol. 4), pp. 435–446). New York: Academic Press.

Sternberg, S., Monsell, S., Knoll, R. L., & Wright, C. E. (1978). The latency and duration of rapid movement sequences: Comparisons of speech and typewriting. In G. E. Stelmach (Ed.), *Information processing in motor control and learning* (pp. 117–152). New York: Academic Press.

West, L. J. (1983). *Acquisition of typewriting skills* (2nd ed.). Indianapolis, IN: Bobbs-Merrill.

West, L. J., & Sabban, Y. (1982). Hierarchy of stroking habits at the typewriter. *Journal of Applied Psychology, 67,* 370–376.

2 A Cognitive Analysis of Exceptional Memory for Restaurant Orders

K. Anders Ericsson
Peter G. Polson
University of Colorado at Boulder

A headwaiter at a restaurant in Boulder (JC) is able to remember complete dinner orders from over 20 people at several different tables without making use of external aids like pencil and paper. JC discovered that people noticed that he was memorizing their orders and that he could serve people better when their orders were stored in his memory. The result was that he received larger tips, which motivated him to further develop his memory skills. This chapter describes our analysis of JC's memory skills.

We jointly began the study of JC's memory skills in the fall of 1980. Results of preliminary studies verified JC's claims concerning these skills. These studies also showed that he was able to generate detailed concurrent and retrospective verbal reports about the processes he used to store orders in memory. These results were integrated into a model of JC's memory skills. Several predictions from this model were evaluated in several experiments, which were carried out over the next 2 years. In addition, the article reports results of experiments from naive subjects attempting to memorize dinner orders.

This chapter and a companion paper (Ericsson & Polson, 1988) are concerned with several issues. First, this chapter presents a detailed model of JC's skills derived from verbal reports on his thoughts while memorizing dinner orders. Second, results are reported comparing JC's performance with college students who had no experience waiting on tables and who had presumably not acquired any of JC's memory skills. Such a comparison is important as the highly redundant and structured dinner orders might be unexpectedly easy to memorize. Third, results are presented that show that JC's memory skills are an example of the Chase & Ericsson (1982) skilled-memory framework. The next section presents summaries of experiments that test empirical predictions of our model of JC's memory skills. Finally, two studies examine the generality of these skills.

THEORETICAL FRAMEWORK

Since Miller's (1956) classic paper shows the subject's memory for briefly presented information to be remarkably limited (around seven unrelated items of information, or chunks) for a wide range of types of information, there have been a large number of demonstrations of vastly superior memory performance for experts within their field of expertise (see Chase & Ericsson, 1982, for a review). Miller's (1956) original explanation for such superior memory was that with practice subjects acquired more complex chunks, wherein each chunk would subsume several of the presented items; and that expert short-term memory capacity would remain invariant in terms of the number of chunks.

Chase and Ericsson (1981, 1982; Ericsson, Chase, & Faloon, 1980) have found empirical evidence suggesting that the chunking hypothesis is insufficient in work on the effects of practice of digit-span. They proposed a model of *skilled memory*. This model asserts that subjects' improvement beyond normal short-term memory capacity involves a more efficient use of long-term memory. According to this framework, subjects generate *long-term memory encodings* of the presented information using existing knowledge, rather than accessing preexisting chunks or patterns as proposed by Miller's chunking model. At the time of encoding, retrieval cues are incorporated in the memory trace, which allow a subject to retrieve the presented information at recall. The empirical evidence with the model of skilled memory comes primarily from detailed analysis of how college students acquire memory skills in the laboratory through extensive practice.

Characteristics of Skilled Memory

Chase and Ericsson (1981, 1982) have examined the acquisition of memory skills in the laboratory, where several subjects improved their digit-span from the normal level (around 7 digits) to over 80 digits. To account for these findings, as well as related findings in the literature on the memory of experts, Chase and Ericsson proposed a framework characterizing skilled memory, which assumes that subjects are able to extend their limited short-term memory by using long-term memory. A memory skill involves the development of rapid and accurate encoding strategies that enable subjects to store and retrieve information at a speed characteristic of much more limited amounts of information in short-term memory by untrained subjects.

They enumerated five characteristics of skilled memory. First, skilled memory requires the subject to efficiently encode the presented information using existing semantic knowledge and patterns. The amount of presented information that can be successfully encoded into a unit or chunk is limited by the capacity of attention, that is, four to five symbols. (The capacity of about seven symbols in memory-span tasks are achieved through sequential rehearsal using a rehearsal buffer rather than simultaneous attention.) Second, the stored information is rapidly accessible through retrieval cues which were associated with the encoding of the presented information during the initial storage. Third, the encoded information is stored in long-term memory and can be retrieved long after immediate tests of retention. Fourth, the speed of encoding can be constantly improved as a function of practice, if subjects are motivated to improve their skills. Lastly, the acquired memory skill is specific to the stimulus domain used during practice and hence does not transfer to a different type of stimuli; for example, there is no transfer from digits to consonants.

The empirical evidence found in support of the theory of skilled memory has been obtained from memory skills acquired in the laboratory (Chase & Ericsson, 1981, 1982). One of the primary motivations of this study is to explore the generality of this theory by examining whether or not real-life memory skills, like those of JC, have the same characteristics.

OUTLINE OF CHAPTER

The first section describes an experimental analog for the restaurant situation. This analog was used for JC as well as for untrained subjects throughout our studies, with only the exception of the experimental conditions of our final experiments with JC. The next section describes our model of JC's memory skill derived from both concurrent and retrospective reports on his cognitive processes. Then JC's performance is compared to untrained subjects' performance. In a subsequent section, JC's performance is examined with specific reference to the characteristics predicted by the model of *skilled memory*. Finally, four experiments are reported: two that tested predictions of our model of JC's memory skill, and two concerned with materials different from dinner orders.

On Method

The first obstacle concerns finding a laboratory analog of the task of memorizing dinner orders in a restaurant. A restaurant corresponds to a number of different tables with different physical characteristics that a given waiter/waitress is responsible for. Each person at the table is unique in be-

havior as well as physical appearance. Hence, the restaurant provides an
environment which is particularly rich in terms of perceptual cues. The first
sessions were spent interactively with JC to design a situation which would
be sufficiently representative of the real memorization task, yet would allow sufficient control of all relevant stimulus variables.

Specific Procedure

At the beginning of each trial, the experimenter laid out a number of cards
containing pictures of people cut out from local newspapers. The cards were
arranged in a characteristic pattern depending upon the number of people
at the table. Subjects were then given a brief period of time to become
familiar with these faces. The orders for all of the customers were presented in a fixed sequence, starting with an initial customer and proceeding
clockwise around the arrangement of faces simulating a table.

A subject initiated the presentation of each order by pointing to a face
and asking for the presentation to begin. At this point, the order for the
designated customer was read by an experimenter. Each order consisted
of four items: an entrée, a cooking temperature of the meat (e.g., medium
rare), a salad dressing, and a starch. The individual items used in all of
these studies are presented in Table 2.1. At any time during the presentation of an order, the subject could ask to review items in the current order
or previously presented orders by pointing at the face and asking to hear
again the complete order or selected items like salad dressing or temperature. A subject signalled the experimenter that the next person's order should
be read by pointing or by saying "next." The presentation of items was terminated after presentation and review of the last order and review of any
previous orders. The trial was terminated when the subject said "done."
Then the subject was instructed to recall the presented items in any order
that he or she wished.

TABLE 2.1
Dinner Orders Consisting of Four Categories of Information with all
Possible Alternatives.

Materials			
Entrée	*Temperature*	*Salad Dressing*	*Starches*
Steak Oscar	Well-Done	Bleu Cheese	Fries
Sirloin Brochette	Medium-Well	Creamy Italian	Baked Potato
Filet Mignon	Medium	French	Rice
Rib Eye	Medium-Rare	Oil and Vinegar	
Bar-B-Que	Rare	Thousand Island	
Boulder Steak			
Teriyaki			

All presented dinner orders were randomly generated by a computer program. The items in each order occurred in a fixed sequence: entree, temperature, salad dressing, and starch. All of the items within a given category had an equal probability of occurring in any given order. However, if two orders for a given trial had more than two items in common, one of the orders was substituted with another randomly generated dinner order.

All sessions were tape-recorded. Study times for individual orders were measured from the request for the presentation of the items in that order until the subject signalled to have the next dinner order presented. Thus, this interval included the total mount of time required to read the current order, to review items in this order or in any of the previously presented orders, and to rehearse or to attempt to encode the presented information. The study time for a complete trial was measured from the beginning of the presentation of the first dinner order until the subject said "done." Subjects' recall protocols were recorded and were later scored for accuracy. The order in which the presented items were recalled was also analyzed. Each experiment with JC involved a series of sessions lasting about an hour with two sessions per week. Each session contained from 6 to 12 trials. A standard trial consisted of memorizing and recalling dinner orders of three, five, or eight customers at a single table.

Ecological Validity

The objective of this research is to study a naturally occurring memory skill. An important question at this point is how adequate is this laboratory analog of a natural restaurant situation. In the analysis presented in the following paragraphs, it is shown that the analog is adequate and in fact defines a more difficult task than that of memorizing orders in a restaurant.

First, a restaurant is a much richer stimulus situation. The physical location of various tables, the dress and behavior of individual customers, and other attributes of the environment permit a much richer and more unique encoding of the relationships between an order and a given customer than do the newspaper photographs used in our studies. Second, there is much more redundancy in actual restaurant orders. Individuals at the same table tend to copy each other. The random stimulus-generation procedure could produce highly atypical combinations that rarely occur in a restaurant. For example, in a restaurant the baked potato is ordered about 90% of the time with a steak, but the stimulus-generation procedure generated one third of the orders with baked potato, one third with rice, and one third with french fries. Finally, the experimental procedure emphasized the speed of memorizing and led to the more rapid presentation of orders than is typically the case when real customers are ordering dinner. JC pointed out that customers often take a relatively long time to make selections. Occasionally customers are ready to give their orders. In such cases, a waiter has some control over the order and speed by asking people to repeat their choices or engaging in small talk while encoding orders given earlier in the interaction.

In summary, the two most salient differences seem to be that, in the laboratory, the stimulus materials are less redundant and the orders are in fact presented more rapidly than in the actual restaurant situation. Let us now turn to a description of a model of JC's cognitive processes in this situation.

A MODEL OF SKILLED MEMORY
FOR DINNER ORDERS

This section presents a model of JC's memory skills which will motivate subsequent experiments. As a first approximation, JC's memory skills can be described as consisting of *encoding* processes, used during the study phase, and *recall* processes, used during the final recall of the information for a given trial. This chapter focusses on the encoding and storage of dinner orders presented in a trial. The model was inferred from an analysis of concurrent and retrospective verbal protocols. The paragraphs that follow describe JC's representation and encoding processes for a table of eight.

Two basic properties determine the overall organization of JC's efforts to encode a sequence of orders. The first is that he deals with orders in groups of four. Thus, he will carefully study and rehearse the first four orders at a table and develop a well-integrated structure for them, and then in effect start over and deal with the second four orders.

Second, JC's internal representation of the orders is a matrix organization as illustrated in Table 2.2. One dimension of the matrix as shown in

TABLE 2.2
Dinner Orders from Five People Arranged by Person Making the Order
(Columns) and by Category of Items (Rows) in a Matrix

	Order 1	Order 2	Order 3	Order 4	Order 5
Entrées	Steak Oscar	Barbeque	Filet Mignon	Filet Mignon	Barbeque
Temperature of meat	Well-Done	Well-Done	Medium-Well	Rare	Medium-Well
Salad Dressing	Thousand Island	Blue Cheese	Thousand Island	Oil and Vinegar	Creamy Italian
Starch	Rice	Baked Potato	Fries	Fries	Baked Potato

the table represents interrelationships among the elements of an order, which are associated with the face of a customer by generating an interactive representation of that individual's entrée and characteristics of the person. Various characteristics of the order were also used to assist JC in associating the four items.

The second dimension of the matrix was by category, as shown in the table. Furthermore, JC had special encoding schemes for each category of the menu. For example, salad dressings were encoded by their first letter, so that bleu cheese was encoded as B , oil and vinegar as O, thousand island as T, and so on. If the first four dressings were bleu cheese, oil and vinegar, oil and vinegar, and thousand island, JC would recode them as B-O-O-T and if possible relate the sequence of four letters to the English word, in this case, BOOT. Temperatures were encoded as a spatial pattern in terms of how well the meat was cooked, exploiting the fact that the temperatures are ordered on an ordinal scale. For example, rare, medium, medium-rare, rare, would have a spatial pattern similar to the one shown in Figure 2.1.

Starches were nearly always encoded as serial patterns, because with only three different starches, there was bound to be at least one repetition in a block of four orders. Entrées were the most variable, and JC reports relying on repetitions and also patterns emerging from a subdivision of the various meat orders into expensive and inexpensive steaks.

Generating within-category encodings requires considerable memory overhead. When a new order is presented, JC has to decide which category to encode, retrieve the earlier items from that category, encode the old items and the new item, and then use the same procedure for the remaining categories. Items in the current order have to be kept in a rehearsal buffer before they are successfully encoded with earlier items in their respective categories. Old and new items in a category must be in attention at the same time in order to permit the recognition of serial patterns in the items. The maximum capacity for attention — that is, four or five items — is con-

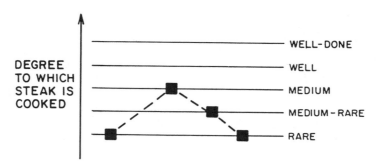

FIGURE 2.1   The spatial pattern corresponding to four temperatures of steaks in sequence: rare, medium, medium-rare, rare.

sistent with the largest within-category chunks used by JC while encoding dinner orders from one table. The assumptions of independent storage in a rehearsal buffer, and of size of units of encodings, are remarkably consistent with the research on memory for digits (Chase & Ericsson, 1981, 1982).

In order to completely describe JC's skill we need to account for how retrieval can occur from long-term memory, where previously presented items are stored. Chase and Ericsson (1982) proposed that a retrieval structure providing sufficient cues for rapid retrieval of the desired information was necessary. When JC wants to retrieve earlier presented items, such as starches, to encode the starch of the current order, these starches can be accessed primarily using the category label. The detailed structure of JC's cognitive processes and structures is being explicated in a computer model.

VERBAL REPORTS EXPERIMENT

Concurrent as well as retrospective verbal reports for selected trials were collected during the first systematic experiment with Ericsson and Simon (1980, 1984) have presented a framework for analyzing verbal reports and encoding these as data. One of the issues concerns whether giving primarily concurrent reports will influence or change the cognitive processes and the performance of the memory task. This may be particularly relevant as Ericsson and Simon found that with "think-aloud" instructions the only changes concern slowing down the process. However, if "thinking aloud" slows down (i.e., increases) the study times, and increases in study times generally lead to improved memory, there may be a change in memory performance.

The first study was directly designed to address the issue of the effect of thinking aloud on JC's cognitive processes in the memory task. The first condition used standard think-aloud instructions (Ericsson & Simon, 1984). In the second condition, JC was asked to count aloud from one through ten during the study phase of the trials. It was assumed that counting is virtually automatic and involves minimal additional cognitive processes. The experiment involved a series of four sessions on different days. Each session consisted of two blocks of trials. Each block contained tables of different sizes (three, five, and eight in random order). The first block was presented with one instruction, and the second block with the other instruction. The order of presenting instructions was counterbalanced over sessions.

An analysis of variance showed no main effect of type of verbalizing condition (F $(1, 18) = 0.13$, $p > .05$) nor an interaction with table size (F $(2,18) = 0.346$, $p > 0.05$). As expected, a significant main effect of table size was obtained (F $(2,18) = 97.439$, $p < 0.001$). In Figure 2.2 the mean study times for each table size are plotted for both verbalizing conditions

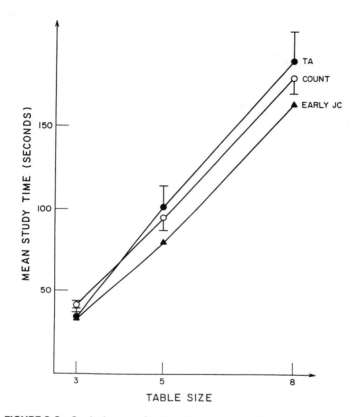

FIGURE 2.2 Study time as a function of table size for Think-Aloud (TA) condition, with counting from 1 to 10 (COUNT) trials and silent control trials from the first experiment.

along with the mean study times for silent control trials obtained in the Category Presentation Experiment (described later under Experiments).

Compared with the silent control performance during sessions recorded immediately after this experiment, both concurrent verbalizing conditions appear slower but the pattern of study times and order of recall are no different. We conclude from this that thinking aloud in this task only slightly slows down the cognitive processes.

In some subsequent studies, it was shown that JC's slowing down could be avoided by restricting the verbalization to thoughts already in oral form, thus explicitly avoiding verbal encoding of thoughts (Ericsson & Simon, 1980, 1984). JC was able to think aloud with these new restrictions and generate study times and accuracy of recall at the level of his silent performance.

The analysis of performance with and without thinking aloud and automatic irrelevant verbalization support the conclusion that no additional cognitive processing during the think-aloud trials (except vocalization) is involved, hence the verbalized information otherwise heeded. In addition, retrospective reports from silent and "think-aloud" trials contained very similar information on a process with the same structure.

PROTOCOL DATA SUPPORTING
THE MODEL OF JC'S MEMORY SKILL

Table 2.3 presents a complete verbatim transcription of JC's think-aloud

TABLE 2.3
Transcribed Think-Aloud Protocol and Retrospective Report
from the Study of Dinner Orders from a Table with Five People

---

E: Why don't you start thinking out loud.

S: Oh, it is five. I thought it was going to be eight. These five people look like they don't fit together. That's unusual. Out of your real estate magazine. This guy, the first guy looks like he's way out of place with this group of people so we'll see how easy his order is. Okay. Go.

E.   Steak Oscar, well done, thousand island, rice.

S: Okay. *Well done and rice seem to fit that guy. Steak Oscar doesn't.* Next.

E.   Barbeque, well done, bleu cheese, baked potato.

S: *That sounds fairly standard. TB is my salad dressing notation* and next.

E.   Filet mignon, medium well, thousand island, fries.

S: *TBT, rice, baker, fries. Temperatures are making an easy pattern.* Next.

E.   Filet Mignon, rare, oil and vinegar, fries.

S: *TB.* What's the salad dressing?

E: Thousand Island.

S: TBTO. Starch for #4?

E: Fries.

S: Fries, okay. Rice, baker, fries, fries, TBTO. Next.

E: Barbeque, medium well, creamy Italian, baked potato.

S: *TBTOH. Barbeque, that's the second barbeque, medium well,* starch?

E: Baked potato.

S: Okay, *fries, rice, starches are easy.* Done. It seems much easier when I'm not counting, by the way. Okay, salad dressings. Thousand, bleu, thousand, oil, creamy Italian. Temperatures: well, well, medium-well, rare, medium-well. Starches: rice, baked potato, fries, fries, baked potato. Steaks: Oscar, barbeque, filet, I have to think a minute on that guy. And the last one is barbeque. Um, #4's steak is rare with fries and he's having oil and vinegar and uh, I have it narrowed down to a filet and a brochette are the two that I'm thinking about. Now, by process of elimination, it seemed to me that there was only one double on this order and that was the barbeques. There were two barbeques, it seemed that everything else was singular, and if there's already a filet that I'm sure of then this guy had a brochette, for #4. And I'll go by that. A brochette. No.

---

protocol for a "five-top" (table with five people). The underlined portions are evidence relevant to the model; the remainder of the protocol is requests for presentations and simple repetitions of the just-presented order.

JC used specialized encoding strategies for each category of item in the dinner orders. Table 2.4 shows statements relevant to salad dressings for the four times that JC memorized tables of eight in this first experiment. JC uses the following letter abbreviations for the five salad dressings: B, bleu cheese; O, oil and vinegar; F, French dressing; T, thousand island; and H, creamy Italian (the house dressing). The most striking result in Table 2.4 is the consistency and reliability of JC's encoding of the salad dressing into groups of four orders. Observe that the dressings from orders 1 through 4 and 5 through 8 are rehearsed together. This pattern of verbalizations provides strong support for the assumptions about the processes that JC used to encode salad dressings. On only four occasions is the letter code not verbalized. Three of these instances refer to immediate repeats of the same salad dressing. On the fourth occasion JC requests information about the previous salad dressing and verbalizes the letter code during the study of the next order.

TABLE 2.4
All segments of Four Think-Aloud Protocols Relevant to Salad
Dressings for Memorization of Dinner Orders from Eight People

	Session			
Order No.	I	II	II	IV
1				
2.	BH	OO	HH	This will be FB to get us started here on that FB
3.	BHF	OOH	HHO	FBH
4.	BHFB			FBHB is an easy salad dressing
5.		T	HHOF	
6.	#5 is also oil & vinegar	TF	BO	HB,HB,HB
7.	OOB	TFO	BOT	HBB
8.	Bleu cheese and baked potato again	TFOO OOHHTFO	BOTH	HBBH

The encoding of starches shows the same groupings but exploits the patterns of run that occur because there are only three starches. Table 2.5 presents all statements relevant to starches during memorization of the same four tables of eight. The major result shown in Table 2.5 is that starches, like salad dressings, are encoded together in groups of four. The primary encodings are patterns using repeats, like AABB, ABBA, ABBB, and so on. JC verbalizes also when three starches in a row are different (III-3 in Table 2.5). He also occasionally verbalizes whether the starch is standard (with meat dishes, baked potato is standard) or deviant, such as rice and fries. Virtually all starches considered are part of groups of items studied, except that at III-6 he notes a relationship between the pattern of the current starches and the pattern of starches for orders 1–4.

The number of verbalizations regarding relations between temperatures and entrées is much smaller. In general, these verbalizations show a pattern of results similar to the data for starches. JC is attempting to exploit

TABLE 2.5
All Segments of Four Think-Aloud Protocols Relevant to Starches
for Memorization of Dinner Orders from Eight People.

	Session			
	I	*II*	*III*	*IV*
1.				
2.			fries, rice	Two different starches from the usual rice, fries
3.		fries, standard, standard	three of its starches in a row—this is the standard	two fries in a row
4.	fries, bake, bake, fries	fries, two standard, rice	"two fries" fries, rice, baker, fries	fries, 3 fries in a row
5.				
6.	baker, rice		rice, fries a reverse pattern from the first two orders	(#5) Teri has a funny starch
7.	rice again	then fries		rice, baker, rice
8.	bleu cheese and baked potato again		rice, fries rice, rice	rice, baker, rice, fries

the patterns that appear in groupings of four orders. For example, JC verbalized twice that the same entrée was presented in direct succession, and twice verbalized repeating entrées that were separated by at least one order. In all but one instance the related items both belonged to orders 1–4 or 5–8.

JC explicitly encodes the dinner orders in terms of groups of four items of each category. With the possible exception of entrées, all relations between items are limited to those contained in a given group.

In the following section we will compare JC's performance with those of untrained subjects, and also try to find observable characteristics that can allow us to infer the cognitive processes used by untrained subjects in this task.

COMPARISON OF JC WITH UNTRAINED SUBJECTS

In order to evaluate whether JC's performance is within the range of normal untrained subjects, eleven subjects from the subject pool performed the same task. The subjects were given an initial training session involving five memorization trials: tables of size three, three, five, five, and eight. Eight subjects returned for the second session, where they memorized orders from tables of three, five, eight, three, five, and eight. All other aspects of the procedure were identical to those used with JC and are described in the General Method section.

The average total study times and percent errors are shown in Figures 2.3 and 2.4. The difference between JC and the naive subjects is actually greater than either of the two graphs indicate, because subjects would probably require substantially longer study times to reduce the number of errors. We will now analyze further data which should give evidence for different processing strategies between JC and the untrained subjects.

Order of Strategy Recall

Subjects were told that they could recall the presented dinner orders in *any* sequence. Hence, there are a large number of possible sequences in which the items of the dinner orders could be recalled. Fortunately, the orders of recall are quite regular for both the untrained subjects as a group, and for JC.

Only two general classes of output sequences were observed in these experiments. The first class involved recall by dinner order. The observed output order for *presented-item* recall is the exact sequence in which the items of the dinner orders were presented. *Presented-order* recall is defined as output of the dinner orders in the presented sequence, with allowed varia-

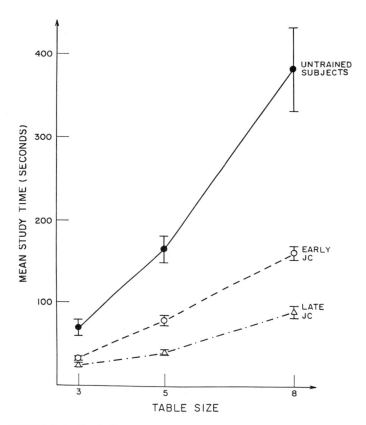

FIGURE 2.3 Study time as a function of table size for untrained subjects and the memory expert (JC), early and late in the experimental investigation.

tions in the serial order of output of items within each dinner order. *Dinner Order* recall requires that all information pertaining to a given order is recalled together, but any sequence of recalled dinner orders is admissible. All these serial orders of recall provide evidence for a memory representation using the orders of people as units.

The second class is output by category; that is, recalling all salad dressings together, all starches together, and so on. *Category* recall is any output sequence by category. The two classes of output sequences lead to virtually non-overlapping sequences with recall of all items.

Five of the eight naive subjects used the presented-item recall strategy. For them, 96.2% of all recalled items were consistent with the exact sequence of initial presentation. The sixth subject recalled the dinner orders in reverse sequence, although the sequence of items within a dinner order was in exact correspondence with the presented sequence of items. This subject was 100% consistent in the application of this strategy. The seventh subject recalled a couple of orders with a modified category strategy, that is, entrées and temperatures together and then salad dressings and finally starches. The last subject recalled information of each dinner order together but with no consistency of items within an order. Hence, all but one subject displayed recall based on dinner orders. For the seven subjects, 99.1% of the items were consistent with such representation. When the deviant subject who occasionally used the category strategy is included, the 95.1% of the items were consistent with recall based on dinner orders.

JC's recall was analyzed for "control" trials for two early periods to provide information about type and stability of recall strategies. JC used

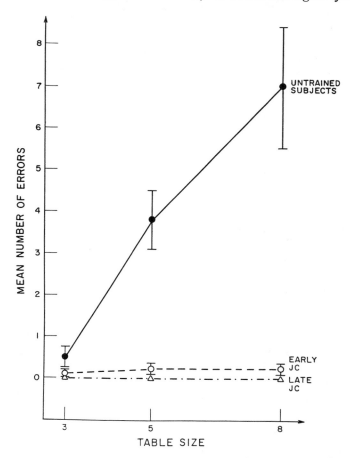

FIGURE 2.4 Mean number of errors as a function of table size for untrained subjects and the memory expert (JC), early and late in the experimental investigation.

category recall without exception, and 95.9% and 100.0% of his recall was described by that recall strategy for the respective periods. The lower value for the first period was due to recalling tables of three with entrée and temperature together. Without that recall, the corresponding percentage is 98.6.

Although JC was quite variable in the sequence in which categories were recalled, he was not random. For the two periods, the average rank of recalling a category was computed. During the first period, the salad dressing tended to be recalled first (average rank = 1.64) and then no preference between entrées (2.68), temperatures (2.77), and starches (2.91). During the second period, salad dressings or entrées were recalled first (1.67 and 1.83 respectively), and then temperatures (2.75), and lastly starches (3.75).

In summary, novice subjects exhibited a wide variety of output sequences but a very large percentage of these sequences were from the first class of recall orders, suggesting that the memory representation was organized by dinner order. The model of JC's memory skills, presented in an earlier section, assumed that JC encoded information by category. Data from concurrent verbal protocols was presented supporting this conclusion. JC's consistent use of category recall is additional evidence of the basic assertion of the model that he encodes items by category.

Errors in Recall

Earlier, it was shown that there are very large differences in error rates between the naive subjects and JC. This section presents a more detailed analysis of the error data for the five subjects who consistently used the presented-order output sequence. JC did not make enough errors at any point during these experiments to permit systematic analysis of his error data.

Table 2.6 shows the average number of errors per item for different serial positions in the list for those five subjects who recalled items in the *presented order* (see previous pages for details). Serial position refers to the order in which the items were first presented, and no corrections are made for later re-presentations of the same item.

TABLE 2.6
Average Number of Errors Per Item as a Function of Order of Initial
Presentation

	Serial Position of First Presentation							
Table Size	1	2	3	4	5	6	7	8
3	0.16	.031	.078					
5	.172	.156	.156	.203	.188			
8	.093	.141	.234	.234	.297	.172	.281	.250

The results shown in Table 2.6 suggest a primacy effect for the tables of eight. This effect for tables of eight cannot be accounted for by a higher frequency of re-presentation of the early items, as shown by the observed average proportion of re-presentation of items from the respective serial positions (1 through 8): 15.2%, 14.9%, 14.9%, 12.7%, 13.8%, 10.9%, 11.2%, and 6.5%. This effect was not mediated by recency, since the first order was re-presented just prior to recall no more often than any other order. There is no suggestion of any recency effect.

In summary, the results presented in Table 2.6 suggest that standard models for free recall, such as those described by Atkinson and Shiffrin (1968), can be employed to explain the data from naive subjects. The data from Table 2.6 show a clear primacy effect. The lack of a recency effect is due to the fact that the five subjects shown in Table 2.6 attempted to recall items in the order in which they were presented, effectively eliminating any items still present in short-term memory. Immediately outputting the contents of short-term memory before going on to attempt to recall the remaining items of the list is a strategy not used by subjects initially in memory experiments (Murdock, 1974, p. 237). Interestingly enough, the naive subjects did not acquire this strategy in two days of practice in this particular task.

Study Times for Individual Orders

The study times for individual orders are measured from the beginning of the presentation of the order until the presentation of the "next" order. This time includes requests for previously presented items of complete dinner orders. The analyses of the naive subject's recall coding and data suggests a sequential memorization of complete dinner orders. Such memorization would lead to a linear increase of the time required for committing each new order.

Figure 2.5 presents the study times for individual orders for the normal subjects. The data strongly supports the sequential hypothesis, as the study times for the first five orders are approximately equal regardless of table size. The study times roughly increase in a linear fashion with the number of earlier presented orders, except for the first order (no previous orders) and the eighth order, which contains a large number of requests of re-presentations of earlier orders. Naive subjects memorized the dinner orders as if they were a list of dinner orders (units of four ordered items) with their cognitive process being independent of length of the list to be presented. It was only at the end of the longer lists (tables 2.5 and 2.8) that they used differential amounts of effort to commit the entire list to memory.

Figure 2.6 shows the average study times for each dinner order where each line corresponds to a given table size for JC's data. Comparison of

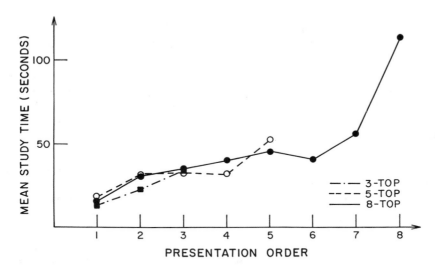

FIGURE 2.5 Average study times for individual dinner orders as a function of serial order of presentation for untrained subjects studying orders from tables of three, five, and eight people.

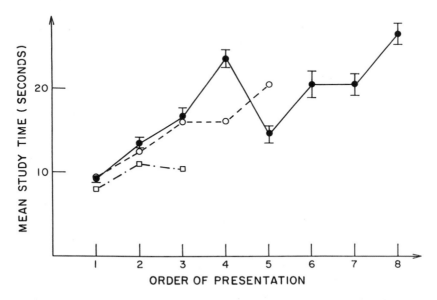

FIGURE 2.6 Average study times for individual dinner orders as a function of serial order of presentation for memory expert (JC) studying orders from three, five, and eight people.

Figures 2.5 and 2.6 shows that both the naive subjects and JC show strikingly different patterns of study times. This is especially apparent for tables of eight. Study time increases linearly across the first four orders and then there is a sharp drop in study time between orders four and five. The study time again increases for orders five through eight, and the first and last half of the serial position curves are strikingly similar. This pattern of study times is exactly what would be predicted from the model of JC's memory skills described earlier. Recall that the model assumes that JC encodes items by category and in groups of four. Study times are predicted to progressively increase *within* a group of four because of larger processing demands for the later orders within each group. With the exception of the first order within the group, storage of items in subsequent orders requires that JC first retrieve earlier presented items of the same category, to allow extracting of patterns involving all items within the group of items of that category.

In summary, JC and the naive subjects use very different encoding processes. The results for recall orders, error patterns, and study times suggest that naive subjects tend to memorize information exactly as presented — that is, as a sub-list consisting of the four items for each individual at a table — and that they proceed sequentially through the list, spending about the same amount of time studying each order, independent of list length. The only exception to this pattern is the rather extensive review and study after the presentation of the last order at a table. We conclude that naive subjects' performance is well described by standard models that have been developed to describe memory for unrelated materials in laboratory tasks. The recall order and the study time data from JC strongly support our model of his memory skill proposed earlier.

IS JC'S MEMORY SKILLLED MEMORY?

Results presented in the previous section showed that normal subjects could be well described by traditional theories for long-term memory (LTM), yet JC appeared to rely on rather different cognitive processes and structures. JC differs from the untrained students in that he has acquired a memory skill through extensive practice. Chase and Ericsson (1981, 1982) have examined the acquisition of memory skill in the laboratory, and have proposed a model of skilled memory to account for these findings as well as for related findings in the literature (Ericsson & Chase, 1982). This model assumes that subjects are able to extend their limited short-term memory by using long-term memory with rapid and accurate encoding and retrieval in such a way that the performance characteristics resemble the use of short-term memory by untrained subjects.

The following section describes JC's memory skills and critically examines whether they have the characteristics proposed for skilled memory. In the introduction the five characteristics of skilled memory were briefly reviewed. For two of these characteristics, ample empirical evidence has already been presented. First, the efficient use of existing semantic knowledge and patterns for encoding has been clearly demonstrated in the different mnemonic procedures for different category items. An experiment reported later in this chapter shows that times required for encoding with these four mnemonic procedures differ markedly from each other. The evidence for restriction of the number of items in each group to 4–5 comes from several sources. The encoding and storage of retrieval cues along with the presented information is equally clear although the empirical evidence for it is less direct. In this section two additional characteristics are examined. By requesting recall of information from a large number of lists after the study session is completed (post-session recall), we can examine if JC stores the information in long-term memory. The speedup of encoding processes will be examined by analyzing JC's performance during the two-year experiment. The fifth and final characteristic, that the acquired memory skill is specific to the stimulus domain used during practice and hence does not transfer, will be evaluated later in two experiments on generalizability.

Long-Term Memory
as Evidenced by Post-Session Recall

One of the most important assertions of the skilled memory framework is that an expert like JC is capable of rapidly encoding material and storing it in long-term memory. Thus one would expect fairly high levels of post-session recall barring any possible proactive or retroactive interference effect. Chase and Ericsson (1981, 1982) have found exactly this pattern of results for strings of random digits. However, it is possible that JC only retains dinner order information for the time required to walk over to the bussing station where he writes the order down for kitchen personnel. It is true that he needs information to later place dishes with the right person, but this could be conceivably done using notes. Thus it is an open question how much of the dinner orders JC remembers at the end of an experimental session during which up to twelve dinner orders have been memorized.

Two kinds of evidence were obtained in assessing the conjecture that JC encodes dinner orders in long-term memory. The first was obtained by asking him for a surprise recall of orders he had taken earlier in the day while working at the restaurant. During the second year of our laboratory study of JC, we had him recall all of the tables he had memorized during a session in an experiment that was designed to evaluate the generality of JC's memory skills.

During one of the first interview sessions JC was unexpectedly asked to recall all orders taken during his work earlier in the day (about 3–4 hours earlier). He recalled information from 15 out of 18 tables. (The restaurant kept all of the waiters' tickets, which allowed us to evaluate the accuracy of his recall.) Out of 61 ordered items (entrées, beverages, etc.) belonging to the 15 tables, he correctly recalled 80%, incorrectly recalled 10%, and omitted 10%. JC thought aloud during his recall, used primarily episodic and spatial (layout of restaurant) cues, and recalled the information by table.

JC's memory for material acquired in the laboratory was evaluated during five sessions of the category list experiment, which was designed to evaluate the generality of JC's memory skills and was carried out toward the end of our studies. The category list experiment is described in detail in a later section. Briefly, this experiment involved two kinds of materials: dinner orders as described in the general methods section, and category lists. The category list experimental materials had a structure identical to the dinner orders and were presented in identical fashion, except that animal names were substituted for entrées, flowers for salad dressings, times for temperatures, and metals for starches. In the discussion that follows, the terms "order" and "table" will be used to refer to either type of material. All five sessions consisted of JC studying and immediately recalling orders from two blocks of six tables each; three were dinner order tables, and three were category list order tables.

At the end of the first session, JC was asked to recall as many orders as possible from the twelve tables presented earlier in the session. JC asserted that he was only able to recall information from the second block of six tables. His recall was organized by tables with the particular kind of materials (dinner orders or category lists) and size (tables of three, five, and eight). The order of recall for any table was exclusively by category. JC got 79.2% of the items correct from those tables that he attempted to recall. His overall performance in the second block of six tables was 59.4% correct. Furthermore, there was some evidence that items from a corresponding table, both in terms of size and of materials, tended to be intruded upon by materials studied during the first block of six tables.

When JC attempted to recall information from the first block of six tables his accuracy of recall for the first block was only 34.4%, but that is reliably higher than chance, 21.5%. The low level of recall from the first block was somewhat surprising, so we decided to change from free recall to cued recall. In two of the following four sessions, we regenerated the pictures corresponding to tables 1 through 6 to serve as cues in the postsession recall; and during the other two sessions, the pictures corresponding to tables 7 through 12 were presented. His accuracy of cued recall is given for both dinner orders and category lists (animal orders) in Figure 2.7. His recall of information about dinner orders is virtually perfect for the second block: 122 of 128 presented items, and reliably less for the first

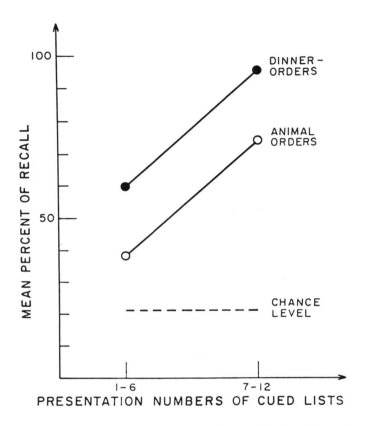

FIGURE 2.7   Mean percent correct recall of lists as a function of presentation number, when JC was given a post-session cued recall for either the first or last half of studied lists.

block. The recall of the analogous category lists have the same pattern, but the level of accuracy is lower. For these lists we noticed a couple of very obvious intrusions from block 1 onto cued recall of block 2. On both occasions with cued recall of block 2, JC recalled one entire sublist of items for a five-top from block 1. (The probability of one such event occurring by chance is less than 1 in 3000.)

Given that recall for dinner orders was virtually perfect for block 2, we examined the recall of dinner orders from block 1 for differences in the amount recalled from each category, such as salad dressings. If systematic differences were found it might suggest that the better recalled category was more closely associated with the pictures of faces. When corrections for incorrect guesses were made, starches were recalled best (72%), entrées and salad dressings second (58% and 50% respectively), and temperatures worst (38%). Hence these results lend no support to the earlier suggestion that entrées are more directly associated with faces.

In sum, the evidence for post-session memory for the studied information is clear and in accordance with the characteristics of skilled memory (Chase & Ericsson, 1982). Furthermore, we observed clear interference from previously studied lists of the same structure and with the same type of information. Passage of time, and other kinds of lists, appeared to have smaller, if any, effect. Hence, only for lists of the same structure and content were massive interference effects (observed in normal laboratory studies) obtained (Underwood, 1957).

Improvement in Performance
During the Year-Long Experiment

During the year-long experiment JC showed a remarkable improvement. After the initial couple of sessions, his recall accuracy was virtually perfect for all the table sizes. His improvement was also exhibited in a steady decrease in the study times. In Figure 2.8 the average study times for four different experiments are given.

The most striking result is steady decrease in study time, along with the

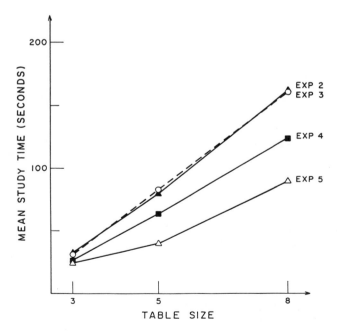

FIGURE 2.8   Mean total study time as function of table size for memory expert (JC) in the four consecutive experiments.

lack of any sign of reaching a stable final performance level. One should also notice that the improvement appears to be proportional over table sizes, and at each level of practice the study times can be described as a linear function of table size. Before turning to a discussion of this practice effect, let us compare the study times for individual orders at different levels of practice, which are given in Figure 2.9. The rather clear increase in latency associated with grouping items into groups of four or five appears to have almost vanished with further practice. However, the reduction of study times, as shown in the previous figure, is essentially unchanged.

This improvement as a function of practice is remarkably similar to the pattern of results found by Chase and Ericsson (1981, 1982). They also found (in their self-paced version of the digit-span task) that remarkable speed up appeared to be most pronounced for longer sequences that initially required a lot of overhead with cognitive processes. As a function of practice these serial cognitive processes appeared to be transformed into processes relying on more direct access. In sum, the first four characteristics of skilled memory have been clearly evidenced in JC's memory skill. The final characteristic, that is, the lack of transfer to other materials, are explored in the two experiments described in the following pages.

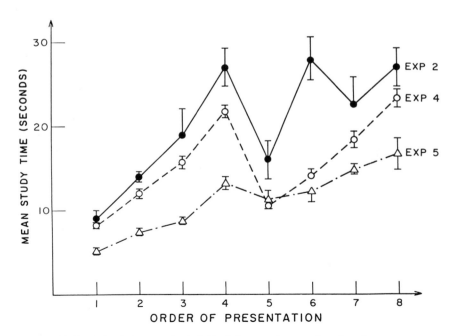

FIGURE 2.9   Study time for individual dinner orders as a function of presentation order for memory expert (JC) in three different experiments.

EXPERIMENTAL STUDIES

Empirical evidence from a wide range of sources (verbal protocols, latencies, order of recall, etc.) gives strong support for our model of JC's memory skill. Our model proposes the existence of encoding operations and retrieval structures whose existence we cannot directly observe. The empirical support for such mediating structures would be radically increased if one could use these constructs to predict the characteristics of performance for *new* and *different* memorization tasks. In the following two experiments the order of presentation of the dinner orders is radically changed. (Later we will report two additional experiments studying memorization of material other than dinner orders, in which the standard presentation method was retained.) For the two experiments described here, experimental conditions were developed that should either enhance or interfere with the encoding processes described by the model. JC's performance in these studies was always compared with the standard method of presenting dinner orders described in the general procedures.

The Category Presentation Experiment

The model of JC's memory skill presented in an earlier section assumes that JC primarily encodes items by category, and only to a lesser degree associates them with an individual. This hypothesis was tested by taking the items generated by the standard method and presenting them by category rather than by complete order for a given person at a table. It was assumed that category presentation should at least not interfere with the encoding process. At best, presentation by category could assist the encoding process since it would avoid retrieval and storage of subgroups of items and allow for a direct storage of the entire group of four items from a category. In addition, with category presentation we can now directly measure the time required to store four items from the same category with the corresponding mnemonic encoding procedures.

During five sessions, JC memorized and recalled six dinner orders, two each of tables of three, five, and eight. One dinner order of each table size (total of three dinner orders) was presented with the earlier-described standard instructions (control condition). The remaining three dinner orders were presented with within-category groups of items (experimental condition) when JC requested information by saying "next." In the experimental condition for a table of three, JC heard a category name, like "salad dressings," and then the list of the three salad dressings. For a table of five, JC was read a category name and five items. However, for a table of eight, the items in a category were split into two groups of four corresponding to the first four people and the last four people. The order of presentation of categories was determined randomly from presentation to presentation. Control trials and experimental trials were randomly mixed and the order of presentation was counterbalanced over sessions.

Results. The detailed method of analysis as well as the actual analysis is presented elsewhere (Ericsson & Polson, 1988) and hence only the major findings are discussed here. No effects were found for the experimental condition (normal vs. category presentation) or its interaction with table size. The effect of table size was large and accounted for most of the variance.

An analysis of the average study time for both conditions showed no difference between conditions even for the first session. The absence of practice effects suggests that JC did not have to adapt to the category presentation, and thus this method of presentation is compatible with his usual encoding processes.

For dinner orders presented by category it is possible to break down the total study time into four component study times corresponding to items from each category. We measured the time from presentation of the first item of a category until JC indicated that the items from the next category should be presented. The detailed analysis of these study times is given in Ericsson and Polson (1988), and only the main results will be described here. No effect of order of presentation of a category *within* a list was found. Hence, the study time for a group of items from a category was no different, when presented as the first category within a list, compared to when presented as the last category. This contrasts markedly with the linear increases of study times observed for individual dinner orders as a function of serial order of presentation order discussed earlier. Hence there is good evidence that storage of within-category groups is direct and noncumulative.

Ericsson and Polson (1988) showed reliable main effects on study time for both the type of category and the number of items presented, as well as a reliable interaction between category and number of items. These results, especially the significant interaction, clearly implicates *different processes of encoding for different types of items*. The mean study times for three, five, and eight items are given for each item type in Figure 2.10. Although all types of items show the expected monotonic increase with the number of presented items, the time for encoding temperatures for five-item sequences appears a little discrepant. One possible reason for this deviation is that five temperatures may in some cases exceed JC's rehearsal buffer, as it would correspond to anywhere from five to ten words. For all other items with multiple words, like entrées (Sirloin Brochette), JC had a one-word abbreviation. In sum, these results show clear differences in study-time patterns for different types of items, which supports the existence of different mnemonic encodings for different categories of items. It also supports the idea of independence of encoding of different item-groups.

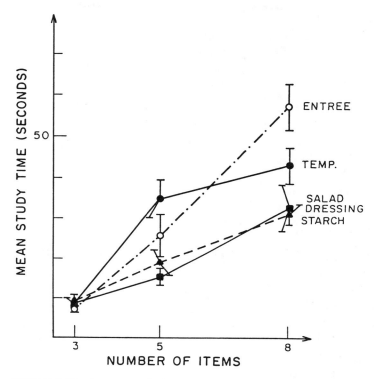

FIGURE 2.10 Average study time with standard error bars for groups of three, five, and eight items from different categories: salad dressings (filled squares), starches (filled triangles), temperatures (filled circles), and entrées (unfilled circles).

Finally, the large differences in required study time suggest that the time taken to encode associations between items and the corresponding person is short, and possibly doesn't take any additional time.

Conclusion. It would have been interesting to show that within-category presentation led to a decrease in overall study times. What is remarkable is that JC, from the *first* session, was able to perform about equally well in the within-category presentation. This suggests that this form of presentation was highly compatible with his normal mode of processing. To the extent that it can be assumed that differences between conditions are small, this suggests that the time required to break up the presented dinner order and associate the items with the other within-category items is small, and that the main portion of the study time is devoted to the generation of a long-term memory code.

Varied Presentation-Order Experiment

One way to disrupt within-category encoding would be to vary the sequence in which people around the table give their orders. Remember that in the standard control situation people were giving their orders in a clockwise sequence around the table. This variation is ecologically valid in the sense that people occasionally give orders out of sequence because of seniority, rank, or sex, and also because they need more time to decide. However, in most situations a waiter or waitress can get the customers to order in sequence by waiting until everybody has made their selections, and then directing his or her attention to them all in sequence. By random variation of the sequence of orders, JC could no longer commit to memory an increasing sequence of within-category items, as was so clearly evidenced in the think-aloud protocol analyzed earlier. This should increase the difficulty of the by-category encoding process.

This experiment was conducted in the same manner as the category-presentation experiment, with differences in instructions and procedure for the experimental condition. In the experimental condition JC was given orders for the Nth customer (going clockwise) as "Order N" and followed by a listing of items, as in the control condition, with the sequence of orders determined randomly. In the control condition JC was given the orders in the same way and with the same words, but the orders were always presented in sequence from Order 1 to Order 8, where 8 is the table size.

The detailed analysis is given in Ericsson and Polson (1988), and only the main results will be described here. The effects of table size were, of course, highly significant, and all the effects reported here were at least significant at 1% level. The main effect of condition (normal vs. varied presentation) was significant as well as its interaction with table size.

Figure 2.11 shows the mean study times for all table sizes for both conditions. A post hoc analysis (Ericsson & Polson, 1988) showed that significant main effects and interaction should be interpreted as a reliable main effect of table size and a significant difference in study time between conditions for *only* the table size of eight. Although the study times for varied presentation order were slower for table sizes of three and five, these differences didn't even come close to being statistically reliable. The errors were exceedingly low for both conditions.

The most readily available index of JC's encoding is his order of recall. An analysis of his order of recall during the first two sessions showed that both for control and experimental conditions he recalled in perfect agreement (100%) with the category recall output sequence, supporting the conclusion that his encoding of the information is the same in both conditions. The only way that this could be achieved would be to recode the information in varied presentation order into the corresponding spatial clockwise order.

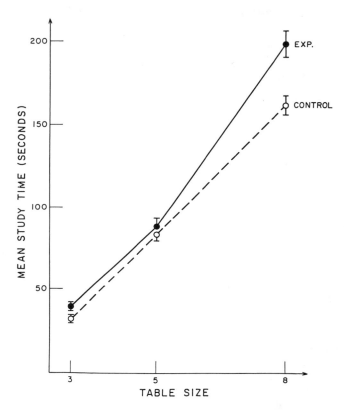

FIGURE 2.11   Mean total study times as a function of table size for control and experimental condition in varied presentation experiment.

In order to better understand JC's cognitive processes in the varied presentation condition, he was instructed to think aloud while he memorized an eight-top. The verbatim transcription of think-aloud protocol is given in Table 2.7. From reading this protocol it is clear that JC relied, as before, on encoding within-category items together. He used a modified list-structure, in which items were encoded in their clockwise order around the table, and items presented later could be inserted. All verbalizations pertaining to salad dressings are shown in Table 2.8, where the last-presented salad dressing is circled.

From Table 2.8 it is clearly seen that JC accumulates items until all the four items corresponding to positions one to four are presented; then all those items are encoded and only the remaining items are retrieved and heeded. JC, in most cases, had to retain more than his preferred four items before he could encode them into a chunk. This is the most likely source

TABLE 2.7

Complete Think-Aloud Protocol from Memorization of Dinner Orders
from Eight People with Varied Presentation Sequence

There's two ladies at the table and the rest are a bunch of guys.
Alright, go.
Order 2. Teriyaki, rare, French, baked potato.
Okay, French and usual starch. Teri, rare, French. Next.
Order 3. Filet mignon, well done, thousand island, rice.
FT. Filet, well, opposite temperature scales. Rice. That's an unusual starch.
FT. They're next to each other. Next.
Order 5. Steak Oscar, medium rare, creamy Italian, baked potato.
Oscar, medium rare, baked potato, creamy Italian. That's FTH and not in order.
   Usual starch. Usual temperature. Temperature.
Order 4. Steak Oscar, medium well, creamy Italian, fries.
FTHH. Two Oscar's in a row. Um, medium well, temperatures all over the place.
   Starch on number 4.
Fries.
Fries. So that's baker, rice, fries, baker. Two unusuals in a bunch. Temperatures all
   over the place. FTHH. Next.
Order 1. Boulder steak, medium well, thousand island, rice.
Boulder steak, medium well, thousand island. Starch?
Rice.
Rice. Boulder steak, medium well, okay. That's TFTHH. Alright, TFTH is the first
   sequence. It's complete. TFTH that's not too bad. Temperature recall. Medium
   well, rare, well done, medium well, okay, medium well's at a 1 and 4. and 2 for
   the steaks. There's three starches that are messed up. Only one usual starch.
   That's 2. Okay. TFTH. Next.
Order 8. Rib eye, medium well, thousand island, fries.
Rib eye, medium well, thousand island, fries. H blank blank T. Temperatures, most
   of the corners are medium well, rib eye for number 8. Fries, that's the first fries,
   no second fries on the bunch. Next.
Order 7. Barbecue, well done, bleu cheese, fries.
Barbecue, well done, bleu cheese, fries. That's two fries in a row, the second well
   done. Barbecue, well done. Bleu cheese, fries, that's HBT on the second go-
   around. HBT. Next.
Order 6. Rib eye, rare, French, fries.
Rib eye, rare, french, fries. Second rare, three fries in a row. HFBT. HFBT.
   Somewhat difficult. HFBT. TFTH. HFBT. HFBT. HFBT. BT. TFTH.

---

of the longer required study times for the tables of eight in the experimental condition.

In a subsequent analysis, we identified for each presented sequence the point at which JC has enough information available to encode a chunk of items 1–4 or 5–8. If the pattern from the control condition (cf. difference between Order 4 and Order 5 in Table 2.7) applies we would expect a reduction in study time for the order following such a successful chunk generation. The mean study time per order, when the encoding of a chunk could

TABLE 2.8
All Segments Relevant to Salad Dressings in Table 2.7, with
a Corresponding Display of Earlier-Presented Salad Dressings

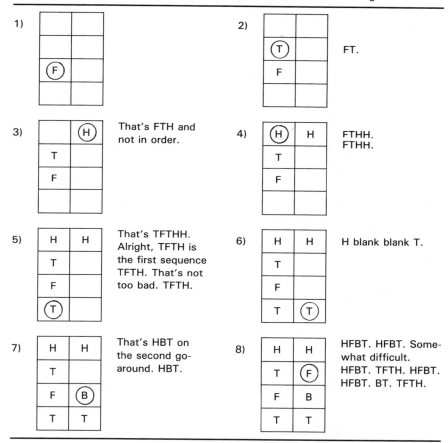

1)

2) FT.

3) That's FTH and not in order.

4) FTHH.
FTHH.

5) That's TFTHH. Alright, TFTH is the first sequence TFTH. That's not too bad. TFTH.

6) H blank blank T.

7) That's HBT on the second go-around. HBT.

8) HFBT. HFBT. Somewhat difficult.
HFBT. TFTH. HFBT. HFBT. BT. TFTH.

be made, was 34.63 (standard error of the mean equal to 4.23) and the subsequent study time was 28.73 (standard error of the mean was 3.13). This analysis showed that the pattern of study times was consistent with the notion of reduced load after a chance to encode chunks of four items.

Conclusion.   The basic result is that JC is not reliably slower in memorizing dinner orders in varied presentation order when all items of a given category are contained in a *single* group, such as a table size of three or five. However, for table sizes of eight, where two groups of items used, a reliable increase in study time was observed.

GENERALIZABILITY AND TRANSFER OF MEMORY SKILL

The above sections describe in detail the cognitive structures and processes used by JC in memorizing dinner orders. The two preceding experiments show that the same cognitive structures were used even when the conditions of presentation were dramatically altered. Hence it is clear that JC's skill is stable and also generalizable. The next two experiments explore the generalizability of JC's skill to information other than dinner orders. Can and/or will JC use the same cognitive structures and mnemonic encoding processes for new stimulus materials?

The Category Materials Experiment

This experiment employed stimulus materials with the same structural characteristics as the dinner orders. The seven entrées were matched with seven animal names. The five temperatures were matched with times (second, minute, hour, day, week) that have the same ordinal relations as rare through well-done. The five salad dressings were matched with five flower names. Finally, the three starches were matched against three metals — iron, copper, and steel. All the items of the respective categories were selected from Battig and Montague's (1969) category norms. The same procedure was followed as in the category presentation and varied presentation order experiments just described. Hence, control trials with dinner orders were intermixed with the trials using the experimental material.

Results.   From the full analysis reported in Ericsson and Polson (1988), the following results have been extracted. The effect of table size was again highly significant and all other effects were significant at the 1% level, unless otherwise stated. The effect of condition (dinner orders vs. animal lists) was significant and its interaction with table size was also significant. The mean study times for table size by experimental condition are shown in Figure 2.12. The interaction in Figure 2.12 is due to an overall slower study rate for animal "tables," which yields total study times proportionally longer for bigger "tables." Figure 2.13 plots the average study time for both conditions as a function of session number. Although both conditions display a clear improvement, the speedup for animal "tables" is much more dramatic.

The order of recall was analyzed in two early sessions for 24 tables or a total of 512 recalled items. Recall followed the category recall strategy virtually perfectly for both experimental and control tables, 98.0% and 99.2% agreement respectively. The order in which the different categories were recalled was remarkably systematic. All twelve control tables were recalled with salad dressings first, entrées second, temperatures third, and

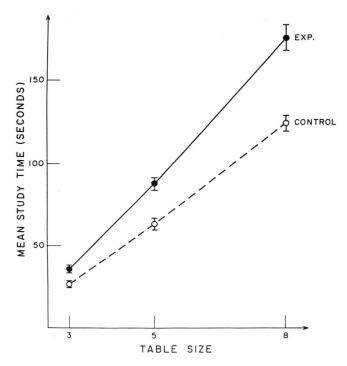

FIGURE 2.12   Mean total study times as a function of "table size" for control and experimental condition in category materials experiment.

starches last. The average rank of recall for the twelve experimental tables was 1.0 for flowers, 2.17 for animals, 3.17 for times, and 3.67 for metals, which is highly systematic.

It appears clear that JC memorized the animal tables by category, and we will now turn to an examination of the pattern of study times for individual orders. Figure 2.14 shows the mean study times for individual orders for control and animal tables. The pattern of study times is remarkably similar for all sizes of tables. The evidence for encoding items in groups of four is equally striking for both the control and the animal condition.

The most detailed evidence on the transfer of encoding processes comes from JC's think-aloud protocols. The two protocols given in Table 2.9 were taken on an identical animal table of 8 studied at two sessions separated by 1–2 weeks.

The two protocols show remarkable consistency of the cognitive processes at the two occasions, and also give strong support for existence of systematic encoding processes, especially for flowers and metals. In order to show more clearly the use of the letter mnemonic for flowers (see earlier use of

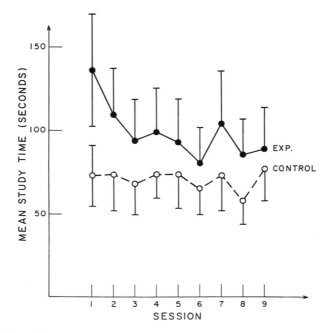

FIGURE 2.13 Average total study times as a function of session number for control and experimental condition in category materials experiment.

that mnemonic for salad dressings), all verbalizations relating to encodings of flowers were extracted and are shown in Table 2.10. They demonstrate the same encoding patterns of four items to a chunk shown earlier for dinner-orders.

The major result of this experiment is that JC's memory skill does generalize to other kinds of information. The source of the transfer is the continued use of the encoding mechanisms and retrieval structures assessed in the dinner order task.

Generality of Skills Experiment

Three types of experimental lists (Type A, B, and C) along with the standard dinner lists were used in this experiment. To construct the lists, eight different categories were selected from the Battig and Montague (1969) association norms, and twelve exemplars were selected for each category. The generation of all list types started with the sampling of four out of the eight categories. Hence, the categories were randomly sampled and therefore changed from trial to trial. Compare this with the stable organization of lists used in the category materials experiment, where the categories were specifically selected to be compatible with JC's different encoding processes.

For Type A lists, seven items were randomly selected for the first category, five items for the second and third categories and three items for the fourth category. Next the materials for a table of three, five, or eight were generated with a structure that was identical to that of the dinner orders. These materials are equally redundant as are the dinner orders, the only difference being that items and categories change from trial to trial.

For Type B lists, seven items were randomly selected for all four categories, and materials for a table of three, five, or eight were randomly generated. Type B lists differ from Type A lists in that they are less redundant. Type C lists were generated from Type B lists by randomly selecting

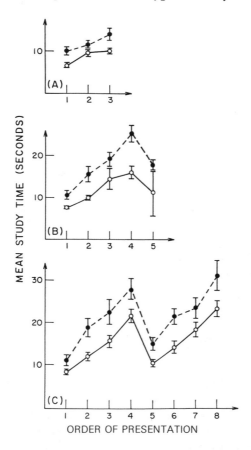

FIGURE 2.14 Study times for individual "dinner orders" as function of serial order of presentation for control and experimental condition in category materials experiment, for lists of three "orders" (upper panel), of five "orders" (middle panel), and of eight "orders" (lower panel).

TABLE 2.9
The First Part of Two Think-Aloud Protocols for Memorization of the
Same Category Lists from Eight People at Two Different Occasions

Occasion I			Occasion II	
1.	S:	Alright. Go.	S:	Alright (knock). Go. Cow, minute, tulip, steel.
	E:	Order 1. Cow, minute, tulip, steel.	S:	Okay. Cow, minute, tulip, steel. Cow, minute, tulip, it's a T system, and steel is the usual, and to refresh myself I've also got iron and copper to think about in the future there. Cow, minute, T, next (knock).
	S:	Cow, minute, tulip, steel.		
2.	E:	Order 2. Elephant, day, violet, steel.	E:	Elephant, day, violet steel.
	S:	Elephant, day V, 2 the same. T, V, elephant, day, T, V.	S:	T, V, two steels in a row, elephant, day, T, V, next (knock).
3.	E:	Order 3. Elephant, week, rose, steel.	E:	Elephant, week, rose, steel.
	S:	T, V, R, elephant, week, next.	S:	T, V, R, elephant, week, (knock) next.
4.	E:	Order 4. Cat, day, tulip, iron.	E:	Cat, day, tulip, iron.
	S:	T, V, R, T, different metal. T, V, R, T, cat, day. Okay. Minute, day, week, day, cow, elephant, elephant, cat, T, V, R, T. Next.		T, V, R, T, cat, day, T, V, R, T, cat, elephant, cow, two days, one week, T, V, R, T, (knock) next.
5.	E:	Order 5. Horse, week, daisy.	E:	Horse, week, daisy, iron.
	S:	Horse, week, daisy, iron, Horse, week, D, 2, D, next.	S:	Horse, week, D, (knock) next.

groups of four items without regard to category membership. For Type A and Type B lists each "order" has exactly the same format; that is, the first item is always from the same category in a given list. However, Type C lists have no such constraint and organization. Table 2.11 shows a sample of each type of list. Tables of three, five, and eight were presented for each of the three experimental conditions and the control condition. The order of presentation of conditions was random and counterbalanced over sessions.

The primary hypothesis was that Type C lists (lacking category organ-

TABLE 2.10
All Segments Relevant to Encoding of Flowers,
in Two Think-Aloud Protocols Shown Partly in Table 2.8

Occasion I	Occasion II
1.	T—T
2. V—T, V—T, V	T, V—T, V
3. T, V, R	T, V, R
4. T, V, R, T—T, V, R, T—	T, V, R, T—T, V, R, T—
T, V, R, T	T, V, R, T
5. D—D	D
6. D, D,—D, D	D, T, D, D—D, D
7. D, D, D	D, D, D
8. D, D, D, V—D, D, V	D, D, D, V, T, V, R, T
	Tulip—T
	Violet—V
	Rose—R
	Daisy—D

ization) would lead to qualitatively different cognitive processing and no facilitation through transfer of generalized skills, as compared to Type A and Type B lists. It was also assumed that Type A lists would require less study time than Type B lists, because the Type A lists are, on the average, more redundant. Finally, less improvement due to practice was expected because the categories from which items were sampled varied from trial to trial.

Results.   A detailed analysis (Ericsson & Polson, 1988) showed a highly significant effect of table size. The significant effects below were at least at the 1% level. There was a significant effect due to list type (control, A, B, C) and the list type by table size interaction. The regression analysis accounted for more than 90% of the variance.

The mean study times for each table size and condition (list type) are plotted in Figure 2.15. Figure 2.15 shows that the experimental conditions' study times have similar relations to table size, whereas the mean study times for the control condition have completely different linear relations. Ericsson and Polson (1988) showed that the planned comparisons between Type C lists and Type A lists, and between Type C lists and Type B lists, were both significant, whereas the comparison between Type A lists and Type B lists was not even close to significance. Given the lack of difference between Type A and Type B lists the data associated with these two types of lists will be pooled together and referred to as *lists with structure* — that is, lists with category structure for each "order."

The mean number of incorrectly recalled items in recall for Type A, B, and C lists were 0.53, 0.60, and 0.47 per table respectively. In the control

TABLE 2.11
Examples of the Three Types of Lists Used in the Different
Experimental Conditions in Generality-of-Skills Experiment

Organized by Category		No Organization
Type A	Type B	Type C
(Isomorphic to Dinner Order)	(Less Redundant)	(Scrambled Type B)
Order 1	Order 1	Order 1
track	potato	Germany
China	hat	dentist
dentist	carpenter	engineer
cherry	apricot	blouse
Order 2	Order 2	Order 2
golf	cabbage	orange
England	blouse	orange
carpenter	plumber	China
lemon	cherry	dentist
Order 3	Order 3	Order 3
baseball	pea	England
Japan	hat	banana
psychologist	dentist	tie
cherry	lemon	teacher
Order 4	Order 4	Order 4
wrestling	spinach	teacher
Germany	shirt	dress
dentist	professor	apricot
banana	apple	hat
Order 5	Order 5	Order 5
lacrosse	pea	tangerine
Japan	hat	Japan
carpenter	doctor	socks
banana	cherry	Spain

condition JC never did make an error. No further analysis of errors was made.

In order to gain a better understanding of how JC was processing Type C lists, the data on order of recall from two sessions were analyzed. The results are quite clear: Control, Type A, and Type B lists were recalled by category. The category recall strategy was used 100%, 72.2%, and 92.9% of the time respectively. The major deviation for Type A lists was a single

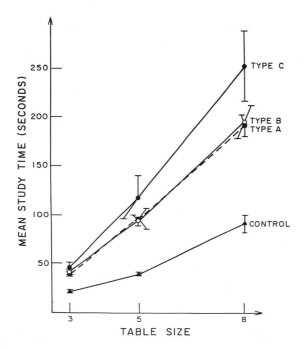

FIGURE 2.15 Mean total study times as a function of "table size" for the three types of lists in generalizability-of-skills experiment.

occurrence of recall of two categories in pairs (compare the similar recall of entrée and temperature in pairs that occurred earlier). Type C lists were recalled in exactly reverse sequence (going backwards) but retaining the sequence of the items within an order. This strategy predicts 84.5% of JC's recall.

JC's sequence of recall for Type C lists was similar to those of naive subjects discussed earlier, except that he recalled two orders backwards. The sequence of recall results suggest that JC cannot use his encoding strategies with Type C lists. This evidence is particularly compelling as JC switched recall strategy between different study lists.

The mean study times of individual orders also suggest that Type C lists were encoded differently. In earlier experiments, the pattern of mean study times per order gave very strong support to the hypothesis that JC encoded items in four item groups, especially data from tables of eight. These earlier studies show a very large drop in study time between orders four and five. Although the evidence for reduction in study time between orders four and five was clearer in earlier experiments, the patterns of mean study times for Type A and Type B lists were different from that of Type C lists. Hence, there is evidence for grouping by fours in Type A and B lists but not in Type C lists.

Conclusion. The generality experiment showed the expected difference in study time between lists with category structure (Type A and Type B) and lists lacking category structure (Type C). The two indices for encoding items by category, that is, serial order of recall and study times of individual "orders", showed clear differences between these two types of lists. No evidence for effects of redundancy was found — that is, no difference between Type A and Type B lists. The differences between lists with category structure (Type A and Type B), where JC could use his retrieval structure and some of his mnemonic encodings, and lists without category structure (Type C), where he could not and did not, was smaller than expected. This result will be discussed below.

DEGREE OF TRANSFER FOR OTHER MATERIALS

Let us now address the general issues of degree of transfer in our last two experiments. We have grouped the three important conditions: isomorphic new category information with (a) the same categories from trial to trial (animal lists, category materials experiment); (b) categories changing from trial to trial (Type A and Type B lists, generality experiment); and finally (c) unstructured presentation of category information changing from trial to trial (Type C lists, generality-of-skills-experiment). Study times for different table sizes are shown in Figure 2.16, and recall errors for different table sizes are given in Figure 2.17. For comparison purposes we have also included the corresponding data for untrained subjects and for JC's early sessions with dinner orders. From Figures 2.16 and 2.17 it is quite clear that JC memorized transfer lists of any kind faster and with fewer errors than did the untrained subjects. In fact, only on the very first session of Type C lists did JC even have study times comparable to those of normal subjects. On the other hand, JC's performance on all of the transfer lists was slower, with somewhat more errors, than was his early performance with dinner orders. The study times in Figure 2.16 support our prediction that fixed category structure is better than varied, and any category structure is better for JC than no such structure.

Given that JC improved quite rapidly on the transfer lists we could, of course, compare his better performance toward the end of the experiment on the transfer lists with his early performance on dinner orders, which did not show any reliable improvement over the five sessions. If we calculate mean study times for the last five sessions of the category materials experiment we find no reliable difference from his early performance. Hence, we feel warranted in arguing that with sufficient practice JC could exhibit his original performance on materials different from dinner orders.

If the best naive subjects' performance (rather than the average perfor-

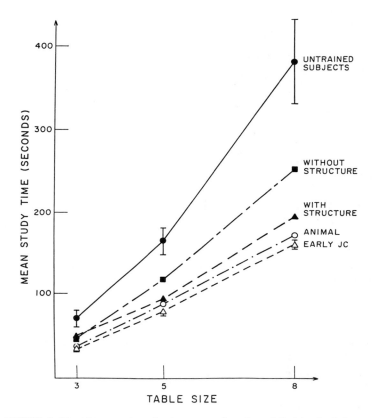

FIGURE 2.16   Mean total study times as a function of "table size" for memory expert (JC) for dinner orders in category presentation experiment (early JC), for fixed category lists in category materials experiment (animals), for category lists with and without structure from generalizability-of-skills experiment and untrained subjects.

mance shown in Figures 2.16 and 2.17) is compared to JC's performance on the lists without category structure (Type C lists), we still see a smaller yet clear difference. However, it is clear that our experimental manipulations have eliminated most of JC's superior memory performance on dinner orders compared to good naive subjects.

In summarizing the results from these transfer experiments we claim that JC showed transfer to new kinds of information—in other words, generalizability over content—and that he was able to use the components of his skill with new and different materials. Later we return to a discussion of the unexpected result, namely that his memory performance appeared to transfer even when essential components of his skill weren't used.

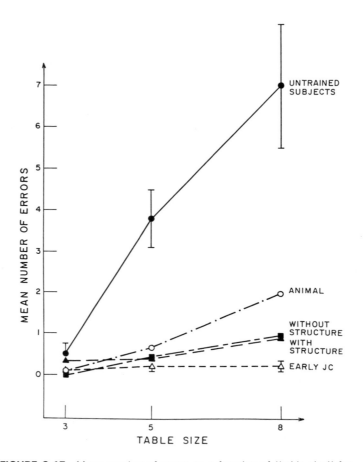

FIGURE 2.17   Mean number of errors as a function of ''table size'' for memory expert (JC) for dinner orders in category presentation experiment (early JC), for fixed category lists in category-list experiment (animals), for category lists with and without structure from generalizability-of-skill experiment and untrained subjects.

SUMMARY OF OUR DESCRIPTION
OF A MEMORY SKILL

Let us first briefly summarize the general findings and point out some issues they raise. JC approaches the task of committing dinner orders to memory in a way that is widely different from that of untrained college students. The latter approached this task in a very predictable manner and

exhibited patterns of results that are very consistent with traditional laboratory studies of memory. JC exhibited characteristics of his performance that
were virtually parallel to those identified for other memory skills by Chase
and Ericsson (1981, 1982). The major point of "apparent" difference between these two studies was the suggestion that JC's skills appeared to transfer to other stimulus materials, whereas the memory experts' skills with digits
did not show any corresponding transfer to other materials, for example
consonants. It is clear that the digit-span task with a fixed presentation rate
is strikingly different from the self-paced procedure with review used in
the dinner order task. We argue that the procedural differences are important in reconciling the differences in result concerning generalizability. These
points are further discussed in the following section.

GENERAL DISCUSSION

This chapter has dealt thus far with two sets of issues. The first involves
the characterization of JC's memory skill. The second deals with the generality of that memory skill. In the following pages we review the major results
presented in this chapter, and then focus on the generality issue.

Characterization of JC's Memory Skill

JC generated explicit descriptions of his encoding processes in both concurrent and retrospective reports while studying lists of dinner orders. He encoded items in groups of four by category, using specialized encoding
schemes for each of the four categories of items in a dinner order. A large
amount of evidence provided strong support for the model derived from
JC's protocols. JC's output orders, patterns of mean study times per order
as a function of order position, and performance in the experimental conditions of the category presentation and varied presentation experiments,
all support this model of his encoding processes.

Comparisons of JC's performance with the performance of naive subjects recruited from introductory psychology courses showed large differences in levels of performance as well as encoding strategies. The data from
naive subjects are well described by standard memory models for laboratory tasks involving ordered recall of unrelated lists (Atkinson & Shiffrin,
1968). Furthermore, there were vast differences in performance in both
study times and error rates.

Finally, it was shown that JC's performance exhibited four out of the
five characteristics of skilled memory as described by Chase and Ericsson
(1981, 1982). The major difference was that JC's skills seemed to transfer
to a rich variety of study procedures and other kinds of experimental materi-

als, whereas memory experts in the digit span task did not show any corresponding transfer to other materials, for example consonants. The digit span task for the fixed presentation rate is very different from the self-pace procedure with reviews used in the dinner order task. These procedural differences are important in reconciling the differences in results concerning generality. These points are discussed further in the remainder of this section.

Generality of Memory Skills

The results from the various experiments presented in this chapter clearly demonstrate the flexibility and the generality of JC's memory skills. He rapidly adapts to variations in input order (category presentation and varied presentation experiments). He deals effectively with novel stimulus material that has a structure very similar to that of dinner orders (the experimental materials in the category materials experiment). Finally, he is able to effectively deal with materials that have a completely different structure, showing clearly better performance than would be expected from naive subjects on Type C lists in the generality-of-skills experiment.

What is the basis for the generality of JC's memory skills? First, it is clear that JC's superior performance with dinner orders and other kinds of materials is in fact mediated by a rich collection of memory skills. At the most specific level, JC has a highly developed set of materials-specific encoding strategies, such as the schemes that he used to encode salad dressings and temperatures of steaks. He is capable of transferring those encoding schemes to novel materials if the structure of those materials permits their application. Units of time and flower names were encoded using varieties of the temperature encoding scheme and the salad dressing abbreviation scheme, respectively, that were used on dinner orders.

At the next level of generality, JC is very skilled in adapting to variations in the organization of the presented items for the dinner order materials. Presenting items by category order had no effect on his performance; variations in the sequencing of presentation for the different dinner orders only slowed him down reliably for tables of eight, where he needed to keep two groups of items active simultaneously. But it had no effect on his recall accuracy or serial order of the output. Such flexibility is a necessary component of JC's memory skill in dealing with people in a restaurant where dinner orders can come in an arbitrary sequence.

At the highest level of generality, JC has a surprisingly sophisticated understanding of his own memory structures and a well developed set of metacognitive skills that he exploits in memorizing any kind of material. From JC's spontaneous comments over the course of our two years in working with him, it is clear that he has a sophisticated understanding of the general architecture of human memory. He is well aware of the basic characteristics of long- and short-term memory. Furthermore, JC understands the importance of multiple redundant retrieval paths in storing material in long-term memory.

Finally, JC has a rather sophisticated and flexible set of strategies for evaluating the quality of his encodings. He explicitly evaluates his encodings by attempting to retrieve material that he has studied earlier during a trial. From our analyses earlier it is clear that previously presented items are rapidly retrievable. In fact, within a group of four to five dinner orders all of the previous items of a given category are virtually instantaneously retrieved to be encoded with the corresponding item of the current order. Hence, encoding of the current order involves automatic checks of previously presented information. The effective utilization of such retrieval checks causes him to slow down when dealing with novel material. He maintains a high level of performance even at the cost of slowing down when dealing with novel material. In comparison, naive subjects have very little understanding of their memory structure or various relevant metacognitive skills, and they are quite surprised when they do poorly during recall.

In summary, the restaurant defines a situation in which JC has developed a great deal of flexibility in encoding dinner orders because of the wide variations in the behavior of groups of people when ordering meals. As a result, procedural variations in the laboratory were relatively trivial for him to deal with. Moreover, JC has developed a very sophisticated understanding of his own memory structure, the properties of long-term memory, and a rather flexible set of metacognitive skills that enable him to evaluate the quality of a particular encoding.

Comparisons Between Digit Span and Dinner Orders

The most obvious difference between digit span and self-paced study of dinner orders is the available time for encoding. In digit span the presentation rate of one digit/second requires extremely fast encoding processes. It is clear that JC's fastest encoding time was 1.5–2.0 seconds/item (disregarding that some items of dinner orders consist of two words). We could argue that use of skilled memory and associated encoding processes in span tasks requires specific practice with the material to achieve sufficient speed. This would account for the lack of transfer between digit span and span with consonants as found by Chase and Ericsson (1981). It is furthermore possible, even likely, that the extreme time pressure in the span task may lead to selection of stimulus-specific processes at the expense of processes relying on a more general representation. In contrast such extreme time pressure doesn't exist in the dinner order task, or in the restaurant situation where

JC originally developed his skill. Most importantly, there are cognitive processes that may speed up the successful memorization of especially large amounts of information, but that are not applicable to the presentation rates used in span studies.

OTHER STUDIES OF GENERALITY

There is a fair amount of documented evidence for transfer to not-previously-seen stimuli. General instruction and minor practice — or even none — in the use of interactive visual imagery, give clear improvement on not-previously-seen stimuli (Bellezza, 1981; Bower, 1972). The speed of forming interactive visual images, which can later be reliably retrieved, has been shown to decrease with practice. One of the most impressive improvements in study times using visual images is reported in a study by Wallace, Turner, and Perkins (Miller, Galanter, & Pribram, 1960). Initially, subjects needed about 25 seconds to encode a paired associate, but after some 500 pairs the study time was less than 5 seconds. The idea that these are generalizable processes is consonant with the generally improved performance on memory tasks for mnemonists, like "S" (Luria, 1968), "VP" (Hunt & Love, 1972) and Professor Ruekle (Mueller, 1911). It should be noted that in all the above-discussed memory tasks the memorization is slow compared to the presentation rates in span tasks.

Improvement through practice in most of the early studies of memorization of nonsense syllables, digits, prose, and text (in verbatim form) is substantial. Since practice effects were generally considered to be theoretically uninteresting and a source of methodological bias, they have received little direct discussion. However, we can extract estimates of improvement. In his study of memory for text, Cofer (1940) found that the number of trials required for verbatim memorization of text at the end of the experiment was reduced to around 40% of the number required for learning at the beginning of the experiment. Harcum and Coppage (1965) found that subjects reduced their number of errors while learning a list of 10 nonsense syllables quite dramatically as a result of practice; one practiced subject made less than one third of his initial number of errors.

There is a line of research initiated by Ebert and Meumann (Meumann, 1913) showing transfer of memorization to a variety of materials from practice on nonsense syllables. Although the research had methodological problems, it stimulated many investigators to conduct research on that issue. In a review of this extensive research Orata (1928) summarized the findings:

> We are therefore justified in concluding that the amount of transfer in memory

from one material to another depends a great deal upon the method used in the practice series. Where it is unintelligent routine, we get very little or no transfer, but where conscious formulation of principles or generalization of techniques of memorizing is made, there is great amount of transfer. (p. 118)

Hence, there is independent evidence for the existence of general methods for memorization, which yield above-baseline performance on new materials.

Returning to JC's performance, we think the most parsimonious account is that he acquired such transferable methods for committing information to memory. Although we cannot and would not argue that his skills were universally transferable, our initial hypothesis, that we could easily arrange an experimental situation in which JC's memory performance could be reduced all the way to an average level, was probably misguided.

Instead we would like to focus on the existence of transferable processes that can improve memory in a wide range of situations. By understanding the structure of mediating processes we should be able to improve instruction in memorization. Furthermore, the enormous individual differences that exist might, at least in part, be understood in terms of such acquired general cognitive processes.

ACKNOWLEDGMENTS

The research has been supported by the Office of Naval Research Grant N00014-81-C-0335 to Carnegie–Mellon University through a subcontract for the first author to the University of Colorado (80785-51113). We want to acknowledge the thoughtful comments on earlier drafts of this chapter by Bill Chase, Gerhard Deffner, and Vic Schoenberg. Finally, we want to thank John Conrad for his enduring enthusiasm and his insightful comments during all phases of our 2-year project.

REFERENCES

Atkinson, R. C., & Shiffrin, R. M. (1968). Human memory: A proposed system and its control processes. In K. W. Spence & J. T. Spence (Eds.), *The psychology of learning and motivation: Advances in research and theory* (Vol. 2, pp. 89–195). New York: Academic Press.

Battig, W. F., and Montague, W. E. (1969). Category norms of verbal items in 56 categories: A replication and extension of the Connecticut category norms. *Journal of Experimental Psychology Monographs*, 80 (3, Pt. 2).

Bellezza, F. S. (1981). Mnemonic devices: Classification, characteristics, and criteria. *Review of Educational Research*, 51, 247–275.

Bower, G. H. (1972). Mental imagery and associative learning. In L. W. Gregg (Ed.), *Cognition in learning and memory* (pp. 51–88). New York: Wiley.

Chase, W. G., & Ericsson, K. A. (1981). Skilled memory. In J. R. Anderson (Ed.), *Cognitive skills and their acquisition* (pp. 141–189). Hillsdale, NJ: Lawrence Erlbaum Associates.

Chase, W. G., & Ericsson, K. A. (1982). Skill and working memory. In G. H. Bower (Ed.), *The psychology of learning and motivation*, (Vol. 16, pp. 1–58). New York: Academic Press.

Cofer, C. N. (1940). *A comparison of logical and verbatim learning of prose passages of different lengths.* Unpublished doctoral dissertation, Brown University.

Ericsson, K. A., & Chase, W. G. (1982). Exceptional memory. *American Scientist, 70*(6), 607–615.

Ericsson, K. A., Chase, W. G., and Faloon, S. (1980). Acquisition of a memory skill. *Science, 208,* 1181–82.

Ericsson, K. A., & Polson, P. G. (1988). An experimental analysis of the mechanisms of a memory skill. *Journal of Experimental Psychology: Learning, Memory, and Cognition, 14*(2), 305–316.

Ericsson, K. A., & Simon, H. A. (1980). Verbal reports as data. *Psychological Review, 87,* 215–251.

Ericsson, K. A., & Simon, H. A. (1984). *Protocol analysis.* Cambridge, MA: MIT Press/Bradford.

Harcum, E. R., & Coppage, E. W. (1965). Serial-position curve of verbal learning after prolonged practice. *Psychological Reports, 17,* 475–488.

Hunt, E., & Love, T. (1972). How good can memory be? In A. W. Melton & E. Martin (Eds.), *Coding processes in human memory* (pp. 237–260), New York: Holt.

Luria, A. R. (1968). *The mind of a mnemonist.* New York: Avon.

Meumann, E. (1913). *The psychology of learning.* New York: D. Appleton and Company.

Miller, G. A. (1956). The magical number seven, plus or minus two. *Psychological Review, 63,* 81–97.

Miller, G. A., Galanter, E., & Pribram, K. H. (1960). *Plans and the structure of behavior.* New York: Holt, Rinehart and Winston.

Mueller, G. E. (1911). Zur Analyse der Gedachtnistatigkeit und des Vorstellungsverlaufes: Teil I. [Studies of memory and cognitive processes. Part I] *Zeitschrift fur Psychologie, Erganzungsband 5.*

Murdock, B. B. (1974). *Human memory: Theory and data.* Hillsdale, NJ: Lawrence Erlbaum Associates.

Orata, P. T. (1928). *The theory of identical elements.* Columbus, OH: The Ohio State University Press.

Underwood, B. J. (1957). Interference and forgetting. *Psychological Review, 64,* 49–60.

3 Skilled Memory and Expert Mental Calculation

James J. Staszewski
Carnegie–Mellon University

1. INTRODUCTION

The subjects of this research are "lightning mental calculators," individuals who solve arithmetic problems such as $74,219 \times 8$, 76×89, or $54,917 \times 63$ with remarkable speed and accuracy. What really makes their skills extraordinary is that they carry out their computations without external memory aids. Because novices typically experience extreme difficulty with this task, most assume that experts must possess either exceptional or "special" abilities to perform at the level they do.

Two related goals motivate this research. A general goal is to understand how experts can perform complex tasks with extraordinary proficiency at levels that most people believe demand capabilities not found in the "normal" population. How can we characterize experts' capabilities? What knowledge do they possess? How do they use their knowledge? This work approaches these issues by trying to characterize the cognitive structures and processes that support the extraordinary skills of these lightning calculators.

A more specific goal is to test the claim that *skilled memory* is a general component of expert-level skill. The basis for this claim is Chase & Ericsson's (1982) Skilled Memory Theory. More a conceptual framework rather than a formal theory, Skilled Memory Theory postulates that expert-level performance depends upon experts' *efficient* use of a vast, domain-specific knowledge base. Through extensive practice in a particular domain, experts acquire knowledge structures and procedures for efficiently encoding and retrieving task-relevant information in long-term memory (LTM). The de-

velopment of highly efficient LTM encoding and retrieval processes enables experts to circumvent basic information-processing limitations,
particularly limited STM capacity and relatively slow LTM encoding
processes (Simon, 1976), that severely constrain novice performance on most
complex tasks. In effect, the development of skilled memory enables experts
to increase their working memory capacity for familiar materials. The enhanced processing capacity that results supports exceptional performance
on tasks that novices find virtually impossible. This work investigates the
extent to which the mental structures and processes employed by expert mental calculators conform to this general characterization of expert knowledge
and the principles related to its use.

The contents of this chapter are organized as follows. First, the theoretical relevance of research on expert mental calculation is discussed, followed
by the central theoretical and empirical issues that this work addresses. A
training study is then described in which two otherwise normal college undergraduates became expert mental calculators through extended laboratory practice. Their performance over the course of practice is described
and their final performance data are compared with data collected from
a lightning mental calculator acknowledged as one of the world's best. These
data set the stage for the theoretical analysis that follows. Findings suggesting that skilled memory plays a central role in expert mental calculation are presented, followed by results that illustrate the contribution of
strategic knowledge to expert mental calculation skill. The chapter closes
by summarizing the conclusions of this work and their implications for understanding the nature of expertise and its development.

2. EXPERTISE AND MENTAL CALCULATION

Why study experts? Truly exceptional performance is intrinsically fascinating, regardless of the domain in which it occurs. Peak performance, the
kind exhibited by the best of the best, the Nobel laureates, Olympians, and
so forth, in essence defines what it means to be human by defining the upper limits of human capabilities. In fact, studies of experts raise the question of whether any fixed, general limits to human intellectual abilities exist.
There are also practical reasons to study how experts are able to do what
they do so well. The foremost is that both people (Staszewski, in preparation) and machines (Feigenbaum, 1977) can use the hard-won knowledge
of experts to facilitate skill acquisition and perhaps even extend the known
limits of performance.

Mental Calculation

What is mental calculation and why should skill in this domain interest cognitive scientists? Quite simply, mental calculation involves solving arithmetic problems without external memory aids. One reason for cognitive scientists' interest in this anachronistic activity becomes apparent when we consider the difficulty that mental calculation poses. To appreciate this difficulty, one needs only to put aside paper and pencil (or any other external memory or computational aids) and try calculating the products of problems such as 47×86 or $48,856 \times 93$. This exercise quickly demonstrates that considerable thought and effort are needed to solve such problems correctly, let alone quickly. In contrast, solving these problems becomes a trivial, seemingly "mindless" exercise when we can use external representations to augment working memory. The point is that mentally solving problems larger than those found in the well-memorized multiplication tables is an extremely demanding task for novices.

What are the demands of mental calculation? When people with basic arithmetic skills face the task of solving problems with operands larger than single digits, most find that maintaining operands and intermediate results in memory while proceeding with computation is the chief difficulty. Fast and accurate solution of problems with multi-digit operands clearly requires sophisticated memory-management strategies. It follows that mental calculation represents an ideal domain for examining the relation between memory processes and expertise, because the basic theoretical problem raised by lightning mental calculators is understanding how they manage the memory load that mental arithmetic imposes.

Theories of Memory Management In Expert Mental Calculation

How do lightning calculators cope with the memory demands of mental calculation? Both Hunter (1962, 1977) and Chase (Chase & Ericsson, 1982) addressed this problem in their studies of exceptionally proficient mental calculators.

Hunter's (1962, 1977) subject was Professor A. C. Aitken, a Cambridge mathematician whose computational feats qualify him as perhaps the most proficient mental calculator ever studied (Chase & Ericsson, 1982; Smith, 1983). Analysis of Aitken's computational procedures led Hunter to attribute Aitken's remarkable ability to two kinds of acquired knowledge that he used to reduce the memory demands of calculation to a manageable level.

First, over a lifetime of practice in squaring, reciprocating, and taking square roots, Aitken devised computational procedures which he applied in a problem-specific manner to minimize the processing load involved in his computations. With a vast repertoire of computational strategies at his disposal, Aitken could select and use what he believed was the best algorithm for solving a particular problem with maximal efficiency.

As a complement to his repertoire of efficient computational strategies, Aitken also used an elaborate mathematical knowledge base to reduce the computational complexity of his solution processes. Armed with an extensive and easily accessible knowledge base of numerical facts, Aitken could use memory retrieval, rather than computation, to solve to a wide variety of problems and subproblems. Analogous to the ability of most people to instantly report that 4×25 is 100 without performing a series of computational steps, Aitken could use his knowledge to reduce the number of simple computations needed to generate a solution considerably.

Recently, Chase's (Chase & Ericsson, 1982) analysis of a semiprofessional calculation expert, called "AB", produced findings that parallel Hunter's in several respects. Like Aitken, AB uses unconventional computational algorithms for squaring and multiplying. Also like Aitken, AB reported discovering algorithms he found more efficient than those conventionally taught in schools, while practicing mental calculation as an adolescent. Curiously, the squaring algorithm AB independently discovered and uses (described in Chase & Ericsson, 1982) is the same as the one discovered by Aitken at the same age, 12.

AB's general strategy for multiplication, which he also discovered independently, happens to be one preferred by most calculation experts who excel in this operation (Binet, 1894; Hunter, 1977; Smith, 1983). The basic difference between this procedure and the conventional procedure typically taught in schools lies in the order in which elementary arithmetic operations are executed. Whereas conventional multiplication iteratively accesses and multiplies pairs of digits from a problem's operands in a right-to-left direction to generate simple, intermediate products, AB's computational strategy proceeds in the opposite direction. The first computational step multiplies the highest magnitude digit in each operand (the left-most digits in a visual display), and computation proceeds by accessing digits from the operands in a left-to-right direction and multiplying all possible pairs. Thus the expert strategy is called "left-to-right multiplication," whereas the conventional strategy is called the "right-to-left strategy". Table 3.1 contrasts the two approaches, illustrating how each is implemented to solve the same problem.

AB's skill also resembles Aitken's in that AB possesses a large and highly interrelated semantic network of easily accessible number facts. "Think-aloud" protocols taken as AB solves multiplication problems show that this knowledge base serves at least three related functions. Like Aitken, AB uses his knowledge (a) to recognize familiar problems or subproblems; (b) to organize efficient solution plans based on his discovery of familiar patterns; and (c) to retrieve the products of familiar problems in the course of executing these plans. In addition, as Chase & Ericsson (1982) have argued, AB's knowledge base enables him to encode numbers within a semantically rich, elaborately interrelated network, thus promoting their retention.

To sum up, analyses of two exceptionally skilled mental calculators re-

TABLE 3.1
Multiplication Strategies:
Left-to-Right Versus Right-to-Left

| | Sample Problem: | 127 | |
| | | × 6 | |
Operation	L-to-R		R-to-L
1	6 × 1 = 6		6 × 7 = 42
2	6 × 2 = 12		6 × 2 = 12
3	60 + 12 = 72		42 + 120 = 162
4	6 × 7 = 42		6 × 1 = 6
5	720 + 42 = 762		600 + 162 = 762

veal that these experts exploit an extensive knowledge base to plan and execute efficient solution procedures adapted to particular problems. In doing
so they exhibit a characteristic of expertise that Bartlett (1932) noted about
expert-level perceptual-motor skills: an expert's ability to precisely tailor
his or her actions to a particular problem to solve it with the greatest possible economy. However, the context-sensitive and idiosyncratic nature of
the solution processes of these two experts does not prevent broad theoretical generalizations about expertise in mental calculation. Rather, the degree
to which Hunter's (1977) and Chase's theoretical conclusions converge with
earlier studies of expert calculators (Bidder, 1856; Bryan, Lindley, & Harter,
1941; Jakobson, 1944; Sandor, 1932; Weinland & Schlauch, 1937) suggests
that it is possible to describe extraordinary skill in this domain in terms of
general theoretical principles.

Theoretical Views on Memory Management

Where Chase and Hunter disagree in their views on expert mental calculation is on the nature of the constraints that working memory capacity imposes upon performance and, particularly, the rigidity of these constraints.
Noting that expert calculators frequently exhibit digit-spans exceeding the
normally accepted limits of STM (Miller, 1956), Hunter's (1977) position
is that exceptional STM capacity accounts, in part, for expert calculators'
exceptional performance. According to this view, the various strategies employed by Aitken and other lightning calculators are used to hold the memory
load related to solving particular problems within their larger-than-normal,
but nonetheless limited, capacity for retaining numerical information. Thus,
the feats of lightning calculators are based upon the efficiency of the strategies they employ and their presumably fixed, but superior capacity to hold
data in temporary storage.

  Like Hunter (1977), Chase took the position that AB's computational strategies cannot alone explain his calculation feats. Although certain strategies can reduce the memory demands of mental arithmetic relative to the more conventional methods, Chase's analysis of AB's squaring procedures indicated that there remains a substantial memory "overhead" in AB's computation that grows with increasing problem size. To manage this burden, AB's protocols show that he augmented his arithmetic strategies with acquired mnemonic strategies that fall under the theoretical rubric of "skilled memory."

Skilled Memory Theory

The fundamental theoretical issue on which Hunter and Chase differ regards the nature of working memory constraints and how they affect the performance of lightning calculators. Whereas Hunter assumes that individuals have a fixed working memory capacity, Chase and Ericsson argue that an individual's working memory capacity is not fixed, but varies with the memory skills an individual develops by working with particular materials on particular tasks.

The empirical foundation for this claim comes from studies that gave normal college students extended practice on the digit-span task. Although novice performance on this task is limited by the sharply limited capacity of STM (Miller, 1956; Newell & Simon, 1972), extended training enabled individuals with otherwise normal memory abilities to increase their spans an order of magnitude (Ericsson, Chase, & Faloon, 1980) and more (Staszewski, 1987, Staszewski, in preparation) beyond the commonly accepted asymptote of 7 ± 2 digits. Moreover, analyses of these mnemonists' performance (Chase & Ericsson, 1981, 1982; Staszewski, 1987) demonstrated that their feats result from learning to encode and retrieve information in LTM efficiently.

Chase and Ericsson (1982) described how experts exploit LTM to expand working memory capacity in terms of three principles of skilled memory:

1. *The Mnemonic Encoding Principle.* This principle states that experts encode new information in terms of an existing knowledge base, thus exploiting information in LTM as a mnemonic aid. For instance, studies of expert mnemonists (Chase & Ericsson, 1981, 1982; Ericsson, 1985; Ericsson, Chase, & Faloon, 1980; Staszewski, 1987, in preparation) and experts from domains such as chess (Chase & Simon, 1973a, 1973b), bridge (Charness, 1979), the games of go (Reitman, 1976) and gomuku (Eisenstadt & Kareev, 1975), electronics (Egan & Schwartz, 1979), architecture (Akin, 1982), and computer programming (McKeithen, Reitman, Rueter, & Hirtle, 1981) all suggest that experts use patterns or chunks of information acquired

through years of practice and stored as semantic codes in LTM to encode new information.

2. *The Retrieval Structure Principle.*   This principle asserts that experts use their knowledge of a domain to develop abstract, highly specialized mechanisms for systematically encoding and retrieving meaningful patterns in LTM. Essentially, these mechanisms enable experts to anticipate the information needs of a familiar task and index information in memory in a way that later facilitates its retrieval at the time it is needed.

3. *The Speed-Up Principle.*   This principle states that practice increases the speed (and reliability) with which experts (a) recognize and encode meaningful patterns and (b) store and retrieve information using retrieval structures. Assuming that LTM storage and retrieval times decrease continuously with practice, albeit in continuously shrinking amounts (Pirolli & Anderson, 1985), this principle implies that with sufficient practice experts can store and access virtually unlimited amounts of information in LTM with the speed and reliability normally associated with STM storage and retrieval.

Together, these theoretical principles offer an explanation of the typically large expert-novice differences in performance. Basically, Skilled Memory Theory asserts that experts increase their working memory capacity for materials within a particular domain by learning to efficiently encode and retrieve information in LTM. The enhanced information-processing capacity that results circumvents the constraints that the sharply limited capacity of STM imposes on novice performance on complex tasks.

Although this theoretical viewpoint holds considerable appeal, its generality can be questioned. Empirical support for the principles of skilled memory is limited to tasks involving intentional memorization; therefore, the viability of Skilled Memory Theory as a general account of what experts know and how they use their knowledge depends upon demonstrating that its principles characterize how experts achieve exceptional performance in tasks in which the performer's goal is something other than intentional memorization.

Mental Calculation as a Test-Bed for Skilled Memory Theory

Mental calculation represents an ideal task for testing the generality of Skilled Memory Theory. Although the goal of this task is obviously not intentional memorization (as in the digit-span task), perfect retention of ordered digit strings is nevertheless required for success. As a result, several predictions can be derived from Skilled Memory Theory regarding the nature of expert-level mental calculation skill.

First, if successful mental calculation depends upon an individual's ability to maintain information in memory over periods filled with computational activity, limited working memory capacity should make solving all but the simplest problems quite difficult for novices. But if working memory capacity for task-relevant materials can be increased through extended practice, as Skilled Memory Theory postulates, substantial improvements in performance should occur with sustained practice in mental calculation. High levels of practice should produce expert-level performance.

Second, if the development of skilled memory is crucial to improving performance in mental calculation, Skilled Memory Theory predicts that improvements in performance should be accompanied by increasingly efficient storage and retrieval of information in LTM. Thus, expert mental calculators should show prolonged retention of information that is actively stored and maintained in working memory in the course of computation.

The third prediction is that experts should use LTM in a manner that is consistent with the three principles of skilled memory. In other words, theoretical analysis of mental calculation expertise should show that (a) experts use LTM to recognize and encode meaningful patterns; (b) they use retrieval structures to encode and retrieve information; and (c) the speed of their encoding and retrieval processes increases with practice.

3. THE ACQUISITION OF MENTAL CALCULATION SKILL

Training Procedures

The opportunity to test these predictions was made possible by the efforts of two Carnegie–Mellon undergraduates who volunteered to participate in a training study of mental calculation. Standardized measures of scholastic aptitude showed that both of the trainees, GG and JA, fell on the high end of the score distributions for a college population. JA scored 620 on the SAT-V (94th %ile) and 750 on the SAT-Q (99th %ile). GG scored 610 on the SAT-V (94th %ile) and 680 on the SAT-Q (96th %ile). In terms of academic achievement, their college grades gave no indication of extraordinary abilities. Based on a 4.0 scale, JA's and GG's GPAs were 3.05 and 3.13, respectively.

Another subject who provided data for this study was AB. His participation in 10 testing sessions provided benchmarks against which the trainees' skills could be measured. All three subjects were paid on an hourly basis for their effort.

GG and JA routinely practiced mental multiplication under laboratory observation for up to 45 minutes a day, three to five days per week. JA attended 268 sessions to accumulate approximately 175 hours of practice over a three-year period. Over four years GG attended 618 sessions resulting in about 300 hours of practice. Practice consisted of solving multiplication problems using the unconventional, general computational strategy employed by AB and the majority of expert calculators whose specialty is multiplication. On some days normal practice was replaced by sessions in which either verbal protocols were taken or experiments were conducted.

In practice sessions two manipulations were used to vary the memory demands of the multiplication problems given. These manipulations involved independently varying problem size and presentation conditions. To vary problem size, the trainees regularly practiced on problems whose multipliers were either one- or two-digit numbers and whose multiplicands ranged from one to five digits in magnitude. These manipulations produced the nine problem-size categories shown in Table 3.2. All problems were

TABLE 3.2
Problem Size Categories

Category	Example
1 × 1 ·············	8 × 6
1 × 2 ············	37 × 4
1 × 3 ············	895 × 9
1 × 4 ···········	1,472 × 8
1 × 5 ···········	91,463 × 7
2 × 2 ···········	73 × 38
2 × 3 ···········	856 × 52
2 × 4 ···········	4,957 × 76
2 × 5 ···········	31,265 × 69

randomly generated and presented in blocks containing one problem from each size category.

Two modes of problem presentation were employed, oral and visual. In the oral condition, problems were read to the subjects. After receiving a subject's ready signal, an experimenter (E) would read first the larger of the operands of the current problem, pause for approximately 2 seconds, and then give the word *times* followed by the second operand. The operands of visually presented problems were typewritten in the center of 3 × 5 cards, according to the display convention shown in Table 3.2. The E would simply display the printed card face to present a problem to the subject in the visual-presentation condition.

An additional procedural difference distinguished the two presentation conditions. Visually presented problems remained displayed until the subject either gave an answer or gave up. Thus, problem operands were available throughout the course of computation in the visual condition, whereas oral presentation required subjects to maintain both operands of a problem in memory to solve the problem successfully. The extra memory load imposed by oral problem presentation was expected, therefore, to increase problem difficulty.

At the start of each trainee's initial practice session, the left-to-right multiplication strategy was described, followed by several illustrations of how this strategy was applied to specific problems. After each subject demonstrated an understanding of this approach by applying it to a set of sample problems, he was instructed to use this strategy to solve all multiplication problems he received as quickly and as accurately as possible. In addition, as an initial performance goal, both trainees were told to aim for an aggregate error rate of 10% or less.

Following each practice trial, feedback was provided on the accuracy of the answer given, and both solution time and accuracy were recorded for each problem. Solution times in the oral condition were measured from the point at which the last digit of the multiplier was read by the experimenter to the subject's statement of the last digit of his answer. In the visual condition, timing started when the problem was displayed. From approximately the 200th session onward, retrospective verbal reports were taken from the trainees on the computational procedures used on each problem. Each session was recorded on audio tape.

For the first 10 practice sessions, 36 problems were presented in four blocks of 9. Within each block a problem from each of the 9 problem-size categories was presented. Order of problem presentation within blocks was randomized and all problems within a block were presented either orally or visually. The number of oral and visual blocks was balanced in each session in which an even number of practice blocks were presented. The order of oral and visual blocks varied within sessions and was counterbalanced across sessions. After 11 practice sessions, improvements in the solution times of both trainees made it possible to present an additional block of problems within a 45-minute session. By their 31st session, the number of practice blocks was increased to 6 per session for both GG and JA, and remained at that level for the remainder of their practice.

Results

Over the course of this study, the trainees generated a huge quantity of data. Given the volume and richness of this database and the aims of this chapter, discussion focuses on findings that bear directly on the predictions of Skilled Memory Theory. Performance data from the trainees are presented first, followed by a theoretical analysis that sketches the cognitive mechanisms underlying their performance.

Practice and Expertise

Skilled Memory Theory postulates that, in principle, people can learn to hold virtually unlimited amounts of information in working memory with sufficient practice. If working memory capacity is the key to mental calculation performance, it therefore should be possible to dramatically improve performance on this task through the development of skilled memory. The improvements that GG and JA made in both the speed and accuracy of their calculation as a result of practice support this prediction.

The effects of practice on the trainees' calculation speed are illustrated in Figure 3.1, where mean solution time is plotted as a function of both problem size and presentation mode for each trainee. The two upper curves in each panel represent the trainees' solution times for the problems presented in the first 10 practice sessions, whereas the lower curves chart the performance of each individual over his final 10 practice sessions. Note that the data points summarize the times for all presented problems, regardless of whether they were solved correctly or not. The initial and final accuracy of the trainees' calculation can be seen in Table 3.3, which presents a breakdown of their error rates for their first 10 sessions and their final 30 sessions.

Consistent with Skilled Memory Theory, a striking practice effect is reflected by improvements in the speed and accuracy of both trainees across all training conditions. The effects of practice are not uniform across treatments, however. As Figure 3.1 and Table 3.3 indicate, the magnitude of the practice effect varies with problem size and presentation mode. Generally speaking, improvements in the trainees' speed and accuracy are proportional to their initial solution times and error rates; the greatest improvement

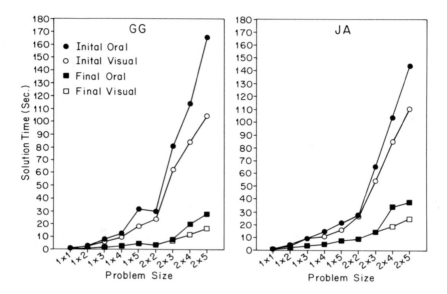

FIGURE 3.1 Trainees' initial and final solution times as a function of problem size and presentation condition. Data points for the initial 10 practice sessions represent the mean of 20 observations (or fewer). Means from the final 10 sessions are based on 30 observations.

TABLE 3.3
Trainees' Errors Rates (%)

First Ten Sessions

Presentation		1 × 1	1 × 2	1 × 3	1 × 4	1 × 5	2 × 2	2 × 3	2 × 4	2 × 5
						Problem Size				
GG	Oral	0	0	10	10	15	25	55	70	90
	Visual	0	5	10	0	25	20	35	30	60
JA	Oral	0	0	15	15	25	15	40	41	75
	Visual	0	0	5	6	0	0	34	15	35

Final Thirty Sessions

Presentation		1 × 1	1 × 2	1 × 3	1 × 4	1 × 5	2 × 2	2 × 3	2 × 4	2 × 5
						Problem Size				
GG	Oral	0	5	0	4	5	7	13	15	15
	Visual	0	0	2	4	7	6	10	13	13
JA	Oral	1	3	4	6	11	9	13	30	29
	Visual	0	5	4	5	6	5	11	9	16

83

occurs where there is the greatest room for improvement, in those treatment conditions that posed the greatest initial difficulty.

Early Performance

A closer look at the trainees' initial solution times and error rates shows that the manipulations of problem size and presentation mode produced substantial variation in problem difficulty. For example, the solution times of both trainees show a clear trend across problem size; holding multiplier size constant, times for both individuals increase monotonically with multiplicand size. A similar pattern of size effects can be seen in both trainees' error rates, but less clearly, probably due to a combination of floor effects (consistent with the emphasis placed on accuracy) and variability in the difficulty of the particular problems sampled within treatment conditions.

Independent effects of presentation mode are seen in both dependent measures as well. Except for GG's times for 1×1 problems, visually presented problems are solved more quickly and more accurately than orally presented problems by both trainees, although this effect eventually disappears with practice for each.

The data also reveal an interaction between problem size and presentation mode on both dependent variables. Figure 3.1 and Table 3.3 indicate that the *difference* between solution times and error rates for the oral and visual conditions increases as problem size increases. In other words, increasing problem size produces a greater performance decrement for orally presented problems than it does for visually presented problems.

To interpret these results, the problem-size effect can be viewed as composite of both task complexity and memory load. Concerning task complexity, analysis of trainees' verbal protocols reveals that the number of arithmetic operations needed to solve a problem is a function of problem size. Assuming that these operations are serially organized, independent of one another, and equivalent in duration and error probability, more operations translate into higher latencies and error rates.[1]

It is argued that memory demands also contribute to the problem-size effect. To understand this relation, consider that both the number and size of intermediate results produced in the course of computation increase as

---

[1]Note that a size effect should appear whether calculations are performed with or without external memory aids, implying that it ought to persist even if the trainees make the maximum possible improvement in memory management. If sufficient practice was available to memorize the answers to all multiplication problems, a problem size effect would still be expected because product size is a function of problem size. Both product retrieval time and output time (included in the solution times) should increase proportionally with product size even in this hypothetical situation.

problems get larger. As a result, larger problems require the trainees to hold larger numbers in memory as computation proceeds.

The faster, more accurate performance of both GG and JA on visually presented problems can also be interpreted in terms of memory load. As suggested earlier, the oral presentation condition adds to the memory load with which the trainees must contend under visual presentation conditions, because problem operands must be held in memory along with intermediate results as computation proceeds. For problems such as 1 × 1s or 1 × 2s, if numbers are represented as quantities (i.e., chunks) rather than digit sequences, the memory load at any point during computation process is probably within the capacity of novices' working memory, estimated to be about three or four symbols or chunks (Broadbent, 1975; Chase & Ericsson, 1982; Simon, 1976). Thus, differences in load for oral and visual problems in this size range should be inconsequential, and the observed oral/visual differences in each trainee's performance support this interpretation. As load approaches and exceeds the capacity of working memory, however, performance in the oral condition should and does fall below that for visually presented problems.

Finally, the interactive effects of presentation mode and problem size on the trainees' early performance can be understood in terms of how these variables affect concurrent memory load. First consider that most of the computation for each orally presented problem proceeds while two problem operands and at least one intermediate result are being held in memory. Next consider that the concurrent load related to maintaining these items grows with increasing problem size. Thus, the task of maintaining problem operands while computation proceeds increases the burden on the memory system and the degree to which memory load increases is a function of problem size. Because a concurrent memory load degrades performance to a greater degree on difficult tasks than on easy tasks (Baddeley & Hitch, 1974), the interactions observed in the trainee's performance are readily interpretable; with oral problems, as problem size grows, the increasing burden of maintaining problems in memory adds to the already increasing size of intermediate results that calculators must also retain.

Evidence supporting this interpretation of the joint effects of problem size and presentation mode comes from an analysis of the errors made by GG and JA during their first 20 sessions. During this period, both failed to produce answers on a number of trials, citing loss of essential information as the reason for failure. Table 3.4 displays the percentage of trials for which forgetting was explicitly reported as the cause of error. The principle finding is that the pattern of forgetting for each trainee closely resembles that seen for their solution times and error rates over the first 10 sessions. The importance of this finding is that it directly relates the probability of memory failure to treatment conditions in a way that is predicted by the

TABLE 3.4

Percentage of Errors Due to Memory Failure

Presentation		*1 x 1*	*1 x 2*	*1 x 3*	*1 x 4*	*1 x 5*	*2 x 2*	*2 x 3*	*2 x 4*	*2 x 5*
						Problem Size				
GG	Oral	0	0	10	5	20	0	45	55	70
	Visual	0	0	0	0	0	0	0	20	30
JA	Oral	0	0	0	10	15	0	15	20	25
	Visual	0	0	0	0	0	0	0	0	0

current account of how problem size and presentation should influence memory demands and, in turn, affect performance.

Finally, the verbal reports taken from both JA and GG during their first few practice sessions indicated that both found the memory demands of this task to be their principal difficulty. Each estimated that the time he spent either rehearsing or trying to recall figures easily exceeded the time spent on actual computation. These reports mirror those obtained by Dansereau's (1969), who used concurrent verbal protocols to analyze the mental processes of novice mental calculators.

In general, the trainees' early performance indicates that the manipulation of problem size and presentation procedures have created a task environment in which problems vary considerably in difficulty. The preceding rather detailed discussion of the trainees' early performance shows how these manipulations relate to memory demands, which in turn affect the difficulty of solving problems in the different treatment conditions. Having established the relations between memory demands and performance, attention now turns to examining how the trainees' performance changed with practice.

Practice Effects

During the first few weeks of practice both JA's and GG's accuracy improved steadily. JA's aggregate error rate dipped below the 10% target criterion by his 10th session, and by his 25th session he reached the level of accuracy he maintained throughout the remainder of his practice (Mean = 9.6%, SD = 2.2).[2] GG took 20 sessions to achieve the 10% criterion, which he never again exceeded, maintaining an average error rate of 5.2% (SD = 1.5) over the rest of his practice. The accuracy achieved by the trainees at this relatively early stage of practice shows that they had devised effective procedures for dealing with the memory demands of mental calculation.

The trainees' solution times show a similar response to practice over a longer time frame. As Figures 3.2, 3.3, 3.4, and 3.5 indicate, both GG and JA showed sizeable decreases in their solution times across all conditions relatively early in practice. Although these plots suggest that solution times for smaller problem sizes asymptote with practice for both trainees, the finding that all practice curves can be well fit[3] by power functions implies that GG's and JA's solution times improved continuously with practice. Of course, this also implies that practice yields diminishing returns.

The general pattern of improvement in the trainees' solution times is one

---

[2]These accuracy statistics are based on data aggregated over blocks of 5 practice sessions.

[3]A more detailed discussion of curve-fitting procedures and results appears in a later section.

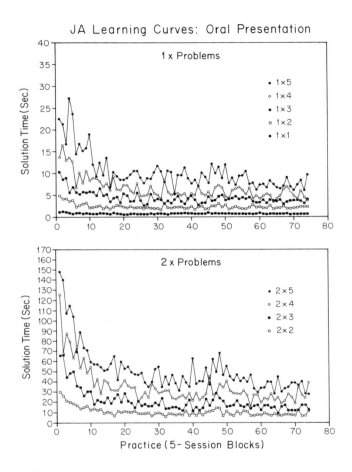

FIGURE 3.2 JA's mean solution times as a function of practice and problem size for orally presented problems. Each data point represents the mean of 15 observations (or fewer for the first 5 practice blocks).

seen in a wide range of cognitive and perceptual motor skills (Fitts & Posner, 1967; Newell & Rosenbloom, 1981). This finding implies that however esoteric the task of mental computation may seem, its underlying mechanisms may well be those common to the acquisition of a wide variety of skills.

Individual Differences

For all the quantitative similarities in the performance of the trainees, there are several interesting qualitative differences in their underlying mental processes. Two are mentioned here because they help to explain differences in the trainees' performance at later stages of their training.

First, within the first 20 practice sessions, JA reported that the externally displayed operands of visually presented problems interfered with his solution processes. To eliminate this distraction, he explicitly chose to ignore the external representations once he had encoded the problem operands they displayed. From that point on, he performed his calculations by accessing needed figures in his internal representations, referring only to the same

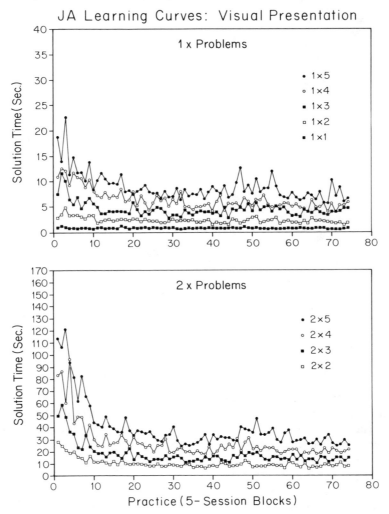

FIGURE 3.3   JA's mean solution times as a function of practice and problem size for visually presented problems. Each data point represents the mean of 15 observations (fewer for the first 5 practice blocks).

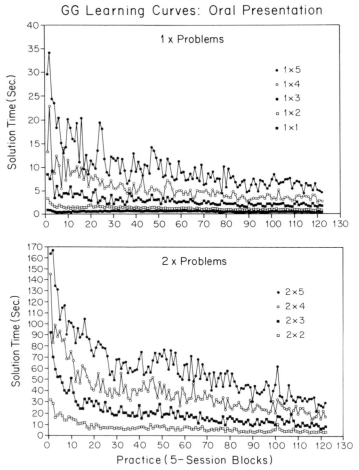

FIGURE 3.4   GG's mean solution times as a function of practice and problem size for orally presented problems. Each data point represents the mean of 15 observations (or fewer for the first 5 practice blocks).

information available in the external representations when memory failed him. As a result, from this point onward JA was only slightly faster in solving visually presented problems, and toward the end of his training, this advantage was evident only for the larger problem sizes (1 × 5s, 2 × 4s, and 2 × 5s).

GG, on the other hand, reported exploiting the externally represented information to the best of his ability throughout his training. As a result, for much of his training his solution times show a substantial, statistically reliable speed advantage for the visual condition. This strategic difference is important, because it later leads to the claim that the eventual disap-

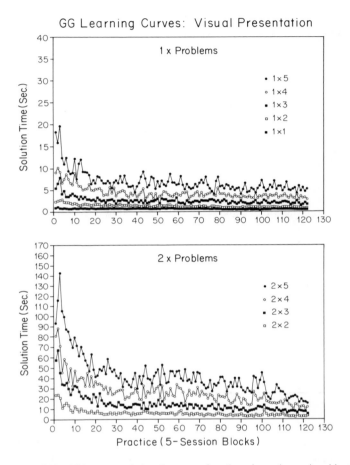

FIGURE 3.5   GG's mean solution times as a function of practice and problem size for visually presented problems. Each data point represents the mean of 15 observations (fewer for the first 5 practice blocks).

pearence of GG's visual advantage is due to his development of skilled memory.

A second interesting difference between the trainees is that each has implemented the left-to-right strategy for two-place (2×) multiplication in different ways. Their methods are contrasted in Table 3.5, which illustrates how each goes about solving the problem 327 × 42. Briefly, GG's strategy uses the smaller of two problem operands as his multiplier, whereas JA uses the larger of the two operands as his multiplier. In terms of arithmetic complexity there is little difference between these two approaches; both require roughly the same number of elementary arithmetic operations. The strate-

TABLE 3.5
Alternative Computational Algorithms for Two-Place Multiplication

327
× 42
_____
13080
+ 654
_____
13734

GG	JA
4 × 3 = 12	3 × 4 = 12
4 × 2 = 8	3 × 2 = 6
120 + 8 = 128	120 + 6 = 126
4 × 7 = 28	2 × 4 = 8
1280 + 28 = 1308	126 + 8 = 134
Reformat 13,080	2 × 2 = 4
Rehearse 13,080	1340 + 4 = 1344
2 × 3 = 6	Carry check
2 × 2 = 4	Say "thirteen thousand"
60 + 4 = 64	7 × 4 = 28
2 × 7 = 14	44 + 28 = 72
640 + 14 = 654	2 × 7 = 14
Retrieve 13,080, 654	720 + 14 = 734
Cherry check 0 + 6 < 9	Say "seven hundred thirty-four"
Retrieve 13, say "thirteen"	
65 + 8 = 73	
730 + 4 = 734	
Say "seven thirty-four"	

gies differ mainly in the sequence in which elementary arithmetic operations are performed. The interesting feature of these strategies is that they differ in terms of their psychological complexity. More specifically, they differ in terms of memory demands.

GG's general approach to 2× calculation resembles the traditional right-to-left multiplication strategy in that it exhibits a similar hierarchical organization of procedures. Computation proceeds by iteratively multiplying the left-most or "tens" digit of the smaller operand against each digit of the larger operand, successively adding the simple products of these operations to an intermediate or "running" product. At the end of this computational "loop" the running product is identical to the second partial product that would be produced using the conventional right-to-left procedure. Then the same sequence of operations is repeated using the second digit of the multiplier to form the second partial product. The partial products are added together in stages, starting with the left-most digits of each. Following each successive step in the addition process, GG reports that portion of the final product just computed.

From the perspective of memory, an important feature of this general algorithm is that the first partial product of a problem must be retained, while the second is computed, and then the second must be held while the first is retrieved. Verbal protocols show that GG's solution to this memory problem is to use retrieval structures to encode his partial products and to rehearse these structured representations at the time of their encoding. The number of rehearsals used to encode each partial product varies with its size, which also covaries with the duration for which it must be retained. Because larger problems produce larger partial products that must be remembered for longer periods, the first partial product of a 2 × 2 seldom receives any rehearsal, whereas that of a 2 × 5 receives between 3 and 5 repetitions.

JA's general 2× algorithm is also hierarchically organized; however, it is structured more efficiently in terms of the memory demands it imposes. Using the larger of the two problem operands as his multiplier, JA multiplies its left-most digit first against the left-most or "tens" digit of the smaller operand and then against the "units" digit, finishing his basic computational loop by adding the two simple products to form a running product. Accessing each digit of the larger operand in order of descending magnitude, JA repeats this sequence of operations, multiplying first against the "tens" digit of the smaller operand and then against the "ones" digit, successively adding each intermediate product to the running product until all elements of both operands have been multiplied and their products added.

Note that as this process proceeds and JA's running products grow in size, the digits of the highest magnitudes in these products are those that appear in the final products, provided that these figures are not altered by carries from future additions. Therefore, at predetermined points in his algorithm, JA decides whether or not future computations are likely to alter his running product, adjusts this product accordingly, and reports that portion of the running product that he assumes will remain unchanged as part of his solution.

It is significant that both GG and JA report parts of final products before finishing all calculation, because doing so reduces the concurrent memory load under which further calculation proceeds. This appears to be one general advantage of left-to-right multiplication. However, differences in their 2× algorithms determine how much of an advantage this general strategy confers. JA's algorithm allows him to report portions of his answers at a much earlier point of this computations than GG can. Thus GG's method imposes a greater burden on memory; he must maintain larger numbers in memory over longer periods of computational activity than JA.

Final Performance Relative to AB

Although the data in Figure 3.1 and Table 3.3 show that both trainees improved their performances substantially with practice, can JA and GG be considered expert mental calculators? This question is answered by comparing their performance to that of the expert, AB.

Figure 3.6 replots the trainees' final solution times from Figure 3.1 along with comparable data from AB. AB's data represent his times on the set of problems given to GG in his final 10 practice sessions,[4] thus facilitating direct comparison. JA's means, however, are based on a different sample of problems. A point to remember in comparing the trainees' data to AB's is that the trainees' performances reflect a few hundred hours of practice, while AB's performance reflects over 18 years of practice at squaring and multiplying.

The level of accuracy achieved by all three individuals was quite comparable. The overall error rates for AB, GG, and JA were 8.9%, 6.7%, and 7.4%, respectively. Consistent with the amount of practice JA received, his overall solution speed is reliably slower than either GG's or AB's. Comparison of GG and AB shows no overall advantage in speed for either individual. Rather, AB is reliably faster than GG on 1 × 3s, 1 × 4s, 1 × 5s, and 2 × 2s and GG is faster on 2 × 4s and 2 × 5s. Comparing verbal protocols from each, it appears that AB's comparative advantage on the smaller problems lis in his ability to retrieve rather than compute answers to a larger number of problems and subproblems than GG. On the other hand, more efficient memory coding and retrieval processes give GG the advantage on the largest problems.

The Specificity of Expertise

Although the preceding data indicate GG is faster than AB on some 2× problems, a theoretically important finding is that his speed advantage does not extend to larger problem sizes such as 3 × 3s and 4 × 4s. In other words, GG's expertise is limited by his experience; his performance drops off sharply when he is presented with problems larger than those regularly presented in practice sessions.

This limitation is illustrated by GG's performance in solving randomly generated 3 × 3s and 4 × 4s problem sizes which AB practiced regularly, but GG had never practiced. Tested on 3 × 3s, GG's average solution time for 12 problems (Mean = 41.23 sec, SD = 25.78) was almost double that of AB (Mean = 21.09, SD = 17.43), while showing comparable accuracy. Presented with 4 × 4s, GG experienced extreme difficulty and quit computation before reaching an answer on all but the last two of eight problems. He correctly solved only the last one. His computation time exceeded five

---

[4]GG's solution times reflect his performance after practicing with JA's 2× algorithm for 100 practice sessions. One consequence of this strategy change is the re-emergence of a visual advantage for 2 × 4s and 2 × 5s that had disappeared by 500 practice sessions.

Comparison of Trainees and AB

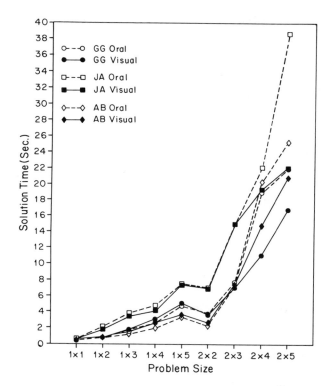

FIGURE 3.6   Mean solution times of GG, JA (replotted from Figure 3.1) and
AB plotted as a function of problem size and presentation condition.

minutes on all of the 4 × 4s, and his overt behavior on all but the last trial
resembled that of a novice struggling to solve a 2 × 5. On all but the last
two trials, GG cited memory overload as the reason for failure, stating specifically that he "didn't have the right schemes for finding and manipulating the numbers." Significantly, after his next-to-last 4 × 4, the first one
on which he was able to achieve an answer, he reported discovering an effective representational scheme.

The finding that GG's expertise is constrained by his practice history is
consistent with the view that expertise is domain-specific (Chase & Simon,
1973a; Feigenbaum, 1977; Reitman, 1976). The size of problems on which
GG demonstrates extraordinary performance is limited to the range of
problem sizes presented to him in practice. The sharp decline in his performance on problems larger than 2 × 5s indicates that his expertise is limited
not to the broad domains such as mental arithmetic or mental multiplica-

tion, but rather to a more circumscribed set of tasks that fall within these domains. Moreover, his protocols reveal that his skill is sharply constrained by the availability of appropriate mechanisms for maintaining information in memory. As a corollary, his expertise is supported by mechanisms precisely tailored to the demands of a specific task environment. The nature and function of these mechanisms are addressed by the following theoretical analysis.

To conclude, comparison of GG's solution times and error rates with those of AB indicates that he has become a world-class mental calculator, at least over the range of problems on which he has trained. JA, whose solution times lag behind those of AB and GG for every problem size, nevertheless has achieved a level of performance that clearly differentiates him from novices. It is noteworthy that these results mark a second occasion (Staszewski, in preparation) in which human expertise has been developed under laboratory conditions using principles derived from a cognitive analysis of expert skill.

4. THEORETICAL ANALYSIS: THE ROLE OF SKILLED MEMORY

The trainees' performance demonstrates that over the course of their training they have devised means to manage the memory load that mental calculation imposes. Attention now turns to the question of how they manage the memory demands of this task and the extent to which their management strategies conform to the principles of Skilled Memory.

LTM Encoding

Skilled Memory Theory claims that experts enhance their information processing capacity by storing and retrieving information in LTM efficiently. Why might expert mental calculators turn to LTM for the storage of information?

One good reason is that the conditions produced by mental calculation resemble those created in studies designed to produce STM forgetting. Consider how closely the task of multiplying $93,472 \times 6$ approximates the conditions of the Brown–Peterson experiments (Brown, 1958; Peterson & Peterson, 1959). These seminal STM studies (see Crowder, 1976, for an excellent review of this work and the many studies that followed) showed that information could be maintained reliably in STM for only a few seconds in the face of interpolated activity. Note that arithmetic calculation served in this paradigm as the task used to prevent rehearsal. Likewise it seems safe to assume that the computational activity intervening between storage and use of the symbols contained in problem operands and intermediate products produces similar effects.[5] Moreover, the similarity of the materials (i.e., digit sequences) being stored within and across trials maximizes the threat that both proactive (Fuchs & Melton, 1974; Wickens, Born, & Allen, 1963) and retroactive (Corman & Wickens, 1968; Landuaer, 1974) interference pose to their retention in STM.

A second reason to suspect that expert mental calculators might use LTM to store task-critical information is the skilled memory effect (Chase, 1986; Chase & Ericsson, 1982;). Studies of experts in a wide variety of domains such as architecture (Akin, 1982), baseball (Chiesi, Spilich, & Voss, 1979), bridge (Charness, 1979), chess (Chase & Simon, 1973a, 1973b; Chi, 1978), computer programming (Anderson, 1985; McKeithen, et al., 1981; Schneiderman, 1976), electronics (Egan & Schwartz, 1979), go (Reitman, 1976), gomoku (Eisenstadt & Kareev, 1975) all exhibit the skilled-memory effect. Essentially, this phenomenon refers to the ability of an expert to retain large amounts of briefly presented material, provided that this material comes from the domain of the individual's expertise.

The generally accepted interpretation of this effect is that experts use LTM representations that they develop through practice in a particular domain to quickly recognize and encode frequently encountered patterns of information. Thus, when presented with familiar materials in an experimental setting, experts use their prior knowledge to create relatively durable memory representations.

Baddeley (1986), however, proposed that expert mental calculators may use means other than LTM storage to retain critical information. His idea is that strategic use of the relatively independent subsystems outlined in his model of working memory (Baddeley, 1986) represents an alternative solution to the memory management problem. For instance, while information needed for ongoing computations is held in one subsystem, information needed for future operations could be stored in the "free" subsystem (e.g., Baddeley's visuo-spatial buffer). The key assumption of this model is that the storage buffers of working memory maintain information in a transient form. Once removed or lost from a buffer, information is irretrievably lost. In support of such a view, Baddeley (1986) cited a study by Hatano and Osawa (1983) in which abacus-based mental calculation experts showed negligible recall for digit lists they had received in a previously presented block of digit-span trials. The implication is that these experts don't rely on LTM storage to perform lightning mental calculation.

To resolve the locus of storage issue, both free recall and recognition tasks

---

[5]Though nothing prevented the trainees from interweaving rehearsal and computation, the demand for speed obviously discourages unnecessary rehearsal. Consistent with this viewpoint, the trainees' verbal reports indicate that they relied on rehearsal extensively at the initial stages of practice and that their improvements in both speed and accuracy during the first few weeks of practice were accompanied by diminishing use of rehearsal.

were used to test the hypothesis that GG and JA used LTM to store vital information during computation. If so, problems presented in the course of practice ought to be retained at a session's conclusion. AB's retention of problems was also tested during the brief period for which he was available.

The basic procedure for testing subjects' recall was straightforward. After solving the final problem of a practice session, the subject was asked to recall as many of the problems presented in the session as accurately as he could. For most sessions, advance notice of the recall task was given prior to the start of calculation practice. On a number of occasions, the trainees received no advance warning. A problem was scored as correctly recalled if the number of digits in both operands was correct and 50% or more of the digits were given in their proper places.[6]

Overall, the results of these studies were consistent with the skilled memory effect. Recall testing began after GG had accumulated 93 practice sessions and JA 136. In the initial testing sessions, GG recalled an average of 31% of the problems presented in the course of a practice session and JA recalled 37%. With further calculation practice, JA's recall gradually rose to 46% near the end of his training and GG's reached 61%. Consistent with Lane and Robertson's (1979) studies of chess experts' recall, the trainees' level of recall was unaffected by whether or not they knew they would be tested for recall on a given day.

Although their ability to recall problems supported the LTM coding hypothesis, it was bothersome that the amount of material GG and JA could recall was small relative to that recalled by the digit-span experts, SF (Chase & Ericsson, 1982) and DD (Staszewski, 1987), in post-practice free recall. A plausible explanation was that problems received later in a session (and the memory representations generated in solving them) interfered with the trainees' recall of early problems. This account was supported by an analysis that showed that the probability of recalling a problem increased as a function of its presentation order for both trainees. In light of this interference, a recognition task was used as a more sensitive means of assessing the calculators' reliance on LTM coding. Following each of two practice sessions, GG, JA, and AB were presented with a set of 108 problems and asked to differentiate between those presented in the immediately preceding practice session and those drawn from randomly-generated set of distractors. The results of this experiment conformed to expectations. All subjects could easily distinguish old problems from new on the majority of trials (GG 92%, JA 87%, AB 82%).

Overall, the results of these problem retention studies suggest that GG,

---

[6]A more stringent scoring that demanded perfect serial recall of the digits in both problem operands reduced the recall scores reported below by an average of about 2% for GG and 4% for JA across recall sessions.

JA, and AB, like experts in a wide variety of other domains, use LTM to represent and maintain task-relevant information. This conclusion leads, of course, to the question of how these expert calculators use LTM to achieve exceptional performance and, more to the point, how adequately the principles of Skilled Memory describe their use of LTM.

RETRIEVAL STRUCTURES

According to Skilled Memory Theory, retrieval structures store material in LTM in a way that makes it easily accessible for later use. Two key functional properties of these mechanisms are (a) their capacity to store long digit sequences in memory in a way that preserves serial order and (b) their ability to provide fast and reliable access to stored information at the time it is needed (Chase & Ericsson, 1982; Staszewski, 1987).

To appreciate the potential value of retrieval structures to an expert mental calculator, consider how their functional properties relate to the memory demands of mental multiplication. First, accurately solving all but the simplest of problems depends upon reliable maintenence of multi-digit problem operands and intermediate results over intervals filled with computational activity. Recall that this intervening activity has a maximally disruptive effect upon STM storage. Second, rapid calculation depends upon *rapid* storage and retrieval of such information at the appropriate junctures in the computational process.

Although the potential advantages of retrieval structures by no means dictate their use, two sources of evidence indicate that both GG and JA use retrieval structures to store and retrieve task-critical information in LTM similar to the way in which the digit-span experts, DD and SF, used retrieval structures to increase their digit spans to unprecedented size. Verbal protocols collected as the trainees solved problems while "thinking aloud" provide the first source of evidence. Data from a detailed analysis of GG's post-practice problem recall provide the second source.

The Protocol Data

Frequently over the course of GG's and JA's training, practice sessions were replaced with sessions in which concurrent verbal protocols were collected. In these sessions problems were presented according to regular practice procedures; that is, problems of varying size and content were presented either orally or visually, and the trainees would proceed to solve them. Unlike regular practice sessions, the trainees were asked to "think aloud" while solving each problem. Their verbalizations were recorded on audio tape, then later transcribed and analyzed.

Table 3.6 contains a transcript of the verbal report given by GG as he solved the visually presented problem 97×266. This particular protocol illustrates several distinguishing properties of retrieval structures that were evident throughout both trainees' protocols. First, one distinguishing characteristic of retrieval structures is that they are used to both encode and retrieve information. A second is that they represent information in a hierarchical format. Together, these characteristics provide straightforward criteria for

TABLE 3.6
Concurrent Verbal Protocol of GG Solving 266 × 97

266
× 97
23940
+ 1862
25802

2 times 9, 18
66 times 9
54
9 times 6 is 54
and 54, 594
18 and 594
18 and 5, 23
retrieve 94
23 94
expand 23 940
23,940, 23,940
ok, 266 times 7
ok, 7 times 2, 14
7 times 6, 42
and 42, it's gonna be 462
so, 14 and 462
14 and 4 is 18
retrieve 62
18 62
retrieve...uh, 29...240, was it?
23 940
23 940 and 18 62
that to . . . 18 62 to 1 862
ummm...940 and 862, carry
uh..., 23, 1, and carry, 25
retrieve 940 and 862
40 and 62 will be a carry, sooo...
umm, gonna be nine, nine-eighty
carry will be 18
strip the 1...8
40 and 62 is 102, strip the 1
8 and 02
802

determining if retrieval structures are employed in a task, because they predict that material encoded and retrieved by these mechanisms should show identical hierarchical organization. For example, findings taken as evidence for DD's use of retrieval structures in the digit-span task were (a) the isomorphic temporal patterns that characterized both his encoding and serial recall of digit lists and (b) results showing that these patterns were well fit by a model of internal representation that postulated hierarchical organization (Staszewski, 1987).

Similar effects can be seen in the protocol found in Table 3.6, which shows that GG's representations of partial products are hierarchically organized and that the same abstract structure is used to both encode and retrieve these products. For example, after GG calculates the subproduct of 9×266 (2,394) and appends a zero to this figure to represent the appropriate magnitude of the first partial product, he then organizes and rehearses the result in two chunks, "twenty-three" and "nine- forty." Similarly, after the second partial product (1,862) is calculated, GG represents it in chunks of "eighteen" and "sixty-two." In each case, the representation of ordered strings of individual digits as two quantities reflects hierarchical organization. Notice in this protocol that neither partial product is used immediately after it is created. Rather, further processing operations intervene between the initial encoding and the later retrieval of each, just prior to their addition. Notice also how the organizational format used to represent each partial product is identical at the time of encoding and retrieval.

The claim that abstract knowledge representations are used to both code and retrieve these products means that the same data structures should accommodate different contents. This claim is supported by the retrieval error that GG makes in the protocol in Table 3.6. After computing the second partial product (1,862), GG attempts to retrieve the first partial product and gets the incorrect figure "twenty-nine" "two-forty." Detecting his error, he immediately retrieves the correct figure. The point is that both the incorrectly and correctly retrieved items exhibit the same abstract structure as the original encoding. This suggests that the structure used to encode and retrieve partial products exists independently of its contents. In this instance, GG correctly retrieves the structure but not the correct contents. Further support for this claim comes from the finding that the representational formats illustrated in this protocol exemplify one of several "canonical" organizational formats (illustrated in Table 3.7) used repeatedly by GG to represent partial products generated by 2×3 multiplications.

A further parallel can be drawn between digit-span experts' representation of random digit lists and the calculation trainees' representation of problems and intermediate results. Like SF and DD, JA and GG use different organizational formats to represent digit sequences that differ in length.

TABLE 3.7
GG's Representational Formats of 2x Partial Products

Problem Size	Formats			
2 × 2	ab c0 +x yz	ab c0 +yz	a b0 + x yz	a b0 +yz
2 × 3	* ab cd0 +w xyz	ab cd0 +xyz	ab c0 +wx yz	ab c0 + x yz
2 × 4	abc de0 +vw xyz	abc de0 +w xyz	ab cd0 +vw xyz	ab cd0 +w xyz
2 × 5	ab cd ef— +u vw x y z	ab cd ef— +vw xy z	a bc de0 +uvw xyz	abc de0 +vw xyz

Note. Notice that the abstract formats of the 2 × 3 structures marked above (*) correspond to the organization of the partial products shown in the protocol presented in Table 3.6.

However, the length of a digit sequence does not alone determine the organizational format that either GG or JA use to represent multi-digit numbers. As illustrated in Table 3.6 by GG's reformatting of "eighteen, sixty-two" to "one, eight sixty-two," the functional role of a particular piece of information within a computation also influences the retrieval structure format selected to store that information in memory. In general, the trainees' protocols show that they have developed a variety of representational structures and that they use these structures in a systematic, flexible, and selective manner.

GG's representational flexibility is implied by the variety of abstract knowledge structures he uses to represent the partial products he generates while solving problems with two-place multipliers (2 × 2s, 2 × 3s, 2 × 4s, and 2 × 5s). These structures, derived from his verbal protocols, are shown in Table 3.7. The contents of this table represent an exhaustive taxonomy of the structures GG uses to represent partial products.

Within this table, the groupings of symbols represent abstract organizational formats GG repeatedly uses to represent partial products. The upper data structure in each pair of structures shows how GG organizes his first partial products, those intermediate results created by multiplying the "tens" digit of a problem's multiplier against the multiplicand. The lower item in each pair shows how partial products generated by the "units" multiplication are formatted. In this table, alphabetic symbols represent locations occupied by numeric values that vary with problems. Note that zeros occupy the units position in all first partial products, except for those from 2 × 5s that would ordinarily consist of seven digits. Claiming that he finds it easier to rehearse such products as three two-digit numbers, GG retrieves the zero reflecting the appropriate magnitude of the first partial only for his final addition operation.

Analysis of the contexts in which these structures are used reveals that GG's selection of a representational format for a given partial product is extremely systematic and depends upon two interacting factors. The first factor is the magnitude of a partial product and the second factor is the order in which a partial is calculated, that is, whether a partial product is generated by the "units" or "tens" digit of the multiplier. These factors interact in the sense that the format of the first partial product constrains which of several representional formats is used to code a second partial product n digits in length.

Although the variety of data structures GG uses suggests considerable representational flexibility, the fact that so few (note the redundancy of structures within Table 3.7) are used to accommodate virtually all of the partial products that can be generated by applying his $2\times$ computational algorithm implies noteworthy economy as well. Overall, GG's development and systematic use of these organizational formats implies (a) his discovery of redundant patterns that occur within his task environment and (b) that he has developed knowledge representations that he uses to exploit these redundancies. In addition, GG's selective use of these structures illustrates how he adapts his processing activities very precisely to the constraints of the task environment that each problem creates.

What is the purpose of such systematic procedures for coding partial products? It appears that GG's formatting strategies enable him, as he says, "to find numbers in the same places" when he turns to adding partial products. Consistent with the view that retrieval structures are mechanisms for indexing[7] information in memory (Chase & Ericsson, 1982; Staszewski, 1987), GG's systematic formatting procedures apparently combine abstract indexing features with his representations of the digits (and digit-groups) to form integrated knowledge representations for addends. Using a retrieval structure to regenerate these abstract relational cues, which then serve as retrieval cues, makes it possible to retrieve pairs of addends sharing similar relative locations within different data structures with a single set of retrieval cues. This view is compatible with the way that GG's representational formats for partial products "align" digits and digit-groups of equivalent magnitude for addition. Within his data structures, to-be-added addend pairs share common abstract locations whose abstract, relational descriptions (e.g., "middle chunk," or first element of last chunk") can serve as retrieval cues for their associated contents.

This discussion of how retrieval structures operate leads to a general point about how experts' strategic use of these mechanisms relates to their ex-

---

[7]See Simon (1976) for a theoretical distinction between LTM "text" or content and its "index" or address.

perience with a particular task. Experts use retrieval structures effectively because they have learned the processing demands of a task and which information is essential for successful performance. In a familiar situation, they know what they will need well in advance of when they need it, and therefore encode critical information appropriately. To be more concrete, consider how GG's reformatting of his second partial product in Table 3.6 anticipates how this information will be used in addition. This instance exemplifies how experts use their familiarity with a task to anticipate future needs and take measures to insure that critical information is maintained for later use. The trainees anticipate their future information needs and maintain task-critical information in working memory by encoding such information in a systematic way that facilitates reliable and efficient retrieval. This is what retrieval structures do.

Before turning to experimental evidence for the use of retrieval structures in expert mental calculation, it is worth noting a ubiquitous feature of retrieval structure organization observed in both trainees' protocols. Without exception, the formats they use to represent either problems or intermediate products are composed of chunks that never exceed three digits. AB's mnemonic system for maintaining intermediate results (described by Chase in his analysis of AB's squaring procedures and also used by AB in multiplication) always codes groups of three digits.

A similar constraint characterizes the retrieval structures used by other experts. Although the structures of SF and DD show more abstract levels of organization, the size of units at each level never exceed three or four elements (Chase & Ericsson, 1982; Staszewski, 1987). Ericsson and Polson's analysis of JC (Chapter 2, this volume), a waiter with exceptional memory for dinner orders, showed that he always encodes dinner orders in groups of four items. This apparent constraint on organizational strategies extends beyond studies of skilled memory. For instance, studies of expert mental calculators and mnemonists report that the organizational strategies used by such subjects never employ chunks that exceed five elements (Ericsson, 1985; Hunter, 1977; Mitchell, 1907; Müeller, 1911).

As Chase and Ericsson (1982) have pointed out, this apparently universal constraint on mnemonic grouping strategies is consistent with Wicklegren's (1964) estimate of optimal chunk size for novices and with independent estimates of the effective working capacity of STM (Broadbent, 1975; Glanzer & Razel, 1974; Simon, 1976). The general conclusion drawn here is that both the external task environment and the internal psychological environment determine the form of the retrieval structures that digit-span experts and mental calculation experts use to represent a particular number in memory. The capacity of STM appears to be one of the principal factors constraining retrieval structure organization.

Experimental Evidence for Retrieval Structures

So far the evidence presented for the use of retrieval structures in mental calculation is based on protocol data and shows that retrieval structures are used to maintain intermediate results in memory. Attention now turns to experimental evidence showing that retrieval structures are used to maintain problem operands in working memory and do so by storing information in LTM.

Recall that the basic claim of Skilled Memory Theory is that experts improve their performance by learning to store and retrieve information in LTM both reliably and efficiently. Retrieval structures represent mechanisms that mediate these processes.

The first step in testing this hypothesis involved using GG's protocols to generate structural models of the retrieval structures he uses to represent problem operands. This analysis showed that the same abstract formats were used consistently to represent operands of a specific length, and that these formats obeyed the same organizational principles that were evident in GG's representations for intermediate results; operands whose length exceeded three digits showed hierarchical organization, and the chunks that defined these structures never contained more than three digits. The tree structure diagrams found in the panels of Figure 3.7 depict the formats hypothesized to code multiplicands three, four, or five digits in length found in both 1× and 2× multiplication problems.

If these abstract structures are used by GG to store and retrieve multiplicands in LTM, his post-practice recall of these items should reflect the organization predicted by these structures. Fortunately for the purpose of testing this prediction, GG recalled a substantial number of items as sequences of individual digits. This made it possible to analyze his recall using the same procedures used to ascertain the organization of DD's retrieval structures (Staszewski, 1987). First, one source of data is used to derive the organization of the structures used to store digit lists of specific lengths. Then the validity of the structural models is assessed by comparing the temporal patterns predicted to characterize the serial recall of lists of a fixed length with the patterns of pauses observed between successively recalled items from many lists.

Applying the reasoning frequently used to infer underlying organization from interitem pauses in free recall (Chase & Simon, 1973a; Patterson, Meltzer, & Mandler, 1971; Pollio, Richards, & Lucas, 1969; Reitman & Reuter, 1980) and serial production tasks (Keele & Summers, 1976; Rosenbaum, Kenny, & Derr, 1983; Staszewski, 1987), GG's hypothesized retrieval structures predict that within-chunk pauses should be roughly equivalent, whereas the additional processing needed to traverse chunk boundaries should produce longer pauses. Thus, the models in Figure 3.7 predict that longer pauses should occur between the second and third digits

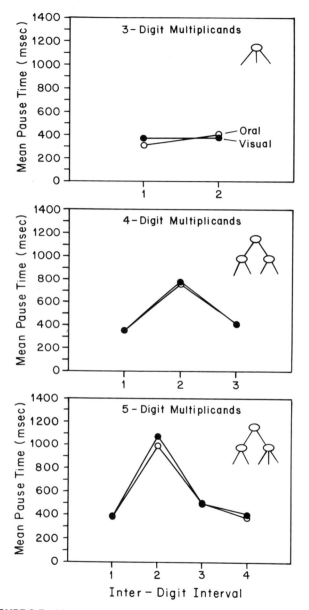

FIGURE 3.7 Mean pause times separating successive digit pairs as a function of their serial position in GG's postpractice recall of problem multiplicands. A schematic model of the retrieval structure governing the encoding and retrieval of multiplicands is shown in each panel. Note that the intervals at which longer pauses occur correspond to the locations of chunk boundaries in the hypothesized structural models.

of both four- and five-digit multiplicands. All other interitem intervals for three-, four-, and five-digit multiplicands should be roughly equivalent.

To test these predictions, interitem pauses were measured between all consecutive pairs of digits for those three-, four-, and five-digit multiplicands recalled correctly and as a sequence of digits. Because GG sometimes recalled pairs of digits as single quantities (i.e., the sequence 7, 5 as "seventy-five"), items containing such chunks were analyzed separately. As a result, 41%, 60%, and 69% of the three- ($N = 128$), four- ($N = 145$), and five-digit multiplicands ($N = 160$), respectively, were used in this analysis.

The data points plotted in Figure 3.7 represent the mean pause times separating the sequentially recalled digits of three-, four-, and five-digit multiplicands. In each panel separate functions are plotted for visually and orally presented problems. In general, the data display the patterns predicted by hypothesized retrieval structure models. Reliably longer pauses occur at the expected intervals for four- and five-digit multiplicands. No reliable differences are observed in pause times between the first and second interdigit intervals of three-digit multiplicands. One unexpected finding, however, occurred for five-digit multiplicands. For such items, GG's pause times at the third interdigit interval are reliably different from all other intervals, regardless of the mode of problem presentation. If this result is replicable, it suggests that what has been assumed to be a chunk of three digits may have a more elaborate internal structure that was not evident in the protocol data. The pattern of pause times implies that the final three digits of five-digit multiplicands may be represented as a chunk composed of smaller chunks of one and two digits. No evidence for similar structure occurs for three-digit multiplicands, however, nothing dictates that minds behave as parsimoniously as theorists would like.

One counterintuitive aspect of these data is the virtually identical pattern of pause times observed for orally and visually presented multiplicands across the three multiplicand sizes. This result suggests that visually presented problems are encoded and retrieved using retrieval structures even though the availability of problem operands throughout practice trials makes their storage unnecessary. A possible explanation is that the operations related to retrieval structure encoding and retrieval are bound tightly to the procedures that make up GG's computational algorithms. In other words, storage and retrieval processes related to specialized, mnemonically effective representational structures may be integral components of the programs governing expert-level mental calculation.

How well do the data excluded from the pause-time analysis support the structural hypotheses pictured in Figure 3.7? Remember that the unanalyzed multiplicands contained sequences of digits recalled as single quantities rather than as sequential digits. Assuming that these quantities are represented in memory as meaningful chunks (that could be unpacked as individual digits), the current organizational hypotheses can be tested by examining whether GG's reported chunks obey the constraints of the retrieval structure models. In other words, how often are the predicted chunk boundaries violated by the chunks GG gives in his recall?

Analysis of where the chunks in GG's recall occur relative to predicted chunk boundary for four-digit multiplicands reveals that the hypothesized boundary is violated once out of 58 possible occasions. In this instance, GG recalled the multiplicand, 8,000, as a single chunk (i.e., "eight thousand").

The predicted boundary between the second and third digits of five-digit multiplicands was violated on 11 of the 49 potential occasions. Analysis of these items showed that 7 of the 11 deviant chunks consisted of duplicate digits (e.g., 11, 22, 88, etc.) and that the remaining four chunks were multiples of five. It is significant that double-digit numbers falling into these two categories also show the highest probability of being recognized and represented by GG as meaningful chunks, because such operands characterize problems that GG most frequently solves using retrieval instead of step-by-step computation. Thus, in the instances that GG violates retrieval structure boundaries, it appears that he trades one mnemonic strategy for another, replacing retrieval structure encoding with encoding that corresponds to Skilled Memory Theory's mnemonic coding principle. At the same time, however, if we consider how frequently these retrieval structure violations occur relative to the total number of five-digit multiplicands recalled (160), the percentage of violations is quite low (6.9%). This suggests that GG tends to use both retrieval structures and meaningful encoding in a complementary way to retain information that is needed to successfully solve problems.

The Development of Retrieval Structures

Before turning to evidence for speed-up and mnemonic encoding, a point regarding the development of retrieval structures is in order. In their discussion of the retrieval structures used by SF and DD, Chase and Ericsson (1982) asserted that these structures require considerable practice to develop. Although little data is available that addresses how retrieval structures develop, several pieces of evidence suggest GG and JA developed retrieval structures fairly early in their training. First, the number of trials on which GG and JA quit computation, citing forgetting as the cause of failure, decreased fairly steadily during the first 30 practice sessions. During the same period they both stabilized their error rates at an acceptably low level and also reduced their solution times substantially. Over this same period, the trainees' verbal reports revealed increasing consistency in their encoding of problem operands and intermediate results, far less rehearsal of these items, and much less time and effort devoted to retrieving needed information. Together, these facts indicate that GG and JA developed and effectively used retrieval structures at a relatively early stage in their training.

Mnemonic Encoding: Recognizing and Encoding Meaningful Patterns

Retrieval structures describe one component of the knowledge that GG and JA have acquired to deal with the memory load mental calculation imposes. In addition, as the earlier discussion of retrieval structures and chunking suggests, the trainees have acquired knowledge of the sort that has been described in prior studies of calculation experts. Evidence indicates that GG and JA use this declarative type of knowledge to improve their performance in ways that are consistent with both Skilled Memory Theory's mnemonic encoding principle and Hunter's (1962, 1977) views of mental calculation expertise.

A characteristic of expert mental calculators repeatedly cited in the literature is an extensive knowledge base of interrelated and easily accessible number facts (Ball, 1892; Bidder, 1856; Binet, 1894; Bryan, Lindley, & Harter (1941), Hunter, 1962, 1977; Jakobsson, 1944; Mitchell, 1907; Müeller, 1911; Sandor, 1932; Smith, 1983). For example, Hunter (1977) reported that Aitken could "automatically" report whether any number up to 1500 is a prime or not and, if so, immediately give its factors. Bryan, Lindley, & Harter (1941) reported that another expert, AG, knew "by heart" the multiplication tables up to 130×130, the squares of all numbers up to 130, the cubes of numbers up to 100, fourth powers up to 20, and more. Consistent with these reports, AB exhibits a similarly elaborate knowledge base of number facts and relations, which he reports to have developed not through intentional memorization but, naturally, through years of practice at squaring and multiplying.

In spite of the limited amount of practice GG and JA have had relative to the experts just cited, several kinds of evidence indicate that each has acquired a store of declarative knowledge which resembles the knowledge acquired by lifelong experts in use, if not in volume.

The first signs of such development occurred for both trainees at a remarkably similar point in their training. Around their 200th session, both showed an increasing incidence of unusually fast solution times on certain 1×2s. The times for these problems were closer to those normally observed for identity problems (whose multiplier is 1) and "decade" problems (whose multiplicands are multiples of 10) than to the times for problems whose products presumably had to be computed rather than retrieved from memory. When questioned about these instances, both GG and JA invariably reported recognizing a familiar problem and consequently altering their usual procedures. In many of these instances, they reported immediately "knowing" an answer upon receipt of a problem. Both further reported occasionally noticing such familiar problems embedded in larger problems and altering their computational plans accordingly. On the basis of these reports, post-trial retrospective protocols were taken from GG and JA during practice sessions on a regular basis to determine the frequency and circumstances under which such events occurred. In addition, the frequency with which concurrently protocols were taken was increased.

Figure 3.8 plots the percentage of practice trials (excluding 1 × 1s) on which each trainee reported detecting one or more familiar patterns within a given problem and modifying his "standard" computational algorithm as a result. The pictured functions indicate that the frequency with which both trainees detected and encoded meaningful patterns of numbers increased fairly steadily as a function of practice.

In what sense are these patterns meaningful? The answer is best revealed by the trainees' protocols. Concurrent protocols show that their recognition of particular patterns leads to the selection of one of a variety of fairly local computational strategies that each has available. These strategies are local in two senses. First, the patterns on which they are based are small and consist of two elements, a multiplier and multiplicand. GG's patterns, even at the conclusion of his training, were rarely larger than 1 × 2. This was generally true for JA, although occasionally he reported encoding patterns as large as 1 × 4. The limited size of these patterns, which falls within estimates of STM capacity, suggests once again the constraint that STM im-

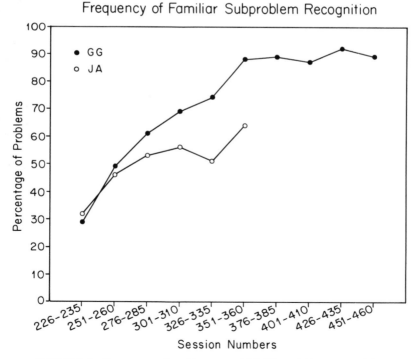

FIGURE 3.8   Percentage of problems on which GG and JA report noticing familiar multidigit patterns that influence their computational strategies. Data are plotted as a function of successive cross sections of practice.

poses on coding processes. Second, these strategies are local in the sense that they are implemented within the larger stereotypic control structures that represent the general left-to-right algorithms that JA and GG use for one- (1×) and two-place (2×) multiplication. Essentially, the patterns that GG and JA recognize and encode represent familiar subproblems which can be solved efficiently with specialized strategies.

Both the patterns and strategies to which particular patterns relate differ for the trainees. In general, JA has a larger repertoire of strategies and a greater variety of pattern classes to which they are related. Like GG, JA has "expanded his multiplication tables" so that there are a variety of 1 × 2s whose products he can retrieve and report in a second or less. His ability to identify quickly the factors of particular numbers enables him to combine factoring and retrieval as a means of solving certain problems and subproblems. In addition, in the course of practice, JA discovered an abstract pattern of results related to an abstract class of problems that led him to devise a computational strategy whose basic procedures resemble those taught in the Trachtenberg system of speeded mathematical computation (Cutler & McShane, 1960). Basically, this strategy is a rule-based computational system applicable to problems or subproblems whose multiplier is 9 and whose multiplicand is a sequence of digits that are either identical (e.g., 9 × 444) or else ascend or descend in units of either 1 or 2 (e.g., 9 × 876, 9 × 579, 9 × 234, etc.). Exploiting the redundancies in the products of such problems, JA's strategy enables him to eliminate addition operations from his computations, thus saving him time.

Although GG's strategies are less varied and original than JA's, his strategies illustrate how rapid pattern recognition and efficient strategy use can improve calculation speed. Table 3.8 presents the principal results of a study that investigated the relation between his strategy use and performance.

In this study the efficiency of GG's strategies was examined by testing him on the entire population of 1 × 2 multiplication problems (excluding problems that use zero as a multiplier). In the oral condition, each of a set of 810 problems was read just as in oral practice blocks. In the visual condition, problems were presented visually on a CRT. Problems in each con-

TABLE 3.8
GG's Strategies for 1 x 2s

Condition		Strategies			
		Identity	Retrieval	Grouping	Calculation
Oral	Mean RT	230	303	430	839
	Proportion of Trials	11.1	25.2	58.6	5.1
Visual	Mean RT	527	631	728	1014
	Proportion of Trials	11.1	24.3	61.0	3.6

dition were presented in random order, and approximately 100 trials were presented in each of 8 sessions conducted on consecutive days. On each trial GG's task was to report the product of the presented problem as quickly as possible and afterward report the strategy he used to solve the problem.

Four basic strategies previously observed in GG's protocols were reported. His *Identity* strategy, applied to problem with a multiplier of one, is intuitively obvious; GG would simply report the multiplicand that had been presented. He described his second strategy, labelled *Retrieval*, as one in which he would report the product that he "immediately knew" upon problem presentation. GG's other two 1 × 2 strategies involved sequential arithmetic operations, in contrast to the two already mentioned. The strategy labelled *Calculation* involved solving 1 × 2s in the way that GG originally solved them at the beginning of his training, just as novices would, using two operations to generate simple products and a third operation to add them. His remaining strategy, labelled *Grouping*, represents an abbreviated version of full computation. According to GG, this procedure involves two consciously controlled steps. The first operation, he reports, is his immediate and simultaneous retrieval of two simple products upon receipt of a problem. The second operation is their addition. Note that with the exception of problems on which the "Full" computation strategy is used, GG's concurrent verbal protocols indicate that he represents multiplicands as single quantities or chunks rather than as discrete symbols. This suggests that the patterns driving strategy selection are specific pairs of quantities.

Table 3.8 shows the proportion of trials on which each strategy was employed for both presentation conditions, and GG's mean reaction times aggregated as a function of reported solution strategy. Because detailed presentation of these results exceeds the scope of the present discussion, the data will be used to make three general points. First, the "full" strategy is used in only about 5% of the situations where GG used it as a novice. Second, the "retrieval" and "grouping" strategies produce solutions much more quickly than full calculation. It is also the case that these strategies produce fewer intermediate results, an important consideration in that such results represent potential sources of interference when it is time to retrieve a product for output. Third, GG's average response latency (the interval between problem presentation and response initiation) for all visually presented 1 × 2s (Mean = 692 msec, SD = 136) approximates solution times that unpracticed adults produce in solving visually presented simple (1 × 1) multiplication problems (Aiken & Williams, 1973; Campbell, 1987). In general, these findings illustrate how knowledge acquired through practice can produce dramatic improvements in calculation speed. The knowledge referred to here consists of meaningful patterns of information associated with specialized computational strategies. These patterns are meaningful in the sense that they are explicitly encoded and used to enable

JA and GG to achieve their principle goal, to solve multiplication problems as quickly and as accurately as possible.

The general point here is that AB, GG, and JA all exhibit a form of mnemonic coding that resembles the pattern recognition capabilities of experts from other domains (Chase & Simon, 1973a, 1973b; Eisenstadt & Kareev, 1975; Reitman, 1976). Through extensive practice with a wide variety of problems, these experts have learned to recognize multi-digit patterns that randomly occur both in isolation and embedded in larger problems. These patterns are meaningful in the sense that they are linked to specific computational strategies that reduce calculation times. In their discussion of the role of pattern recognition in the play of chessmasters, Simon & Chase (1973; Chase & Simon, 1973b) suggested that the patterns experts hold in memory are linked to plausible "good" moves. As a result, their ability to rapidly recognize familiar patterns enables them to select moves more efficiently than less skilled players. The current work shows that similar knowledge-based pattern recognition capabilities enable expert mental calculators to employ computational algorithms that decrease solution times. Thus, this work explicitly links complex pattern recognition with strategy selection and high-level performance.

It is theoretically significant that Siegler's studies of children's arithmetic (Siegler, in press; Siegler & Jenkins, in preparation; Siegler & Shrager, 1984) show that children's skills parallel those of GG and JA in several respects. For instance, children discover and employ a variety of computational strategies for solving simple arithmetic problems. In addition, there is good evidence that their strategy selection is apparently determined by their recognition of specific familiar combinations of problem operands. Finally, as their skills improve with practice, memory retrieval replaces multi-step computation as the preferred solution strategy for an increasing number of problems. These parallels suggest a fundamental continuity in the skill acquisition process across age levels, practice levels, and tasks.

To sum up, it appears that expert mental calculators use semantic memory in three principal ways to achieve fast and accurate performance. First, consistent with Skilled Memory Theory's mnemonic encoding principle, they use an elaborately interrelated knowledge base to recognize and encode meaningful patterns of numbers that occur either as problems or embedded subproblems, thus promoting their retention. Second, much like chessmasters apparently use their pattern recognition capabilities to efficiently select effective chess moves, calculation experts use their unique pattern recognition capabilities to select efficient computational strategies on a problem-by-problem basis. Finally, experts use their knowledge to replace computation with retrieval as a means of generating products and intermediate results, thereby decreasing solution times. Just as SF and DD became expert mnemonists by learning to use semantic memory to encode meaningful patterns of digits, this work shows that GG and JA have developed knowledge bases which they use in a similar fashion to become experts in the domain of mental calculation.

SPEED-UP AND SKILLED MEMORY

What evidence is there that the trainees' memory processes speed up with practice? Data consistent with Skilled Memory Theory's speed-up principle is shown in Figures 3.2 through 3.5, where learning curves graphically describe the effects of extended practice on the trainees' solution times.

The general form of these curves is familiar to students of skill acquisition, because negatively accelerated functions of the sort shown here characterize the relation between speed and practice for a wide range of cognitive and perceptual-motor skills (Anderson, 1983; Crossman, 1959; Fitts & Posner, 1967; Newell & Rosenbloom, 1981). This relation is known as the *power law of practice*. Essentially, this empirical law predicts that the function relating speed of performance to practice is approximately linear when both variables are transformed logarithmically.

Evidence that the trainees' performance conforms to this empirical law can be seen in Table 3.9. Shown here are the parameters and fits obtained when a power function of the form

$$T = A + BN^{-\alpha}$$

is fit to the curves plotted in Figures 3.2 through 3.5.[8] In this function, T represents total problem solution time (calculation time + answer recitation time). A is a fixed value approximating asymptotic solution time for each problem size.[9] The parameter B represents an estimate of calculation time for the first practice block, N represents the number of completed practice blocks at any point in training, and α is the estimated learning rate (i.e., the slope of a linear function in log-log coordinates).

Table 3.9 shows the learning functions obtained by fitting this generalized power function to the data in each problem size/presentation mode

---

[8]The program STEPIT (Chandler, 1965) was used to fit this general function to the data.

[9]Values for the asymptotes were estimated experimentally. On each of a series of trials, each trainee was given a product from a randomly generated problem which he was to memorize so that, upon an experimenter's cue, he could report it aloud as quickly as possible, just as if it had been calculated on a regular practice trial. The products were sampled from the population of products for each of the 9 problem sizes on which GG and JA trained. Total response time (reaction time + recitation time) was measured for each of 30 products taken from each problem size category. The mean response time for each problem size was used as an estimate of asymptotic solution time. The assumption is that such a value represents the average solution time for all problems of a given size, assuming that infinite practice would make all of their products directly accessible.

TABLE 3.9
Trainees' Learning Functions

Problem Type	GG					
	Oral			Visual		
	Function	R^2	RMSD	Function	R^2	RMSD
1 × 1	$T = 0.43 + 0.35N^{-.25}$	.188	0.09	$T = 0.43 + 0.73N^{-.30}$	.590	0.08
1 × 2	$T = 0.64 + 2.57N^{-.41}$	.755	0.19	$T = 0.64 + 2.56N^{-.35}$	.764	0.19
1 × 3	$T = 0.86 + 8.65N^{-.40}$	.746	0.65	$T = 0.86 + 6.07N^{-.34}$	.734	0.45
1 × 4	$T = 1.07 + 17.77N^{-.38}$	.707	1.50	$T = 1.07 + 10.08N^{-.30}$	.775	0.66
1 × 5	$T = 1.28 + 34.67N^{-.38}$	.793	2.28	$T = 1.28 + 18.10N^{-.32}$	.777	1.16
2 × 2	$T = 0.86 + 33.09N^{-.45}$	.870	1.61	$T = 0.86 + 25.42N^{-.43}$	.836	1.39
2 × 3	$T = 1.07 + 95.19N^{-.44}$	.925	3.46	$T = 1.07 + 67.70N^{-.43}$	.888	3.04
2 × 4	$T = 1.28 + 143.31N^{-.37}$	.878	6.76	$T = 1.28 + 91.51N^{-.35}$	.838	5.04
2 × 5	$T = 1.50 + 192.77N^{-.32}$	.852	10.17	$T = 1.50 + 140.20N^{-.33}$	.785	9.37

(Continued)

TABLE 3.9
(Continued)

JA

Problem Type	Oral			Visual		
	Function	R^2	RMSD	Function	R^2	RMSD
1 × 1	$T = 0.32 + 0.82N^{-.15}$	.379	0.09	$T = 0.32 + 0.78N^{-.08}$	.174	0.10
1 × 2	$T = 0.79 + 3.76N^{-.26}$	.588	0.37	$T = 0.79 + 3.04N^{-.20}$	.406	0.40
1 × 3	$T = 1.32 + 8.80N^{-.33}$	.729	0.70	$T = 1.32 + 8.01N^{-.29}$	.501	0.99
1 × 4	$T = 1.74 + 15.30N^{-.36}$	.738	1.27	$T = 1.74 + 12.36N^{-.31}$	.714	1.06
1 × 5	$T = 2.15 + 24.82N^{-.35}$	.689	2.32	$T = 2.15 + 17.28N^{-.30}$	.615	1.74
2 × 2	$T = 1.31 + 28.34N^{-.35}$	.785	1.96	$T = 1.31 + 27.63N^{-.37}$	.836	1.65
2 × 3	$T = 1.71 + 70.72N^{-.42}$	.828	4.50	$T = 1.71 + 56.40N^{-.40}$	.800	3.87
2 × 4	$T = 2.22 + 116.04N^{-.40}$	.828	7.28	$T = 2.22 + 93.92N^{-.42}$	.787	6.83
2 × 5	$T = 2.64 + 155.39N^{-.37}$	.847	8.98	$T = 2.64 + 130.72N^{-.40}$	.834	8.14

Note. Estimates of parameters A and B given in seconds.

condition and measures of their fit. Each function accounts for a statistically reliable proportion of the variance in the solution times, and the R^2 values indicate that the functions fit the data quite respectably in most cases. The exceptions are the functions for smaller problem sizes. A reasonable explanation for their poor fits is that prior experience with mental multiplication and addition, particularly on problems whose size makes their solution fairly tractable for novices, may have produced improvements in trainees' solution times that occurred prior to their participation in this study. Generally, both the quality of the fits and the reasonable parameter estimates obtained indicate that the power law provides a good characterization of the trainee's learning.

The speed-up seen in the trainees' solution times implies an underlying increase in the speed with which meaningful patterns are recognized, encoded with retrieval structures, and later retrieved. The data do not provide completely unambiguous support for the speed-up principle, however. As findings presented later in this chapter show, improvements in solution speed can result also from the discovery and use of efficient computational algorithms that decrease both the processing and memory demands related computing solutions. Fortunately, clearer support for the speed-up principle comes from data that relate speed-up more directly to memory encoding and retrieval processes.

Figure 3.9 replots GG's learning curves shown in Figures 3.4 and 3.5., combining curves for orally and visually presented problems of corresponding problem size in a single plot.[10] The shaded area in each plot depicts the *visual advantage*, that is, the amount of time by which mean solution time for orally presented problems exceeds the mean for visually presented problems. This measure is obtained by subtracting the mean solution time for visually presented problems from the mean for orally presented problems for each block of 5 practice sessions. Unshaded areas between the two functions indicate blocks in which problems presented orally were solved more quickly than visual problems.

The relevant difference between these presentation conditions lies in the demands they place upon memory. Recall that, in the visual condition, problem operands are constantly available for inspection while the solution process proceeds, whereas in the oral condition getting the correct answer to a problem depends on perfect retention of problem operands. Thus, it seems reasonable to assume that the visual advantage stems from the extra time used to encode and retrieve problem operands (and their constituent elements) in the oral condition.

The most salient common feature of these plots is the reduction in shad-

---

[10]Note that the curves in Figure 3.9 are truncated after 500 practice sessions, the point at which GG was instructed to use a new computational strategy for $2\times$ multiplication.

Speed-up in Memory Access

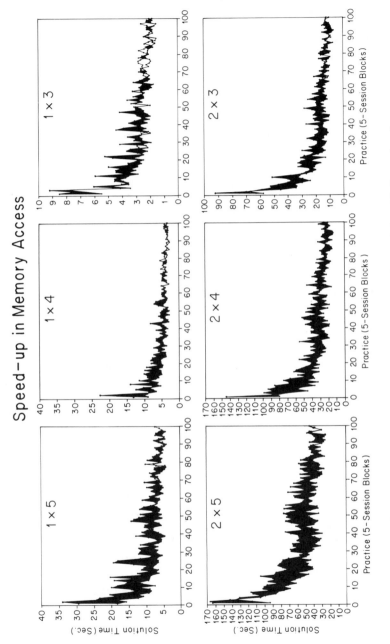

FIGURE 3.9 GG's mean solution times (replotted from Figures 3.4 and 3.5) as a function of problem size, presentation condition, and practice through session #500. Shaded areas between the functions represent the degree to which the mean for orally presented problems exceeds that for visually presented problems at each level of practice.

ed area as a function of practice. This reflects a gradual convergence of solution times for the oral and visual presentation. Statistical comparison of oral and visual solution times from sessions 476-500 reveals that a reliable difference between means occurs only for 1 × 1s; here, orally presented problems are solved more quickly. In addition, a consistent but nonsignificant oral advantage is observed for 1 × 2s and 1 × 3s. Considering GG's ability to use direct retrieval to solve a good proportion of 1 × 2 problems, presentation of the first problem operand in the oral condition may prime associated patterns in semantic memory and lead to faster retrieval times than those found in the visual condition. For all other problems sizes, the means still reflect a slight visual advantage that is swamped by the variability in solution times. The main point, however, is that the visual advantage evident in the early stages of practice diminishes in all cases with practice. The interpretation of this trend is that GG's skills at storing and retrieving problem information in LTM have improved with practice to a point where he encodes and operates upon internal representations nearly as quickly as he processes external representations.

A less obvious but theoretically interesting feature of the data plotted in Figure 3.9 is the slight increase in solution times that can be seen between sessions 200–250 for both presentation conditions. This is also the period in which GG's protocols showed that his recognition and encoding of 1 × 2 patterns increased in frequency. The coincidence of these events, along with GG's reports of actively searching problem operands for familiar patterns on practice trials, suggests that the observed increase in solution times around sessions 200–250 reflects additional processes related to searching for familiar patterns and effectively encoding those found. Assuming that this interpretation is correct, one may infer that reductions in the visual advantage prior to session 200 might be attributed to the increasingly efficient use of retrieval structures with practice. Past this point, continuing improvement in the use of retrieval structures *and* speed-up in the detection and encoding of familiar patterns may both contribute to the observed speed-up in performance.

Note that accounting for speed-up in solution times in terms of improvements in the efficiency of different mechanisms is consistent with Newell and Rosenbloom's (1981) theoretical interpretation of the power law. Essentially, they argue that the power functions that describe complex skill learning come about through practice-related speed-up in the operation of local, specialized processing mechanisms that mediate performance and develop at different points on the practice continuum. The claim here is that retrieval structures and complex memory codes developed over the course of practice and stored in semantic memory represent such mechanisms. However, these are by no means the only mechanisms contributing to the pattern of improvement GG shows. As the following pages show, GG's adoption of an algorithm for two-place ($2\times$) multiplication that is more efficient than his original method played a significant role in reducing his calculation speed for this class of problems to AB's level.

COMPUTATION STRATEGIES, MEMORY MANAGEMENT, AND EXPERT PERFORMANCE

The foregoing theoretical analysis provides strong support for Skilled Memory Theory, showing that the ways that GG and JA handle the memory demands of mental calculation are consistent with the principles of skilled memory.

Nevertheless, there is more to becoming an expert mental calculator than developing skilled memory. Skilled Memory Theory does not provide a complete account of the trainees' expertise, nor does it fully describe how they manage memory. Consistent with Hunter's (1962, 1977) views on lightning mental calculation, the use of efficient computational strategies has a substantial effect on performance. This claim is supported by the results of an experiment in which GG was instructed to abandon the general algorithm for two-place ($2\times$) multiplication he had used for 500 practice sessions, and adopt the algorithm devised and used by his cohort, JA.

The idea for this manipulation arose with the discovery that the general algorithms the trainees used to perform $2\times$ multiplication differed both in computational complexity and in the memory demands they imposed. This discovery prompted the construction of process models of the trainees' procedures based on the protocol and experimental data on hand. The purpose was to represent the trainees' thought processes in a way that the relative efficiency of their computational strategies could be measured objectively.

Briefly, these models were designed with control structures that mirrored the sequence of operations that characterized each trainee's solution procedures across different problems of varying size. A key feature of these models was the well-supported assumption that both GG and JA used retrieval structures to encode and retrieve problem operands and intermediate results in working memory during their calculations. Because the protocols indicated that most of their arithmetic operations involved only elements of operands and intermediate results, the current models assume that (a) all multiplication and addition operations are carried out on pairs of symbols representing single digits[11], and (b) retrieving individual symbols, nested within hierarchically organized knowledge representations, carries with it the overhead of traversing the abstract architecture used to organize and

---

[11]These first-approximation models make no provisions for either trainee's ability to retrieve solutions to familiar 1×2s or encode and operate upon their double-digit operands as unitary quantities. Therefore, despite the encouraging results obtained using these models as analytic tools, they face further development and testing before they can be regarded as valid models of the trainees' skills.

access these symbols. Thus, basic memory search and retrieval operations that access the inputs for arithmetic operations constitute a major portion of the processing needed to execute each simple arithmetic operation involved in solving a problem. A measure of task complexity related to solving a particular problem is obtained by summing the number of elementary memory operations needed to execute the arithmetic, rehearsal, or reformatting operations that a particular solution algorithm dictates.

Once the trainees' procedures for solving $1\times$ and $2\times$ problems were captured in such first-approximation simulation models, these programs were given $2\times$ problems of varying size to solve. Analyses comparing their performance on identical problems showed that JA's method was more efficient than GG's in terms of the number of symbol-processing operations it required to produce solutions. A more detailed examination of the models' performance as a function of problem size showed that the relative advantage of JA's strategy varied proportionally with problem size; JA's strategy was only marginally more efficient than GG's in solving 2×2s, but its margin of superiority increased monotonically with each increase in multiplicand size.

These findings were consistent with the pattern of results shown repeatedly when JA's and GG's solution times were compared at equivalent levels of practice using samples taken between sessions 100 and 300. GG's average solution times were faster than JA's for all levels of $1\times$ problems, roughly equivalent to JA's times for 2×2s, and slower by an increasing margin as problem size increased to 2×5s.

To test the validity of these models more directly, the same problems that the trainees received in practice were fed into the simulation programs. The strategy was to obtain estimates of task complexity for each problem-size category and use these measures to predict the trainees' solution times. The results of these regression analyses were both encouraging and informative. First, across several samples both GG's and JA's models could consistently account for about 80% of the variance in their respective solution times. In addition, the parameter estimates produced by these analyses consistently showed that JA took more time to execute a single processing operation than GG. From this finding, it follows that GG's solution times should be faster than JA's on problems whose solutions required approximately the same number of operations. Moreover, because the models show that GG's solutions for 2×3s, 2×4s, and 2×5s require increasingly more operations than JA's solutions, it also makes sense that his solution times should fall farther and farther behind JA's as the size of $2\times$'s increase. Thus, the results of these model-based analyses offered an explanation for the differences observed in trainees' performance. GG's relative advantage over JA in processing speed is reflected in his faster solution times on $1\times$'s, but this advantage is negated on the larger $2\times$ problems by the additional processing operations that his $2\times$ algorithm requires.

To directly test the hypothesis that the differences in the efficiency of JA's and GG's 2× computational algorithms might account for this pattern of performance, the following experiment was performed. At the beginning of GG's 501st practice session, JA's method for 2× calculation was described to him and he was instructed to use this new method in all subsequent practice sessions. In order to compare GG's performance using the two strategies in as controlled a fashion as possible, the problems presented in sessions 401–500 were re-presented in sessions 501–600 in the same order and under their original presentation conditions.

Figure 3.10 plots GG's average solution times for sessions 476-500, sessions in which he was still using his original 2× algorithm, and sessions 576-600, sessions in which he was fairly well practiced in using JA's 2× algorithm. Comparison of the functions shows an improvement in solution times for all problems sizes with practice. The average improvement for 1× problems is approximately 7% and represents a baseline against which

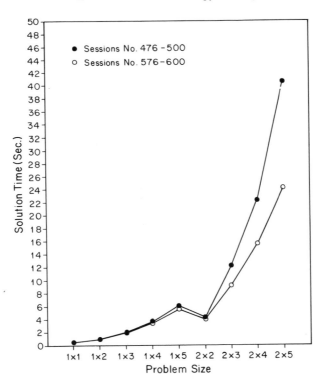

FIGURE 3.10 GG's mean solution times as a function of problem size before and after adopting a new strategy for two-place (2×) multiplication. Means in each condition are based on 75 observations.

improvements due to the experimental manipulation can be measured. Focusing on the times for $2\times$'s, the effects related to switching strategies are interesting in several respects.

First, the general pattern of improvement was predicted in advance by the simulation models' estimates of task complexity; solution times for $2 \times 2s$, $2 \times 3s$, $2 \times 4s$, and $2 \times 5s$ showed decreases of 9%, 25%, 31%, and 40%, respectively. Note that the greatest decreases occur for the problem sizes on which GG's solution times are faster than AB's (2×3's, 2×4's, and 2×5's). The implication is that GG, left to his own devices, would have required considerably more practice to achieve the level of performance that instructional intervention has produced. This result demonstrates how information obtained by analyzing expert performance can be used to "engineer" human expertise in cognitive skills as well as perceptual skills (Biederman & Shiffrar, 1987).

Second, GG was able to adapt to the new algorithm with surprisingly little difficulty. Quantitatively, close inspection of GG's $2\times$ learning curves in Figures 3.4 and 3.5[12] show a relatively small and temporary increase in GG's solution times immediately after switching strategies. A small (2%) and temporary increase in his $2\times$ error rates also occurred at the same point. Qualitatively, concurrent verbal protocols taken during the first few days of the strategy switch also showed a corresponding decrease in the fluency of GG's sequence of operations. In retrospective reports, he mentioned having to pay "a little closer attention" to sequencing his operations on each $2\times$ trial, which he believed slowed him down. Significantly, both types of protocols revealed that GG could encode problem operands and intermediate results via his retrieval structures and execute his pattern-driven computational strategies within the new algorithm without any apparent difficulty.

Theories of skill acquisition (Fitts & Posner, 1967; Schneider & Shiffrin, 1977; Shiffrin & Schneider, 1977) that emphasize the development of automaticity predict that high levels of practice under stable conditions produce relatively inflexible skills. Although there is some evidence for the negative transfer predicted by such theories in the current experiment, the performance decrement related to GG's switch from a familiar strategy to a novel one is trivial compared to that shown when the task environment in which subjects had automatized their skills was altered radically (Experiment 1, Shiffrin & Schneider, 1977). The relative absence of negative transfer is not entirely surprising, because the high variability built into the trainees' practice environment is not conducive to the development of automaticity (Schneider, Dumais, & Shiffrin, 1984).

Although it seems likely that automatization of relatively low-level processes (pattern recognition, memory retrieval) makes an important con-

---

[12]Note the upward inflections in GG's learning curves at practice block #101.

tribution to GG's impressive performance, the ease with which he adapted to using a new algorithm indicates a considerable degree of control and flexibility in his skill. This finding supports Bartlett's (1932) views on expertise and flexibility. This experiment also shows that the acquisition of expert-level skill is a complex process involving more than the automatization of mental operations (Cheng, 1985) and the development of skilled memory. Strategy discovery and use play important roles.

CONCLUSION

What does this work contribute to our understanding of human expertise?

Empirically, the levels of performance achieved by JA and GG as a result of extended training support the view that experts are made, not born. Like the studies of the exceptional mnemonic skills acquired by SF and DD under laboratory conditions, this work shows that knowledge acquired through long and steady practice is the essential ingredient of expertise (along with the motivation to endure extended training, of course). Although intuitions suggest a relation between general aptitude measures and the development of expertise, no clear relation is evident either in this work or in previous studies of expert mental calculators (Hunter, 1962). This observation is consistent with studies of digit-span expertise and chess expertise (Chase & Simon, 1973a, 1973b; deGroot, 1965, 1966; Simon & Chase, 1973). Like Chase and Simon's (1973a, 1973b) demonstration of the domain-specificity of chess expertise, exploration of the boundaries of GG's skill shows the extent to which expert-level performance is specific to particular training conditions. In general, this work adds to the empirical data indicating that expert-level performance in cognitive skills can be achieved by individuals who possess intellectual abilities within the normal range and the motivation to acquire the requisite knowledge through practice.

If experts can be "made," how can we speed up the process? The achievements of GG and JA, and DD's achievement of a level of mnemonic skill never before seen (Staszewski, 1987, in preparation), demonstrate the value of expert strategies as tools for training cognitive skills. In both cases, strategies identified through detailed cognitive analyses of expert skills were used to train novices to achieve exceptional levels of skill. Although the practical value of expert strategies as training tools has been intuitively obvious for centuries (as illustrated by the development of craft guilds in medieval times), the success observed in this study and with DD establishes the identification, description, evaluation, and use of expert strategies as instructional tools as a scientific endeavor. GG's successful adoption of JA's 2× calculation algorithm is a particularly important finding in this regard. It shows that our empirical and theoretical understanding of human expertise can be used to substantially improve the performance of individuals

who are already highly skilled. Moreover, it shows that experts can successfully modify highly-practiced skills without suffering the dramatic drop
in performance that Shiffrin and Schneider (1977) have shown can occur
when changes in a task environment dictate changes in behavior.

From a theoretical perspective, analyses of JA's and GG's skills provide
strong empirical support for the claim that skilled memory is a critical component of mental calculation expertise, showing that the principles of skilled
memory characterize the means by which these mental calculation experts
manage the memory demands that arise in doing mental arithmetic. At the
same time, this work demonstrates that there is more to expert-level performance than experts' efficient use of memory. The strategies that experts
devise influence both the memory demands and computational complexity
of problem solving. As a result, peak performance levels are constrained
by the efficiency of the strategies that experts employ.

Finally, this examination of mental calculation experts extends the generality of Skilled Memory Theory from the domain of expert-level mnemonic
skills to the domain of skill-based expertise. The studies presented in this
chapter provide a detailed sketch of the knowledge that two lightning mental
calculators acquired through training. They dissect this knowledge and show
how its components contribute to the trainees' remarkable capabilities.
Although strategic knowledge and extensive factual knowledge of numerical relations represent important components of expertise in the domain of
mental calculation, skilled memory appears to constitute its foundation. This
conclusion suggests that an important part of developing expert skill involves
learning how to use content knowledge effectively *and* efficiently. Thus,
the current studies suggest that skilled memory represents a general component of expert knowledge across a wide range of cognitive skills.

ACKNOWLEDGMENTS

This study was initiated by Bill Chase and carried out under his direction
until his untimely death occurred in its first year. This chapter is dedicated
to his memory.

GG and JA deserve special thanks for their long hours of dedicated practice. They give new meaning to the phrase "heroic subjects." I also thank
AB for his valuable participation in this research.

I am grateful to Ruth Day, Herb Simon, and Bob Siegler for their valuable comments on this work. Ruth Day also contributed many helpful
editorial suggestions after reading an early draft of this chapter.

I thank John Allen, Rebecca Deuser, Richard Eastman, Patricia Feather,
and Norene Pfeffer, all of whom helped with the preparation of materials,
data collection and scoring, and database management at different points
in this study. John Allen's skillful programming and Rebecca Deuser's technical assistance in the preparation of this chapter deserve special ac-
knowledgment.

Special thanks also go to David Klahr, Chair of the Carnegie-Mellon University Psychology Department for his encouragement and support of this project.

This research was funded by the Personnel & Training Division of the Office Naval Research with ONR Contracts N00014-81-0335 to Bill Chase and N00014-84-K-0249 to David Klahr and N00014-85-K-0524 to Jim Staszewski. ONR's sustained support of this work merits special acknowlegment.

REFERENCES

Aiken, L. R., & Williams, E. N. (1973). Response times in adding and multiplying single-digit numbers. *Perceptual and Motor Skills, 37,* 3-13.

Akin, O. (1982). *The psychology of architectural design.* London: Pion.

Anderson, J. R. (1983). *The architecture of cognition.* Cambridge, MA: Harvard University Press.

Anderson, J. R. (1985). *Cognitive Psychology and Its Implications.* New York: Freeman & Co.

Ball, W. W. R. (1892). Mathematical recreations and problems of past and present times. London: McMillan.

Baddeley, A. D., & Hitch, G. J. (1974). Working memory. In G. Bower (Ed.), *Recent advances in learning and motivation.* New York: Academic Press.

Baddeley, A. (1986). *Working memory.* Oxford: Clarendon Press.

Bartlett, F. C. (1932). *Remembering.* London: Cambridge University Press.

Bidder, G.P. (1856). On mental calculation. *Minutes of Proceedings, Institute of Civil Engineers,* pp. 251-280.

Biederman, I., & Shiffrar, M. M. (1987). Sexing day-old chicks: A case study and expert systems analysis of a difficult perceptual-learning task. *Journal of Experimental Psychology: Learning, Memory, and Cognition, 13,* 640-645.

Binet, A. (1894). *Psychologie des grands calculateurs et joueurs d'echecs.* Paris: Librarie Hachette.

Broadbent, D. A. (1975). The magical number seven after fifteen years. In A. Kennedy & A. Wilkes (Eds.), *Studies in long-term memory.* New York: Wiley.

Brown, J. (1958). Some tests of the decay theory of immediate memory. *Quarterly Journal of Experimental Psychology, 10,* 12-21.

Bryan, W. L., Lindley, E. H., & Harter, N. (1941). *On the Psychology of Learning a Life Occupation* Bloomington, Indiana: Indiana University.

Campbell, J. I. D. (1987). Production, verification, and priming of multiplication facts. *Memory & Cognition, 15,* 349-364.

Chandler, P. J. (1965). Subroutine STEPIT: An algorithm that finds the values of the parameters which minimize a given continuous function (Computer program). Blooming-ton: Indiana University, Quantum Chemistry Program Exchange.

Charness, N. (1979). Components of skill in bridge. *Canadian Journal of Psychology, 33,* 1-50.

Chase, W. G., & Ericsson, K.A. (1981). Skilled memory. In J.R. Anderson (Ed.), *Cognitive skills and their acquisition.* Hillsdale, NJ: Erlbaum.

Chase, W. G., & Ericsson, K.A. (1982). Skill and working memory. In G. Bower (Ed.), *The psychology of learning and motivation, Vol 16.* New York: Academic.

Chase, W. G., & Simon, H.A. (1973a). Perception in chess. *Cognitive Psychology, 4,* 55-81.

Chase, W. G., & Simon, H. A. (1973b). The mind's eye in chess. In W. G. Chase (Ed.), *Visual information processing* (pp. 215-281). New York: Academic.

Chase, W. G. (1986). Visual information processing. In K. R. Boff, L. Kaufman, & J. P. Thomas (Eds.), *Handbook of Percpetion and Human Performance, Vol 2: Cognitive*

Cheng, P. W. (1985). Restructuring versus automaticity: Alternative accounts of skill acquisition. *Psychological Review*, 92, 414–423.

Chi, M. T. H. (1978). Knowledge structures and memory development. In R. S. Siegler (Ed.), *Children's thinking: What develops?*. Hillsdale, NJ: Erlbaum.

Chiesi, H. L., Spilich, G. J., & Voss, J. F. (1979). Acquisition of domain-related information in relation to high and low domain knowledge. *Journal of Verbal Learning and Verbal Behavior*, 18, 257–273.

Corman, C. N., & Wickens, D. D. (1968). Retroactive inhibition in short-term memory. *Journal of Verbal Learning and Verbal Behavior*, 7, 16–19.

Crossman, E. R. F. W. (1959). A theory of the acquisition of speed-skill. *Ergonomics*, 2, 153–166.

Crowder, R. G. (1976). *Principles of learning and memory*. Hillsdale, NJ: Erlbaum.

Cutler, A., & McShane, R. (1960). *The Trachtenberg speed system of basic mathematics*. New York: Doubleday & Co.

Dansereau, D. (1969). *An information processing model of mental multiplication*. Doctoral dissertation, Carnegie–Mellon University, Unpublished doctoral dissertation.

deGroot, A. D. (1965). *Thought and choice in chess*. Paris: Mouton & Company.

deGroot, A. D. (1966) Perception and memory versus thought: Some old ideas and recent findings. In B. Kleinmuntz (Ed.), *Problem solving* (pp. 19–50). New York: Wiley.

Egan, D. E., & Schwartz, B. J. (1979). Chunking in recall of symbolic drawings. *Memory and Cognition*, 7, 149–158.

Eisenstadt, M., & Kareev, Y. (1975). Aspects of human problem solving: The use of internal representations. In D. A. Norman & D. E. Rumelhart (Eds.), *Explorations in cognition*. San Francisco, CA: Freeman.

Ericsson, K. A. (1985). Memory skill. *Canadian Journal of Psychology*, 39, 188–231.

Feigenbaum, E. A. (1977). The art of artificial intelligence: Themes and studies of knowledge engineering. *Proceedings of the International Joint Conference on Artificial Intelligence*, pp. 1014–1029.

Fitts, P. M., & Posner, M. I. (1967). *Basic concepts in psychology. Human Performance*. Belmont California: Brooks/Cole Publishing.

Fuchs, A. F., & Melton, A.W. (1974). Effects of frequency and stimulus length on retention in the Brown-Peterson paradigm. *Journal of Experimental Psychology*, 103.

Glanzer, M., & Razel, M. (1974). The size of the unit in short-term storage. *Journal of Verbal Learning and Verbal Behavior*, 13, 114–131.

Hatano, G., & Osawa, K. (1983). Digit memory of grand experts in abacus-derived mental calculation. *Cognition*, 15.

Hunter, I. M. L. (1962). An exceptional talent for calculative thinking. *British Journal of Psychology*, 53, 243–258.

Hunter, I. M. L. (1977). Mental calculation. In P. N. Johnson-Laird & P. C. Wason (Eds.), *Thinking: Readings in Cognitive Science*. New York: Cambridge University Press.

Jakobsson, S. (1944). Report on two prodigy mental arithmeticians. *Acta Medica Scandinavica*, Vol. CXIX.

Keele, S. & Summers, J. J. (1976). The structure of motor programs. In G. E. Stelmach (Ed.), *Motor Control: Issues and Trends* (pp. 109–142). New York: Academic.

Landauer, T. K. (1974). Consolidation in human memory: Retrograde amnestic effects of confusable items in paired-associate learning. *Journal of Verbal Learning and Verbal Behavior*, 13, 45–53.

Lane, D. M., & Robertson, L. (1979). The generality of levels of processing hypothesis: An application to memory for chess positions. *Memory and Cognition*, 7, 253–256.

McKeithen, K. B., Reitman, J. S., Rueter, H. H., & Hirtle, S. C. (1981). Knowledge organization and skill differences in computer programmers. *Cognitive Psychology*, 13, 307–325.

Miller,G. A. (1956). The magical number seven, plus or minus two. *Psychological Review*, 63, 81–97.

Mitchell, F. D. (1907). Mathematical prodigies. *American Journal of Psychology*, *18*, 61-143.

Müeller, G. E. (1911). Zur analyse der gedächtnistätigkeit und des vorstellungverlaufes: Teil I. *Zeitschrift fur Psychologie*, Vol. 5.

Newell, A., & Rosenbloom, P. S. (1981). Mechanisms of skill acquisition and the law of practice. In J. R. Anderson (Ed.), *Cognitive skills and their acquisition*. Hillsdale, NJ: Erlbaum.

Newell, A., & Simon, H. A. (1972). *Human problem solving*. Englewood Cliffs, NJ: Prentice-Hall.

Patterson, K. E., Meltzer, R. H., & Mandler, G. (1971). Inter-Response Times in Categorized Free Recall. *Journal of Verbal Learning and Verbal Behavior*, *10*, 417-426.

Peterson, L. R., & Peterson M. J. (1959). Short-term retention of individual verbal items. *Journal of Experimental Psychology*, *58*, 193-198.

Pirolli, P. L., & Anderson, J. R. (1985). The role of practice in fact retrieval. *Journal of Experimental Psychology: Learning, Memory, and Cognition*, *11*, 136-53.

Pollio, H. R., Richards, S., & Lucas, R. (1969). Temporal properties of category recall. *Journal of Verbal Learning and Verbal Behavior*, *8*, 529-536.

Reitman, J. (1976). Skilled perception in Go: Deducing memory structures from inter-response times. *Cognitive Psychology*, *8*, 336-356.

Reitman, J. S., & Rueter, H. H. (1980). Organization revealed by recall errors and confirmed by pauses. *Cognitive Psychology*, *12*, 554-581.

Rosenbaum, D. A., Kenny, S. D., & Derr, M. A. (1983). Hierarchical control of rapid movement sequences. *Journal of Experimental Psychology: Human Perception and Performance*, *9*, 86-102.

Sandor, B. (1932). Die Gedächtnistätigkeit und Arbeitsweise von Rechenunstlern. *Charakter*, *1*, 47-50.

Schneider, W., & Shiffrin, R. M. (1977). Control and automatic human information processing: I. Detection, search, and attention. *Psychological Review*, *84*, 1-66.

Schneider, W., Dumais, S. T., & Shiffrin, R. M. (1984). Automatic and control processing and attention. In R. Parasuraman & D. R. Davies (Eds.), *Varieties of attention*. Orlando, FL: Academic.

Schneiderman, B. (1976). Exploratory experiments in programmer behavior. *International Journal of Computer and Information Sciences*, *5*, 123-143.

Shiffrin, R. M., & Schneider, W. (1977). Control and automatic human information processing: I. Detection, search, and attention. *Psychological Review*, *84*, 1-66.

Siegler, R. S., & Jenkins, E. (in press). *The process of strategy discovery*.

Siegler, R. S., & Schrager, J. (1984). Strategy choices in addition and subtraction: How do children know what to do? In C. Sophian (Ed.), *Origins of cognitive skills* (pp. 229-291). Hillsdale, NJ: Erlbaum.

Siegler, R. S. (in press). Strategy choice procedures and the development of multiplication skill. *Journal of Experimental Psychology: General*.

Simon, H. A., & Chase W. G. (1973). Skill in chess. *American Scientist*, *61*, 394-403.

Simon, H. A. (1976). Neural Mechanisms of Learning and Memory. In M. R. Rosenzweig and E. L. Bennett (Eds.), *The Information-Storage System Called "Human Memory"*. New York: M.I.T. Press.

Smith, S.B. (1983). *The great mental calculators*. New York: Columbia University Press.

Staszewski, J. J. (1987). *The psychological reality of retrieval structures: A theoretical and empirical investigation of expert knowledge*. Doctoral dissertation, Cornell University,

Staszewski, J. J. (manuscript in preparation). Engineering human expertise.

Weinland, J. D., & Schlauch, W. S. (1937). Examination of the computing ability of Mr. Salo Finkelstein. *Journal of Experimental Psychology*, *21*, 382-402.

Wickens, D. D., Born, D. G., & Allen, C. K. (1963). Proactive inhibition and item similarity in short-term memory. *Journal of Verbal Learning and Verbal Behavior*, *2*, 440-445.

Wicklegren, W. A. (1964). Size of rehearsal group and short-term memory. *Journal of Experimental Psychology*, *68*, 413-419.

4 Knowledge and Processes in The Comprehension of Computer Programs

Elliot Soloway
Beth Adelson
Kate Ehrlich
Yale University

INTRODUCTION

We have been investigating the cognitive underpinnings of how programmers — novices and experts — read and write computer programs. Our approach has been to employ a cycle of constructing theory, carrying out
empirical studies (Bonar & Soloway, 1983; Soloway, Bonar, & Ehrlich 1983;
Soloway, Ehrlich, 1984; Soloway, Ehrlich, & Greenspan, 1982), and building and testing AI programs that embody our theory (Johnson & Soloway,
1984). In this chapter we present our current view on the knowledge and
processing strategies programmers employ in attempting to comprehend
computer programs. We first present an experiment that supports our claims
as to the composition of an expert programmer's knowledge base. Next, we
propose processing strategies that may be at work in comprehending programs. As support for these latter mechanisms, we draw on our experience
in building a computer program that attempts to understand computer programs written by novices.

TYPES OF PROGRAMMING KNOWLEDGE

What is it that expert programmers know that novice programmers don't?
We would suggest that the former have *at least* two types of knowledge
that the latter typically do not:

- *Programming Plans:* program fragments that represent stereotypic ac-

tion sequences in programming, such as a RUNNING TOTAL LOOP
PLAN, an ITEM SEARCH LOOP PLAN (see also Rich, 1981).

- *Rules of Programming Discourse:* rules that specify the conventions
  in programming, such as that the name of a variable should usually
  agree with its function; these rules set up expectations in the minds
  of the programmers about what should be in the program. These rules
  are analogous to discourse rules in conversation.

In our view, programs are composed from programming plans that have
been modified to fit the needs of the specific problem. The composition of
those plans is governed by rules of programming discourse. Thus, a program can be correct from the perspective of the problem, but be difficult
to write and/or read because it doesn't follow the rules of discourse; that
is, the plans in the program are composed in ways that violate some discourse rule(s).

Our approach to programming borrows directly from at least two con-
verging sources: research on text processing in artificial intelligence and psychology, and research on problem solving with experts and novices. Our
first claim, that text comprehension research informs program comprehension research, is based on the following observation: although programs can
be *executed* for effect, they can also be *read* as communicative entities. This
implies that the notion of *schemas*, one of the most influential notions to
have emerged from recent research on text comprehension (e.g., Bartlett,
1932; Bower, Black, & Turner, 1979; Graesser, 1981; Schank & Abelson,
1977) should be useful in the study of program comprehension. As stated
in Graesser's (1981), "Schemas are generic knowledge structures that guide
the comprehender's interpretations, inferences, expectations, and attention
when passages are comprehended." Our notion of programming plan corresponds directly to this notion of schema.

Second, research with experts and novices in various technical domains
(chess (Chase & Simon, 1973; deGroot, 1975), physics (Larkin, McDermott, Simon, & Simon, 1980), and electronic circuitry, Egan & Schwartz,
1979) have shown that the experts seem to possess *chunks* that represent
functional units in their respective domains, while the novices do not. Similar
results have been obtained in the programming domain (Adelson, 1981;
McKeithen, Reitman, Rueter, & Hirtle, 1981; Schneiderman, 1976). The
work reported in this chapter builds on and extends the aforementioned
research in the programming domain, by examining whether or not
programmers have and use specific programming plans and rules of
programming discourse in the process of comprehending computer
programs.

The study presented here was conducted to evaluate the preceding claim,
and to investigate the programming plans and discourse rules of expert

programmers. Programs that do not conform to the plans and discourse rules should violate the programmers' expectations: for example, if they see a variable initialized to zero ($N := 0$) at the top of a program, since variables are usually updated in the same fashion as they are initialized, programmers would expect N to be updated via an assignment statement. They would therefore be surprised to see it being changed via a read statement (**READ(N)**) later in the program. While this type of situation won't create an unrunnable program, it certainly violates the accepted conventions of programming. In addition, programmers don't like to include statements that have no effect: A **READ** statement destroys whatever is in the variable initially, and thus the initial setting of **N** to zero is suddenly seen to be superfluous if **READ (N)** is encountered. We claim that these violations in expectations — the surprises due to violations of conventions — can make such programs much more difficult to comprehend. Thus, if advanced programmers have knowledge about plans and discourse rules, then programs that do not conform to the rules of discourse (*unplan-like programs*) should be harder for them to understand than programs that do conform to these rules (*plan-like programs*). In contrast, we would not expect novice programmers to have acquired as many of the plans and conventions in programming; by definition a novice programmer has less knowledge than an advanced programmer. Thus we would not expect novice programmers to be as sensitive as experts to violations of conventions, as they don't know what the conventions are in the first place. Therefore, in a task that requires understanding a program, we expect advanced programmers to do much better on the programs that do conform to the plans and rules than on the programs that do not. We also expect novice programmers to perform at a consistent level whether or not the programs violate the plans and the discourse rules.

DESCRIPTION OF FILL-IN-THE-BLANK EXPERIMENT

Rationale for Experiment Design

The design of the experiment reported here was modelled after the classic Chase and Simon chess experiment *with one key difference*. In (1973), Chase and Simon created two types of stimulus materials: (a) chessboards that were real game boards, and (b) chessboards that were randomly composed. Expert chess players were able to recall the former type better than novices; however, the experts performed no differently than novices on the latter type. While we have expert programmers and novice programmers in our studies, the stimulus materials are different: we created (a) a set of programs that were *plan-like* — that is, programs whose plans were composed to conform to the rules of programming discourse; and (b) a set of *unplan-like* programs — that is, programs that were runnable and produced desirable results, except that their plan structure did not conform to the rules of programming discourse. The latter programs (the Beta versions), were created from the former programs (the Alpha versions) by violating one (or sometimes two) of the discourse rules.[1] An example of an Alpha version and a Beta version for a programming problem is given in Figure 4.1. (In a later section we describe in detail how these programs were constructed, and why we would consider the Beta versions to be unplan-like.) Notice that both the Alpha version and the Beta version are runnable programs that in almost all cases compute the *same* values.[2] Moreover, to an untrained eye their differences may even not be apparent: they always differ only by a very few textual elements. Other studies have been conducted (Adelson, 1981; McKeithen et al., 1981; Schneiderman, 1976) that were also modelled after the Chase and Simon experiment, and they too used one set of stimulus materials that were runnable programs, and another class that were randomly composed programs. While those studies demonstrated the basic effect — that advanced programmers have strategies for encoding and remembering programs better than do novice programmers — we see our work as focusing on the *detailed knowledge* that programmers have and use.

Description of Study

The study reported here uses the "fill-in-the-blank technique": here we take out one line of code from the program and replace that line with a blank. The task required of our experimental subjects, who were both novice and advanced student programmers, was to fill the blank line in with a piece of code that, in their opinion, best completed the program. An example of the programs with blank lines is given in Figure 4.1. Note carefully that we do *not* tell the subjects what problem the program is intended to solve. However, since there is only one blank line per program, a great deal of context is still left. If advanced programmers do have and use programming plans for stereotypic programming situations, then they should be able to recognize the program fragment in the plan-like versions as an example of programming plan X, and they should all fill in the blank line with the same piece of code. However, in the case of the unplan-like programs, advanced programmers should be more unsure of what plan is being indicated; they should be less likely to complete the program in the correct fashion. On the other hand, novice programmers should not be as surprised by the

---

[1]Clearly the unplan-like versions are not totally unplan-like; in fact, they have many plans in common with the plan-like versions. The term *unplan-like* is thus one of degree.

[2]In only one program type, **MAX** (e.g., Figure 4.1), do the Alpha and Beta versions compute different values.

Version Alpha

```
PROGRAM Magenta(input, output);
VAR Max, I, Num  INTEGER;
BEGIN
     Max := 0;,
     FOR I := 1 TO 10 DO
         BEGIN
             READLN(Num);
             IF Num > Max THEN Max := Num
         END,
         WRITELN(Max);
END.
```

Version Beta

```
PROGRAM Purple(input, output);
VAR Max, I, Num : INTEGER,
BEGIN
     Max  := 999999;
     FOR I := 1 TO 10 DO
         BEGIN
             READLN(Num);
             IF Num < Max THEN Max :=Num
         END,
         WRITELN(Max);
END.
```

```
PROGRAM Magenta(input, output);
VAR Max, I, Num  INTEGER;
BEGIN
     Max  := 0;
     FOR I := 1 TO 10 DO
         BEGIN
             READLN(Num);

     IF Num  [    ]  Max THEN Max  := Num
            [____]

         END;
         WRITELN(Max);
END.
```

```
PROGRAM Purple(input, output);
VAR Max, I, Num : INTEGER;
BEGIN
     Max  := 999999;
     FOR I := 1 TO 10 DO
         BEGIN
             READLN(Num);

     IF Num   [    ]   Max THEN Max  := Num
              [____]

         END;
         WRITELN(Max);
END.
```

Program type 1

Basic plan: search plan (max, min)

Discourse rule: A variable's name should reflect its function (1)

How construct
Beta version: violate discourse rule (1)

Alpha case: variable name agrees with search function

Beta case: variable name does NOT agree with search function

FIGURE 4.1 Example: program type 1.

unplan-like programs since they have not as yet acquired the programming conventions. Thus, we expect that the advanced programmers will be more affected by the unplan-like programs than will the novices.

Subjects

A total of 139 students participated in the experiment. These students were recruited from programming classes and were paid $5 for participating in the experiment. There were 94 novice-level programmers and 45 advanced-level programmers. Novice programmers were students at the end of a first course in Pascal programming. The advanced-level programmers had completed at least three programming courses, and most were either computer science majors or first-year graduate students in computer science; all had extensive experience with Pascal.

Materials

We created two pairs of programs (an Alpha version and a Beta version comprise one pair) for each of four program types, one of which is described in detail as follows, while the other three program types are described in detail in the Appendix.[3] Thus, there were eight pairs of programs, two pairs for each program type.

What makes a program plan-like rather than unplan-like is the way in which plans are *composed* in a program. The composition is governed by *rules of programming discourse*, which are analogous to discourse rules both in conversation and underlying the structure of stories. In Figure 4.2 we depict a set of programming discourse rules that we have identified. Individually, they look innocuous enough, and one would hardly disagree with them. While these rules are typically neither written down nor explicitly taught, we claim that programmers have and use these rules in the construction and comprehension of programs. If programmers do use these rules and expect other programmers to also use them, then programs that violate these rules will be harder to understand than programs that do not.

One key point to notice in the following discussion is that the unplan-like version (the Beta version) *is only slightly* different from the plan-like one (the Alpha version). That is, the idea is to take a plan-like program and modify it ever so slightly, by violating a discourse rule, so as to create an unplan-like version. Both versions are executable programs that usually compute the same function. Moreover, both versions have about the same surface characteristics: about the same number of lines of code, about the same number of operands and operations, and so on. Thus, we rule out potential artifacts. In addition, while more traditional methods of calculating program complexity (e.g., lines of code, or Halstead metrics, Halstead, 1977) would predict no difference in the difficulty of understanding for the two programs (the Alpha version and the Beta version), we base our predictions on the use of discourse rules and therefore are able to predict performance differences in this task.

Program Type 1: MAX.   In Figure 4.1, version Alpha is the plan-like version

---

[3]In order to better enable the reader to evaluate the claims we draw from the experiment herein described, we provide access to a detailed description of all the stimulus materials used in this experiment.

Nature of Expertise Conference

(1)   Variable names should reflect function.

(2)   Don't include code that won't be used.

(2a)   If there is a test for a condition, then the condition must
        have the potential of being true.

(3)   A variable that is initialized via an assignment statement
        should be updated via an assignment statement.

(4)   Don't do double duty with code in a nonobvious way.

(5)   An IF should be used when a statement body is guaranteed to
        be executed only once, and a WHILE used when a statement body
        may need to be repeatedly executed.

FIGURE 4.2   Rules of programming discourse.

of a program that finds the *maximum* of some numbers. In our plan vocabulary, it embodies the MAXIMUM SEARCH LOOP PLAN which in turn uses a RESULT VARIABLE PLAN. Notice that the RESULT VARIABLE is appropriately named *Max*; that is, the name of the variable is consistent with the plan's function. In contrast, version Beta is unplan-like since it uses a MINIMUM SEARCH LOOP PLAN in which the RESULT VARIABLE is inconsistent with the plan's function: the program computes the *minimum* of some numbers using a variable named *Max*. To create the Beta version, we violated the first rule of programming discourse in Figure 4.2: *Variable names should reflect function.* (See also Weissman, 1974, who did exploratory empirical studies on the role of variable names.)

The fill-in-the-blank versions of both these programs are also given in Figure 4.1. Our hypothesis is that programmers will see the variable name *Max* and thus "see" the program as a MAXIMUM SEARCH LOOP PLAN. In other words, the name of the variable will color how they understand the rest of the program. Therefore, in the Beta version, where the function of the procedure is inconsistent with variable *Max*, we predict that programmers will fill in the blank with a $>$, rather than a $<$ — indicating that they see the program as computing the maximum of a set of integers, instead of the minimum.

As mentioned earlier, we created two instances (two pairs of programs) of each type of program. Both instances were similar. For example, the second instance of the program type **MAX** (Figure 4.3) searched for an integer whereas the first instance searched for a character.

```
PROGRAM Green(input, output);
VAR I : INTEGER;
     Letter, LeastLetter  :  Char;
BEGIN
     LeastLetter  := 'z';
     FOR I := 1 TO 10 DO
          BEGIN
               READLN(Letter);
               IF Letter < LeastLetter
                    THEN LeastLetter := Letter;
          END;
     Writeln(LeastLetter);
END.
```

```
PROGRAM Yellow(input, output);
VAR I : INTEGER;
     Letter, LeastLetter  :  Char;
BEGIN
     LeastLetter  := 'a';
     FOR I := 1 TO 10 DO
          BEGIN
               READLN(Letter);
               IF Letter < LeastLetter
                    THEN LeastLetter := Letter;
          END;
     Writeln(LeastLetter);
END.
```

```
PROGRAM Green(input, output);
VAR I : INTEGER;
     Letter, LeastLetter  :  Char;
BEGIN
     LeastLetter  := 'z';
     FOR I := 1 TO 10 DO
          BEGIN
               READLN(Letter);

          IF Letter  | ___ |  LeastLetter
                     | ___ |

               THEN LeastLetter  := Letter;
          END;
     Writeln(LeastLetter);
END.
```

```
PROGRAM Yellow(input, output);
VAR I : INTEGER;
     Letter, LeastLetter  :  Char;
BEGIN
     LeastLetter  := 'a';
     FOR I := 1 TO 10 DO
          BEGIN
               READLN(Letter);

          IF Letter  | ___ |  LeastLetter
                     | ___ |

               THEN LeastLetter  := Letter;
          END;
     Writeln(LeastLetter);
END.
```

Program type 1 -- Instance 2

Basic plan:	search plan (max, min)
Discourse rule:	A variable's name should reflect its function (1)
How construct Beta version:	violate discourse rule (1)
Alpha case:	variable name agrees with search function
Beta case:	variable name does NOT agree with search function

FIGURE 4.3 Example: program type 1—instance 2.

Design

The three independent variables in this study were:

1. Version — Alpha (plan-like), Beta (unplan-like).
2. Program Type — 1 **MAX**, 2 **SQRT**, 3 **AVERAGE**, 4 **IF/WHILE**.
3. Level of expertise — novice or advanced.

There were two dependent variables:

1. Accuracy of the response; a correct response was one that completed the intended plan.[4]
2. Time to complete a problem.

Procedure

Each subject was given eight programs, four Alphas and four Betas. We also counterbalanced version with program type such that if a subject received an Alpha version for one program of a type, then the subject would receive the Beta version for the other program of the same type. The test programs were presented as a booklet in which the order of the programs was randomized for each subject. Subjects were instructed to work through the booklet in the given order. As we mentioned earlier, each program was presented along with one blank: the subjects were not told what problems the programs were intended to solve. The subjects were given the following instruction: *Fill in the blank line with a line of Pascal code which in your opinion best completes the program.* They were given as much time to do the test as they wanted; almost all finished within an hour.

RESULTS AND DISCUSSION

Using an analysis of variance we found:

- the experts performed better than the novices (61% vs. 48% $F_{1, 137}$ = 17.27, $p < 0.001$).
- all the subjects correctly answered the Alpha versions more often than they did the Beta versions (88% vs. 31%, $F_{1, 137}$ = 375.22, $p < 0.001$).

---

[4]Strictly speaking, filling in the blank line with an answer that differs from the plan-like one would not necessarily be *incorrect*. For example, filling in the blank line in Beta of Figure 1 with a > would still result in a running program. However, it would be a strange program. Thus, by *correct* we actually mean the line of code that in our judgment best fulfills the overall intent of the program.

- there was a significant difference in accuracy for the four program types ($F_{3,\,411} = 26.81$, $p < 0.001$).
- the interaction between program version and expertise was significant ($F_{1,\,137} = 6.78$, $p < 0.01$).
- the differences between the Alpha and Beta programs was not constant over the four program types. This interaction between program type and version was significant ($F_{3,\,411} = 68.39$, $p < 0.001$).
- there was also a significant three-way interaction between program type, version, and expertise ($F_{3,\,411} = 3.12$, $p < 0.05$).

Moreover, using a Newman-Keuls test the difference in performance between the novice and the advanced subjects for the Alpha versions was significant at the .05 level. No significant difference was found between the two groups of subjects on the Beta versions. Thus, as we see in Figure 4.4 the performance of the advanced students was no longer significantly different from that of the novices when dealing with the unplan-like versions of the programs.

The change in the level of performance for the advanced programmers across the versions of the programs is impressive (Figure 4.4): The advanced programmers performed about 50% worse on the Beta versions than they did on the Alpha versions. (This difference was significant at the .01 level using a Newman-Keuls test.) Given that the only difference between the two versions was a violation of one (or possibly two) rules of programming discourse, the size of the effect is striking. Clearly, discourse rules in programming have a salient effect on programmers' abilities to comprehend programs.

Turning to the three-way interaction of program type, version, and expertise, a breakdown by version and program type is given in Table 4.1 for each level of expertise. Here we see the percentage of subjects that answered each program correctly. An intuition for this interaction can be gleaned from the results presented here: Performance on the Beta version of the **SQRT** program type was better than performance on Beta versions of the other program types. (This difference was statistically significant at the .01 level using a Newman-Keuls test.) Why was the performance on the Beta version of this one program type so high? The most plausible explanation is based on a practice effect: Since in every other program that the subjects saw, data was input via a **READ** statement, subjects simply did not notice that **READ** was not appropriate to this particular program and immediately filled in the blank line with a **READ**.

In Table 4.2 we display a breakdown of the number and type of errors that subjects made. There were, of course, more errors made on the Beta

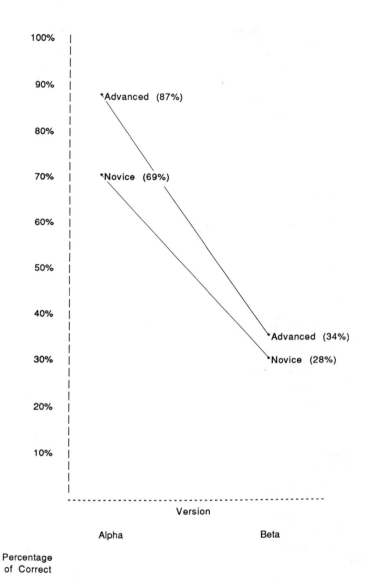

100% ⎮
       ⎮
       ⎮
 90% ⎮
       ⎮   •Advanced (87%)
       ⎮
 80% ⎮
       ⎮
       ⎮
 70% ⎮   •Novice (69%)
       ⎮
       ⎮
 60% ⎮
       ⎮
 50% ⎮
       ⎮
       ⎮
 40% ⎮
       ⎮   •Advanced (34%)
       ⎮
 30% ⎮   •Novice (28%)
       ⎮
       ⎮
 20% ⎮
       ⎮
 10% ⎮
       ⎮
       ⎮
       ⎮- -
                              Version

              Alpha   Beta

Percentage
of Correct

FIGURE 4.4   Interaction: expertise and program type

TABLE 4.1
Percentage of Correctness by Program Type

	Novices (N = 94)	
Program Type	Alpha	Beta
1 MAX	78%	12%
2 SQRT	69%	61%
3 AVERAGE	80%	01%
4 IF/WHILE	48%	38%
	Advanced (N = 45)	
1 MAX	93%	13%
2 SQRT	87%	84%
3 AVERAGE	96%	06%
4 IF/WHILE	73%	31%

versions (390) than on the Alpha versions (140) ($p < .001$ by a sign test). More interesting, however, was the type of error usually made on the Beta versions. Our theory makes a strong prediction about the type of incorrect response that subjects will make on the Beta versions: it predicts that errors will be the result of an attempt to encode programs as instances of well formed plans. Thus, whenever subjects do not recognize that the Beta versions are unplan-like, they will simply use plans and discourse rules to guide their responses. In such cases we expect them, having perceived the Beta version as just being an Alpha version, *to provide the plan-like response*; that is, to provide the response for the Alpha version. For example, as discussed earlier, Program Purple in Figure 4.1 actually computes the minimum of a set of inputs; it appears, however, because of the key variable name *MAX*, to be a program that computes the *maximum* of some input values. The correct fill-in-the-blank answer for Program Purple was '<'. However, our theory predicts that those subjects who fill in the blank incorrectly will do so by saying '>'—which *is* the correct answer for the plan-like (Alpha version) form for that program type.

The data (Table 4.2) do bear out that prediction: On the Beta versions, 66% (257/390) of the incorrect responses were one specific response—the response that would have been appropriate for the corresponding Alpha

TABLE 4.2
Error Data: Fill-in-the-Blank Study

ERRORS on Alpha and Beta Versions:

Alpha Versions:
  Total number of errors by Novice and Advanced Subjects: 140
Beta Versions:
Total number of errors by Novice and Advanced Subjects: 390

ERRORS on Only Beta Versions:

Plan-like Errors:
  Total number on Beta versions by Novice and Advanced Subjects: 257
Unplan-like Errors:
  Total number on Beta versions by Novice and Advanced Subjects: <u>133</u>
                                                                    390

---

version of the program. (The difference between the number of incorrect responses that were plan-like and the number that were not was significant at $p < .01$ by a sign test):[5]

Another effect of the unplan-like versions on our subjects' performance can be seen by examining the amount of time it took subjects to provide a *correct* response to the Alpha and the Beta versions. Figure 4.5 depicts this relationship. It took approximately 50% more time to respond correctly to the Beta versions than it did to respond correctly to the Alpha versions; this difference in response time was significant ($F_{1, 288} = 35.1$, $p < 0.001$). The difference between novice and advanced programmers was also significant ($F_{1, 288} = 8.6$, $p < 0.01$); however, the interaction between expertise and program version was not significant ($F < 1$).

Our interpretation of these data is as follows: A correct response to the Alpha versions required only that programmers use their knowledge of programming plans and rules of programming discourse. However, in order to arrive at a correct answer to the Beta versions, subjects needed to employ additional processing techniques, such as trying to run the program on some sample numbers mentally. (In the next section, we describe in more detail processes that may underlie the comprehension of both plan-like and unplan-like programs.) This additional processing time corresponds to the increase in response time needed to bring in additional problem-solving strategies in order to compensate for the explanations.

In sum, then, the data from this experiment support our claim as to the

---

[5]The p value of .01 reduces the likelihood that we are affirming a chance result from having partitioned the data.

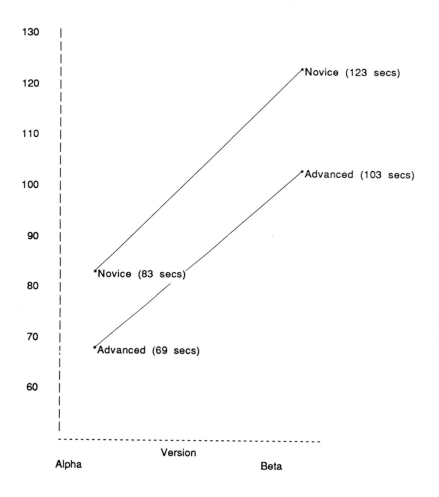

130 —

120 —   ↗Novice (123 secs)

110 —

100 —   ↗Advanced (103 secs)

90 —

80 —   ↖Novice (83 secs)

70 —

60 —   ↖Advanced (69 secs)

- -
                        Version
      Alpha   Beta

Time To Answer
   Problem
   Correctly
(In Seconds)

FIGURE 4.5   Time to respond correctly: Alpha versions vs. Beta versions

importance of knowledge of programming plans and rules of programming discourse. As predicted, we saw that:

- the performance of the advanced programmers was reduced to that of the novices only on the unplan-like programs.
- significantly more time was needed to answer the unplan-like programs correctly.
- when subjects answered the unplan-like programs incorrectly, they typically responded by providing the plan-like answer to the unplan-like program.

Similar performance results were obtained using professional programmers as subjects, rather than novice and advanced student programmers (Soloway & Ehrlich, 1984).

PROCESSES UNDERLYING COMPREHENSION

How were our subjects processing the programs in the preceding experiment? Initially, subjects most likely started reading at the beginning of the program using a bottom-up strategy, since they were not supplied with the goals of the program. However, once programming plans were recognized in the program, and the corresponding goals realized by these plans were retrieved, the subjects then went into a predictive, top-down mode. This strategy is one that has been posited for the reading and comprehension of text (Black, 1985; Schank & Abelson, 1977). We call this type of strategy *shallow reasoning*, since the process is one of matching programming plans to code, without significant causal reasoning about the relationship between the parts of the program. This type of strategy was fine for the Alpha versions — the plan-like programs — since it was these programs that were purposefully constructed to match programmers' plans and expectations. For example, the line Max : = 0 in the Alpha version of the programs in Figure 4.1 would be a *beacon* for the *MAXIMUM SEARCH LOOP PLAN*; that is, this line is representative of the *MAXIMUM SEARCH LOOP PLAN* and should be used to index into it in plan memory. The line **IF Num >** **Max THEN Max** : = **Num**, would be predicted by the *MAXIMUM SEARCH LOOP PLAN*. Thus, reading this line later in the program should provide confirmatory evidence that indeed the goal of the program under consideration is to find the maximum of a set of input numbers.

However, the Beta — unplan-like — programs were more problematic: To effectively comprehend them, we hypothesize that programmers employed a *deep reasoning strategy*. In this type of strategy, a programmer reasons causally about the relationship of the goals of the program to the code in the program. For example, in the Beta version of the programs in Figure 4.1, the subject would need to override the expectation that this program computes the maximum of the integers' input in order to see that it computes the minimum. We hypothesize that the subject would need to consider what was actually being computed in the program, and not be able to rely on stereotypic, stored plan knowledge to provide the answer. In order to see what the program did actually compute, the programmer most likely went back to some bottom-up technique, such as running the program on some specific input values. After such simulation, the subject should be able to make the inductive step to the goal of the program. In effect, then, causal knowledge about (a) the actual flow of information in the program, and (b) the relationships between the parts of the program, has been compiled into the already stored programming plans. Unless forced, the programmer does not need to deal explicitly with these levels of detail.

The evidence we have for these observations is twofold. First, as shown in Figure 4.5, it took much longer for our subjects to correctly answer the Beta programs than to correctly answer the Alpha programs. We interpret the increase in response time for the Beta versions as reflecting an increase in the number of steps needed to answer the Beta versions correctly. While consistent with the above hypotheses, these timing data frankly do not provide direct evidence for them; nor do they rule out potential alternative explanations.

The evidence that bears more directly on the above hypotheses comes from the workings of an AI simulation of program understanding. In particular, we have built a system, called *PROUST* (Johnson & Soloway, 1984), that attempts to identify the nonsyntactic bugs in novices' computer programs; currently it can correctly identify approximately 75% of the bugs in programs generated by actual students for a relatively complex introductory programming assignment. The design of *PROUST* was based on our observations of how humans went about the task of understanding correct and buggy programs. In order to attain this rate of performance, *PROUST* employs both shallow and deep reasoning techniques. When a novice's program is written in a plan-like fashion, then *PROUST* understands such a program primarily by a process of retrieving programming plans from its knowledge base, matching them against the program in question, and retrieving further plans based on the expectations set up by the previous matches; this technique corresponds to the shallow reasoning technique we claim was being used by our subjects on the plan-like (Alpha) programs.

The majority of programs we have analyzed written by novice students are unplan-like (Johnson, Soloway, Cutler, & Draper, 1983). To understand programs of this sort, *PROUST* must expend significant resources trying to reason causally, first about the intentions of the programmer, and then about how those intentions were realized in the program. Aspects of this process differ from those we claim were used by our human subjects in coming to a correct understanding of the unplan-like (Beta) programs. For example, rather than running a program on some test cases and inductively discovering the program's goals, *PROUST* has heuristics built in the attempt to recognize goals based solely on the code in the program. Despite this difference, the act of reasoning about the intentions of the program and the programmer, which in turn is based on some bottom-up processes operating on the code itself, provides the common ground between *PROUST's* mechanisms and those we hypothesize our subjects use on the unplan-like (Beta) versions. The success of *PROUST* suggests that the mechanisms proposed in this section are useful in accounting for performance in unplan-like situations.

CONCLUDING REMARKS

Our goals in this paper have been, first, to describe how our group is going about studying the process of computer programming; and second, to provide a status report on our efforts. To this end we described two types of knowledge that we believe are used by expert programmers, and one key experiment we conducted that provided empirical support for that claim. We also suggested processes that might underlie the comprehension of programs. As evidence on this point we cited our experience with our system called *PROUST*, that can understand a class of correct and buggy novice programs.

There are a number of directions in which we are continuing to pursue this research. For example, we are working on a more fine-grained description of various levels of representation underlying a computer program: Programming plans and discourse rules are only a beginning. Based on the deep representation of a program, we are also exploring the development of a computable measure of program complexity: Counting, as we have been, surface features of a program — though they are easily computable — does not necessarily provide an accurate assessment of the program's complexity. More importantly, our goal is to develop a complexity measure that can explain why a program is complex (Soloway, Ehrlich, & Black, 1983). We also feel that this effort can contribute to the development of more effective complexity measures of text. Finally, we are continuing to develop a model of the processes that are used in the reading and writing of programs and in the design of programs. In conclusion, we see that the study of programming has both *practical* value, in that results of the sort reported here should have some interest to software engineering, and *theoretical* value, in that programming is an exemplar of a semantically rich, complex-problem-solving task.

APPENDIX

While in previous pages we described how and why we constructed plan-like (Alpha) and unplan-like (Beta) versions of one type of program (type **MAX**), in the following pages, we describe the how and why for the Alpha and Beta versions of each of the other three program types:[6]

1. **SQRT**
2. **AVERAGE**
3. **IF/WHILE**

Program Type 2: SQRT

The Alpha and Beta programs in Figure 4.6 are both intended to produce the square root of **N**. Since **N** is in a loop which will repeat 10 times, 10 values will be printed out. The question is: How should **N** be set? In version Alpha the *DATA GUARD PLAN* constrains what should be filled in on the blank line. That is, the **Sqrt** function must be protected from trying to take the **Sqrt** of a negative number; thus, the immediately preceding **IF** test checks to see if the number is negative, and makes it positive if necessary. Besides protecting the **Sqrt** function, the *DATA GUARD PLAN* exerts influence on what could reasonably be filled in on the blank. The very presence of the *DATA GUARD PLAN* implies that the numbers might be negative, and thus the manner in which **N** is set *must allow for it to be negative*. A typical way of realizing this constraint is via a **Read (N)**; the user decides what values should be entered. In contrast, setting **N** via an assignment statement, such as **N := I**, would *never* result in a negative number — thus making the *DATA GUARD PLAN* totally superfluous. The influence of the *DATA GUARD PLAN* over the blank line stems from a rule of programming discourse: *If there is a test for a condition, then the condition must have the potential of being true.* Thus, the blank line must be filled in with something that does not make the *DATA GUARD PLAN* superfluous, such as **Read (N)**.

In version Beta, however we have added an additional constraint on the

---

[6]The names given to each of the four types carry no deep significance; they are meant only to aid the reader.

```
PROGRAM Violet(input, output);
    VAR Num : REAL,
          I : INTEGER;
    BEGIN
       Num := 0;
       FOR I := 1 TO 10 DO
           BEGIN
               Read (Num);
               IF Num < 0 THEN Num := -Num;
               Writeln ( Num, Sqrt(Num)  );
               (* Sqrt is a built-in
               function which returns the
               square froot of its argument*)
           END;
END.
```

```
PROGRAM Violet(input, output);
    VAR Num : REAL;
          I : INTEGER;
    BEGIN
       Num := 0;
       FOR I := 1 TO 10 DO
           BEGIN
           --------------------------------
           |                              |
           |                              |
           --------------------------------
               IF Num < 0 THEN Num := -Num;
               Writeln ( Num,  Sqrt(Num)  );
               (*  Sqrt is a built-in
               function which returns the
               square root of its arguments*)
           END;
END.
```

```
PROGRAM Beige(input, output);
    VAR Num : REAL,
          I : INTEGER;
    BEGIN
       FOR I := 1 TO 10 DO
           BEGIN
               Read (Num);
               IF Num < 0 THEN Num := -Num;
               Writeln ( Num, Sqrt(Num)  );
               (* Sqrt is a built-in
               function which returns the
               square froot of its argument*)
           END;
END.
```

```
PROGRAM Beige(input, output);
    VAR Num : REAL;
          I : INTEGER;
    BEGIN
       FOR I := 1 TO 10 DO
           BEGIN
           --------------------------------
           |                              |
           |                              |
           --------------------------------
               IF Num < 0 THEN Num := -Num;
               Writeln (Num, Sqrt(Num)  );
               (*  Sqrt is a built-in
               function which returns the
               square root of its arguments*)
           END;
END.
```

Program type 2

Basic plan	guard plan; variable plan
Discourse rule	Don't include code that won't be used (2)
	If there is a test for a condition, then the condition must have the potential of being true. (2a)
	A variable that is initialized via an assignment statement should be updated via an assignment statement. (3)
How construct Beta version	include two incompatible discourse rules (2) and (3).
Alpha case	guard plan predicts read initialization
Beta case	guard plan predicts read update, but initialization plan predicts assignment update.

FIGURE 4.6 Example: program type 2

blank line: The *VARIABLE PLAN* for N starts off with an assignment type of initialization (**N** := **0**) and sets up the expectation that **N** will also be updated via an assignment statement, such as **N** := **N** + **I**, or **N** := **N** + **1**. However, this expectation conflicts with the expectation set up by the *DATA GUARD PLAN* (namely, **Read (N)**). Moreover, there is an additional level of conflict: The expectation of the *DATA GUARD PLAN* is now in conflict with the initialization of **N** to **O**. This latter conflict is due to a violation of the following rule of programming discourse: *A variable that is initialized via an assignment statement should be updated via an assignment statement.*

Program Type 3: AVERAGE

The programs in Figure 4.7 calculate the average of some numbers that are read in; the stopping condition is the reading of the sentinel value, **99999**. Version Alpha accomplishes the task in a typical fashion: Variables are initialized to **0**, a read-a-value/process-a-value loop (Soloway et al., 1983) is used to accumulate the running total, and the average is calculated after the sentinel has been read. Version Beta was generated from version Alpha by violating another rule of programming discourse: *Don't do double duty in a nonobvious manner.* That is, in version Beta, unlike in Alpha, the initialization actions of the *COUNTER VARIABLE* **Count** and *RUNNING TOTAL VARIABLE PLANs* **Sum** in Beta serve two purposes:

- **Sum** and **Count** are given initial values.
- The initial values are chosen so as to compensate for the fact that the loop is poorly constructed and will result in an off-by-one bug: the final sentinel value (**99999**) **will be incorrectly added into the** *RUNNING TOTAL VARIABLE*, **Sum**, and *COUNTER VARIABLE*, **Count**, will also be incorrectly updated.

We felt that using **Sum** and **Count** in this way was most nonobvious, and would prove very hard for advanced programmers to comprehend.

Program Type 4: IF/WHILE

The difference between an **IF** statement and a **WHILE** statement in Pascal is that the latter executes a body of statements repeatedly, while the former only executes the body once; note that both have a testing component. In looking at programs written by novice programmers, we found that novices sometimes used a **WHILE** statement when the body would

```
PROGRAM Grey(input, output);
VAR Sum, Count, Num : INTEGER;
        Average : REAL;
BEGIN
      Sum  := 0;
      Count  := 0;
      REPEAT
            READLN(Num);
            IF Num <> 99999 THEN
                              BEGIN
                              Sum  := Sum + Num;
                              Count  := Count + 1;
                              END,
         UNTIL Num = 99999;
         Average  := Sum/Count;
         WRITELN(Average);
END.
```

```
PROGRAM Grey(input, output);
VAR Sum, Count, Num : INTEGER;
        Average : REAL;
BEGIN
      Sum  := 0;
      ---------------------------------
      |                               |
      |  _____|
      REPEAT
            READLN(Num);
            IF Num <> 99999 THEN
                              BEGIN
                              Sum  := Sum + Num;
                              Count  := Count + 1;
                              END,
         UNTIL Num = 99999;
         Average  := Sum/Count;
         WRITELN(Average);
END.
```

```
PROGRAM Orange(input, output);
VAR Sum, Count, Num : INTEGER;
        Average : REAL;
BEGIN
       Sum   := -99999;
       Count  := -1;
       REPEAT
               READLN(Num);
               Sum  := Sum + Num;
               Count  := Count + 1;
          UNTIL Num = 99999;
          Average  := Sum/Count;
          WRITELN(Average);
END.
```

```
PROGRAM Orange(input, output);
VAR Sum, Count, Num : INTEGER;
        Average : REAL;
BEGIN
       Sum   := -99999;
      ----------------------------------
      |                                |
      |                                |
      ----------------------------------
       REPEAT
               READLN(Num);
               Sum  := Sum + Num;
               Count  := Count + 1;
          UNTIL Num = 99999;
          Average  := Sum/Count;
          WRITELN(Average);
END.
```

Program type 3

Basic plan	read/process, running total loop plan
Discourse rule	don't do double duty in a non-obvious way (4)
How construct Beta version	violate discourse rule (4)
Alpha case	initialize to standard values
Beta case loop	initialize to non-standard values to compensate for poorly formed

FIGURE 4.7 Example: program type 3

149

Version Alpha

```
PROGRAM Gold(input,output);
    CONST
         MaxSentence=99;
         NumOfConvicts=5;
    VAR
         ConvictID, I, Sentence  :  INTEGER;

    BEGIN
         FOR I :=1 TO NumOfConvicts DO
             BEGIN
                 READLN(ConvictID, Sentence);
                 IF Sentence > MaxSentence
                     THEN  Sentence  := MaxSentence;
                 WRITELN(ConvictID, Sentence);
             END;
    END.
```

Version Beta

```
PROGRAM Silver(input,output);
    CONST
         MaxSentence=99;
         NumOfConvicts=5;
    VAR
         ConvictID, I, Sentence  :  INTEGER;

    BEGIN
         FOR I :=1 TO NumOfConvicts DO
             BEGIN
                 READLN(ConvictID, Sentence);
                 WHILE Sentence > MaxSentence;
                   Do Sentence  := MaxSentence;
                 WRITELN(ConvictID, Sentence);
             END;
    END.
```

```
PROGRAM Gold(input,output);
    CONST
         MaxSentence=99;
         NumOfConvicts=5;
    VAR
         ConvictID, I, Sentence  :  INTEGER;

    BEGIN
         FOR I :=1 TO NumOf Convicts DO
             BEGIN
                 READLN(ConvictID, Sentence);
                 WHILE Sentence > MaxSentence

             THEN  [_____]

                 WRITELN(ConvictID, Sentence);
             END;
    END.
```

```
PROGRAM Silver(input,output);
    CONST
         MaxSentence=99;
         NumOfConvicts=5;
    VAR
         ConvictID, I, Sentence  :  INTEGER;

    BEGIN
         FOR I :=1 TO NumOf Convicts DO
             BEGIN
                 READLN(ConvictID, Sentence);
                 IF Sentence > MaxSentence

             DO  [_____]

                 WRITELN(ConvictID, Sentence);
             END;
    END.
```

Program type 4

Basic plan	reset to boundary condition
Discourse rule executed	An IF should be used when a statement body is guaranteed to be only once and a WHILE used when a statement body may need to be repeatedly executed. (5)
How construct Beta version	violate discourse rule. (5)
Alpha case	use IF for testing and one time execution
Beta case	use WHILE for testing and one time execution

FIGURE 4.8   Example: program type 4

only be executed once: It was as if novices had a rule such as *when a body needs to be executed only once, then either a* **WHILE** *or an* **IF** *could be used.* We felt that advanced programmers would be horrified by such a rule, and, moreover, would be confused in seeing a **WHILE** in a situation that "clearly" called for an **IF**.

The programs in Figure 4.8 were developed to test the above hypothesis. Both these programs test to see if some variable contains a number that is greater than a maximum; and if so, the variable is reset to the maximum. The Alpha version uses an **IF** test; the Beta version uses a **WHILE** statement. The Beta version was generated from the Alpha version by violating the following discourse rule: *An* **IF** *should be used when a statement body is guaranteed to be executed only once, and a* **WHILE** *used when a statement body may need to be repeatedly executed.* If the advanced programmers do have this rule than we predict that they would not recognize the **RESET PLAN** in the Beta version nearly as often as they would in the Alpha version.

ACKNOWLEDGMENT

This work was sponsored by the National Science Foundation, under NSF Grants MCS-8302382 and IST-8310659.

Portions of this chapter appear in the IEEE Transactions on Software Engineering, September, 1984.

REFERENCES

Adelson, B. (1981). Problem solving and the development of abstract categories in programming languages. *Memory and Cognition, 9*, 422–433.

Bartlett, F. C. (1932). *Remembering: A study in experimental and social psychology.* Cambridge, England: University Press.

Black, J. (1985). An exposition on understanding expository text. In Britton & Black (Eds.), *Understanding expository text.* Hillsdale, NJ: Lawrence Erlbaum Associates.

Bonar, J., & Soloway., E. (1983). Uncovering principles of novice programming. *Proceedings of the Tenth Symposium on the Principles of Programming Languages.* Palo Alto, CA: Morgan-Kaufmann.

Bower, G. H., Black, J. B., & Turner, T. (1979) Scripts in memory for text. *Cognitive Psychology, 11*, 177–220.

Chase, W. C., & Simon, H. (1973). Perception in chess. *Cognitive Psychology, 4*, 55–81.

DeGroot, A. D. (1965). *Thought and choice in chess.* Paris: Mouton & Company.

Egan, D., & Schwartz, B. (1979). Chunking in recall of symbolic drawings. *Memory and Cognition, 7*, 149–158.

Graesser, A. C. (1981). *Prose comprehension beyond the word.* New York: Springer-Verlag.

Halstead, M. M. (1977). *Elements of software science.* New York: Elsevier.

Johnson, L., & Soloway, E. (1984). Diagnosis and understanding in novice programs. *Proceedings of the American Association for Artificial Intelligence Symposium*, Austin, TX.

Johnson, W. L., Soloway, E., Cutler, B., & Draper, S. (1983, October). *Bug catalogue: I.* (Tech. Dept. #298). Yale University, Dept. of Computer Science.

Larkin, J., McDermott, J., Simon, D., & Simon, H. (1980). Expert and novice performance in solving physics problems. *Science, 208,* 140–156.

McKeithen, K. B., Reitman, J. S., Rueter, H. H., & Hirtle, S. C. (1981). Knowledge organization and skill differences in computer programmers. *Cognitive psychology, 13,* 307–325.

Rich, C. (1981). *Inspection methods in programming.* (Tech. Rept. AI-TR-604). Massachusetts Institute of Technology, Artificial Intelligence Lab.

Schank, R. C., & Abelson, R. (1977). *Scripts, plans, goals and understanding.* Hillsdale, NJ: Lawrence Erlbaum Associates.

Shcneiderman, B. (1976) Exploratory experiments in programmer behavior. *International Journal of Computer and Information Sciences, 5,* 123–143.

Soloway, E., Bonar, J., & Ehrlich, K. (1983). Cognitive strategies and looping constructs: An empirical study. *CACM, 26,* 853–861.

Soloway, E., & Ehrlich, K. (1984). Empirical studies of programming knowledge. *IEEE Transactions on Software Engineering, 5,* 595–609.

Soloway, E., Ehrlich, K., Black, J. (1983). Beyond Numbers: Don't ask "how many". . . ask "why." *Proceedings SIGCHI Conference on Human Factors in Computer Systems, SIGCHI,* Boston, MA.

Soloway, E., Ehrlich, K., Bonar, J., & Greenspan, J. (1982). What do novices know about programming? In A. Badre & B. Shneiderman, (Eds.), *Directions in human–computer interactions* (pp. 87–122). Norwood, NJ: Ablex, Inc.

Weissman, L. (1974). Psychological complexity of computer programs: An experimental metho odology. *SIGPLAN Notices, 9.*

5 Learning to Program Recursive Functions

John R. Anderson
Carnegie–Mellon University

Peter Pirolli
University of California

Robert Farrell
Yale University

INTRODUCTION

To iterate is human. To recurse, divine.
-Logout message on the Carnegie–Mellon CMUA computer.

Learning to write recursive programs is notoriously difficult. It is likely that students learning to program LISP would almost unanimously agree that writing recursive functions is the biggest hurdle they face. This chapter discusses (a) why learning recursive programming is so difficult, and (b) how it is successfully mastered.

To provide a framework for later discussion, we first describe how the recursive programming behavior of an expert is modeled in GRAPES (Goal-Restricted Production System), a production system developed (see Anderson, Farrell, & Sauers, 1982, 1984) to model programming in LISP. Second, we will discuss why recursive programming is so difficult to learn. To foreshadow this, our conclusion will be that it is difficult both because it is a highly unfamiliar mental activity and because it depends on developing a great deal of knowledge about specific patterns of recursive programs. Third, we will offer a general proposal as to how recursive programming is typically learned. In line with the learning of other aspects of LISP, recursive programming seems to be learned by analogy to example programs and by generalization from these examples. Fourth and last, we will discuss a series of protocols used by one subject trying to learn recursive programming. We discuss these protocols in the light of GRAPES simulations of her behavior. This last exercise is intended to provide evidence both for our proposals about recursive programming and for our GRAPES model of LISP programming behavior.

SIMULATION OF LISP PROGRAMMING

We developed GRAPES to model how subjects write functions (i.e., programs) in the LISP language, and how subjects learn from their problem-solving episodes. GRAPES is a production system architecture which emulates certain aspects of the ACT* theory. Each production in GRAPES has a condition which specifies a particular programming goal and various problem specifications. The action of the production can be to embellish the problem specification, to write or change LISP code, or to set new subgoals. The details of the GRAPES production system are described in Sauers and Farrell (1982). The architecture of GRAPES differs from that of other production systems (e.g., Anderson, 1976; Newell, 1973), primarily in the way it treats goals. At any point in time there is a single goal being focused upon, and only productions relevant to that goal may apply. In this feature, GRAPES is like ACT* (Anderson, 1983) and other recent theories (Brown and Van Lehn, 1980; Card, Moran, & Newell, 1983; Rosenbloom and Newell, 1983).

To give a sense of what a GRAPES production system is like, let us consider some examples of productions that have been used in our simulations. A representative example of a production[1] that a pre-novice might have is:

R1:   IF the total is to write a structure
                and there is a template for writing the structure
        THEN set a goal to map that template to the current case.

R1 might be invoked in a nonprogramming context such as when one uses another person's income tax form as a template to guide how to fill out his own. Productions like R1 serve as a basis for subjects' initial performance in LISP. A production that a novice might have after a few hours of learning is:

R2:   IF the goal is to add List1 and List2
        THEN write (APPEND List1 List2)

This production recognizes the applicability of the basic LISP function APPEND. With experience, subjects become more and more discriminating about how and when to use LISP functions. A rule that an expert might have is:

---

[1]Here and throughout the paper we will give English-like renditions of the production rules. A technical specification of these rules (i.e., a computer listing) can be obtained by writing to us. Also available is a user's manual (Sauers & Farrell, 1982) that describes the system.

R3:   IF the goal is to check that a recursive call to a function will terminate and the recursive call is in the context of a MAP function

        THEN set as a subgoal to establish that the list provided to the MAP function will always become NIL after some number of recursive calls

All programs in LISP take the form of functions that calculate various input–output relations. These functions can call other functions or call themselves recursively. A programming problem is solved in GRAPES by decomposing an initial goal of writing a function into subgoals, and dividing these subgoals into others, and so on, until goals are reached which correspond to things that can be directly written. The decomposition of goals into subgoals constitutes the AND-level of a goal tree — each subgoal must be successful for the goal to be successful. Alternative ways of decomposing a goal constitute the OR-level of the goal tree — any decomposition can be successful for the goal to be successful.

One of the basic observations we have made, of learning to program in LISP, is that subjects do not seem to learn much from the abstract instruction they encounter in textbooks. Rather they learn in the process of trying to solve problems. Our GRAPES simulations have therefore focussed on modeling problem-solving and the resultant learning (see Anderson, Farrell, & Sauers, 1982, 1984). We have developed in GRAPES a set of *knowledge compilation* learning mechanisms which create new production operators from the course of problem solutions (Anderson, 1983; Anderson, Farrell, & Sauers, 1984). Knowledge compilation summarizes extensive problem-solving attempts into compact production rules. These knowledge compilation mechanisms have successfully simulated a number of the learning transitions we have observed in our subjects. We will discuss in this paper some other simulations of learning transitions.

Simulation of a Recursive Solution

Here we would like to describe the GRAPES simulation of an expert's solution of a particularly interesting recursive problem called POWERSET. GRAPES' solution to POWERSET is arguably the prescriptively "ideal" solution. Having this ideal solution as a reference point, we will be in a position to make a number of important points about the nature of writing recursive programs.

Figure 5.1 illustrates the POWERSET problem as we present it to subjects. The subject is told that a list of atoms encodes a set of elements, and that he or she is to calculate the powerset of that set — that is, the list of all sublists of the list, including the original list and the empty list NIL.

(POWERSET '(A B C))
= ((A B C) (A B) (A C) (B C) (A) (B) (C) ( ))

FIGURE 5.1.   The POWERSET problem requires the student to write a recursive program that produces all possible subsets of an input set.

Each subject is given an example of the POWERSET of a three-element list. All subjects come up with basically the same solution. This solution is given in Table 5.1. The definition in Table 5.1 involves a secondary function ADDTO which takes as arguments a list-of-lists and an atom. ADDTO returns a list of lists composed by adding the atom to each list in the original list-of-lists argument. We have not provided a definition for ADDTO because the definition varies with the level of expertise of the programmer[2]. The basic structure of the POWERSET definition, however, does not change with expertise although there is easily a greater than a 10:1 ratio in the time taken by novices versus experts to generate the code.

Figure 5.2 presents the goal tree for the solution to the POWERSET problem produced by GRAPES. Each node in this tree (e.g., "try CDR-recursion") is a specific programming goal. Arrows show the decomposition of a goal into subgoals. For example, the goal "try CDR-recursion" decomposes to the subgoals "do terminating condition" and "do recursive step." The goals in this tree are set in a left-to-right, depth-first manner. The code presented in Table 5.1 is the product of carrying out the plan specified in Figure 5.2.

With the first goal set to code the function POWERSET (the topmost goal in Figure 5.2), the first GRAPES production to apply is:

P1:   IF the goal is to code a function
              and it has a single level list as an argument
        THEN try to use CDR-recursion and set as subgoals to:

    1. Do the terminating step for CDR-recursion.
    2. Do the recursive step for CDR-recursion.

TABLE 5.1
Powerset solution

(Defun powerset (l)
       (cond ((null l)(list nil))
             (t (append (powerset (cdr l))
                        (addto (car l) (powerset (cdr l)))))))

---

[2]In fact some programmers insert a MAPCAR call without naming an auxiliary function.

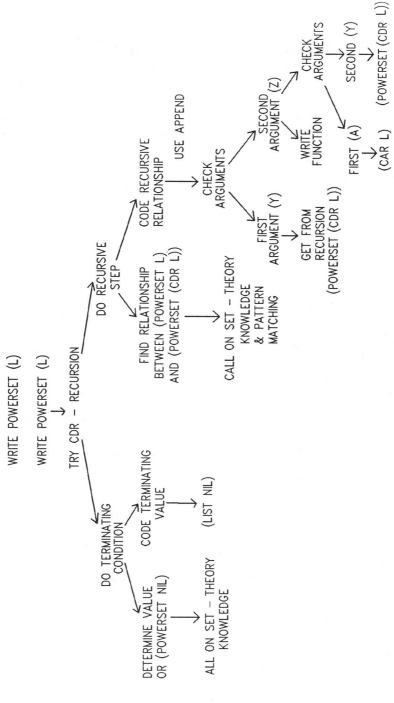

FIGURE 5.2. The goal tree for the "ideal" POWERSET solution. Arrows point from goals to their subgoals. In this tree, all of a goal's subgoals must be successful for the goal to be successful. Goals are activated in a depth-first, left-to-right manner.

CDR-recursion is a type of recursion that can apply when one of the arguments of the function is a list. It involves calling a function recursively with successively smaller lists as arguments. It is called CDR-recursion because it utilizes the LISP function CDR which removes the first element of a list. Thus, each recursive call is passed the CDR of a current argument list. Production P1 sets up the plan to call (POWERSET (CDR LIST) within the definition of (POWERSET LIST). The standard terminating condition for CDR-recursion involves the case in which the list argument becomes NIL. In this case a special answer has to be returned. So note that this "expert" production is relatively specialized — it is only concerned with a special case of recursion and only applies in the special condition that the argument list is a one-level list. Production rules are selected for application by *conflict resolution principles* in GRAPES, and one of these principles involves specificity: Productions with more specific conditions (i.e., more conditions and/or less variables) tend to be selected over productions with less specific productions. Because of this specificity principle, P1 would not apply in many situations where there was a one-level list argument. For instance, if the goal was to write a function that returned a list of the first and second elements in a list argument, other more special case productions would apply.

Activating goals in a left-to-right, depth-first manner, GRAPES turns to coding the terminating condition. In the case of CDR-recursion this amounts to deciding what the correct answer is in the case of an empty list — that is, when the list becomes NIL. The answer to this question requires examining the definition of POWERSET and noting that the POWERSET of the empty set is a set that contains the empty set. This can be coded as (LIST NIL). Each goal decomposition under "do terminating condition" is achieved by a production. We have just summarized their application here. The important feature to note is that coding the terminating condition is extremely straightforward in a case like this, where the answer can be derived from a semantically correct definition of the function. In particular, writing such code does not require an analysis of the recursive behavior of the function.

After coding the terminating condition, GRAPES turns to coding the recursive step. This is decomposed into two subgoals. One is to characterize the recursive relationship between POWERSET called on the full list and POWERSET called on the CDR or tail of the list. The other goal is to convert this characterization into LISP code. The only nonroutine aspect of applying the CDR-recursion technique is discovering the recursive relationship. Figure 5.3 illustrates what is involved. In that figure the symbol X denotes the result of POWERSET on a typical list and Y denotes the result of POWERSET on the CDR of that list. The critical insight involves noticing that Y is half of X and the other half of X is a list, denoted Z, which

```
L = (A B C)                            Y = (POWERSET (CDR L))
                                         = ((B C)
X = (POWERSET L)                            (B)
  = ((A B C)                                (C)
     (A B)                                  ( ))
     (A C)
     (A)
     (B C)
     (B)
     (C)
     ( ))
X = Y + Z              WHERE       Z = ((A B C)
                                        (A B)
                                        (A C)
                                        (A))


       Z IS FORMED FROM Y BY ADDING A TO EACH
       MEMBER OF Y.
```

FIGURE 5.3. The POWERSET insight involves determining what must be done with the result of the recursive call, (POWERSET (CDR SETT), in order to get the result for the current function call (POWERSET SETT).

can be gotten from Y by adding the first element of the list (A in Figure 5.3) to each member of Y. Thus, $X = Y + Z$. We have developed GRAPES simulations which will produce this "correct" POWERSET characterization if given the goal to compare concrete examples of X, Y, and Z. Generally, novice LISP programmers consider this comparison only after performing many other types of comparisons of concrete examples. In contrast, experts often do not need to consider any concrete example; when they do, they typically choose almost immediately to compare a concrete example of X, the POWERSET of a whole list, and Y, the POWERSET of the CDR of the list, and search for an appropriate characterization of this relationship.

The actual coding of the recursive relationship is extremely straightforward. One production recognizes that the LISP function APPEND is appropriate for putting the two sublists Y and Z together to form the answer X. This leaves the subgoals of coding the first and second arguments, Y and Z, for the function. Another production recognizes that Y can be calculated simply as a recursive call — (POWERSET (CDR L)). There is no LISP function that will directly calculate Z, and this evokes a default production which sets a subgoal to write an auxiliary function, ADDTO, which will calculate Z given the first element of the list L and given Y.

POWERSET is one of a large class of recursive functions that lend themselves to straightforward solution in this manner. There are a number of
standard recursive paradigms in LISP in addition to CDR-recursion but
they all have the same straightforward character. It is the case that not all
LISP recursive functions are so straightforward. One reason for complexity is that the function may not have as precise a semantics as POWERSET,
and part of the problem-solving is to settle on that semantics. Part of the
trick is to settle the semantics in a way that makes the coding easy. Another
reason for complexity concerns recursion in nonstandard paradigms. For
instance, production R3 described earlier deals with one such nonstandard
recursion. However, the important observation is that standard recursion
as in POWERSET causes novices great difficulty. The students we have
looked at spent from just under two to over four hours arriving at the solution to POWERSET that an expert can produce in under ten minutes.

WHY IS RECURSIVE PROGRAMMING DIFFICULT?

A starting point for understanding the difficulty of recursive programming
is to note that recursive mental procedures are very difficult — perhaps
impossible — for humans to execute. For instance, center-embedded structures in language, while perhaps grammatical, are impossible to understand.
Interestingly, the same degree of difficulty does not arise when different
types of constructions are embedded within each other — only when the same
construction is embedded within itself (Anderson, 1976; Dresher & Hornstein, 1976). For instance, sentence 1 below involves the embedding of two
relative clauses; sentence 2, the embedding of two complement clauses; sentence 3, the embedding of a relative clause within a complement clause;
sentence 4, the embedding of a complement clause within a relative clause.
Sentences 1 and 2, which involve self-embedding, are much more difficult
to understand:

1. The boy whom the girl whom the sailor liked hit ran away.
2. The fact that the shepherd said that the farmer had given the book
   to the child to the police was to be expected.
3. The fact that the shepherd reported the girl whom the sailor liked
   to the police was to be expected.
4. The boy who told the girl that the farmer had read the book ran away.

This pattern makes sense if we assume that distinct procedures are responsible for understanding distinct expressions. The human mind seems incapa-
ble of doing what LISP does — creating a copy of a procedure and embedding

it within itself, and keeping track of what is happening in both copies. It is also interesting that right embedding of one linguistic construction within itself does not create the same difficulty. It seems that the mind can treat such tail recursive procedures with an iterative control structure.

Indeed, it seems that it is a typical "programming trick" in the mind to change what is naturally a recursive procedure into an iterative one. A good example is the evaluation of arithmetic expressions like $4 * [(3 - 2) * (5 + 7)]$. The "logical" procedure for evaluating such expressions would be a top-down recursive evaluation as one would perform in LISP. The actual procedures that people use are iterative. For instance, a frequent procedure is to scan for an embedded expression that has no embeddings (e.g., $3 - 2$), evaluate it, replace the expression by its evaluation, and reiterate.

In observing how students mentally simulate recursive functions in LISP, we see some of the clearest evidence for the difficulty of recursion. The evidence is particularly clear because the evaluation process is sufficiently slow that it can be traced as it progresses in time. Students frequently show no difficulty in simulating a function making recursive calls to itself and passing control down. However, when they have to simulate the return of results and combine the partial results they get completely lost. It seems that the human mind, unlike the LISP evaluator, cannot suspend one process, make a new copy of the process, restart the process to perform a recursive call, and return to the original suspended process. In particular, it seems impossible to hold a suspended record in our mind of where we were in a series of embedded processes.

If it is the case that minds can iterate and not recurse, then it might seem obvious why recursive programming is difficult — the mind is not capable of it. We have frequently heard various forms of this argument, but they all have a serious fallacy: Writing a recursive procedure is not itself a recursive procedure! Consider that the construction of the definition of POWER-SET in Figure 5.2 was not performed by a recursive mental procedure. We would like to claim that the human inability to *execute* recursive procedures is not the direct source of difficulty in *programming* recursive functions.

The Unfamiliarity of Recursion

We feel that the fundamental reason for the difficulty of recursive programming is the unfamiliarity of the activity. People have had prior preprogramming experience with following everyday procedures (e.g., recipes) and, more importantly, with specifying such procedures to others. However, because these preprogramming procedures typically had to run in human heads, they were never recursive. Therefore, recursive programming is most people's first experience with specifying a recursive procedure. Interestingly, we have only observed one student who had no difficulty with learning recursive programming. Significantly, this was a graduate student in mathematics who had done a fair amount of work in recursive function theory.

A major source of difficulty in learning recursion is an instructional one. Every textbook we have examined gives students no direct help in how to generate a recursive function. Textbooks explain what recursion is, explain how it works, give examples of recursive functions, give traces of recursive functions, and explain how to evaluate recursive functions; but they never explain how to go from a problem specification to a recursive function. Thus, students have a major induction problem: How to go from the information they are given to a procedure for creating recursive functions. Textbooks are no more lucid about how to create iterative procedures, but here the student has prior experience in structuring such an induction problem.

Another difficulty is that students often think of iterative procedures for solving recursive problems. For example, many novices coding POWER-SET solve the problem at hand according to the following procedure: Place the null set in the result list, then all subsets of length one, followed by all subsets of length two and so on, until the whole set is reached[3]. This procedure of successively gathering all subsets of length N is radically different from the ideal POWERSET procedure in LISP. Such a plan is difficult to achieve in code and tends to interfere with seeing the easy-to-code solution. Thus, having nonrecursive solutions to problems tends to blind students to recursive solution.

A further exacerbating factor is that there are really many different types of recursive functions in addition to CDR-recursion. Integer recursion requires recursively calling the function with a progressively smaller integer argument. CAR and CDR recursion requires calling a function recursively on the CAR (first element) and the CDR of the list. Soloway and Woolf (1980) have argued that each of these major types of recursion has many subtypes. The student is not going to be an effective recursive programmer until he learns to deal with each type. Again, typical textbooks offer the student no help; they encourage the belief that there is just one type of recursion — a function calling itself.

The Duality of a Recursive Call

Another source of difficulty (especially in LISP) is the duality of meaning in a recursive procedure call. On the one hand the call produces some resultant data; on the other hand it specifies that an operation be carried out repeatedly. Thus, the written form of a recursive call is the symbolic ana-

---

[3]The ordering varies somewhat from student to student.

log to a Necker cube: It can be data or complex operations, depending on your view.

Because students often perseverate on one view of recursion, they are often blinded to solutions that could be easily attained from the other view. For example, it is often useful to determine what has to be done to the result produced by a recursive call in order to get a result for the current function call. This is a key component in the POWERSET insight (see Figure 5.3) where one must determine what has to be done with the list produced by the recursive call, (POWERSET (CDR SETT)), in order to get the current function result, (POWERSET SETT). Students often miss such insights because they perseverate on the view of the recursive call as a complex flow of control. They will often attempt to trace out the flow of control rather than consider what result will be produced by a recursive call.

Complexities Which Exacerbate the Difficulty of Recursive Programming

There are other factors that really have nothing to do with recursion per se but which nonetheless complicate recursive programming. For instance, textbook problems for recursive programs are typically more difficult than for iterative ones. The POWERSET example is an instance of this phenomenon. Students frequently have problems in fully understanding the input-output relations in the first place, and then face the difficulty of maintaining this complex relation in memory. Another, presumably independent difficulty is that the data structures being operated upon are often unfamiliar. For instance, students' prior experience with list structures (critical to CDR-recursion and some other forms of recursion) is weak. It has been shown (Anderson & Jeffries, 1985) that making one part of the problem difficult impacts on the difficulty of a logically separate part.

So, in summary, recursive programming is difficult principally because it is an unfamiliar activity, with hidden complexities, that must be induced in an unfamiliar and difficult domain. The unfamiliarity of creating recursive procedures can be traced to the mental difficulty of executing recursive procedures, but the mental difficulty is not the primary reason.

Having said all this, we should point out that there is one secondary problem in recursive programming that is directly related to the mental difficulty of creating recursive procedures. This concerns checking and debugging recursive programs. This requires evaluating the programs with sample arguments, and evaluation is a recursive procedure—in contrast to program generation. Of course, students learn procedures that convert recursive evaluation into an iterative procedure, such as writing down intermediate results and states in linear stack-like structures. However, dealing with logically recursive evaluation does make it harder for students to detect errors in recursive programs. So, though initial program generation does not involve the mental difficulties of recursion, program debugging does. However, it needs to be stressed that the major problems of novices are with initial program generation, and not with debugging.

PROPOSAL FOR THE LEARNING OF RECURSIVE PROGRAMMING

So how do students learn the unfamiliar procedure of generating recursive programs? Explicit procedures are not given to the student. In the absence of explicit procedures, our hypothesis is that the primary means available to students is learning from examples. By this, we mean two things. First, students can try to look at worked-out examples, and map by analogy the solution for these problems to a solution for the current problem. This is learning by analogy. Second, they can try to summarize their solution to one problem by new problem-solving operators (GRAPES productions), and apply these operators to another problem. This is learning by knowledge compilation. We believe that these two learning mechanisms are logically ordered — that the first problems are solved by analogy and that solutions to these early problems give rise to the operators that can apply to later problems. The following protocol analyses provide support for our application of this analysis to recursion. For successful application to other domains of learning LISP, see Anderson, Farrell, and Sauers (1984).

PROTOCOLS AND SIMULATIONS

We will discuss the behavior of one subject, SS, as she solved her first three recursive functions. The first recursive function was SETDIFF which took two list arguments and returned all the members in the first list that were not in the second list. The second was SUBSET, a function of two list arguments which tested if all the elements of the first list were members of the second. The third function was POWERSET. All three functions may be solved by the CDR-recursion technique. (The first two are easily and more efficiently solved by iterative techniques, but SS's textbook, in the manner typical of LISP pedagogy, does not introduce iteration until after recursion.)

SS's textbook was Siklossy's (1976) *Let's Talk LISP*, which is a somewhat singular book in regard to the amount of discussion it contains of programming technique issues. It is also designed for the programming novice and attempts a very careful introduction to all relevant concepts. It does not, however, instruct directly on how to write recursive functions, but rather it instructs on "considerations" relevant to good recursive functions and gives many examples — many of which involve set theory. SS had spent over 15 hours studying LISP at the time of these protocols. In this time she had studied basic LISP functions and predicates, conditionals, and function definitions.

Solving these three problems took SS a total of five hours. In following SS through this protocol, we can see her improving from one function to the next. We cannot say that by the end she had induced all the components required to do CDR-recursion — although she had some of them. SS continued to do LISP problems long after we finished studying her, and she eventually became quite effective at writing a wide variety of recursive functions. We can only guess that she reached her proficiency by use of more learning steps of the variety we were able to document in these protocols. It is clear that it takes a great deal of time to learn recursive programming in the traditional learning situation.

SETDIFF

The first function SS tried to write was SETDIFF. She took a little over an hour to solve the problem. Table 5.2 gives a schematic protocol of her

TABLE 5.2
SS's SETDIFF Protocol

---

1. SS reviews code for INTERSECTION1 function (previous problem).

2. SS reads SETDIFF problem and forms the analogy
   SETDIFF:INTESECTION::CDR:CAR. SS also proposes the following relation:

   SETDIFF (SET1, SET2)
   =MINUS (SET1, INTERSECTION(SET1, SET2))

3. Writes (DEFUN SETDIFF (SET1 SET2).

4. Decides to code SETDIFF by rearranging INTERSECTION1 code.

5. Decides to code simple cases found in INTERSECTION1.

6. Considers case (NULL SET1), decides the action will be NIL. Code is now

   (DEFUN SETDIFF (SET1 SET2)
     (COND ((NULL SET 1) NIL)

7. Considers case (NULL SET2), decides action will be SET1. Code is now

   (DEFUN SETDIFF (SET1 SET2)
     (COND ((NULL SET1) NIL)
       ((NULL SET2) SET1)

8. SS formulates plan to check each element of SET1 to see if it is NOT a member of SET2. Gives up on this plan.

(Continued)

TABLE 5.2
(Continued)

---

9. Decides to code the relation MINUS (SET1, INTERSECTION(SET1, SET2)). Realizes that MINUS is equivalent to SETDIFF and gives up on this plan.

10. Returns to using INTERSECTION1 code as an analogy. Considers case (MEMBER (CAR SET1) SET2), decides action should be "something with nothing added to it."

11. Refines action to the code (SETDIFF (CDR SET1) SET2). Code is now:

```
(DEFUN SETDIFF (SET1 SET2)
    (COND ((NULL SET1) NIL)
          ((NULL SET2) SET1)
          ((MEMBER (CAR SET1) SET2)
           (SETDIFF (CDR SET1) SET2))
```

12. Considers case in which (CAR SET1) is not a member of SET2. Formulates plan to add (CAR SET1) to the answer for SETDIFF.

13. Decides to look at INTERSECTION1 code again. Notes that 4th action of INTERSECTION maps onto 3rd action of SETDIFF, ponders whether 3rd action of INTERSECTION1 will map onto 4th action of SETDIFF. Decides that the code will work. Final code is:

```
(DEFUN SETDIFF (SET1 SET2)
    (COND ((NULL SET1) NIL)
          ((NULL SET2) SET1)
          ((MEMBER (CAR SET1) SET2)
           (SETDIFF (CDR SET1) SET2))
          (T (CONS (CAR SET1)
                   (SETDIFF (CDR SET1) SET2)))))
```

14. Checks code visually and on the computer.

---

solution to the problem. This is an attempt to identify the critical steps in that problem-solution episode. Very important to her solution is the example which just precedes this problem in Siklossy's book. It is a definition for set intersection and is given as:

```
(INTERSECTION1 (LAMBDA (SET1 SET2)
    (COND ((NULL SET1) ())
          ((NULL SET2) ())
          ((MEMSET (CAR SET1) SET2)
           (CONS (CAR SET1) (INTERSECTION1 (CDR SET1)
           SET2)))
          (T (INTERSECTION1 (CDR SET1) SET2)))))
```

The basic LISP control construct in this function is the conditional

COND. It evaluates a set of conditional clauses. Each conditional clause consists of a condition test and an action. The COND function executes the action of the first conditional clause it encounters whose condition part is true. There are four clauses here with the condition of the last T which stands for true. So if none of the preceding three evaluate to true, then the last will. The logic of the function is presented in Figure 5.4: If the first set is empty return the empty set; if the second set is empty return the empty set; if the first member of the first set is a member of the second set, return a set consisting of the first member added to the result of a recursive call with the CDR of the first set; otherwise just return the result of the recursive call. Note that INTERSECTION1 is a bit unusual in that there is an unnecessary test for SET2 being empty. Significantly, SS carries this unusual test into her definition of SETDIFF.

Our GRAPES simulation of SS was provided with a representation of INTERSECTION1 at multiple levels of abstraction, a specification of the SETDIFF relation and a somewhat quirky relationship that our subject recognized as she read the problem. This latter relation, which later caused some difficulty for SS, was stated as: The SETDIFF of SET1 and SET2 is SET1 minus the intersection of SET1 and SET2. Our simulation was then

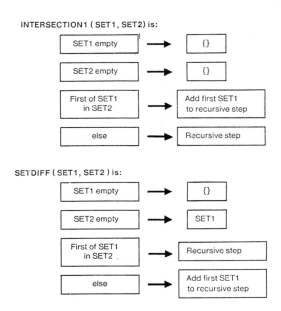

FIGURE 5.4.   A schematic view of the logic of the INTERSECTION1 and SET-DIFF functions. Arrows point from conditions to actions. Conditions are examined from top to bottom. The first condition that is true triggers its corresponding action to be evaluated.

given the goal of writing SETDIFF. Since it did not have any means of directly solving the problem, the following default rule applied:

IF the goal is to to write a structure
and there is a previous example
THEN set as subgoals:

1. Check the similarity of the example to the current problem.
2. Map the example structure onto the current problem.

This production sets goals to first check the similarity of the specifications of INTERSECTION1 and SETDIFF, and then map the code structure of INTERSECTION1 onto the SETDIFF code. This is an instance of setting AND subgoals. If the first subgoal fails the second subgoal is not attempted.

A set of comparison productions matched features from INTERSEC-TION1 and SETDIFF. These productions found that both functions take two sets, both perform some membership test, and both are recursive[4]. These productions found a sufficient similarity (the criterion is arbitrarily set in GRAPES) between INTERSECTION1 and SETDIFF, so the first subgoal was satisfied. Next, the following structure-mapping production matched the goal to map INTERSECTION1's conditional structure and the fact that such structures generally have several cases:

IF the goal is to map an example structure
onto the current problem
and that structure has known components
THEN map those components from the example
to the current solution

This production sets up subgoals to map each INTERSECTION1 conditional clause. Our subject gave clear evidence in her protocol of also intending to map the cases of the conditional. The basic rule we assume for mapping each conditional clause is:

IF the goal is to map a conditional clause
THEN map the condition of that clause
and set as subgoals:

---

[4]Subjects frequently state that they know a solution will be recursive because the problem is in the recursion section of the text.

1. To determine the action in the current case given the mapped condition.
2. To code the new condition–action clause.

There is some evidence that SS had acquired this rule from earlier problems involving non-recursive conditional functions.

Her mapping of the first two clauses of INTERSECTION1 were relatively straightforward. For the first clause she decided the condition would be (NULL SET1) and the action NIL. This is a verbatim copy of the first clause of INTERSECTION1, but from her treatment of later clauses we do not think she was simply copying symbols. The second clause had (NULL SET2) as its condition, just as in INTERSECTION1, but for the action she put SET1 which does not match INTERSECTION1. Her protocol at this point included ". . . if there are no elements in SET2 then all the elements in SET1 will not be in SET2, so if SET2 is the null set the the value of SET-DIFF is SET1." So, it seems pretty clear that she was reasoning through the semantics of the condition of the clause and what the implications were for the action of the condition. Our simulation, working with mappings of meaningful abstractions of the conditional clauses of INTERSECTION1, produced the same problem-solving behavior as did SS.

Our GRAPES representation of the meaning of the third clause was "test if the first element should be added to the answer" — which is a rather liberal interpretation of the third condition. Our principal justification for this representational assumption is that it allows us to simulate the behavior of the subject. Both the simulation and SS refined this condition further to the condition "test if the first element is NOT a member of the second set." The problem with this representation of the condition is that neither the simulation nor the subject can directly code this in LISP, and thus the attempt fails. This led both to try to refine the alternate "quirky" definition in working memory: The SETDIFF of SET1 and SET2 is SET1 minus the INTERSECTION of SET1 and SET2. This led both the subject and simulation to set a subgoal of trying to refine "minus." In trying to refine the semantics of minus, both simulation and subject realized that it was equivalent to SETDIFF, the function they were trying to define. Thus the subject had refined the goal of defining SETDIFF into the goal of defining SET-DIFF. This is another failure condition, and so simulation and subject attempted to map another representation of the third clause of SETDIFF.

At this point both simulation and subject mapped a very literal translation of the INTERSECTION1 clause: "Test if the first element of SET1 is in SET 2." Thus, the third clause of INTERSECTION1, (MEMSET (CAR SET1) SET2), was used nearly literally as the clause for SETDIFF. Using the specification of SETDIFF, both simulation and subject decided that the output result should not contain the currently tested first element of SET1, and that SETDIFF should repeat over all elements of SET1. SS decided to simply call SETDIFF on the rest of SET1 in this case. Thus, her action became (SETDIFF (CDR SET1) SET2). The coding of the action was produced in GRAPES by another structure-mapping production:

> IF the goal is to code a relation
>   and a code template exists for relation
> THEN map the code template.

This production matched to a template which states: "To repeat a function over the elements of a set, call the function again with (CDR set)." The resulting code matched that of SS.

SS and the simulation then turned to coding the last conditional clause of SETDIFF. Both were still mapping a relatively literal copy of INTERSECTION1 and consequently both copied the T as the condition for the fourth clause of SETDIFF. The semantics of this condition were refined by both SS and the simulation to the case "the first element of SET1 is NOT is SET2." Again working from the semantics of the SETDIFF specification, both GRAPES and SS decided that this condition implies that "the tested element should be added to the result." Our subject floundered at this point because, once again, she did not know how to code the relation she had refined. She inspected the superficial structure of the relationship between SETDIFF as she had written it and INTERSECTION1. She noticed that, while the conditions of clauses 3 and 4 of INTERSECTION1 could be mapped onto the conditions of clauses 3 and 4 of SETDIFF, the action of INTERSECTION1 clause 4 had been mapped onto the action of SETDIFF clause 3. She solved the structural analogy and wrote the action from the third clause in the position of the fourth clause. We gave GRAPES the goal of solving the structural analogy between the last two clauses of the production. Having this goal given, it then set about solving the analogy just as had our subject.

After solving the problem, GRAPES goes into a knowledge compilation phase during which it compiles into single production segments of the problem-solving episode. The details of compilation are discussed in Anderson, Farrell, & Sauers (1984). For present purposes, we are interested in the products of the compilation process. A number of production rules were formed but two important ones that were invoked in the later problem-solving are the following:

C1:   IF the goal is to code a relation on two sets SET1 and SET2
           and the relation is recursive
       THEN code a conditional and set as subgoals to:

1. Refine & code a clause
   to deal with the case when SET1 is NIL.
2. Refine & code a clause
   to deal with the case when SET2 is NIL.
3. Refine & code a clause
   to deal with the case when the first
   element of SET1 is a member of SET2.
4. Refine & code a clause
   to deal with the else case.

C2:   IF the goal is to code a relation causing a function
           to repeat on the rest of a list
         and this occurs in the context of writing a function
           that codes the relation on the list
    THEN insert a recursive call of a function with the argument
       the CDR of the list

The first production compiles the analogy to INTERSECTION1 into a single rule. The second production was learned in the context of coding the third clause of SETDIFF. It is the first recursive rule that the subject has. Note however that its condition does not have a recursive semantics. Rather, SS conceives of the recursive call as causing the function to *repeat*.

It should be noted that C1 and C2 above constitute a fragment of CDR-recursion, and an approximation at that. C1 is the first step to setting up the case structure that is needed in CDR-recursion. C2 provides the recursive control. However, this is a long way from the control structure that we saw in the ideal model's solution to POWERSET.

Conclusions

There are three important conclusions that this example illustrates. First, we see the absolutely critical role that analogy plays in enabling the problem solution. The analogical mapping from INTERSECTION1 to SETDIFF is never a mindless symbol-for-symbol mapping. Rather, it takes advantage of the subjects' knowledge of LISP and a representation of the meaning of what is mapped. Still, we see the subject struggling with exactly what representations to map. The process of problem-solving by analogy is hardly trivial.

The second conclusion is the importance of compilation of this problem-solving episode to future performance. In looking at the solution to the next problem, SUBSET, we will find the compiled productions C1 and C2 absolutely critical. The related third conclusion is about the development of recursive programming skill. It is developing piecemeal and by approximation. With successive problems, we will see the simulation developing a set of productions that handle recursive programming with increasing completeness.

SUBSET

The SUBSET problem is specified in Siklossy as:

> Define a predicate SUBSET of two sets SET1 and SET2. The value of (SUBSET SET1 SET2) is T if SET1 is a subset of SET2; otherwise it is NIL. SET1 is a subset of SET2 if all elements of SET1 are members of SET2.

The schematic protocol of SS solving this problem is given in Table 5.3. SS took under half an hour to solve this problem in contrast to more than one hour that she spent on SETDIFF.

The first production to apply in simulating this protocol was C1 formed in SETDIFF. It sets out the case structure for the conditional. Both subject and simulation consulted the semantics of the subset relation and determined that the answer for the first case, when SET1, should be NIL. SS considered the case when SET2 is NIL but decided to omit this case for reasons that are unstated in her protocol. At the analogous point in our simulation we simply deleted the goal to refine and code the second conditional clause. The third case is one in which the first element of SET1 is a member of SET2. Both subject and simulation, consulting the definition of SUBSET, decided that the program must go on to check whether the other members of SET1 are part of SET2. Setting this goal evoked C2 in the simulation and led it to code the recursive call (SUBSET (CDR SET1) SET2). Finally, the program and subject determined that in the else case, the correct value is NIL.

Thus, we see that the coding episode progresses without the search associated with the first episode. The subject already had a set of rules adequate to handle a small set of CDR-recursive functions, of which SUBSET is one. From this episode one additional relevant production was compiled to reflect the three-clause solution to this problem:

C3:   IF the goal is to code a relation on two sets SET1 and SET2
            and the relation is recursive
        THEN code a conditional and set as subgoals to:

        1. Refine & code a clause
           to deal with the case when SET1 is NIL.

TABLE 5.3
SS's SUBSET Protocol

1. Reviews SETDIFF solution.

2. Reads SUBSET problem.

3. Writes

```
(DEFUN SUBSET (SET1 SET2)
    (COND
```

4. Considers case (NULL SET1). Decides action should be T. Code is:

```
(DEFUN SUBSET (SET1 SET2)
    (COND ((NULL SET1) T)
```

5. Decides not to worry about the case (NULL SET2).

6. Considers case (MEMBER (CAR SET1) SET2). Decides that the function must go on to check the rest of SET1 to see if it is a SUBSET of SET2. Code becomes:

```
(DEFUN SUBSET (SET1 SET2)
    (COND ((NULL SET1) T)
          ((MEMBER (CAR SET1) SET2)
           (SUBSET (CDR SET1) SET2))
```

7. Considers T case—(CAR SET1) is not a member of SET2. Decides value is just NIL. Code is:

```
(DEFUN SUBSET (SET1 SET2)
    (COND ((NULL SET1) T)
          ((MEMBER (CAR SET1) SET2)
           (SUBSET (CDR SET1) SET2))
          (T NIL)))
```

8. Checks code visually and on the computer.

---

2. Refine & code a clause to deal with the case when the first element of SET1 is a member of SET2.
3. Refine & code a clause to deal with the else clause.

POWERSET

The POWERSET problem is specified in Siklossy as:

Define the POWERSET of a set SETT to be a function that calculates the set of all subsets of SETT.

Example: (POWERSET (QUOTE (YALL COME BACK))) has as value the
set ((YALL COME BACK)(YALL COME)(YALL BACK)(COME
BACK)(YALL)(COME)(BACK)()).
Hint: If a set has N elements, its POWERSET has 2-to-the-n elements.

The schematic protocol for SS's solution is given in Table 5.4. In contrast to the SUBSET problem, SS took three hours to solve the POWER-
SET problem. We take this as evidence that she was rather short on general
recursive programming skill.

Our GRAPES simulation was presented the goal to write POWERSET,
and production C3 partially matched in this situation. It was only a partial match because C1 applies to two-argument functions and POWER-
SET takes only one. The second goal set by C3 involved a test of whether
the first element of SETT was a member of the uninstantiated second list.
SS actually did momentarily consider a test of the first element when she
reached this point in her coding. However, she gave up and turned to the
else case. Note that the evidence is that C3, formed after SUBSET, was
the one to apply here, and not C1, formed after SETDIFF. If C1 had applied we would also have expected to see mention of the (NULL SET2) test
in her protocol—which had been considered and rejected in the SUBSET
protocol. Instead, we only saw consideration and rejection of the (MEM-
BER (CAR SET1) SET2) test from C3. As with any protocol evidence, this
is of course only circumstantial.

Not surprisingly, the case that caused SS difficulty was the else clause.
She originally failed with efforts to enumerate all members of the answer.
Eventually, the experimenter led her through an inspection of the relationship between (POWERSET (SETT) and (POWERSET (CDR SETT). She
came to the insight illustrated in Figure 5.3 and clearly articulated that
insight. Our simulation was similarly interrupted and given the goal to induce the POWERSET relation by performing the same comparison. It also
came up with the critical POWERSET insight.

The experimenter intervened to tell SS to assume she had a magic function, CONST, which calculated Z in Figure 5.3 from Y—that is, it adds
the first member of the input list to Y. The effect of this intervention in
the simulation is to have GRAPES postpone the coding of CONST and complete the coding of POWERSET—which corresponds with the flow of control that we see in our subject.

The subject, in trying to code the recursive step, at first just wrote
(CONST (CAR SETT) (POWERSET (CDR SETT))). Only when the ex-
perimenter pointed out that this would not include the subsets without (CAR
SETT) did she change her code to (UNION (POWERSET (CDR
SETT))(CONST (CAR SETT)(POWERSET (CDR SETT)))). We were able
to simulate this in GRAPES by letting the insight $X = Y + Z$ in Figure

TABLE 5.4
SS's POWERSET Protocol

1. Reads problem.

2. Writes (DEFUN POWERSET (SETT).

3. Uses the example POWERSET ((YALL COME BACK)) to define the answer as the set of all sets of one element, all combinations of two elements, the whole list and the null list.

4. Considers case (NULL SETT). Decides that result will be NIL.

```
(DEFUN POWERSET (SETT)
    (COND ((NULL SETT) ())
```

5. Considers T case. Decides result will be the set containing SETT, the null list, the (CAR SETT) and the (POWERSET (CDR SETT)). Omits the null list since it is the action of the first clause. Code is:

```
(DEFUN POWERSET (SETT)
    (COND ((NULL SETT) ())
        (T (SETT (CAR SETT)
            (POWERSET (CDR SETT)))))))
```

6. Realizes that function will not obtain all combinations of two elements.

7. Decides that (CDR SETT) is one combination. Begins to rewrite final clause as

```
(T (SETT (CAR SETT) (CDR SETT))
```

8. Realizes that other combinations of two elements will not be easily obtained.

9. Attempts to plan a way of getting the combinations of two elements by taking the UNION of each pairwise combination of set elements. Has difficulty generalizing beyond example.

10. Decides that for N-element list, the result contains the UNION of the (CAR SETT) with all successive CDRs of the list and all CARs of the CDRs, and with all of the combinations of each. Still cannot plan a way of getting the combinations.

11. Tutor gives a hint: Assuming that POWERSET works for a set of a certain size, how would it work for the next larger size? SS doesn't use hint.

12. Tutor asks SS to write out the answer for the POWERSET of the (CDR SETT).

13. Tutor instructs SS to compare the POWERSET (CDR SETT) with the POWERSET (SETT).

14. SS realizes that POWERSET (SETT) is the POWERSET (CDR SETT) plus all the sets containing the (CAR SETT).

15. Tutor instructs SS to make an explicit comparison between the sets in the POWERSET (CDR SETT) and all the sets containing the (CAR SETT).

16. SS realizes that the sets containing the (CAR SETT) can be obtained by CONSing the (CAR SETT) into each set in the POWERSET (CDR SETT).

(Continued)

TABLE 5.4

(Continued)

17. SS wonders how she is going to CONS the (CAR SETT) into each element in a list of lists. Tutor tells SS to assume that she has a subfunction that will do this.

18. At the tutor's prompting SS names the subfunction CONST, specifies that it will take two arguments (an atom and a list of lists), and returns a list of lists in which each element list contains the atom argument.

19. Decides that the value of POWERSET in the T case will be

(CONST (CAR SETT) (POWERSET (CDR SETT)))

20. Begins to work through examples. Tutor points out that the POWERSET of () is not just () but (()).

21. Tutor points out that the current function will not return the sets in POWERSET that don't contain the (CAR SETT).

22. SS decides that the T case should result in the union of the POWERSET (CDR SETT) with the (CONST (CAR SETT) (POWERSET (CDR SETT))). Code is:

(DEFUN POWERSET (SETT)
    (COND ((NULL SETT) (()))
        (T (UNION (POWERSET (CDR SETT))
            (CONST (CAR SETT)
            (POWERSET (CDR SET))))))))

23. Tries out examples of length one and two. Hand solutions work.

24. Realizes that CONST is undefined as POWERSET is being typed in. Begins definition of CONST.

25. Formulates plan to CONS the first argument to CONST into each element of the second argument. Writes:

(DEFUN CONST (SIL LIS)

26. Decides that function does not need any conditional statements.

27. Decides that the value of CONST will be the UNION of the (CONS SIL (CAR LIS)) with (CONST (CDR LIS)). Code is:

(DEFUN CONST (SIL LIS)
    (UNION (CONS SIL (CAR LIS)) (CONST (CDR LIS))

28. While typing in function, realizes that recursive call to CONST is missing an argument. Replaces (CONST (CDR LIS)) with (CONST SIL (CDR LIS)).

29. Works through examples by hand. Types in CONST.

30. Tries out example on computer. Gets an error message indicating an infinite recursion taking place.

(Continued)

TABLE 5.4

(Continued)

31. Traces CONST. Realizes that function does not stop when second argument is empty.

32. Decides to use conditional statements. Considers case of (NULL LIS) and decides that result will be (CONS (SIL ())). Then decides that this result is equal to (SIL). Code is:

```
(DEFUN CONST (SIL LIS)
    (COND ((NULL LIS) (SIL))
```

33. Considers T case and realizes that the result will be returned by the previously written code.

```
(DEFUN CONST (SIL LIS)
    (COND ((NULL LIS) (SIL))
        (T (UNION (CONS SIL (CAR LIS))
            (CONST SIL (CDR LIS))))))
```

34. Tries out function on computer. Gets error message stating that SIL is an undefined function. Changes (SIL) back to (CONS SIL ()).

35. Tries out function again. Answer is not the right list of lists.

36. Traces UNION and CONS and tries function again. Cannot understand why the function is not returning the desired result.

37. Tutor intervenes and prods SS into reconsidering the first condition—(NULL LIS). Convinces SS that action should be ().

```
(DEFUN CONST (SIL LIS)
    (COND ((NULL LIS) ())
        (T (UNION (CONS SIL (CAR LIS))
            (CONST SIL (CDR LIS))))))
```

38. Tries out function on the computer. Answer is still not in right form.

39. Tutor prods SS into realizing that UNION should be CONS. SS has difficulty because she believes that CONS takes an atom as its first argument. Code is:

```
(DEFUN CONST (SIL LIS)
    (COND ((NULL LIS) ())
        (T (CONS (CONS SIL (CAR LIS))
            (CONST SIL (CDR LIS))))))
```

40. Tries out CONST on computer and it works.

41. Tries out POWERSET on computer and gets error message saying that NIL is an undefined function.

(Continued)

TABLE 5.4
(Continued)

---

42. Quotes the list of () in the first condition of POWERSET. Code is:

```
(DEFUN POWERSET (SETT)
    (COND ((NULL SETT) '(())) )
        (T (UNION (POWERSET (CDR SETT))
            (CONST (CAR SETT)
                (POWERSET (CDR SET)))))))
```

43. Tries out POWERSET again and function works.

5.3 degrade to $X = Z$. This was produced simply by a loss of features in the working-memory representation of the insight. The experimenter's intervention was simulated by replacing the full $X = Y + Z$ into working memory.

The simulation formed a production rule to summarize the two-clause solution to this problem:

C4:   IF the goal is to code a relation on one list SET1
            and the relation is recursive
    THEN code a conditional and set as subgoals to:
    1. Refine & code a clause
        to deal with the case when SET1 is NIL.
    2. Refine & code a clause to deal with the else case.

This is very much like the production for setting up CDR-recursion in the ideal model, but we will see that there still is a critical issue of having it evoked in the right situations.

For purposes of our analysis of recursion, the important observation is that the recursive calls to POWERSET were not generated by the production C2 compiled in the context of doing SETDIFF. Rather the code was generated by structure-mapping over the representation built up in the formation of the POWERSET insight.

Another production learned in the POWERSET episode has an impact on future performance:

C5:   IF the goal is to add result1 and result2 to form a list
    THEN write (UNION result1 result2)

This production is a compilation of the problem-solving involved in coding the final action of POWERSET, and it applies when there is a goal to combine the results of two function calls into a list. As we will see in the coding of CONST, this production is overly general. Often in synthesizing recursive function one must consider more specific details concerning the results of function calls and the form of the list being constructed.

CONST

After defining POWERSET, SS went to the solution of CONST. Here she immediately saw an iterative plan for performing CONST: "I've got to take successive CARs of the second argument and each time CONS the CAR of SETT into that set and the final value of CONST will just be the set of all those CONSes." SS refined this iterative conception further into a plan to perform a CONS operation with the first element of the input list and to make the function CONST repeat on the rest of the list. She then wrote two separate segments of code to instantiate this plan. First, she wrote (CONS SIL (CAR LIS)), which satisfies the first component of her plan. Next, she wrote the recursive call (CONST SIL (CDR LIS)) which satisfies the plan to make CONST repeat. Our simulation, which was provided with a representation of SS's plan for iterative solution, wrote the same code segments. The simulation first applied a production coding CONS and its arguments (learned in previous sessions). It then applied the production C2 learned in SETDIFF to code the recursive call. We should point out that the semantics of production C2 imply "something that causes repetition to happen," and this appears to be the meaning SS associated with the recursive call that she coded.

At this point in her protocol, SS decided to combine the results produced by her two code segements and she used UNION to perform this operation. Our simulation also selected UNION to combine function results by applying the newly learned production C5. The code produced by SS and the simulation was:

```
(DEFUN CONST (SIL LIS)
    (UNION (CONS SIL (CAR LIS))(CONST SIL (CDR LIS))))
```

This solution lacks a feature critical to all recursive programs. It does not specify a terminating condition for the recursive process. Without a terminating condition the above function leads to an infinite recursion. It is interesting that the subject notes that her definition of CONST differs from previous recent function definitions in that it does not have a COND structure, but is adamant that such a structure is not needed.

Note that the application of C4 in this case would have led to the correct control structure. We have assumed that the reason why C4 did not apply can be traced to the way SS identified recursive programs from problem specifications. We believe that she characterized SETDIFF, SUBSET, and POWERSET as recursive functions because they were implicitly identified as such in the textbook's problem section on recursion. CONST, however, was simply identified by SS's tutor as a helper function to POWERSET. It has been noted in other studies (e.g., Larkin, McDermott, Simon, & Simon, 1980) that novices often have the skills required to solve a problem, but are inept at characterizing the problem features in an appropriate manner to evoke those skills. Thus it is not enough to just have the right operators; they have to be invoked in the right circumstances.

SS and our simulation tried out the above version of CONST, and an error message was generated indicating infinite recursion. By using LISP facilities which trace out the recursive operation of a function, SS's tutor pointed out that the function did not stop when the input list LIS was empty. This led SS and the simulation back to the goal of redefining the function. This time SS characterized the function as having two cases: when the input set is empty, and in the else case. She and the simulation then each set goals to determine and code the conditional clause for the (NULL LIS) case, and to simply copy the already written recursive code into the action for the else case.

The remainder of the protocol was devoted to working through her misconceptions about the code. One of SS's misconceptions concerned the use of UNION to combine the results of (CONS SIL (CAR LIS)) with the recursive call to CONST. The function UNION combines the elements from two lists into a single list. However the appropriate action in this case is to insert the result of (CONS SIL (CAR LIS)) into the result of the recursive call. To illustrate this more clearly, the UNION of the lists (A B) and (C) is (A B C). CONSing the same lists yields ((A B) C). This difference often confuses students (Anderson & Jeffries, 1985). When SS ran the version of CONST which contained UNION, she obtained an output list that differed from the desired result. Her tutor assisted her by pointing out that the terminating recursive case would return the empty set NIL, and that the most appropriate plan was to insert elements returned by (CONS SIL (CAR LIS)) into the result of recursive calls. Given this information, both SS and our simulation substituted CONS for UNION to produce the correct code:

```
(DEFUN CONST (SIL LIS)
    (COND ((NULL LIS) ()))
        (T (CONS (CONS SIL (CAR LIS))
            (CONST SIL (CDR LIS)))))))
```

The important production compiled from this final episode of debugging is:

C6:   IF the goal is to code a relation adding result1 and result2
            and the code occurs in the context of writing a function
            and the result2 is produced by the function repeating
                an operation on a list
            and the function returns NIL when given NIL as an ar-
            gument
       THEN write (CONS result1 result2)

Thus, the simulation has learned a rule which uses CONS to add data elements to a list constructed by CDR-recursion. This is a fairly standard code
pattern seen in CDR-recursive functions (see Soloway & Woolf, 1980). Thus
we see the learning of another important component of recursive
programming.

SUMMARY

This POWERSET episode gives further evidence for the gradual accrual
of a set of productions that will adequately apply CDR-recursion. We see
the formulation of a basic CDR-recursion procedure involving two cases — a
terminating case and a recursive case. The latter production is highly similar to the expert's general recursion production P1. We should note however
that the productions learned in POWERSET do not generalize to the full
space of CDR-recursive functions. Although SS got noticably better at coding later recursion problems, there were still many unfamiliar patterns and
instances that forced her to fall back on general problem-solving skills.

POWERSET also provides another example of the importance of analogical processes in LISP problem-solving and learning. This time, a complex interrelation of worked-out concrete examples provides the source of
the mapping. However, because the goals regarding the exact comparisons
to be made were generated by an external source (SS's tutor), they are not
compiled into any productions which specify a more general means of
characterizing recursive relations.

GENERAL CONCLUSIONS

We see a fair bit of evidence for our analysis of the difficulty of recursion
in these protocols. Specifically:

1. Recursion is difficult because it is unfamiliar. The subject is forced
to try to work by analogy from examples.

2. Recursion is difficult because of imprecise instruction. The subject was really forced to learn almost everything from her mistakes. An interesting issue is what would happened if the text had provided her directly with the rules that she instead had to induce. These rules would have been in English, rather than in production form, and so there would still be some learning in converting them; but we would predict more rapid and less painful and error-ridden learning.

3. Recursion is difficult because of interference from other methods of solution. SS initially characterized recursion as a form of iteration. This eventually led to her failure to correctly code CONST on her first attempt.

4. Recursion is difficult because it is complex. The subject is still learning the patterns that define the application of CDR-recursion to various problems. It is also worth noting that she is only learning about CDR-recursion. In other research we have done, we have shown that there is little transfer from CDR-recursion to other types of recursive functions.

5. Recursion is difficult because it is exacerbated by the difficulty of LISP. We saw numerous examples, particularly in POWERSET, in which the subject's difficulty with the nonrecursive aspects of LISP programming complicated the learning of recursion.

It is interesting that nowhere in these protocols from SS do we find her trying to perform a recursive mental operation. This is further evidence for our claim that the difficulty of recursive programming does not directly arise from the difficulty of performing recursive mental operations.

Finally, we would like to note that the success of GRAPES in simulating the protocols of SS is further evidence for our theory of how LISP functions are typically programmed. Specifically, the basic flow of control is top-down problem decomposition. Initial problems are solved by structural analogy to worked-out examples. Subjects summarize these solutions by new compiled operators. These operators are keys to the solution of later problems.

ACKNOWLEDGMENT
This research was supported by the Personnel and Training Research Programs, Psychological Services Division, Office of Naval Research, under Contract No.: N00014-81-C-0335.

REFERENCES

Anderson, J. R. (1983). *The Architecture of Cognition.* Cambridge, MA: Harvard University Press.

Anderson, J. R. (1976). *Language, Memory, and Thought*. Hillsdale, NJ: Lawrence Erlbaum Associates.

Anderson, J. R., Farrell, R., & Sauers, R. (1982) *Learning to plan in LISP* (Tech. Rep. ONR-82-2). Pittsburgh, PA.: Carnegie–Mellon University.

Anderson, J. R., Farrell, R., & Sauers, R. (1984). Learning to program LISP. *Cognitive Science*, 8, 87–129.

Anderson J. R., & Jeffries, R. (1985). Novice LISP errors: Undetected losses of information from working memory. *Human Computer Interaction*, 1, 107–131.

Brown, J. S., & VanLehn, K. (1980). Repair theory: A generative theory of bugs in procedural skills. *Cognitive Science*, 4, 379–426.

Card, S. K., Moran, T. P., & Newell, A. (1983). *The psychology of human–computer interaction*. Hillsdale, NJ: Lawrence Erlbaum Associates.

Dresher, B. E., & Hornstein, N. (1976). On some supposed contributions of artificial intelligence to the scientific study of language. *Cognition*, 4, 321–398.

Larkin, J. H., McDermott, J., Simon, D. P., & Simon, H. A. (1980). Models of competence in solving physics problems. *Cognitive Science*, 4, 317–345.

Newell, A. (1973). Production systems: Models of control structures. In W. G. Chase (Ed.), *Visual information processing* (pp. 463–526). New York: Academic Press.

Rosenbloom, P. S., & Newell, A. (1983). The chunking of goal hierarchies: A generalized model of practice. In R. S. Michalski (Ed.), *Proceedings of the International Machine Learning Workshop* (pp. 183–197). University of Illinois at Urbana-Champaign.

Sauers, R., & Farrell, R. (1982). *GRAPES user's manual* (Tech. Rep. ONR-82-3). Pittsburgh, PA.: Carnegie–Mellon University.

Siklossy, L. (1976). *Let's talk LISP*. Englewood Cliffs, New Jersey: Prentice-Hall.

Soloway, E. L., & Woolf, B. (1980). *From problems to programs via plans: The content and structure of knowledge for introductory LISP programming* (Tech. Rep. Coins 80–19). Amherst: University of Massachusetts.

6 A Model of Software Design

Beth Adelson
Tufts University

Elliot Soloway
Yale University

1. INTRODUCTION

In this chapter we present a cognitive model of the process of software design. Our goal was to develop a model of expert problem-solving skills for a task in which domain knowledge played an extensive role. In order to observe problem-solving skills we provided expert designers with a challenging task. Otherwise we only would have seen them fall back upon "routine cognitive skill" (Card, Moran, & Newell, 1983). In order to allow domain knowledge to play its role, we developed a task which was within our subjects' domain of expertise; we therefore presented these expert software designers with a problem which was both novel and complex, and from a domain familiar to them. We collected and analyzed the protocols taken from our subjects; and as a result of our protocol analysis we have built a model which unites several recurring behaviors into a coherent whole. The behaviors we account for include the building of mental models, mental simulation, and balanced development.

Organization

In Section 2 we present a description of our methodology. In Section 3 we present several recurrent and intriguing behaviors. In Section 4 we present our model of expert design. In Section 5 we present some issues our model and our data raise.

2. METHOD

Subjects.   Three expert software designers served as subjects.[1] Each of our experts had worked for at least eight years in commercial settings designing a wide variety of software.

Procedure.   We presented each of the designers with the following design task:

> **TASK** — Design an Electronic Mail System (EMS) around the following primitives: READ, REPLY, SEND, DELETE, SAVE, EDIT, and LIST-HEADERS. The goal is to get to the level of pseudocode that could be used by professional programmers to produce a running program. The mail system will run on a very large, fast machine so hardware considerations are not an issue.

The task we gave the subjects had several important properties: (a) It was nontrivial, requiring close to two hours of the subjects' time. (b) It was novel; none of our designers had designed a solution to the problem previously. These two properties meant that we would have the opportunity to see not only "routine cognitive skill," but some problem-solving as well. (c) The problem we chose was similar to the types of problems which the subjects had to deal with professionally. As a result we would be able to see them turn to already existing knowledge stores.

3.   RECURRENT BEHAVIOR LEADING TO OUR MODEL OF THE DESIGN PROCESS

Here we present behaviors which we found our subjects exhibited repeatedly. All of the designers generated a model-in-progress of the system they were attempting to design. These working models were internal representations of the mailer as a functional, but not yet fully specified entity. The behaviors presented in following pages reflect the way in which our experts manipulated and transformed the mental model in the process of creating the design.

Observation I: Transformation of Mental Models

The use of mental models was quite pervasive. The designers used them throughout the design process, even when their conception of the problem

---

[1]The protocols from all three subjects were analyzed. In Appendix I we present a long section of the protocol of S1. S1's protocol is representative of the protocols of all three subjects and is focussed on most heavily in this chapter.

was still quite abstract. The models began as very abstract versions of a mail system and then became increasingly concrete as the design progressed. The following quotes from designer S3 illustrate the progression from an abstract to a concrete model. Early in the task S3 said, "What we have here is information flowing through a system". We consider this description to be abstract in that it specifies neither the nature of the information flowing through the system nor the mechanism which implements the flow; the description is an accurate description of a mail system, but it is vague with respect to implementation details. At 20 minutes into the task S3 said:

> I'm making an assumption down here . . . . There's some stream of input come in. I've found the key word "mail" embedded in there. I'm assuming that the user has put blanks in between words. So, having done that, presumably in going from one end of the string to the other I've also found other strings of characters which I haven't analyzed for what this means yet, but I've got them separated out . . . .

We consider this description to be concrete in that it specifies some of the implementation details of the data and processes of the mail system. The designer addresses the nature of the data flowing through the system, referring to it as a "stream of input" in the form of "strings of characters." He or she addresses the processes of the mail system as well. When S3 states, "I've found the key word *mail* embedded in the {input stream}," he is referring to a token extraction which must take place in order to control the flow of information which he spoke of in the previous quote.

Observation II: Balanced Development

At any point in time, the resolved processing modules[2] of the design were all defined at approximately the same level of detail. The following quotes are representative of this phenomenon:

> Addresses, routing of messages are *all hidden inside in some of these seven primitives*. The primitives are working on messages as an object. I say send a message — that primitive gives me, it implies there's enough power in the system in order to send [the message] or not. *So I don't have to worry about that.*

---

[2]We define a processing module as an element which has a clearly coherent function within the system being designed. For example the commands given to the subjects in the problem statement (READ, SEND, SAVE, etc.) are all processing modules. Additionally, these modules may also be decomposed into coherent submodules. For instance SAVE may be decomposed into two modules, a "write" module which writes the message under consideration into a file in memory, and an "erase" module which erases the message from the user's store of messages which have just arrived.

This quote from S1 shows an important aspect of balanced development.

> We must be able to prepare, send, receive. In receiving, a number of choices and decisions have to be made as to the disposition of it. *We'll get into that later.* The system must be able to store.

Here we see that although S1 is concerned with going into greater detail in order to achieve a complete definition of "receive", he is even more concerned with first dealing with all of the issues at the level of detail at which he is currently working. This tension between processes that push the design ahead, and processes which insist on taking care of the current issue, results in balanced development. The successful management of this tension seems to be one of the marks of expertise.

Note also that when S2 said the following he was transforming his model from an abstract to a concrete state, but he was also using the notion of balanced development as a guiding principle in the transformation process:

> This will help us structure our solution to the problem at a higher level. Then we will go into each one of the building blocks that help us write the processing step at each step in the state diagram.

In Section 5 we discuss the mechanism which underlies balanced development and how it is realized in our model.

Observation III: Notes

We found that the expert designers would frequently make "notes" to themselves about things to remember later in the design process. These notes had to do with constraints, partial solutions, or potential inconsistencies which eventually needed to be handled in order to produce a successful design. An example from S1's notes follows:

> At this stage, I need the functional specifications. *I'll come back and do that in a little while*, time permitting, and carry on making some other assumptions here. Store, Read, OK. That's good enough for the user view of it.

The reason that these notes were not handled immediately was that they were concerned with a level of detail which was greater than the level of detail of the current state of the design. This means that incorporating them into the design when they were thought of would have caused a departure from balanced development. We also found that the expert designers would be reminded of previously made notes once the current state had reached a level of detail which would allow the note to be incorporated into the design without violating balanced development.

Observation IV:
Simulation Runs of Mental Models

We observed all of our subjects repeatedly conducting mental simulation runs of their partially completed designs. They would consult the state of the design and then conduct a simulation of it at its current level of abstraction. Thus we observed simulations that became increasingly concrete as the design progressed. For example, in S3's early simulation he saw the mailer as "information flowing through a system"; this is an accurate but very weakly specified instantiation of a mail system. In a later simulation, when considering his module for the READ function, S1 drew a state diagram for all of the states which could be reached from READ. These simulations, which also appear in the protocols of Kant and Newell (1982), have a central functionality as explained in the next section.

4. A MODEL OF THE DESIGN PROCESS

In order to give the reader an overview of the nature of the model we are proposing, we want to point out several of its properties. First, the process of design is captured via goals and operators interacting with a knowledge base. Second, we have defined the goals and operators as ones which are general to design, rather than specific to the current task. Third, we have structured the atomic level operators so that they are able to access domain-specific knowledge acquired through experience. Together, the second and third points enable both general processes and domain-specific knowledge to play critical roles in producing any particular design. Finally, the reader will notice that the model has very little to say about recovering from errors. This follows from the almost error-free performance of our subjects.

Our model of the design process has three major components:

1. *The Sketchy Model.* This is the working representation of the object being designed. It is manipulated and expanded upon during the design process.
2. *The Knowledge Base.* This reflects the various types of information needed to produce a successful design. It includes knowledge about strategies useful to the design process, and examples of familiar mail systems and how they function.
3. *The Goals and Operators.* These are the mechanisms which underlie the design process.

In what follows we present a description of these components of the model and of the relationships among them.

4.1. The Sketchy Model

The main representation used by our model of the design process is the "Sketchy Model" (MODEL). This construct reflects the subjects' use of mental models. The MODEL resides in working memory. The MODEL is initially sketchy in that the expert has not yet specified its functionality down to a level of detail which would be sufficient to produce an implementable program.

4.2. The Knowledge Base

An expert designed draws on many types of knowledge both about the designer process and about objects being designed. For example:

- An expert designer has and uses knowledge about strategies which can be used to produce a successful design. An example of such a strategy, which was used by our subjects, was to think about the system as it would appear to the user. The following quote illustrates S1 drawing on this knowledge as he begins to simulate the states that a user moves through as he enters the mail system:

    "O.K. Let me start looking at the states of a user first of all. How in the world is this going to be seen from the view of the user?

- Our subjects used knowledge about exemplars of mail systems in order to add the properties of these exemplars to their designs. The following quote from S1 illustrates the use of a property of an exemplar in order to fill out the design.

    "I think of Unix, the dead-letter concept—the store of messages that we can't do anything with if we want to store them."

- Our designers also possessed knowledge about functional requirements of systems in general. An example of this type of knowledge is provided in the following words from S1, noting that issues of concurrency must be resolved:

    "Throughout the system, it is going to be handling concurrency, so that is the initial event I need to address.

The purpose of these stores is to provide the general goals of the model with the necessary task-specific information.

4.3. Goals and Operators

Here we describe the goals and operators of the model and the relationship between them. Figure 6.1 illustrates the hierarchical relationship that exists among the goals. The description of the goals and operators that follows is organized as a breadth-first traversal of the goal tree. Appendix I presents a protocol onto which the goals of the model have been mapped.

Goal: EXPAND NEXT LEVEL

The entire design process is driven by the repeated achievement of the top-most goal, EXPAND NEXT LEVEL (EXPAND).[3] The purpose of EXPAND is to transform the model of the object being designed from its original abstract state into the concrete goal state. Each successive achievement of EXPAND not only carries the design further from the abstract toward the concrete, but is also an appropriately sized step from the last. We argue that this systematic choice of appropriate-sized steps is the underlying cause of the observed balanced development.

As just mentioned, EXPAND is repeatedly achieved until the design is complete. Each repetition of EXPAND can be viewed as an episode result-ing in the integration of new information into the current model. Processes are shown in upper-case letters, inputs and outputs in italics. EXPAND results in the MODEL becoming increasingly well specified after each suc-cessive episode. For example, in an early episode S3 defined and then in-tegrated three categories of EMS functions: a category that sent mail, a category that received mail, and a category that moved mail out of an "in-box." The successful integration that occurred in this first episode allowed him to go on and further specify his MODEL in the next episode. In this next episode he removed one of his original categories, the one for moving mail out of the "in-box," and replaced it with the more specific functions *save* and *delete*. These two new functions were then integrated into the MODEL.

The three sub-goals underlying EXPAND are:

1. EVALUATE CURRENT SKETCHY MODEL (EVAL). The purpose of EVAL is to assess the differences between the behaviors of the current and the goal states and to make some decisions about how to close that gap. First the differences between the components of the current and the goal states are evaluated in terms of what processing components need to be better specified in the current MODEL. As a result of this evaluation, the design-er understands what needs to be worked on. Therefore, an appropriate view of the EMS can be chosen. Finally, using this view as a constraint, descrip-tions are formed of the information that needs to be retrieved and added to the MODEL. These descriptions reflect a systematic, incremental increase over the level of detail just dealt with. Since the descriptions formed here act as the input to the next subgoal, the retrieval and integration that fol-low are all constrained to be at the appropriate level of detail.

---

[3]The names of goals are capitalized.

GOAL HIERARCHY FOR THE DESIGN PROCESS

EXPAND

EVAL   PREPARE   INTEGRATE

DIFF   CHOOSE   RETRIEVE   CHECK   INTERACTIONS   EXPLORE   CHECK

STRAT   DESCRIP   INTERNAL   EXTERNAL   COMPLETENESS   INTERNAL   EXTERNAL   COMPLETENESS

KEY:
EXPAND = EXPAND NEXT LEVEL
EVAL = EVALUATE CURRENT SKETCHY MODEL
PREPARE = PREPARE NEXT LEVEL OF CURRENT SKETCHY MODEL
INTEGRATE = INTEGRATE INTO CURRENT LEVEL OF SKETCHY MODEL
DIFF = DETERMINE DIFFERENCES BETWEEN CURRENT AND GOAL STATE
CHOOSE = CHOOSE A MEANS
RETRIEVE = RETRIEVE INFORMATION RELEVANT TO THE CURRENT SKETCHY MODEL
CHECK = CHECK CURRENT MODEL
INTERACTIONS = INSTANTIATE INTERACTIONS BETWEEN ELEMENTS OF SKETCHY MODEL
EXPLORE = EXPLORE PROPERTIES OF ELEMENTS OF THE CURRENT SKETCHY MODEL
STRAT = PICK A STRATEGY
DESCRIP = FORM A DESCRIPTION
INTERNAL = INTERNAL CONSISTENCY
EXTERNAL = EXTERNAL CONSISTENCY

FIGURE 6.1. Goal hierarchy of the model of the design process.

2. PREPARE NEXT LEVEL OF THE CURRENT SKETCHY MODEL (PREPARE). The purpose of PREPARE is to retrieve a new set of elements which will then be included in the MODEL in order to increase its specificity. These elements may be new functional components of the model (such as a READ module) or properties not yet specified in already existing components (such as the nature of the parameter for READ). PREPARE uses the description formed by EVAL and the state of the MODEL in order to retrieve the new set of elements.

3. INTEGRATE CURRENT LEVEL OF THE SKETCHY MODEL (INTEGRATE). The purpose of INTEGRATE is to incorporate into the design the elements chosen by the proceeding PREPARE. This is done by simulating the function of each element in the context of the others. This simulation is necessary since the task is novel, which means that the designer has not previously seen this set of elements functioning together and cannot therefore predict the interactions which will occur.

We present the control structure of EXPAND as follows, noting that EVAL and PREPARE may be triggered repeatedly until a sufficient amount of information has been accumulated, at which point INTEGRATE will fire.

To achieve EXPAND NEXT LEVEL

Repeatedly
   Achieve EVALUATE CURRENT SKETCHY MODEL
Achieve PREPARE FOR NEXT LEVEL OF THE CURRENT SKETCHY MODEL
Until all elements at current level of detail have been retrieved

Achieve INTEGRATE CURRENT LEVEL OF THE SKETCHY MODEL

Integrating through EVAL and PREPARE before attempting to achieve INTEGRATE captures the alternating retrieval and integration of sets of elements which we observed in the protocols. An example of waiting to retrieve a set of elements before integrating the entire set (rather than integrating each element as it is retrieved) is provided by the first six minutes of the protocol presented in Appendix I. There we see S1 first retrieve several elements: prepare, send, receive, and store. Not until this set is retrieved does he begin to integrate them.

The chain of events which comprise an episode is presented in the following diagram. There we see that the designer uses his *current model* as input to EVAL, which results in outputting a *description* of what information should be added to the *model*. PREPARE then takes this output and uses it to retrieve a *set of elements* whose properties will add the appropriate detail to the *model*. These elements are then integrated by INTE-GRATE. This results in a new, more specific *model* at the conclusion of the episode.

Current sketchy model— > EVAL— > *description*— > PREPARE— > *set of elements*— > INTEGRATE— > *new sketchy model*[4]

Goal: EVALUATE CURRENT SKETCHY MODEL

The purpose of EVAL is to evaluate the current state of the designed object in order to form a description of the objects PREPARE needs to retrieve. This result is accomplished by achieving the following two subgoals in succession.

1. DETERMINE DIFFERENCES BETWEEN CURRENT AND GOAL STATE (DIFF). DIFF compares the behavior of the current MODEL to the desired behavior of the goal state, and then returns differences between the two in terms of what components need to be elaborated in the current MODEL.[5]
2. CHOOSE A MEANS (CHOOSE). The purpose of CHOOSE is to formulate a description of what information needs to be added to the current MODEL. The description may be of a processing module that is missing, a property that needs to be added to an existing module, or some global constraint that must be incorporated. The description is arrived at by the following sequence of events: The output of DIFF is used to determine what, at this point, will be a useful way to view the EMS. This view is then used as a constraint in forming a description of what to retrieve next. CHOOSE is achieved through the subgoals of:
    a. PICK A STRATEGY (STRAT). As input, STRAT takes the differences between the current and the goal state DIFF returned. Then, using task-specific knowledge about the nature of the particular object being designed, STRAT selects a strategy (a view of the EMS) which will decrease the differences. Picking a view is useful as an aid in decreasing the differences, because it uncovers properties that currently are lacking. The following illustrate the task-specific rules used by STRAT to form a strategy:
        • The mail system can be viewed as a set of functions and a set of data objects.

---

[4]Processes are shown in upper-case letters, inputs and outputs in italics.

[5]Simulation is the appropriate mechanism for determining these differences.

- The mail system can be viewed from the perspective of the user.
- The mail system can be viewed from the perspective of the operating system.

b. FORM A DESCRIPTION (DESCRIP). DESCRIP takes the strategy output by STRAT and forms descriptions of elements to be retrieved. Task specific knowledge is used in forming the descriptions of the items to be retrieved, since DESCRIP has rules as to what type of information should be retrieved at different stages in the process. These stage-specific retrieval rules control the size of the change in level of detail dealt with on each episode. As a result, the phase-specific retrieval rules are the mechanisms which underlie balanced development. The following illustrate the task-specific rules used by DESCRIP in forming descriptions for PREPARE:

- In the early stages of design, retrieve relevant exemplars of other mail systems from long-term memory.
- In the middle stages of design, retrieve relevant exemplars of mail functions and mail objects (messages) from long-term memory.
- In the late stages of design, retrieve relevant exemplars of specific properties of mail functions and mail objects from long-term memory.

Here we present a single excerpt from the protocol of S1. It has been divided into two parts which illustrate DIFF and STRAT respectively. In the first, as DIFF is triggered, S1 considers his current definition of a mail message and then compares this to what needs to be known about a message in order for the system to function properly:

> I'm thinking, what is the form of these [mail messages]. When we save them off in a file like that, are we going to save them as mail objects, or are we going to just append them onto some file where they're not distinguishable...

The following part of the excerpt illustrates STRAT. Now that S1 has evaluated what properties messages must have in a fully functioning EMS, STRAT is triggered so that S1 can select a view of the system in order to retrieve appropriate information; this will help him elaborate his MODEL. As a result of STRAT's triggering, he takes the operating system's view of the EMS and so the meaning of READ as "read a line" comes to mind:

> I now need to start making some decisions on that. Let me look back at my primitives.

Read.
Read a mail message . . . .
as well as to *read a line of something.*

Here we present control structure of EVAL:

To achieve EVALUATE CURRENT SKETCHY MODEL STATE
  achieve DETERMINE DIFFERENCES BETWEEN CURRENT
  AND GOAL
  achieve CHOOSE A MEANS

Goal: *PREPARE NEXT LEVEL OF CURRENT SKETCHY MODEL*

The purpose of PREPARE is to retrieve information that will be incorporated into the design during the next stage. Here objects are gathered in order to be assembled in the simulation done in the next stage of the design process. In achieving PREPARE the designer uses the description formed in the preceding EVAL and therefore only retrieves information appropriate to the level of detail of the current MODEL. Using the description formed by EVAL constrains the model to conform to balanced development.

PREPARE consists of the following two subgoals which are achieved in order. The sequence may be repeated if all of the information relevant to the current level of specificity has not been gathered after the first retrieval:

1. RETRIEVE INFORMATION RELEVANT TO THE CURRENT SKETCHY MODEL (RETRIEVE). RETRIEVE considers the descriptions passed to it by DESCRIP and fetches the described information from long-term memory. Retrieval continues until all of the information relevant to the description has been retrieved.
2. CHECK CURRENT MODEL (CHECK). CHECK takes the elements just retrieved by RETRIEVE and checks that they form an appropriate set, given the current and the goal states. This is done through the subgoals of:
   a. INTERNAL CONSISTENCY (INTERNAL). INTERNAL checks that the set of elements being considered do not have conflicting functions. For example, that READ does not cause a message to be deleted, which would prevent it from then being saved.
   b. EXTERNAL CONSISTENCY (EXTERNAL). EXTERNAL checks that adding the properties currently being considered will not move the functionality of the model further from the goal state in some unexpected way.
   c. COMPLETENESS (COMPLETENESS). COMPLETENESS

checks that given the current specifity of the Sketchy Model, all elements are present. This contributes to the balanced development of the design.

The following quote from S1 is broken into three sections. Each illustrates one of PREPARE's subgoals. First RETRIEVE triggers as the subject considers what functions the mailer should have:

> We must be able to prepare, send, receive.

Next COMPLETENESS triggers and the subject checks what else should, at this point, be included as part of receive:

> In receiving, a number of choices and decisions have to be made as to the disposition of it. We'll get into that later.

Then INTERNAL and EXTERNAL trigger and he checks that his conception of receiving is internally and externally consistent:

> The system must be able to store them, the system must be able to handle abnormalities throughout it.

Following is the control structure of PREPARE. We see that RETRIEVE and CHECK may be triggered repeatedly until all of the information that conforms to the description formed by DESCRIP has been retrieved:

To achieve PREPARE
    Repeatedly
        Achieve RETRIEVE (Using the description formed by EVAL)
        Achieve CHECK CURRENT MODEL
    Until all elements specified by EVAL's description have been retrieved

Goal: *INTEGRATE INTO CURRENT LEVEL OF SKETCHY MODEL*

The purpose of INTEGRATE is to integrate the information retrieved during the preceding PREPARE into the MODEL. This is done by the subgoals:

1. INSTANTIATE INTERACTIONS BETWEEN ELEMENTS OF SKETCHY MODEL INTERACTIONS). INTERACTIONS causes a simulation of each element in the MODEL to be run. A simulation is necessary because elements are being combined in a novel way and so their interactions can only be predicted in context. Various types of interactions need to be explored such as enablement (**READ** ena-

bles **REPLY**), disenablement (**DELETE** precludes **SAVE**), and causation.

2. EXPLORE PROPERTIES OF ELEMENTS OF THE CURRENT SKETCHY MODEL (EXPLORE). During the simulation the existence of poorly understood elements will trigger the goal EXPLORE, which causes retrieval to be done from long-term memory. Retrieval is only done until the element is understood, or until no elements are retrieved which are relevant to the description formed earlier by DESCRIP. The presence of the description constrains the model behavior, and this results in balanced development. If retrieval is constrained and therefore stops before the element is understood, the element is placed in a demon which will then fire when the level of detail of the sketchy model matches the level of detail needed to understand the element.

3. CHECK CURRENT MODEL (CHECK). As a result of the simulation, each element is again checked by the subgoals of CHECK: INTERNAL, EXTERNAL, and COMPLETENESS. This check ensures that the properties which are uncovered when the element is functioning *in the context of the other elements* are consistent with the properties desired in the goal state. This check is necessary since side effects may arise in this novel context. These side effects cannot be anticipated out of context when CHECK CURRENT MODEL is triggered during the preceding PREPARE, since this object has not been designed before. That is, when information must be combined from different scripts, routine cognitive skill will not suffice and simulation becomes necessary.

The following diagram reproduces the state diagram gradually drawn by S1 during the following excerpt from his protocol.

LIST-HEADERS — > READ — > INITIAL STATE

The excerpt is divided into four parts, each illustrating a subgoal of INTEGRATE. The excerpt begins when S1 is in the process of simulating his current MODEL. He has just considered the **LIST-HEADERS** function and will now trigger INSTANTIATE in order to examine the control flow relationship between LIST-HEADERS and READ. S1 draws:

LIST-HEADERS

S1 says:

This [**LIST-HEADERS**] brings him to new state where he knows what mail he has—he can choose at this state to exit and get out to some other place we don't know yet where it is. Going to read mail, read monitoring.

He expands the diagram to:

LIST-HEADERS—>READ

INTERNAL is now triggered and we see S1 checking the effects of **READ**. S1 says:

> When he reads it, he's got to make a disposition of it, what he's got to do with it. Most of those are going to get him back to his initial state. Whatever disposition we decide—destroy, hold, reply, whatever else will get him back there.

He further expands the diagram to:

LIST-HEADERS—>READ—>INITIAL STATE

At this point S1 does not fully understand the states leading out of **READ**. As a result, EXPLORE is triggered; we see that he is about to unpack **READ** but stops, since the descriptions previously established by DESCRIP are still constraining EXPLORE. As a result, a demon is created to store the suspended issues.

> I think it will be very obvious now that I've got to decide what those functions are from the users point of view before I can continue much farther with this design. So let me note that.
> (Makes a note)
> At this stage, I need the functional specifications. I'll come back and do that in a little while, time permitting . . . .

S1 now completes the current INTEGRATE as COMPLETENESS is satisfied:

> . . . . and carry on making some other assumptions here. Store, Read. OK, that's good enough for the user view of it.

Here we present the control structure of INTEGRATE:

To achieve INTEGRATE INTO CURRENT LEVEL OF SKETCHY MODEL
    For each element in the current Sketchy Model begin:
      achieve INTERACTIONS

```
    if the current element is poorly understood then
        achieve EXPLORE
    achieve CHECK CURRENT MODEL
end
```

5. DISCUSSION

In what follows we will comment on several issues raised by our research:

- First the simulation process raises two questions: Why is balanced development found so frequently in expert behavior? What role does it play? In order to answer these questions, we need to examine another behavior that has been observed repeatedly: namely, that experts check their design-in-progress by conducting simulations of the design. In order to effectively carry out a simulation, it is important to have *all the elements in the simulation at the same level of detail*. If an input has been insufficiently specified by a preceding element, the level of detail of the input needed to simulate the current element will not be present. Additionally, if an input is too highly specified, in the worst case the current element will not be able to function and in the best case extra computation will be needed to bring the input to the appropriate level of abstraction. If the development of the designed object is balanced, elements will be generated which are at the same level of description, and effective simulation will be possible.

- How is balanced development achieved? The decision of how to increase the level of detail dealt with from one episode to the next happens during DESCRIP. DESCRIP forms a description of what needs to be added to the MODEL, given the current state in the design process. This one decision then constrains the way that the design is elaborated during RETRIEVE and EXPLORE, as it constrains the nature of the elements that can be retrieved. Balanced development then results, because the only elements that can then be retrieved are those which conform to the level of detail chosen by DESCRIP. In our model, balanced development is achieved by the repeated firing of a single decision rule which then constrains the choice of elements at each point in the design. The decision rule fires and the effects are then felt through the remainder of the episode. Note that balanced development is achieved implicitly rather than explicitly, as the rule concerning what description to form says "at this point retrieve something of type x," rather than "retrieve something only if it is in keeping with balanced development."

- We believe that note should be taken of a particular aspect of the behavior termed breadth-first *expansion* of the problem statement (Jeffries et al., 1981). We suggest that the behavior that has been observed should be viewed as an *integration* rather than an expansion. We believe this is the case because in our protocols subjects first retrieved sets of elements and then integrated these sets only after they had been retrieved. (For example, in the first 6 minutes of the protocol in the Appendix at the end of this chapter, S1 retrieves information. In the next 5 minutes he integrates it.) The reason that the observed behavior has been interpreted as breadth-first expansion is that integrating an already retrieved set of elements, each of which is at the same level of detail, is an orderly process which gives rise to a breadth-first behavior. We feel that it is more useful to view breadth-first expansion simply as an integration which is enabled by a prior, appropriately constrained retrieval. We then need to address separately the unanswered issue of whether or not the prior retrieval is breadth-first.

• We mentioned earlier that since the task we chose was from the designers' domain of expertise and was also novel, the designer understood the elements of the design but had not previously used them in concert. The simulation process became, to a certain extent, necessary since with a novel *combination* of elements it was not possible to predict what interactions would occur. A comparison of the range of tasks from those which are totally novel to those which are totally routine would be an interesting one, as it would allow us to see on the one hand to what extent simulation can be relied upon, and on the other hand to what extent it can be done away with.

• We feel our model is domain-independent in the sense that its goal structure would be appropriate for modeling a large class of design tasks. There is a sense, however, in which it is not domain-independent since ultimately the goals can only be achieved by operating on knowledge bases which are relevant to the particular task at hand. If ur claim of domain independence is correct, we should be able to apply this model to other types of design problems. We are planning to evaluate this claim by studying hardware designers.

• A major issue that our research leaves unresolved concerns the mechanisms that facilitate the interaction of the domain-independent model with the domain specific knowledge. There are in fact a number of related subissues here. For example:

  • All the operators that realize the goals at the leaves of the goal hierarchy tree access domain-specific knowledge; for example, the operators for the goals RETRIEVE, EXPLORE, and INSTANTIATE must access long-term memory. How do these operators gain access to the "appropriate" knowledge? Similarly, how do the evaluation operators for the goal CHECK CURRENT MODEL access the relevant knowledge?

  • Notice that during simulation information is combined in novel ways. How is this integration accomplished? Since the design task we gave our subjects was one for which they did not have a complete "canned" design, they needed to integrate pieces of other stored designs in order to produce an effective solution to the assigned task. We do not understand the mechanism used here. In addition, a piece of one previously stored design could usually be easily combined with a piece of another stored design: The output of a piece from one served as the input to a piece from another. Occasionally, however, this combination process was problematic, such as when, for instance, one function in an otherwise well understood set was less familiar than the others. The conditions under which the recombination of knowledge is easy or difficult need to be explored.

We plan to focus on these issues in subsequent research.

6. CONCLUDING REMARKS

We have presented here a model of the design process. This model attempts to Account for behaviors that we, as well as others, have repeatedly observed in analyzing protocols taken from expert designers (Atwood, Turner, Ramsey, & Hooper, 1979; Collins & Gentner, 1982; Jeffries, Turner, Polson, & Atwood, 1981; Kant & Newell, 1982).

While the domain-independent aspect of our model is intellectually pleasing, the interaction of the model with domain-specific knowledge is critically important and remains to be worked out. Toward this end, we are planning to collect protocols of expert designers performing a variety of design tasks (e.g., a completely novel task and a completely routine task). Such data should enable us to develop richer, more fine-grained models of the design process. Understanding "design" is a major undertaking; in complementing work that has already appeared, we see our effort as continuing the progress toward this goal.

ACKNOWLEDGMENTS

We gratefully acknowledge the contribution of Ruven Brooks to this project: His energy and support have played an important role in this resarch. We would also like to thank Larry Birnbaum and Jim Spohrer for their detailed and insightful comments. This research was supported by grants from ITT and the National Science Foundation.

REFERENCES

Atwood, M., Turner, A., Ramsey, R., & Hooper, J. (1979). *An exploratory study of the cog-*

nitive structures underlying the comprehension of software design problems. (ARI Tech. Report #392). SAI-79-100-DEN.

Card, S., Moran, T. & Newell, A. (1983). *The psychology of human–computer interaction.* Hillsdale, NJ: Lawrence Erlbaum Associates.

Collins, A., & Gentner, D. (1982). Simulations of mental models. *Proceedings of the Cognitive Science Society.* Norwood, NJ: Ablex.

Jeffries, R., Turner, A., Polson, P., & Atwood, M. (1981). The processes involved in designing software. In J. Anderson (Ed.), *Cognitive skills and their acquisition* (pp.255–284). Hillsdale, NJ: Lawrence Erlbaum Associates.

Kant, E., & Newell, A. (1982). *Problem-solving techniques for the design of algorithms.* (Tech. Report No. CMU-C S-82-145). Pittsburgh: Carnegie–Mellon University.

APPENDIX
ANNOTATED PROTOCOL

Here we present an annotated version of the first 11 minutes of S1's protocol. On the left we see the subject's statements. On the right the goal structure of the model has been mapped onto the statements. The key in Figure 6.1 defines the abbreviations used here for the goals. Reading down the right-most column we see that, in two successive episodes, EVAL PREPARE and INTEGRATE occur in the order predicted by the model.

EPISODE I:
ELAPSED TIME = 0 MIN

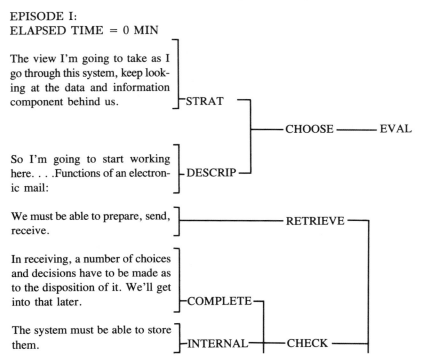

The view I'm going to take as I go through this system, keep looking at the data and information component behind us. — STRAT

CHOOSE ——— EVAL

So I'm going to start working here. . . .Functions of an electronic mail: — DESCRIP

We must be able to prepare, send, receive. ——— RETRIEVE

In receiving, a number of choices and decisions have to be made as to the disposition of it. We'll get into that later. — COMPLETE

The system must be able to store them. — INTERNAL — CHECK

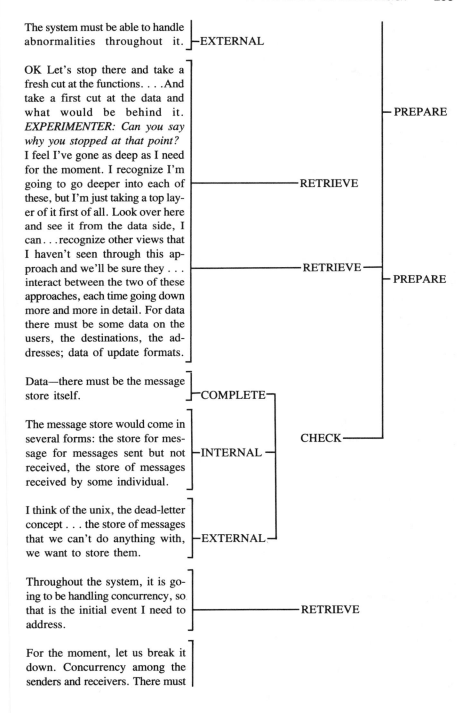

The system must be able to handle abnormalities throughout it. —EXTERNAL

OK Let's stop there and take a fresh cut at the functions. . . .And take a first cut at the data and what would be behind it. *EXPERIMENTER: Can you say why you stopped at that point?* I feel I've gone as deep as I need for the moment. I recognize I'm going to go deeper into each of these, but I'm just taking a top layer of it first of all. Look over here and see it from the data side, I can. . .recognize other views that I haven't seen through this approach and we'll be sure they . . . interact between the two of these approaches, each time going down more and more in detail. For data there must be some data on the users, the destinations, the addresses; data of update formats.

Data—there must be the message store itself.

The message store would come in several forms: the store for message for messages sent but not received, the store of messages received by some individual.

I think of the unix, the dead-letter concept . . . the store of messages that we can't do anything with, we want to store them.

Throughout the system, it is going to be handling concurrency, so that is the initial event I need to address.

For the moment, let us break it down. Concurrency among the senders and receivers. There must

PREPARE

RETRIEVE

RETRIEVE — PREPARE

COMPLETE

INTERNAL

CHECK

EXTERNAL

RETRIEVE

be some function other than senders and receivers, which is periodically monitoring what is happening to our message store; I think of unix.

├─COMPLETE ─

We have to make strategy decision on how we deliver messages to the receiver of it. Whether we deliver when the receiver logs on or when the message is sent, or whether we deliver through having some continuously running program . . . some demon type of program that comes in periodically, looks around and says, "Can I do anything with the message?" So there must be some sort of dispatching philosophy.

└─ CHECK ───────── INTEGRATE

├─INTERNAL

EPISODE II:

What's coming to mind is that here we've got, in fact we can look at the states for our messages, the states of this whole system, and take another view as well as the function-data view. Think of it as a big state machine, what is happening to it, so that we can see that for awhile.

├─STRAT ───────── CHOOSE ───────── EVAL

States . . . What are the things we are dealing with? Objects. Terms of events . . . Objects, we've got users, we've got message mail. Events, new mail ready, receivers log on.

├─────────── RETRIEVE ────── PREPARE

OK Let me start looking at the states of a user first of all. How in the world is this going to be seen from the view of the user? He starts out, start him out with some state of, let's look at a reception scenario and through log on, he's becomes capable of receiving

├─────────── INTERACTIONS ─┐

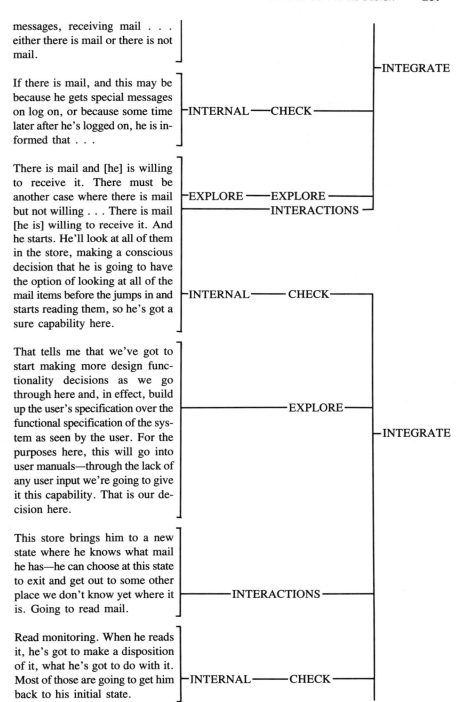

messages, receiving mail . . .
either there is mail or there is not
mail.

If there is mail, and this may be
because he gets special messages
on log on, or because some time
later after he's logged on, he is in-
formed that . . .

There is mail and [he] is willing
to receive it. There must be
another case where there is mail
but not willing . . . There is mail
[he is] willing to receive it. And
he starts. He'll look at all of them
in the store, making a conscious
decision that he is going to have
the option of looking at all of the
mail items before the jumps in and
starts reading them, so he's got a
sure capability here.

That tells me that we've got to
start making more design functionality decisions as we go
through here and, in effect, build
up the user's specification over the
functional specification of the system as seen by the user. For the
purposes here, this will go into
user manuals—through the lack of
any user input we're going to give
it this capability. That is our decision here.

This store brings him to a new
state where he knows what mail
he has—he can choose at this state
to exit and get out to some other
place we don't know yet where it
is. Going to read mail.

Read monitoring. When he reads
it, he's got to make a disposition
of it, what he's got to do with it.
Most of those are going to get him
back to his initial state.

INTEGRATE

INTERNAL——CHECK

EXPLORE——EXPLORE
——————INTERACTIONS

INTERNAL——CHECK

EXPLORE

INTEGRATE

INTERACTIONS

INTERNAL——CHECK

Whatever disposition we decide—destroy, hold, reply, whatever else will get him back there. I think it will be very obvious now that I've got to decide what those functions are from the user's point of view before I can continue much farther with this design. So let me note that.

————EXPLORE————

At this stage, I need the functional specifications. I'll come back and do that in a little while, time permitting, and carry on making some other assumptions here. Store, Read, OK . . .That's good enough for the user view of it.

⌐COMPLETNESS————CHECK⌐

ELAPSED TIME = 11 MIN

7 Expertise and Decision under Uncertainty: Performance and Process

Eric J. Johnson
The Wharton School, University of Pennsylvania

INTRODUCTION

In everyday life, we encounter many individuals we consider expert decision makers. Experts, whether they be physicians, security analysts, commodity traders, or bookies, all appear to possess an important talent: They make more accurate decisions than do other people in environments that are characterized by uncertain information. The commonplace belief is that they possess superior ability resulting from extensive training, hard work, practical experience, and professional dedication.

This opinion of expert judgment seems to be shared by cognitive science and artificial intelligence. Chapters in this volume, for example, examine experts in many domains ranging from computer programming and software design to medicine. Modeling expert performance has emerged as an important and difficult challenge for cognitive science.

In contrast, empirical research in behavioral decision theory presents a very different view of expertise: In many studies, experts do not perform impressively at all. For example, many expert judges fail to do significantly better than novices who, at best, have slight familiarity with the task at hand. This result has been replicated in diverse domains such as clinical psychology (Goldberg, 1970), graduate admissions (Dawes, 1971), and economic forecasting (Armstrong, 1978). Not surprisingly, this has led to strong recommendations. Consider for example, Armstrong's advice about experts' forecasts:

> People are willing to pay heavily for expert advice about the future. . . . The evidence is that this money is poorly spent. Expertise beyond a minimal level

in the subject area is of almost no value. . . .The implication is obvious and clear cut: Do not hire the best expert you can — or even close to the best. Hire the cheapest expert. (pp. 84–85)

Indeed the results in the area are so uniformly negative that one wonders why Armstrong suggests hiring the expert at all: As Goldberg (1968, p. 484) stated ". . . [the] surprising finding — that the amount of professional training and experience of the judge does not relate to his judgmental accuracy — has appeared in a number of studies." More recently a dissertation has announced ". . . the end of the mystique of expertise" (Camerer, 1980a, p. 5).

Clearly these two divergent views warrant attention. In this paper, I describe the characteristics of experts as portrayed in these two literatures, concentrating on the behavioral decision literature. Two subsequent sections present an overview of research which examines the decision processes of two different kinds of experts. A final section attempts to use this research to help resolve the paradox presented by the two views of expertise held by cognitive science and behavioral decision theory.

Expert Judgment: Evidence

What are the essential properties which define an expert? There are many characteristics we associate with expertise: quick, confident judgments made under pressure, a reassuring manner, and an eye for the unusual or rare variable. However, one consideration seems tantamount: that experts make better — that is, more accurate — judgments than do untrained novices. In other words, expertise should provide both superior decision processes and superior performance.

Cognitive science has documented clear differences in experts' and novices' behavior. The specifics naturally depend upon the task, but it is clear that experts often have better and more complete representations of the task domain (Chi, Feltovich, & Glaser, 1982). These representations, in turn, allow experts to encode new information more quickly and completely (Chase & Simon, 1973; Johnson & Russo, 1984; Spilich, Vesonder, Chiesi, & Voss, 1979; Voss, Vesonder & Spilich, 1980). Experts apparently also have a richer repertory of strategies, and appropriate mechanisms for accessing and applying these strategies (Larkin, McDermott, Simon, & Simon, 1980). These strategies, and the appropriate organization of knowledge, often allow experts to perform tasks more quickly than novices.

Experts in domains such as physics problem-solving produce more accurate solutions than novices. However this focus on experts' performance is secondary, and problem-solving research often assumes the superiority of expert performance; it usually evaluates performance, if at all, on a small number of problems, concentrating instead upon difference in process.

Research in decision and judgment provides a marked contrast. These tasks are characterized by an uncertain relationship between inputs and outcomes, task domains which are described by the term *decision under uncertainty*. The results in this literature present a rather pessimistic appraisal of experts. Experts are often found to perform no better than novices in the tasks studied. Consider, for example, Goldberg's (1959) result, comparing the ability of psychiatrists and their secretaries to diagnose brain damage using a common test, the Bender-Gestalt. He found no difference. Other studies may appear to be only slightly more heartening. Goldberg (1968) also compared undergraduate students and experienced clinical psychologists and psychiatrists in their ability to diagnose psychosis using the Minnesota Multiphasic Personality Inventory (MMPI). He found that experts were more accurate, making the correct diagnosis 65% of the time, compared to undergraduates' performance of 58%. A random responder would be right 50% of the time.

Much more devastating, however, are comparisons to simple statistical models, provoked originally by the "Clinical–Statistical" controversy in clinical psychology (Meehl, 1954). Here, experts are compared to simple regression models. The independent variables are the attributes describing a particular case, such as scores on a clinical test — for example, the scores on the Minnesota Multiphasic Personality Inventory. The dependent variable is an outcome, such as the eventual diagnosis of the patient as psychotic or neurotic. Such a model has no explicit knowledge of the environment, but combines the available numeric variables, using weights estimated through Ordinary Least Squares.

How well do these models perform? In almost every case, the models' predictions are more accurate than those of the expert judges. The experts in Goldberg's MMPI study made accurate diagnoses in 65% of the cases, the regression model in 70% of the cases. This finding has been replicated in many other domains, far beyond its original setting in clinical psychology. Einhorn (1972), for example, compared the ability of physicians to predict the severity of cases of Hodgkin's disease to the ability of a simple linear model. While the correlation of physicians' judgments with the observed outcome was no better than chance, cross-validated linear regressions performed modestly well, $r = .24$. Similarly, linear regressions have been shown to be superior to human experts in judging bankruptcy (Libby, 1976), predicting success in graduate school (Dawes, 1971), and predicting security prices (Wright, 1979).

These disappointing results have led to the comparison of experts to an even more limited mechanical combination rule. Here, rather than estimate weights, all important variables are weighted equally. Because no statistical estimation is involved, such prediction schemes are termed *improper linear models*. These models have no prior experience in the domain, and possess an almost trivial form. Often these models are superior to experts (Dawes, 1979). For example, in Einhorn's study of radiologists, an equal-weighted model was superior to all four physicians; and in Libby's (1976) study of bankruptcy judgments, a simple one-variable model predicted business failure more accurately than 31 of the 43 experts (Dawes, 1979, p. 579).

In sum, the behavioral decision literature does not present a flattering view of expert judgment. The superiority of experts to novices is often surprisingly small, or, in some cases, nonexistent; more disturbing may be the superiority of trivial linear representations to the performance of carefully trained human judges. These effects appear to be both robust and large: The surprisingly poor performance of experts has been replicated across a broad range of seemingly unrelated task domains, and models are often twice as good (in terms of variance explained) as expert judges.

Whereas the decision-making literature has evaluated the performance of experts in many domains, it has much less to say about process. Thus we have, at best, an incomplete picture. While process differences have been well documented in cognitive science, we know little about performance differences. The behavioral decision literature presents the opposite imbalance, with an emphasis upon performance and not process.

Expert Judgment: Process Explanations

Why do experts in these domains do so badly? The behavioral literature, with its emphasis on performance, does not offer much in the way of answers. Why is the performance of these experts so remarkably poor in comparison to those in domains such as physics? First, note the obvious differences in the tasks. Most problem-solving research examines well-structured tasks. Expertise consists of identifying a correct procedure for obtaining a solution and applying it. The procedure, whether learned through experience or instruction, is usually known to provide a correct answer, and often provides some means of checking if the answer is correct. In decision under uncertainty no single correct procedure exists, and there is no definitive way of assessing the correctness of a rule based upon the outcome of a single case. There is no *optimally* correct rule, for example, to predict psychosis, bankruptcy, or the severity of Hodgkin's disease; there are only rules which are *relatively* more accurate. Thus, the tasks may make radically different demands upon experts' abilities.

While there may be no single way of being right in these tasks, there seems to be more than one way of being wrong. At least three different hypotheses suggest themselves:

1. *Experts are fallible linear models.* Experts might attempt to behave

like a linear model, but, because of their limited ability to process information, fail. Dawes (1979), for example, speculates that linear models perform well in these tasks "because people — especially experts in a field — are much better at selecting and coding information than they are at integrating it." This theme, that the human judges are deficient in combining information, appears in a number of studies. Here experts are seen as noisy regressions, who can identify important variables, but who fail to combine them accurately. "People are good at picking the right predictor variables. . . . People are bad at integrating information from diverse and incomparable sources (Dawes, 1979)." Thus even expert judges might use inappropriate weights, or apply those weights in an inconsistent or unreliable fashion. It is important to emphasize that even the most pessimistic researcher would not eliminate experts from these tasks. Experts' strength is in the selecting and coding of relevant variables; their weakness seems to be in combining them.

2. *Experts use nonlinear rules.* According to this view, experts may use the same variables as statistical models, but combine them differently. Experts' discussions of their judgment processes, whether gathered informally, as in much of this literature, or using concurrent verbal reports (Kleinmuntz, 1963), do not fit the picture of the expert as a noisy linear combination rule. Rather, experts report that they use complex *configural* rules: The impact of one variable depends upon the level of another, in a fashion that is analogous to an interaction in an analysis of variance. The impact of one scale of the MMPI depends, for example, upon whether or not the other scales also have high values. These rules often sound very similar to the if–then form used in production system models of experts.

However, arguments for configurality must address two rather distressing facts: First, the judgments of most experts are well predicted by linear representations, with interactions representing, at best, a minor part of their judgments. Second, these regression models of judges (called *bootstrap models*) do better at predicting the criterion than do the judges themselves. This first finding, that judges who claim to be configural are well modeled by simple regressions, may well be epiphenomenal: Linear models can predict nonlinear processes under a wide variety of well-defined conditions (Dawes & Corrigan, 1974; Einhorn, Kleinmuntz, & Kleinmuntz, 1979; Johnson & Meyer, 1984). However, the second finding, that experts are less accurate than linear models based upon their judgments, suggest that whatever the experts *are* doing does not improve their performance.

3. *Experts attend to different variables than do models.* Meehl (1954), a central actor in the clinical–statistical debate, suggested the following example: Imagine that we had to predict whether or not a faculty member would attend the movies on a given night. We might construct a sophisticated linear model consisting of variables such as marital status, whether

or not our colleague was tenured, age, number and age of children, and so on. However, if we found out that the faculty member had just broken his or her leg, then we would confidently discard our model and make our prediction based on this fact.

Such events, which we term *broken leg cues*, are not included in the regression because they occur too infrequently to be estimated. Yet when they are present, such cues can be quite diagnostic. Experts, according to this different-variable hypothesis, might tend to use such cues rather than those included in the regression model. Their resulting poor performance occurs because these cues are less predictive than those in the model.

Currently, it would be difficult to ascribe experts' poor performance to one of these causes or another. Decision theory's emphasis upon performance has allowed it to assess the performance of judges, but, unfortunately, it has less to say about the causes of that performance. While regression models can provide a good account of the outcomes of a decision process, they are relatively uninformative about the psychological process producing these outcomes. The actual nature of these processes deserves closer examination, using the methods that reveal the information examined by the judges, and the methods judges use to combine this information. Emphasizing process may also help reconcile the two views of expertise we have encountered. Do experts in decision-making behave like experts in other domains? Do they possess superior information-processing skills?

The next two sections present an overview of a series of studies which examine expert performance and processes in two different domains: The first, evaluating applicants for medical internships, is similar to what has become a standard task in the decision literature: graduate admissions judgments (Dawes, 1971). The second task is the prediction of stock prices by expert security analysts and by novice MBA students. In both studies we have changed the standard methodology used in decision research in two ways: (a) We have presented the decision-makers with an environment that is richer in information than that normally used in studies which evaluate experts' performance; and (b) we also have collected verbal reports on some subsets of the trials, which allow us to examine these experts' decision processes. Additional details are available in Johnson (1980) and in Johnson and Sathi (1988), respectively.

EXPERT JUDGMENT: PHYSICIANS' SELECTION OF HOUSE OFFICERS

The Task

Each year, applicants for internships and residencies (collectively termed *house officers*) participate in a program which matches applicants to post-graduate positions in teaching hospitals. The applicants express their preferences by ranking desirable positions. The hospitals, in turn, must submit a rank ordering of candidates to ensure the admission of desirable applicants. The rank-order preferences of both applicants and hospitals is processed through the National Internship and Residency Matching Program, which uses a complex algorithm to make the assignments. Because the hospitals are blind to the preferences of the applicants, their ranking of applicants represents their only means of maintaining the quality of their house staff. Consequently, the physicians expend considerable effort at this process; each of the twelve physicians on the admissions committee we studied examined the folders for each of 200 applicants, and attended two day-long meetings in which final ranks were computed. Although administrative staff might perform this task, the physicians believe that they have the inherent expertise which justifies their expenditure of about one person-week apiece.

Information about each applicant is contained in a folder, which consists, on average, of 13 pages of material. The contents of the folders include an application form supplied by the Department of Medicine, letters from the dean and faculty of the applicant's medical school, transcripts of course work, two summaries of interviews conducted with the applicant, and the results of a standardized exam, the National Boards. Tallying the number of separate statements contained in these folders shows that there are over 400 potentially relevant facts to be considered.

The goal for each judge was to simply rate the applicant on a five-point scale using information in the application. These ratings are then summed to form an initial rank ordering of all applicants, which is then slightly modified following discussion.

Our analysis of these experts involved two sources of data: (a) Concurrent verbal reports collected from two of the physicians and two undergraduate novices as they reviewed six of the applications; and (b) The overall ratings of all twelve physicians and a single novice on 156 applications. In both cases, subjects provided ratings of non-numeric items such as the letters of recommendation, and we coded for each applicant a set of objective variables, such as National Board scores, listed in the applicant's folder. More detail is available in Johnson (1980).

Process Differences

To examine differences in the processes employed by experts and novices, each protocol was segmented into a series of complete thoughts, and coded into one of six categories, each representing a category of cognitive process. The categories and definitions are presented in Table 7.1. We also identified, for each occurrence of a retrieval operator, the actual statement which

TABLE 7.1
Description of Statement Types

Retrievals	Nonevaluative statements consisting of verbatim or paraphrased quotation of information presented in the folders.
Recall	Statements of similar nonevaluative information obtained from memory.
Evaluation	Statements which result in the judgment of some aspect of the applicant, his or her medical school or other object. This excludes judgments made in response to a question on the response form, or evaluations read from the folder.
Scaling statements	Responses made in completing the form provided with each application.
Inferences	Nonevaluative statements, based on retrieved information, but which clearly go beyond the presented information.
Goal statements	Statements of intentions or actions to be performed. Search for a source of information, etc.
Miscomprehension	Statements reporting difficulty in understanding presented information.
Comment	An uncodable statement or one irrelevant to the task.

was read. This allowed us to compare the experts and novices, both in terms of the information search and in the cognitive processes used to evaluate information.

These protocols reveal several qualitative and quantitative differences. Most striking are the differences in the time required to perform the rating task: The two experts averaged about 7.8 minutes per applicant, while the novices took almost twice as long, about 15 minutes per applicant. There was almost no overlap in the two distributions of time. These differences were due, in part, to the smaller amount of information examined by the experts. The novices' protocols contained almost twice as many retrievals as the experts' (126.5 vs. 64.2 retrievals per protocol). While the novices examined over 43% of all the statements that were available in the folder, experts examined about 22%. The experts also examined *different* information than the novices. Transcripts, for example, were barely examined by the experts. Only 3% of the statements contained in the transcript were examined by the experts, while the novices examined about 13%. The experts also seemed to limit their examination of the letters, concentrating upon one or two key sentences in each letter. The only item examined more closely by the experts was the application form. Here expert subjects examined about 42% of the statements and the novices about 38%.

These differences in search appear to reflect experts' belief that certain items provided by the applicant are relatively uninformative: The transcript, and the grades provided, often reflect a pass/fail system. An expert seems to know that any graduate of these programs has passed these courses. The dean's letter, in contrast, often contains a series of key phrases describing the students' progress in each course. There are several phrases that, like grades, indicate differential performance in class work. The experts appear to use their knowledge of medical education to focus upon more diagnostic information.

Experts not only search for different information, they also have different patterns of search. By and large, the novices examine the information present in the folders the way it is presented, reading one item at a time, moving sequentially down the page. The experts search much more actively: They return to previously examined information much more often, and change the focus of their attention from one part of the folder to the other much more frequently. The tendency of experts to examine the information in a more active, flexible manner also manifests itself in the frequency in which they apply certain operators. Specifically, more goal statements appear in the experts' protocols. About 3% of all statements in experts' protocols are coded as goal statements, while novices' protocols contain less than 1%. Similarly, experts make more extensive use of their knowledge of medical education. About 10% of all the information used by experts appears to be recalled from memory, and by novices, about 3%.

In sum, the experts appear to examine this information in a top-down fashion, using their knowledge of medical education to structure their search. The increased use of goals in their protocols, along with the greater use of knowledge retrieved from memory and their more active search patterns, presents a picture consistent with the portrait of experts in other domains. Our expects appear to use their knowledge to examine only information that they consider diagnostic, limiting their search to a smaller subset of the available information. Thus, although admissions tasks such as this have often resulted in rather disappointing evaluations of expert performance, these results suggest that the processes used by these experts are much like those used by experts in other domains.

More importantly, these processes do not resemble a linear regression model. Rather than being fallible approximations to a linear model, these judges seem to use information in a quite different manner. While there are occasional references to configural effects among the cues, there seems to be marked use of information which applies only to the particular case at hand. Consider the following example taken from one of the experts' protocols:

At Hopkins the thing to look for is the Ossler Clerkship
It's really a sub-internship in medicine

He did very well there . . . Honors.
I'd think he would therefore do well here. . . .

However mundane, this inference would be impossible to model within
a regression framework. While one could include the complex interaction,
the clerkship in question is available to only a few students at one particular medical school. There would be far too few observations to estimate
a coefficient. Interpreting the impact of this information does not require
statistical estimates of covariation, but rather the realization that the duties
of the clerkship are similar to those of a house officer. The process data
often seems to more closely resemble the different-variable model of expert
judgment: Experts seem to pay attention to relatively rare variables, applicable to only the case under consideration.

Experts and Novices in Admissions Judgment: Performance

While we have seen important differences in the decision processes used
by experts and novices, an important question remains: Do experts perform
more accurately? An important aspect of the matching process used to as-
sign house officers is that it allows some evaluation of the individual decision-
makers. The National Residency and Intern Matching Program provided
the rankings of these applicants at 32 teaching hospitals, which represents
a large majority (> 80%) of the hospitals in which the applicants sought
positions. We can then identify, for each applicant, the rank which max-
imized the probability of the applicant being assigned to these experts' hospital. Deviations from this rank may be suboptimal: Either a candidate is
ranked more highly than necessary to insure admission, or a candidate is
ranked too low, increasing the probability of his or her assignment to a competing hospital. Although other, more sophisticated definitions of accurate
judgment in this task are possible (Roth, 1984), the simple comparison of
a judge's rankings to those that optimized a candidate's chances of being
assigned to the physician's hospital represents a useful first step. To further
ensure the relevance of this criterion, we collected ratings of the applicants'
performance for that subset who eventually joined the Department of Medicine. The chairperson of the admissions committee and the head of the training program both rated and ranked each intern at the end of the first year
of training. The resulting correlation between this measure and the committee ranking, $r = .48$, suggests some relationship between the criterion
we use and eventual success as an intern.

To evaluate the performance of these experts we can compare their rank
orderings of the applicants to one which would have given the training program the best chance at matching with each applicant. The simple correlation of the experts with this criterion ranges from .50 to .29 with a mean

of .37. Although this appears to be a disturbingly low level of performance, it is typical to that found in similar tasks: Wiggins and Kohen (1971) reported an average correlation of .33 between predicted and actual freshman Grade Point Averages for incoming college students; and Dawes reported that faculty rankings at the time of admission correlated .19 with a measure of eventual success in graduate school.

One evaluation of the experts in this study is the comparison of their performance with that of an undergraduate novice who had rated the 151 applicants. This novice performed as well as two of the physicians, ranking eleventh out of the total of thirteen judges. His correlation with the criterion was .33. Thus, although we find marked differences in the processes that are used by novices and experts in this task, these differences appear to have a relatively small impact upon performance. We also compared the expert judgments to a cross-validated linear regression model of the outcome. Recall here that the results are a uniformly disappointing assessment of expert performance: Experts never perform as well as the model. In this study, the cross-validated model performs well, $r = .48$, but here a single expert performed as well as the model. The model is quite simple, and uses only three predictor variables selected by a stepwise regression: the quality of the applicant's medical school, an interviewer's rating of an on-campus visit, and a variable indicating membership in an honorary society.

In sum, the evaluations of these experts presents, at best, a slightly more optimistic view of expertise: Most experts are slightly better than an undergraduate novice, and a single expert actually performs about as well as a simple linear regression. These results are summarized in Figure 7.1 which

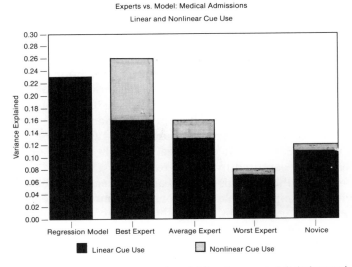

FIGURE 7.1 Experts, novices, and models' performance: Admissions task.

displays the performance of the best and worst expert judge, the novice, and various statistical models.

Yet these results present us with a quandary: How can a simple regression model be as accurate as the apparently complex processes revealed in the verbal reports? The regressions are more accurate than most experts, yet they consider only three variables. The regression and the judges seem to be doing different things. Unlike the experts, the models look at the same information for every case. In contrast, the verbal reports indicate that the physicians examine many more cues, and the pattern of their search seems to be contingent upon the information at hand.

This paradox suggests that the fallible regression hypothesis is wrong. The experts' strategies seem quite different than that portrayed by the regression. To examine this further, we explicitly tested the noisy regression hypothesis. Using stepwise regression, we constructed linear models of the judges (i.e., "bootstrap" models), which fit moderately well, explaining between 41% and 77% of the variance in judgments. If these models represent all the systematic variations in judgment, the residuals of these models should have no relationship with the outcome (Camerer, 1980b). If, on the other hand, judges are using cues in a valid configural fashion, or making use of broken-leg cues, we would expect a positive correlation between residuals (what the regression model cannot explain) and outcomes. In essence, this statistical technique divides the accuracy of the judgments into a linear component, modeled by a regression, and a nonlinear component, due to the valid use of configural and broken-leg cues. It also allows us to attribute the accuracy of each judge to two different sources: (a) a linear component, and (b) a nonlinear component, consisting of valid configural and broken-leg cues.

On average, the correlation between the residuals and the criterion was positive, $r = .124$, and statistically significant. The maximum, $r = .314$, belonged to the most experienced physician. This nonlinear cue usage was an important part of these experts' judgments, accounting on average for 15% of their predictive validity. The best judge also showed the most valid use of configural and broken-leg cues, accounting for 37% of his valid judgment. Figure 7.1 reflects the division of performance into linear and nonlinear cue usage by dividing total accuracy into two components. The top section represents nonlinear cue usage, while the bottom half represents linear cue usage captured by the regression.

In sum, the data from this study clearly weakens the notion that the expert judges are simply fallible regressions. One source of evidence is the verbal reports. The goal-driven, knowledge-intensive, and contingent search patterns are inconsistent with a regression model's focus upon one set of cues. A second source of evidence is the regression analyses, which show that a linear model fails to capture a significant part of the experts' valid judgments. Why then do linear models do so well? Apparently because the model uses information that the expert ignores, and because that information is important.

We must be somewhat cautious about interpreting the relative importance of linear and nonlinear information. Our analysis to date has been correlational; this study does not experimentally manipulate the presence of broken-leg cues. Thus, the regression models may over- or underestimate nonlinear cue usage. More importantly, we have not separated the two types of nonlinear information usage: configurality and broken-leg cues.

In the next section we describe a study addressing these issues in a task possessing a real-world criterion, and obvious real-world incentives: the prediction of security prices. This domain allows us to experimentally manipulate the presence or absence of potential broken-leg cues — in this case, summaries of news items from the *Wall Street Journal* — allowing us to better assess the importance of such cues.

EXPERT JUDGEMENT: PREDICTING SECURITY PRICES

The Task

In a recently completed study (Johnson & Sathi, 1988), we have compared predictions of changes in security prices made by experienced security analysts and by inexperienced MBA students. Each of the subjects in this study predicted year-end closing prices for 40 securities. The securities were described on a set of 22 variables similar to those usually available to analysts engaged in predicting security prices. Half of these securities were accompanied by news items which were summaries of stories about the company that had appeared in the *Wall Street Journal*. Whereas the financial information and the news items described actual securities in 1980, the names of the securities were not revealed to the subjects, ensuring that they would have to predict, and not simply recall, the year-end closing prices. In both expert and novice groups there was, in addition to normal compensation, a sizable prize awarded to the most accurate judge. This provided an additional incentive for accurate judgment.

Process Differences

Our expert subjects represent an average of four years of experience, and were employed as research analysts in three different companies. Our novices were students studying for their Masters degrees in administration, who had taken only an introductory course in finance. Our analysis, although still in progress, replicates several of the process differences observed in the previous study. A comparison of the time required to make a prediction demonstrates that experts were faster than novices, averaging about 144 seconds per security compared to the novices' 162 seconds. A coding scheme similar to that used in the previous study has yet to show substantial differences in the types of operators used by experts and novices. Differences do appear, however, when we examine the information examined by experts and novices. Experts concentrate on certain variables: They examine certain financial descriptors such as the earnings per share and the previous year's closing price more intensely than do novices. These two variables represent 22% of all information examined by the experts, and only 5% of that examined by novices. Again experts appear to focus upon fewer cues than do novices: While novices, as a group, examined 21 out of 22 possible variables, the experts examined only 13. Apparently, like the physicians, they ignored cues they believed to be redundant. Although these results are quite tentative, differences in the processes used by experts and novices in this task are marked, and consistent with those described in the previous study.

Performance Differences

A important advantage of security pricing as a task is the existence of a clear-cut standard for the measurement of performance: actual price changes. To evaluate the experts and novices, we can compute the average absolute size of their errors, that is:

| actual price - predicted price | / actual price.

Of course with this error measure, the smaller the mean, the better the performance, and perfect performance would yield a mean error of zero. Overall, experts did perform better than novices: Their average error was 61.5% compared to a mean error of 65.3% for the novices, a statistically significant difference. More interesting is the interaction between expertise and the presence of the news items. This interaction, which is presented in Figure 7.2, demonstrates that the presence of the news items does not help the novices, but increased the accuracy of the experts. Thus the news items appear to aid expert judgment, at least in part because the experts seem able to comprehend the impact of these items.

Despite the advantage apparently provided by the news items, these experts do not approach the performance of a simple regression. A cross-validated regression of the cues, upon the criterion of percentage change in price, shows that the model is still superior to the mean of the expert judge, having an average error of only 52.4%. Thus, although experts do better in the presence of news items, they still are inferior to a relatively simple linear regression.

We next divided the experts' predictive validity into linear and nonlinear

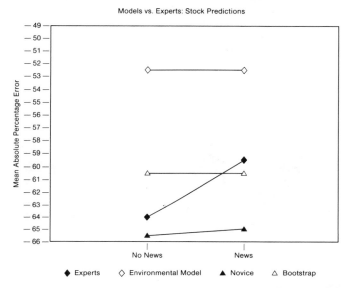

FIGURE 7.2 Experts, novices, and models performance: Security pricing with and without broken-leg cues.

components, using the bootstrapping technique used previously. Figure 7.3 shows that without the news items, the experts were well modeled as linear combination rules. However, the presence of the news items increased their ability to predict, largely through the use of nonlinear information. In contrast, the novices use nonlinear information less, and their nonlinear cue usage is largely independent of the presence of the news items. Thus, the experts seem to depend heavily upon the presence of news items to increase the accuracy of their predictions. In contrast the novices appear to use the information in some nonlinear fashion that appears to be configural and independent of the news items.

In terms of our three models of expert performance, the data from this study tend to support the different-variable hypothesis to the detriment of the configural cue hypothesis. Our experts only show significant nonlinear cue use when the news items are present. It then seems logical to attribute this nonlinearity to the presence of the news items. Over half of the experts' predictive validity is due to this information. Accurate judgment of the impact of these rare events seems essential to their expertise. The key findings of this research are therefore:

1. That experts in these ill-structured tasks behave in many ways like experts in well-structured domains.
2. That experts concentrate on the interpretation of rare events.
3. While this aids their predictions it leads, in the tasks we have exa-

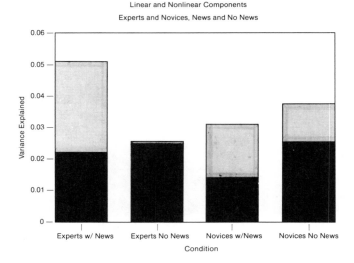

FIGURE 7.3 Experts and novice security analysts: Linear vs. nonlinear cue usage.

mined, to performance inferior to that provided by simple linear models.

DISCUSSION

Experts' Strengths, Experts' Weaknesses

These two studies clearly show experts' strengths: the interpretation of cues that apply to these particular cases. The experts' weakness, and the strength of regression models, is the ability to combine the more mundane information available for every case. Note that this distinction is analogous to another in the behavioral decision literature, that of base-rate versus case-specific data (Kahneman & Tversky, 1973). In this literature it is apparent that base-rate data is often underweighted, relative to case-specific data.

Why is case-specific data overweighted? Experts appear to interpret rare events through inference, and, more specifically, through causal reasoning. The ability to assess the impact on the price of security of a rare event such as the death of a Chief Executive Officer in a plane crash does not lie in lessons learned from experience. Instead, it seems that experts can assess the event's impact because they have some knowledge of the company and the CEO's role within it, and understand the potential market reactions. This general ability to learn better pattern-matching and reasoning skills is consistent with the development of expertise in other domains. P. Johnson and his colleagues (1981), for example, have shown that expert physicians seem to be better able to identify the patterns of symptoms which are linked to a disease. Knowledge of the symptoms alone is not enough: "A failure in human subjects does not reflect the lack of a disease model in memory, but rather a lack of knowledge for using that model in particular situations" (P. Johnson et al., 1981, p. 274). This knowledge of patterns, and their application, seems to be the key to expertise in many domains (Larkin et al., 1980). While this is a useful skill in the domains characterized as decision under uncertainty, there is also other useful information available.

Why then is base-rate data neglected? Whereas we may be impressed with the performance of "simple" regression models, we must attribute their performance to their ability to properly weight base-rate data. Although perhaps simple in statistical terms, the cognitive processes represented by the regression model are not "simple" at all. Because the relationship between the independent variables (cues) and the dependent variables is stochastic, we need a large number of cases to evaluate their covariation. Without written records, such a task overwhelms the abilities of the decision-maker. The ability of individuals to judge covariation is severly limited, as documented in the literature on covariation (Crocker, 1981), multi-cue probability learning (Brehmer, 1980), and even judging covariation in a simple two-by-two table (Jenkins & Ward, 1965). The origins of the neglect of base-rate data seem to stem from the inherently burdensome information-processing demands of the task. In retrospect, it seems obvious that neglect of base-rate information is the key to the relative weakness of experts, as compared to models.

Implications

This tendency for decision-makers to examine broken-leg cues and to neglect other information represents an important opportunity for those who would wish to design aids to decision-making for experts. Specifically, we might design aids which help decision-makers by combining the information that they currently underweigh, and providing an estimate of its impact. An expert might then adjust this initial estimate to account for information not considered by the model, such as broken-leg cues. We are currently exploring this possibility. For details, see Johnson & Sathi (1988). Such an aid illustrates one of the payoffs of a process analysis of expert judgment. By decomposing prediction tasks into components, we can isolate those that are easily accomplished by a human judge from those which present difficulty. This then allows us to consider the design of aids which assist the judge with the more difficult components of the task.

This research also raises some interesting questions for the development of systems which capture human expertise in the form of a computer program. Much work in these expert systems seems to focus upon mimicking the performance of a human judge (Duda & Shortliffe, 1983). The present results suggest that the appropriateness of modeling a human judge may depend on the task. Because we cannot easily identify those tasks which are heavily dependent upon broken-leg cues, we need to approach the modeling of judges with caution. Specifically, if an expert system attempts to mimic a human expert, it may fail to exploit much of the information available in the task, such as the base-rate information captured by a simple regression model. For some tasks we may find ourselves in the ironic position of having developed a useful model of human performance, which also captures the experts' foibles — specifically, their tendency to emphasize broken-leg cues while neglecting other information.

This is a particularly troublesome observation since the protocols generated by our judges sound suspiciously like the productions contained in many expert systems. We might encode our physician's observation concerning students from Hopkins in the form:

If   (Applicant is from Johns Hopkins and has Ossler
      Clerkship and grade is equal to an A)
Then (increase certainty that applicant is a good
      intern)

This is probably valid, leading to an increase in the accuracy of judgment. However, this may miss more valid but mundane relationships like those between grades and performance. This observation should emphasize, therefore, the importance of evaluating the performance of expert decision-makers, whether they be humans or machines, against simple alternative models. Simple linear models can serve as interesting baselines for the evaluation of expert systems.

Finally, the current research has barely started to examine the psychology of expert judgment. We have failed to examine specific facets of experts' cognitive abilities. Although there is an increasing understanding of experts' abilities in many domains, the current work has not specifically examined some of these, such as the role of their possibly superior encoding and recall skills in their performance.

ACKNOWLEDGMENT

This work has been supported by a grant from the Risk, Decision and Management Science Program at the National Science Foundation, while the author was at Carnegie-Mellon University. Comments on earlier drafts by Colin Camerer, John Payne, Anthony Pratkanis and J. Edward Russo are very much appreciated.

REFERENCES

Armstrong, J. S. (1978). *Long range forecasting: From crystal ball to computer*. New York: Wiley.

Brehemer, B. (1980). In one word: Not from experience. *Acta Psychologica, 45*, 223–241.

Camerer, C. (1980a). *The psychology of expert judgment*. Unpublished doctoral dissertation, University of Chicago, Graduate School of Business.

Camerer, C. (1980b). Conditions for the success of bootstrap models. *Organizational Behavior and Human Performance, 24*, 411–422.

Chase, W. G., & Simon, H. A. (1973). Perception in chess. *Cognitive Psychology, 4*, 55–81.

Chi, M., Feltovich, P., & Glaser, R. (1982). Categorization in experts and novices in R. Sternberg (Ed.), *The Handbook of Intelligence*, Earlbaum: Hillsdale, N.J.

Crocker, J. (1981). Judgment of covariation by social perceivers. *Psychological Bulletin, 90(2)*, 272–292.

Dawes, R. M. (1971). A case study of graduate admissions: Application of three principles of human decision making. *American Psychologist, 26*, 180–188.

Dawes, R. M., & Corrigan, B. (1974). Linear models in decision making. *Psychological Bulletin, 81*, 95–106.

Dawes, R. M. (1979). The robust beauty of improper linear models in decision making. *American Psychologist, 34*, 571–582.

Duda, R. O., & Shortliffe, E. H. (1983). Expert systems research. *Science, 220*, 261–268.

Einhorn, H. E. (1972). Expert measurement and mechanical combination. *Organizational Behavior and Human Performance, 7*, 86–106.

Einhorn, H. J., Kleinmuntz, D. N., & Kleinmuntz, B., (1979). Linear regression *and* process-tracing models of judgment. *Psychological Review, 86*, 465–485.

Goldberg, L. R. (1959). The effectiveness of clinicians' judgments: The diagnosis of organic brain damage from the Bender–Gestalt test. *Journal of Consulting Psychology, 23*, 25–33.

Goldberg, L. R. (1970). Man versus model of man: A rationale, plus some evidence for a method of improving clinical judgment. *Psychological Bulletin, 73*, 422–432.

Goldberg, L. R. (1968). Simple or simple processes? Some research on clinical judgments. *American Psychologist, 23*, 483–496.

Jenkins, H. M., & Ward, W. C. (1965). Judgment of contingency between responses and outcomes. *Psychological Monographs, 79*, 11,15,19.

Johnson, E. J. (1980). *Expertise in admissions judgment*, unpublished Doctoral Dissertation, Carnegie–Mellon University, Department of Psychology.

Johnson, E. J., & Meyer, R. M. (1984). Compensatory choice models of Noncompensatory Processes: The Effect of varying Context. *Journal of Consumer Research, 11*, 528–541.

Johnson, E. J., & Russo, J. E. (1984). Product familiarity and learning new information. *Journal of Consumer Research, 11*, 542–550.

Johnson, E. J., & Sathi, A. (1988). *Expertise in security analysts*. Manuscript in preparation.

Johnson, P. E., Duran, A. S., Hassebrock, F., Moller, J., Prietula, M., Feltovich, R. J., Swanson, D. B. (1981). Expertise and error in diagnostic reasoning. *Cognitive Science, 5*, 235–283.

Kahneman, D., & Tversky, A. (1973). On the psychology of prediction. *Psychological Review, 80*, 237–251.

Kleinmuntz, B. (1963). Personality test interpreted by digital computer. *Science, 139*, 416–418.

Larkin, J., McDermott, J., Simon, D. P., & Simon, H. A. (1980, June). Expert and novice performance in solving physics problems. *Science, 208*, 1335–1342.

Libby, R. (1976). Man versus model of man: Some conflicting evidence. *Organizational Behavior and Human Performance, 16*, 1–12.

Meehl, P. E. (1954). *Clinical versus statistical prediction: A theoretical analysis and a review of the evidence*. Minneapolis: University of Minnesota Press.

Roth, A. E. (1984). The evolution of the labor market for medical interns and residents: A case study in game theory. *Journal of Political Economy, 92,* 991–1016.

Spilich, G. J., Vesonder, G. T., Chiesi, H. L., & Voss, J. F. (1979). Text processing of domain-related information for individuals with high and low domain knowledge. *Journal of Verbal Learning and Verbal Behavior, 118,* 275–290.

Voss,, J. F., Vesonder, G. T., & Spilich, G. J. (1980). Text generation and recall by high-knowledge and low-knowledge individuals. *Journal of Verbal Learning and Verbal Behavior, 19,* 651–667.

Wright, W. F. (1979). Properties of judgment models in a financial setting. *Organizational Behavior and Human Performance, 23,* 73–85.

Wiggens, N., & Kohen, E. S. (1971). Man vs. model of man revisited: The forecasting of graduate school success. *Journal of Personality and Social Psychology, 19,* 100–106.

8 Expertise on the Bench: Modeling Magistrates' Judicial Decision-Making

Jeanette A. Lawrence
Murdoch Universty, Western Australia

Legal judging is a problem-solving domain where problems are always ill-structured. Solutions are inconclusive, and important features of the problem space become apparent only after initial processing has begun. The information that is available comes from different sources at different stages of the judging process, and is constrained by legal rules and by other people. In Australian criminal courts, the stipendiary magistrate usually judges cases alone, sometimes against the intentions and efforts of other participants. Thus, the disposition of people's affairs is dependent on the magistrate's expertise at forming solutions as judgments and penalties in indefinite and externally constrained problem spaces.

The ill-structuredness and indeterminateness of judicial problem-solving is well documented in the archival data of disparities in penalties that have been handed down for similar offenses across different courts, and even within the same court (Diamond, 1981; Homel, 1981; Hood & Sparks, 1972; Lawrence & Homel, 1987). The appeals court system bears witness to the inconclusiveness of decisions which can be overturned by higher courts. The legal criterion for a good judgment is the magistrate's personal satisfaction beyond reasonable doubt, with a public statement of reasons for the use of the appeals court. Therefore, judging can be regarded as a specialized professional problem-solving domain amenable to cognitive modeling, but with special features related to the ill-defined nature of its problem space.

CRITERIA FOR REPRESENTING JUDICIAL PROCESSES

In order to represent expertise in judicial problem-solving, a cognitive model should meet certain basic criteria. First, the representational scheme should be comprehensive enough to deal with the cognitive perspectives that magistrates bring to individual cases, as well as with the procedures they use in court. Then, the scheme should reflect the realities of problem-solving as it happens in the judicial domain; and finally, the concepts and linkages of the scheme should clearly represent basic intentional-reasoning structures and their content for critical scrutiny.

Perspectives and Procedures

All professional problem-solvers approach new tasks with personal expectations and goals; the initial representations which come from these goals then affect subsequent processes and solutions (Revlis, 1975; Voss, Greene, Post, & Penner, 1983). Personal perspectives influence problem-solvers to make intuitive leaps and to selectively process available information (Kahneman, Slovic, & Tversky, 1982; Svenson, Lawrence, & Willis, 1983). Perspectives are especially influential in judging where the work is individualized and where time and case loads demand fast, decisive solutions. The expert judge represents each new case against his or her acquired frames of reference or constructions of reality (Berger, Berger, & Kellner, 1973; Berger & Luckman, 1966; Lawrence, 1984). One very experienced magistrate commented on the way his colleagues acquired their own norms and patterns in the courtroom:

> They adopt a style . . . that style might have elements which are questionable, but I believe, basically, finally, that sentencer develops a pattern and he follows that pattern . . .

People's implicit cognitions are not usually represented together in the same model as the procedural steps that they take to solve specific problems. We need to describe how an expert's a priori perspectives operate in interaction with procedures for making sense of data and generating solutions. The same magistrate also identified the necessity of extracting the significant features of individual cases rather than routinely operating on well-used patterns:

> This is a terrible danger in our field, that we grab everything and put it within that kind of circle . . . we ought to see outside that circle, that this is a new situation and ought to be dealt with differently . . . So I think that a good sentencer has got to be alive to the unusual. (Lawrence, 1984, p. 326).

On-the-job reactions and extractions of new information are also defining characteristics of expertise, and should be represented along with prior frames of reference and expectations (Hayes-Roth & Hayes-Roth, 1979; Lawrence, Dodds, & Volet, 1983). Capturing the mix of experts' perspectives and operations on information is most important in judging because there are certain regularities, and those regularities can be upset by unusual factors at any stage in a case.

In the model, magistrates' prior perspectives are called "Frames of Reference" in order to show how they define a problem space, set limits on what it contains, and focus attention on its features. The concept picks up the way shared values and outlooks place certain constructions on reality for professional and cultural groups (Berger, Berger, & Kellner, 1973). Immediate procedures are defined as magistrates' activities for selecting portions of available evidence as relevant information, and the inferences and decisions they construct from that information (Hood and Sparks, 1972; Lawrence & Browne, 1981; McKnight, 1981).

Domain Realism

Representational schemes can be imposed on legal processes or they can be formulated in the types of cognitive activities that already identify expertise in the profession (Haney, 1980; Konečni & Ebbeson, 1981). The elegance of top-down models is costly if it means neglecting some of the messier aspects of professional expertise.

Each professional task exerts its own demands on the expert, and these task demands will need to be represented realistically in the model in order to describe the contingencies that help engineer the nature of expertise in that domain. For example, if snap perceptions are used, as on the auctioneer's platform, then the cognitive model should reflect the perceptual speed of the expert auctioneer. Since the judge's problem-solving is essentially ill-structured and requires a satisfying decision outcome, then the prior and procedural cognitions he or she uses should be the defining concepts of the model.

Representing Judicial Expertise

The rich and detailed data of expert problem-solving behaviors present some special representational difficulties if we are seeking to represent framing and procedural cognition of the same ill-structured problem space. If only classes of propositions are extracted from verbal protocols, then chains of inferencing and connectors are missing. If only goal structures and connecting links are drawn, then it is difficult to reveal the contents of specific nodes. Voss and his colleagues (1983) use a dual representational system of goal and reasoning structures in order to account for the complexities of problem-solving in ill-structured social science issues. I will describe a technique for reducing the verbal protocols of judging problems by identifying information-selection propositions that can be reduced to their basic forms and connected to consequent inferences and decisions.

Once propositions and links in a protocol are identified, they can be tabulated in inferential chains, and the formal structure can be represented diagramatically. Voss et al. (1983) represent goal structures and reasoning structures of total protocol in a Problem Behavior Graph. This system shows how subjects create their own goals and subgoals for ill-structured problems, and how they support their goals and solutions with assertions, arguments, and elaborations. The existence of supporting reasoning is marked on the goal structure graph, but reasoning content is shown in a separate table. I have tried to show actual inferencing structures together with their input information in the tables. Since subjects' objectives and views were elicited in direct questions, I have not drawn goal structure models as such. Instead, the general form or structure of the solution of a case can be stated as an *IF–THEN* implication of formal logic. This resembles the Condition–Act structures by which Chi, Glaser, & Rees (1981) represent propositions in their physics solution protocols. I will illustrate the reduction of a section of protocol in discussing the drunk driving case.

A MODEL OF JUDICIAL PROCESSES

The general form of the *IF p THEN q* implication specifies two nodes of the conditional p, and a chain of consequences as q:

Structure

$$
\text{IF} \xrightarrow{\quad THEN \quad} \qquad \xrightarrow{\quad THEN \quad}
$$

$$
\left\{ \begin{matrix} \text{Frames of} \\ \text{Reference} \end{matrix} \;\&\; \begin{matrix} \text{External} \\ \text{Constraints} \end{matrix} \right\} \left\{ \begin{matrix} \text{Information} \\ \text{Selection} \end{matrix} \left[\text{Inferences} \left(\begin{matrix} \text{Judgment} \\ \text{and sentence} \end{matrix} \right) \right] \right\}
$$

The figure is a simplification of an earlier composite model, abstracted from magistrates' accounts of their courtroom cognitions (Lawrence, 1984; Lawrence & Browne, 1981). Fifteen stipendiary magistrates spontaneously described their judgment processes in terms that could be grouped into the two types of cognitive activity. These comprised personal frames of reference and information procedures under the influence of external constraints.

Procedural steps are shown in the center of Figure 8.1 as information selected on offense, defendant, inferences, and decisions. Green (1961) and other researchers found that details concerning offense and defendant ex-

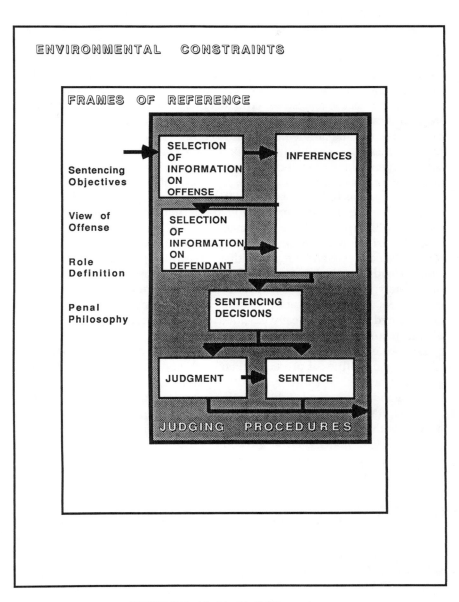

FIGURE 8.1 Model of judicial processes.

ert significant influence on sentencing variance, especially when analyzed in relation to judges' perspectives and views (Homel, 1981; Hood & Sparks, 1972). Information about the offense is typically obtained from police facts and reports on such things as blood alcohol levels in drunk driving cases, a defendant's statement to the police, witnesses' testimonies, and exhibits. Psychological and presentence reports on defendants may be requested by the magistrate in addition to police records and verbal testimonies.

The border of the magistrate's frames of reference encloses the procedural steps to illustrate how they give focus and perspective to the information procedures. Frames of reference or implicit theories can intrude at any point in the process, and can be illuminating as well as containing. In the literature, influential framing perspectives have included the penal philosophies or decision rules of individual judges, the immediate sentencing objectives, a judge's view of the severity of a particular crime, and his or her definition of the judging role in relation to particular cases (Gibson, 1978; Hogarth, 1971; Kapardis & Farrington, 1981; McKnight, 1981).

The outside parameter of the model illustrates the environmental factors which constrain and interact with a magistrate's processing. Our original subjects had expressed awareness of the possible effects of larger contextual parameters, and of their own ways of handling input from statutory or human forces. Legal constraints include the law of evidence and the range of legislated penalties. Heavy caseloads impose further physical contextualizing factors.

Human constraints exert inhibitive or facilitative influence, as the intentions and abilities of prosecutor, counsel, and witnesses expose or cloak pertinent details. One of our magistrate subjects observed, "The facts are only as good as the people who give them. That's the problem in our area." A skilled magistrate must recognize the limits imposed on him, and try to maximize the quality and quantity of information he uses. "All you can do is push the sides out . . . you are still constricted at some stage," was his way of expressing his efforts not to be contained by externals.

The three types of concept are interactive, and the model can trace input through the levels illustrated in the figure to judgment and sentence solutions. For example, a sentencing objective influences the information that is selected as relevant, and information selection affects the inferences that are made about the defendant. The structure and content of inferences determine the outcome judgment. Thus expertise can operate at several levels; in responding to external forces, in structuring one's own processes, and in choosing and transforming case details.

ANALYZING SENTENCING PROCESSES

The model was used to analyze how two experienced magistrates and one novice solved three simulated sentencing cases. Initially it was applied to the processing of a case with relatively little available data, and then to two more complicated cases containing probation officers' presentence reports.

A particular type of simulation technique was used for the first empirical application of the model. I have called it a "chambers simulation" to reflect the environmental setting and the closeness of the sentencing simulation task to magistrates' actual cognitive work and usual context. Jury and parole simulations of judicial thought processes often have to use contrived tasks. My cases were extracted from files of cases completed in the previous six months by other magistrates in the same court where the three experimental subjects presided. Actual file data were read and tendered to each magistrate as they would be in court. Magistrates were accustomed to processing file data and to receiving case details on the spot, without preparation. Although natural human sources of information and exchange were not present, the chambers simulation provided a way of getting verbal reports of magistrates' problem-solving of typical cases, without interfering with sensitive court proceedings.

Case and Subjects

Three representative offenses and defendants were chosen from the court archives. Henry was a 51-year-old homeless man who pleaded guilty to a charge of driving with more than the higher prescribed limit of alcohol, 0.280, when the prescribed level was 0.110. Sarah was a Middle Eastern migrant who pleaded guilty to stealing goods worth under $14 from a large city store. She had sufficient money with her to pay for the goods. Robert was a young baker who pleaded guilty to charges of supplying and possessing Indian hemp.

Subjects were two experienced stipendiary magistrates and an aspiring magistrate, all of whom worked in the same large Australian city court. The aspirant was a special kind of novice as he had completed all his legal training and service as a clerk of the court. He was currently working as a clerk and chamber magistrate giving informal legal advice to the public, and he hoped to be selected as a stipendiary magistrate in the future. The magistrates processed these three cases among others and discussed their work over three separate interviews within a two-week period.

First each magistrate was asked his general approach and frames of reference for the particular offense, with clinically probed questions about his view of its seriousness and implications, and his objectives when sentencing offenders. He then worked on the case as he would normally, or in the novice's case as he expected he would, while thinking out loud. Subjects dictated the order for tendering file data. They were asked to explain what they would do with any information they requested that was not on file, and then to work with the information that was available.

Data Analysis

Verbal protocols of audio tapes were analyzed by propositions in which pieces of data were verbalized, for all information mentioned and all inferences made about a case. Then the information points and inferences were reduced to their basic concepts to permit comparison of each of the three magistrates' handling of each case. Comparisons were made visible by the tabulation of the reduced form of the protocols. The tabulations are shown as Tables 8.1, 8.2, and 8.3. In each table, sentencing objectives and views of offenses are shown for each magistrate across the top of the columns. Information selected about offenses are in rows $O1$ to Oo, and about the defendants in $D1$ to Dd. Inferences and sentencing decisions are shown in rows $I1$ to Ii and $SD1$ to $SDsd$, respectively.

For example, the following section of Expert One's protocol is separated into reduced propositions of Column One, Table One.

Er, he's probably been on an all-night binge. Finishing at, er, 10 or midnight or so, when the beer supply, um, er, ran out or closed up, and got onto the bottles of wine and stayed on the wine until sometime before driving.	$I1$. All-night binge
There's no indication in the facts as to when he had his last drink prior to the, oh yes, there, is, nine last drink, nine-thirty A.M.	$\emptyset 3$. Times of events (and in other segments)
Well, that may be right, it may not, because his um, faculties aren't going to be extremely good at .280. Er, but it does indicate an all-night binge which in turn indicates in a man of er, what, er, 51 years, a serious alcohol problem.	$I2$. Defendant is alcoholic

I will describe the analysis of the simplest case on which the tabulated scheme was developed, and then show how the model accounted for similarities and differences in the experts' and novice's approaches to more complex cases.

Sentencing a Drinking Driver

In the case of Henry, the drunk driver, the experts differed from the novice in their frames of reference for the case, and in the inferences they made about the available data. They did not differ dramatically from the novice in the information about Henry that they extracted from the file data. The reductions of the three protocols are shown in Table 8.1.

Frames of Reference.   The two experts' frames of reference were similar to each other's, but different from the novice's both in their sentencing objectives and views of the drunk driving offense. Reading across the top of the columns shows that experts expressed objectives of individualized treatment of Henry with the explicit purpose of deterring him from repeating his offense. Expert One emphasized intervention and treatment; Expert Two mentioned individualized penalties as his ideal. In Henry's case this meant treatment of his alcoholism. Both defined the offense as serious because of its danger and monetary cost to the community. In contrast, the novice mentioned "deterrence" as his aim, but gave no explanation of whether he meant specific avoidance of Henry's reoffense or generalized deterrence of any potential offenders. Later he added that he wished to keep within a reasonable middle range of penalties for that court.

Selection of Information.   The three magistrates mentioned similar details about the offense and the defendant, although Expert One typically mentioned more information. Expert–novice differences were in the inferences they made about the file data, and in their sentencing decisions.

Inferences.   Both experts built up a picture of Henry as an alcoholic (*I1, I2*), and saw the collision as a direct result of his alcohol problem (*I3*). He was a danger to the public (*I4*). Expert One concluded that Henry's personal condition meant that he had no motivation for changing his life-style, such as a job to attend next morning or a family to go home to (*I5*). Expert Two commented that the heavy fine for the previous offense would automatically mean jail by default for an unemployed man without money to pay (*I6*). Both experts said the previous sentence was ineffective and jail would be no deterrence (*I7*). In contrast, the novice said only that he saw no basis for mitigation of a heavy sentence, because of a similar previous incident and this reoffense (*I9*). However, he added that the earlier fine had been too harsh and he would settle for a middle-range heavy fine (*I10*).

Sentencing Decisions.   Both experts preferred to adjourn and seek presentence reports than to hand down a penalty from the data that were available (*SD1*). Each said he would personally assess any reports (*SD2*). The novice

TABLE 8.1

Expert and Novice Magistrates' Processing of a Drunk Driving Case

STATED FRAME OF REFERENCE	Magistrate		
	Expert One	Expert Two	Novice
Sentencing Objective	Treatment to prevent reoffense	Treatment to prevent reoffense	'Deterrence' (unspecified) Reasonable, parity penalty
View of Offense	Serious, danger to public	Serious, danger to public	Minor unless dangerous
Information Selection			
On Offense			
01. Blood Alcohol Level very high, .280	+	+	+
02. Circumstances of offense: Collision	+	+	+
03. Times of events: Last drink 9.30am, collision 11.25am	+	.	.
On Defendant			
D1. Previous offense in year, Blood Alcohol Level, .300	+	+	+
D2. Unemployed, homeless, living in motor vehicle	+	+	+
D3. Previous sentence: Heavy fine, $600	+	+ heavy	+ heavy, $600
D4. Unlicensed driver because disqualified	+	.	.

Inference			
I1.	All-night binge	+ from 01,03	+ from 01, D1	.
I2.	Defendant is alcoholic	+ from 01, 02, D1, I1	+ from 01, I2	.
I3.	Alcoholism, drunkenness cause of collision	+ from 01, I2	+ from 02, I2	.
I4.	Defendant is danger to the public	+ from 02, I2		.
I5.	Defendant has other problems, no motivation for change	+ from 02, 03		.
I6.	Heavy fine would mean jail	.	+ from D2, D3	.
I7.	Previous penalty was ineffective	+ from 01, D1, D3	+ from 01 D1, D3	+ from 01, D1, D3
I8.	Jail would not deter	+ from I7	+ from I7	+ from D3
I9.	No mitigation of penalty possible	.		.
I10.	Last fine high by current court standards	.		
Sentencing Decisions				
SD1.	Adjourn, ask for presentence, medical, social reports	+	+	.
SD2.	Assess reports	+	+	.
SD3.	Ask defendant for explanation of life circumstances		+	+
SD4.	Penalty	drug clinic probation supervision three-year disqualification	drug clinic or weekend jail and community service three-year disqualification	fine, $400 . three-year disqualification

did not seek a presentence report, but said he would immediately seek further details about Henry's circumstances, and especially ask why a man of 51 was living in his car (SD3).

As penalty, Expert One said he would impose attendance at a daily drug clinic and long-term probation supervision as interventions in Henry's lifestyle, or one month's "short, sharp" imprisonment as a final attempt to avoid reoffense. Expert Two's penalty was similar, except that he included weekend detention and community service as possible additions to treatment. The novice decided that a $400 fine was reasonable (SD4). All imposed the usual three-year driving disqualification.

In summary, expertise was exhibited in the objectives and views that the experienced magistrates had built upon the bench, and in their handling of the case data to prevent Henry's reoffense. The two experienced men had similar ways of approaching the case, and of generating penalties from the available information. They both wanted more information and were unwilling to sentence finally without it. The first expert stated his commitment to an intervention and treatment goal. The second expert's individualized approach included a desire to know if a family would be adversely affected by jailing Henry, even though no family was mentioned in the file. Individualization was his ideal, but time constraints sometimes meant using a tariff penalty with new offenders. In this case an individualized sentence coincided with the treatment approach of his colleague. The novice's bureaucratic processing was revealed in his more rigid and sparser inferencing and his monetary tariff penalty.

If these men were following individualized styles, then the experts' treatment goals and the novice's bureaucratic approaches may be observable in other cases. If their approaches were artifacts of Henry's case, or of drunk driving offenses, then they may not generalize. For example, Expert One may not try to intervene in the life-style of other offenders. The novice saw drunk driving as a minor offense with a wide range of potential offenders. What would emerge in other cases where he did not readily identify with the defendant? Would his bureaucratic concern with generating a sentence on a parity with other courtrooms persist for cases with more information, and for cases other than a traffic offense? Concepts of the model and the data-reduction scheme were applied to the other two cases where there was more information in probation officers' presentence reports. Analysis of these cases allowed examination of the interactive features of magistrates' processing when more data were injected after the initial file material had been processed.

Sentencing a Shoplifter

Features of the shoplifting case which distinguished the experts' protocols from the novice's were their initial sentencing objectives, and their inferences. Magistrates' processes are shown in Table 8.2.

Frames of Reference.   Each expert said his main objective in sentencing shoplifters was to prevent reoffense. That objective was associated with their shared perception that there was too much stealing from stores. In ultimate costs to the community, Sarah's offense was more serious than merely a minor act of theft. Both experts sought to achieve deterrence by treatment which would assist individuals to change their life-styles.

The novice saw his task as devising a fine that would fit court norms. Shoplifters could be penalized with tariff fines, and did not elicit the kind of treatment approach he would use on drug addicts who needed help. This view changed when the presentence report revealed that Sarah was under psychiatric care. He immediately adopted a treatment objective like the experts', when this extra information was given.

Information Selection and Inferencing.   Expert One selected the most information from the files, mentioning legal and personal details. Expert Two paid more attention to legal details such as the defendant's plea and prior offenses, than to her personal characteristics. Initially the novice noticed only that goods were taken from several parts of the store (O1), and he extracted only some information about the mother's illness from the file (D4). The presentence report data influenced his processing perspective (D5,6,8).

Both experts, but not the novice, inferred that Sarah's plea of guilty was acceptable because she was represented by a solicitor (I1). Expert One's attention to details was sustained in the kinds of inferences he made about the shoplifter. He drew his own conclusions about Sarah's personal problems and emotional state, and her intention to steal the goods. Inferences I2, I3, and I4 show that he had a patterned expectation which was activated as soon as the charge was read, and the defendant's name, sex, and age were revealed. She would be an ordinary shoplifter (I4), and

> She's undoubtedly married. Yes, and probably got two children, and I'll be told all this later. There's an immediate suspicion that things aren't good at home and that she's in fact a repressed housewife, which may be the root of the offense.

He had to change his assumption when the file revealed that Sarah was a single, Lebanese migrant. But he had another script for that. "Why was she staying in Australia if she was a single, Middle Eastern woman, and alone?" These inferences activated a well-used script which, with his objective of treatment to prevent her reoffense, led him to look for additional clinical data about her problems; those data took him to a sentence which involved treatment and supervisory help (I5,SD1 and 2, to SD4).

TABLE 8.2
Expert and Novice Magistrates' Processing of a Shoplifting Case

	Magistrate		
STATED FRAME OF REFERENCE	Expert One	Expert Two	Novice
Sentencing Objective	Treatment to Prevent Reoffense	Treatment to Prevent Reoffense	'Deterrence' (unspecified) Reasonable, Parity, Middle-Range Fine
View of Offense	Economic Cost to Public, Prevalence	Ecomonic Cost to Public, Prevalence	Not an Offense for Treatment (Change After D6)
Information Selection			
On Offense			
O1. Took goods from several parts of store	+	.	+
O2. Goods of minor value, $14	+	.	.
On Defendant from Files			
D1. Plea of guilty	+	+	.
D2. Represented by solicitor	+	+	.
D3. 34-year-old migrant woman, poor English	+	.	.
D4. Mother's illness	+	.	+
On Defendant from Presentence Report			
D5. There was a previous offense	+	+	+
D6. Depression, under psychiatric treatment	+	+	+
D7. Outgoing, intelligent	+	.	.
D8. Mother's death	+	.	+

Inference

I1. Plea acceptable because represented	+ from D1, D2	+ from D1, D2	·
I2. Average, ordinary shoplifter	+ from O1 (assumption)	·	·
I3. Housewife with home problems	+ (assumption, changed)	·	·
I4. Deliberate theft, not forgetfulness	+ from O1, D1	·	+ from O1
I5. Long-standing problem, caused by life-style	+ from O1, D5, D6	·	·
I6. Inconsistencies in presentence report	+ (D6 vs D7, D4 vs D8)	·	·
I7. Police report deficient	·	+ from D5	·
I8. No sympathy possible	·	·	+ from O1, I4
I9. Mitigating circumstances exist	·	·	+ from I8, D6 (change)

Sentencing Decisions

SD1. Adjourn, ask for presentence, psychiatric reports	+	+	·
SD2. Assess reports	+	+	·
SD3. Ask police about mother's illness			+
SD4. Penalty	bond, 3–5 yrs probation supervision psychiatric treatment	bond probation supervision psychiatric treatment	bond probation supervision psychiatric treatment

In contrast, the other expert focussed on legal information (*I1, I7*). He used the presentence report to confirm his early decision that if Sarah was under psychiatric care, he would order its continuation (*SD4*). He was perturbed that the police report had not documented a prior offense (*I7*). Her depression, and the poor police information, led Expert Two straight to a Presentence Report, and from that — with his treatment-oriented approach — to the same sentence as his colleague (*D6, I7, SD1 and 2, to SD4*).

The novice's inferences show the interactive nature of the sentencing process. His inferencing and solutions were changed by extra information. Originally, because Sarah took goods from several different parts of the store, he induced deliberate theft (*I4*). He had no sympathy for her (*I8*). However, once he knew of her illness he interpreted that as a mitigating factor, and consciously adapted his approach. The switch is shown at (*I9*), with his view of the offense. He turned to a treatment frame for the case once he saw the mitigating circumstances of her depression, and therefore, in this case, his final sentence agreed with the experts' (*D6, I9, to SD4*).

Sentencing Decisions and Penalties.   The experts differed from the novice in their early request for a presentence report that they would assess (*SD1,2*). The novice, instead, again said he would seek special information from the police officer in court (*SD3*). Once the novice had the details about Sarah's problems, he called for the same penalty as the experts — bond, supervision, and continuation of psychiatric treatment (*SD4*).

Sentencing a Drug Offender

There was agreement in the three magistrates' views of the drug offense. This time, however, expert/novice differences were found at the level of information selection, inferencing, and decisions even when the same objectives were stated. The magistrates' processing is shown in Table 8.3.

Frames of Reference.   All three magistrates considered supplying drugs more serious than their possession, and no one defined an Indian Hemp case as a serious drug offense. Expert Two defined possession as something which "doesn't affect the rest of society" except in terms of selling. Nevertheless he thought it was less serious in its effects on the community than drunk driving. All three had the objective of preventing Robert's reoffense. Technically this is called "specific deterrence." All three added the objective of general deterrence of other potential offenders, in the penalties they handed down for Robert's two charges.

Information Selection and Inferencing.   Both experts noticed more information

TABLE 8.3

Expert and Novice Magistrates' Processing of a Drug Supply and Possession Case

	Magistrate		
STATED FRAME OF REFERENCE	Expert One	Expert Two	Novice
Sentencing Objective	Deterrence, treat to change life-style, general deterrence	Specific and general deterrence	'Deterrence' from supplying
View of Offense	Supply is a crime, possession is not	Supply is worse than possession, not serious case	Supply is worse than possession
Information Selection			
On Offense			
01. Quantity of hashish for sale	+ $600 worth	+	.
02. Not cooperative, withheld details	+	.	.
03. Defendant selling from home	+ one month	+	.
04. Two charges: Supply and possession	+	+	+
On Defendant from Files			
D1. Plea of guilty to supply	+ from 01	.	.
D2. Single, 23 y.o., baker, $160 per week	+	.	.
D3. Hashish, but defendant not Eastern European	+	+	.
D4. Prior offense for possession, minor fine	+	.	+ ($70)
D5. Prior offense, withheld details	+	.	.
D6. Prior traffic offenses	+	.	.
On Defendant from Presentence Report			
D7. Disturbed family background	+	.	+
D8. Insecure, emotionally disturbed	+	.	+

(Continued)

245

TABLE 8.3
(Continued)

Stated Frame of Reference	Magistrate		
	Expert One	*Expert Two*	*Novice*
Sentencing Objective	Deterrence, treat to change life-style, general deterrence	Specific and general deterrence	'Deterrence' from supplying
View of Offense	Supply is a crime, possession is not	Supply is worse than possession, not serious case	Supply is worse than possession
Inference			
I1. Professional supplying for profit, not self-use	+ from O1, O3, D3	.	.
I2. Motive is greed	+ from O1, I1	.	.
I3. Attitude poor on prior offense and now	+ from O2, D5	.	.
I4. Prior use led to supply	+ from O4, D4	.	.
I5. Reason for involvement is personality	+ from D7, D8	.	.
I6. Reason for withholding information, family background	+ from D5, D7	.	.
I7. Personal problems	+ from O2, D5, D7, D8	+ no source	.
I8. Disregard for drug laws	.	+ from presentence rpt	.
I9. Prior offense not serious to that magistrate	.	.	+ from D4
I10. Nothing extenuating or different in this case	.	.	+ from D7, D8
Sentencing Decisions			
SD1. Case is minor, can be heard summarily	+ from O1	.	.
SD2. Presentence recommendation agreeable	+ from D8	.	.
SD3. Needs constant supervision	.	.	+
SD4. Penalty On supply:	bond, probation supervision	bond, probation supervision	bond, probation supervision fine, $150
SD4. Penalty On possession:	community service	community service	

than did the novice, who only mentioned that there were two charges (*O4*). Expert Two's attention to details was sparser than Expert One's, but he reached a similar conclusion that Robert had personal problems (*I7*), and that his behavior indicated disregard for drug laws (*I8*). Expert One attributed Robert's offense to motivational and environmental causes (*I1 to I7*); he believed Robert's interest in drugs was commercial because the type of hemp was hashish, implying either Eastern European nationality or professional involvement (*I1*). To this expert, Robert's disturbed family background and a previous possession case explained his current involvement with drugs (*I5, I6*). The novice's inferences were to establish the level of the prior sentence (*I9*), and to conclude that there were no mitigating circumstances (*I10*).

Sentencing Decisions and Penalties.   Two charges meant that magistrates could impose a bond and supervision for the supply charge, and another penalty for possession. Legal guidelines made community service possible for the second charge, so the experts used it and avoided jailing Robert. Expert One had deterrence of other potential offenders in mind:

> To simply put him on a bond would be seen by him and his peers as being not anything strong in the way of penalty. . . . But when he goes home all he's got to say is that "I've got to work on Saturday for the next fifty-two weeks." They'll see that as the penalty for the supply.

Although Expert Two said less, he was responding to an overall assessment of the minor nature of the offense, an individualized penalty, and Robert's problem. The novice used a fine. Supervision meant for him a chance to have Robert watched, in contrast to Expert One who wanted the officer to positively intervene in Robert's problems.

In summary, the three protocols revealed several places where experience made a difference. The experts' intentions and perspectives were different from the novice's and influenced the types of inferences they made about case details. They saw the defendants as individuals to be dealt with according to their circumstances.

The novice worked from a tariff approach which paid lip service to deterrence, but actually defined outcome penalties against his own intention of keeping within court norms. With that kind of goal, he had little need to make inferences about causes of offenses beyond determining any mitigating circumstances which would reduce standard penalties. He reacted to extra presentence information by changing his standard tariff objective to a treatment approach he had previously said was inappropriate. Now he saw the shoplifter as someone to be helped. Although he had alluded to drug offenders as candidates for help in contrast with shoplifters, when it came to the drug offender, he could find no mitigating circumstances to suggest treatment, and again imposed a standard fine.

Hints of external influences arose in the two cases with extra data. Both experts were conscious of possible influence of other people's input. Expert Two was not prepared to accept the probation officers' presentence reports, especially when he found a discrepancy in the content. He did not want an officer to interpret a psychiatrist's report. He would do that himself and not be influenced. Statutory laws were influential in their breakdown of the penalties for the two drug charges.

We are now in a position to indicate the distinguishing features of the expert and novice protocols. An *IF–THEN* structure can be shown. The *p* of the relationship comprises both the frames of reference and the external constraints. The *q* is a string of implications. The proposition states that sentencing objectives and theories of crimes' seriousness influence choice of relevant information, the inferences from that information, consequent decisions, judgment, and sentence.

The experts' protocols have the following structure:

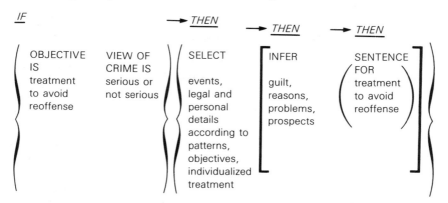

The novice's protocols have the structure:

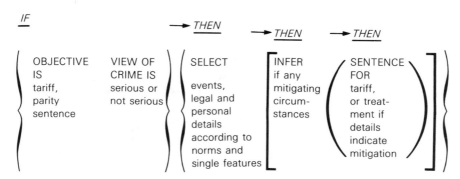

Major expert/novice differences occurred at the levels of what the magistrates brought to the three cases as their objectives, and at levels of inferencing and of deciding on sentencing solutions. There were hints of difference in the manner of expert/novice selection procedures rather than in the content of the information. Experts had more patterned approaches, and were directed by their treatment of objectives to assess the cause of the defendants' behaviors, and their prospects of responding to treatment and individualized approaches. Although the novice knew and responded to ritualized evidence-gathering procedures, he seemed to work with single details. The low-level seriousness of these offenses did not provoke extreme reactions, and think-aloud readings of files may not be the most illuminative sources of subjects' emphases. Direct questions can be used in follow-up studies to check these hints with cases of varying severity.

Perhaps expert/novice differences could be explained as the consequences of the degree of familiarity with cases, the number of cases, quality and consistency of patterns for common offenses, and experience with procedures for interpreting details. The area yields no easy criteria for assessing expert behavior. A judge whose decisions are seldom taken to appeals courts may be more inefficient than another judge with frequently challenged judgments. Imposition of standard tariff penalties like the novice's would probably not provoke strong reactions. Peer evaluation is not common. The concepts of the model contribute to ways of discerning expertise, but otherwise we have to rely on years of experience as a rule-of-thumb descriptor. There were consistent trends in these experts' approaches, as well as indications of personal styles.

Now that inter- and intraindividual consistencies and inconsistencies can be demonstrated schematically, we can look at courtroom expertise in action. *In situ* interactive and constraining influences can be analyzed. So the generality and usefulness of the model was examined by applying it to one experienced magistrate's judging of two actual defended court cases. Unwillingness to take models out of the laboratory is partly due to the difficulties of obtaining naturalistic data that can be represented in a detailed way (Scribner, 1983; Scribner & Cole, 1981). I used a technique for obtaining on-site reports and observations of courtroom expertise.

APPLICATION TO ACTUAL COURT CASES

The subject was a magistrate with over ten years' experience on the bench. He presided in another Australian city court, and had been interviewed informally twelve months previously. The two defended cases he heard were eight months apart, and each took a full day's summary hearing. Similar charges gave a basis for observing a single subject in different working contexts. The magistrate made no connections between the cases, but I observed that it was the same defense counsel on both occasions.

Each defendant pleaded not guilty to the charge of dangerous driving with serious human consequences. The first defendant, Karen, was a woman of middle years who was charged with dangerous driving causing grievous bodily harm. She was accused of driving her car onto a grass verge beside a suburban road and injuring a young boy who was sitting on the grass with his friends. Paul, a truck driver in his thirties, was charged with dangerous driving causing death. His semitrailer collided head-on with a car on a country road, resulting in death for the three occupants of the car.

To obtain verbal and observational data of the magistrate's processing, I interviewed him in his chambers prior to the hearing, attended court myself and took notes, and interviewed the magistrate in chambers again after the conclusion of each day-long case. Pre-court questions were designed to find out the magistrate's sentencing objectives, view of the crime, and definition of his own role in the proceedings. He had to make two decisions in each case, a judgment and a sentence if necessary. I asked for his expectations about the type of information he expected to emerge during the hearing, and how he would handle that information. Attendance in court allowed me to note the information that was presented and the contextual factors that influenced how the magistrate worked, and to generate post-court questions and problems.

Transcripts and courtroom notes were analyzed in the concepts of the model by coding each statement the magistrate made about his views, role, and objectives, and his comments about external constraints and the courtroom proceedings. Statements could be spontaneous or in response to probing questions from my courtroom observations. His identification of each piece of useful, missing and misleading information was reduced to basic concepts, together with his expressed inferences and decisions. All transcripts and my courtroom notes were coded independently by an anthropology graduate, and interpretations were discussed.

There is greater focus on the events of the actual offense in a defended case. Sentencing is secondary to judging guilt. Therefore Table 8.4 sets out the concepts of the original model to show the double-headed aspects of the problem space. Facts about the event will be especially important as the magistrate proves beyond his doubt that the reputed offense took place, and was done by the defendant and in the manner as charged. Inferences about the defendant's characteristics are more closely related to the determination of an appropriate sentence if the defendant is judged guilty.

Frames of Reference.   These were elicited prior to court, and discussed after. For both cases the magistrate defined his judging objectives as determining the single issue of whether or not the actual driving was dangerous. In the bodily harm case, dangerousness overruled any side issues about what caused the defendant to drive onto the verge. Whether or not she had been drink-

TABLE 8.4

An Experienced Magistrate's Judging of Two Dangerous Driving Cases Causing:

	Grievous Bodily Harm	Death
State Frame of Reference		
Judging Objective	Determine if driving dangerous, not causes, establish facts situation	Juggle issues to determine one; if driving dangerous, find facts situation
View of Offense	Traffic offense, wide range of offenders, defined as single issue	More serious than other traffic offenses only in grave consequences, single issue
Role of Magistrate	Put self there, familiarize with events, environment	Postpone decision till all data are in, associate and disassociate self
External Constraints		
Statutory	Inflexible rules for sentencing	Strong guidelines for sentencing
Human	Defense counsel's strategies, quality of police testimony	Defense counsel's strategy of conceded evidence, prosecution weak
Information selection		
On Offense		
O1. Police evidence available	+ Officer A's + B's	. conceded by defense
O2. Witnesses' testimony	+ children's	+ elderly lady's
O3. Exhibits: Maps, photos, etc.	+	+
On Defendant		
D1. Prior convictions	+ minor traffic	+ minor, 10 years ago
D2. Occupation	+ entertainer, social work	+ truck owner
D3. Characteristics	+ emotional, drinking	+ aged parents, remorse

(Continued)

TABLE 8.4
(Continued)

	Grievous Bodily Harm	Death
State Frame of Reference		
Judging Objective	*Determine if driving dangerous, not causes, establish facts situation*	*Juggle issues to determine one; if driving dangerous, find facts situation*
View of Offense	*Traffic offense, wide range of offenders, defined as single issue*	*More serious than other traffic offenses only in grave consequences, single issue*
Role of Magistrate	*Put self there, familiarize with events, environment*	*Postpone decision till all data are in, associate and disassociate self*
External Constraints		
Statutory	*Inflexible rules for sentencing*	*Strong guidelines for sentencing*
Human	*Defense counsel's strategies, quality of police testimony*	*Defense counsel's strategy of conceded evidence, prosecution weak*
Inference		
I1. On police evidence	+ A's unreliable (from O1 & past experience) B's useful on time, locations	not available to court (from O1)
I2. On witnesses' testimonies	+ children's; "ring of truth," corroborative (from O2, O3)	+ elderly lady confused, uninformative (from O1)
I3. One exhibits	+ useful; confirmed testimonies on car's tire, slow speed, stopping (from O2, O3)	+ useful; explained conditions, driver's behaviors & intentions (from O3, O1)
I4. On priors	+ not against mitigation (from D1)	+ previous good record, mitigation (from D1)
I5. On occupation	+ irrelevant is a stripper (from D2)	+ dependent on driving for livelihood (From D2)
I6. On characteristics	+ disturbed, alcoholic (from D3, O3, I3)	+ has dependent, signs of self-justification to follow (from D3)
Decisions		
JD1. Driving dangerous	+ and unintentioned, children innocent (from I2, I3)	+ and culpable (from I3)
JD2. Mitigation	+ on condition, tire, car (from I3, I5)	+ on record, characteristics (I4, I5, I6)
Judgment	Guilty (from JD1)	Guilty (from JD1)
Sentence		
Penalty	$250 (qrt max) (from JD2) 1-year disqualification	$3600 (half max) (from JD2) 18-month disqualification

ing was irrelevant to the charge of the dangerous manner of her driving. In the case of the death of several people, the magistrate expected a number of factors to arise, but to converge again on one central issue of whether the truck driver actually drove dangerously on the wrong side of the road across double lines on a bend. The gravity of the consequences was not at issue, but whether those consequences were caused by behavior beyond carelessness, to the point of unnecessary danger. When asked, he defined his own role — in very similar terms on both occasions — as one of trying to put himself in the situation, familiarizing himself with environment and events in order to be able to assess the degree of danger.

External Constraints. Another special feature of the defended case is the significance of external constraints. Legal statutes set limits on possible penalties, and therefore define official interpretations of the seriousness of a case. Someone charged with repeated drunk driving offenses could incur a penalty similar to someone charged with driving that caused such grave human consequences. The magistrate kept that in mind in his view of the crimes and when fixing on the lowest penalty that the community would stand.

Human intentions and abilities influenced how the magistrate worked. Some useful information was denied him, as in the truck driver's case by the defense counsel's clever concession of all police reports, and the police prosecutor's ineptitude. Consequently the number dead and the condition and positions of the vehicles were never stated. Although I was present throughout the case, I did not know how many people were killed until I asked after court. The prosecutor allowed the defense counsel to concede the data and so to "disrupt the case" the magistrate said. This meant that he as judge had to "go digging for information" which should have been made clear for him. So some of his cognitive work was in response to influences outside his power.

Information, and Inferences. These are placed together in the table to show the magistrate's inferences about the information, as it emerged. Information on the actual offense is *O1 to O3*, and about the defendants is *D4 to D6*. Inferences *I1* to *I6* are alongside the information, and Judging Decisions are *JD1,2*.

On the actual events of the bodily harm case, three constables gave evidence of varying usefulness (*O1*). Officer A's evidence was considered unreliable, because of previous encounters and because of his "premeditated evidence." Officer B's was useful in establishing that the woman was driving the car at established times and locations (*I1*). The children's testimonies (*O2*) were convincing, because when the defense counsel accused them of playing "chicken" on the road, their innocent reactions were credible (*I2*). Police exhibits and maps (*O3*) indicated to the magistrate that the car had stopped and was traveling slowly, and had a tire problem. This was supported by testimony of the boy's minor injury (*I3*). But the corroboration of the children's evidence led to the inference that they were sitting on the verge (*I2*). As the magistrate told me after the hearing:

> But because the later children confirmed each other . . . I was happy to feel that I knew the children were . . . not on the curb but a short distance from it. . . . But I found myself accepting their version because they corroborated each other so well and I did feel I ended up with a fact situation that I could rely on.

Evidence was readily available from witnesses for this case, and the exhibits gave the magistrate a feeling of participant observer, and confirmed the verbal evidence. The magistrate judged the woman guilty of dangerous driving (*JD1*). In the other case, the magistrate had to carefully work through the exhibits himself. Police reports were absent (*O1*) because the evidence was conceded and therefore was not read out (*I1*). Eyewitness reports were not helpful (*I2*) because the elderly aboriginal woman witness could not describe the situation (*O2*). Maps and photographs (*O3*) formed the only substantial evidence. When the conditions of the road with skid marks and double lines were read off, "everything else jelled into place." The magistrate estimated speed and locations, reconstructed the scene from exhibits (*I3*), and judged the defendant guilty of driving on the wrong side of the road and unnecessarily dangerously (*JD1*). In reflection, he described the scene:

> And when the brake lights (of the leading car) came on, as no doubt they did, he decided, "Well I'm not going to put up with this," and he just signalled and moved over to the other side of the road. Eventually he caught up with that other car and started to pass it on the wrong side of the road into a bend, over the double line.

Information about both defendants (*D4,5,6*) was used to determine the grounds for setting penalties within Parliament's prescribed range. This segment of the protocol is reminiscent of the selection of defendant characteristics in the sentencing simulations. Absence of prior convictions (*D1*) was significant in both cases for determining any mitigation, and the penalties (*I4*). The woman's occupation was considered irrelevant, the truck driver's occupation was significant because driving was his livelihood. (*D5* to *I5*). Her emotionality and early-morning drinking implied a disturbed state and probable alcoholism to the magistrate, but also that she would be driving slowly. The truck driver's aged parents and his injuries established his commitments and predicted future good behavior (*D6* to *I6*). Other mitigating factors were her car's bad tire, and his good record (*JD2*). In both cases the magistrate felt he had met society's demands without being punitive. He considered his fine to be reasonable, or even light; he was forced to work with the evidence that was made available.

The analysis reveals the features of the magistrate's predictive and retrospective reports. Some major consistencies were in his objectives for the hearings and in his own involvement; his perception of the offenses' gravity, not based on consequences but on the legal definition of driving dangerously; and his active follow-through on the task of accruing information that would prove that single issue of dangerous behavior. *IF–THEN* structures of the two protocols set out schematically the similarities of the magistrate's perspectives and procedures, and his responses to the contingencies of the cases.

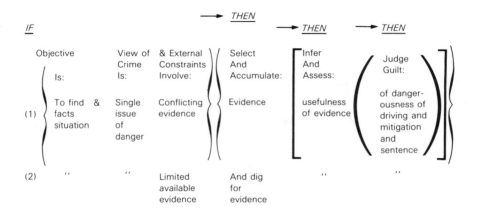

The analysis gives some insight into the way experience or expertise brought this magistrate to two similar judgments in distinct problem spaces. He anticipated some of the features of his problem, and handled others as they arose.

A problem-solver's anticipatory patterns and responsive moves may be even more important in ill-structured problem spaces than in those where fewer properties are free to vary. Ultimately there may be few problems where experts do not have to impose individualized perspectives and structures on data. Whatever the case for well-structured problems, this is so in a complex situation with conflicting intentions and procedural rituals.

This magistrate anticipated regularities in his approaches across the cases:

> You're going to follow a pre-existing pattern where whatever does happen is going to fit between extremes of what you've dealt with before.

His expectation and coping strategies were illustrated in the magistrate's perceptions of the defense counsel's moves. It was the same well-known attorney. In the first case, the magistrate did not know his identity until they were in court; but in the second case he did know, and was prepared for the counsel's tactic of raising doubts about who was at fault.

> And I suppose it's mentally preparing for the kind of procedures that are going to be followed, and the kind of procedures that I'll need to be ready for.

In the post-court interview he interpreted the defense counsel's attempts to shift fault as a tactic designed to determine positive grounds for mitigation of sentence, and he explained how counsel had been effective within legal boundaries. Counsel's obfuscation of the collision events prepared the ground for mitigation of sentence.

One way to deal with uncontrollable features of a problem is to hold certain possibilities in tension, and not foreclose early (deGroot, 1965). The magistrate had predicted that he would need to do that, and in the post-court report described how he had to wait to be sure that the boy was not out on the road. The ring of truth in the later children's testimony convinced him, and he re-examined the other data.

The ability to search for significant features in uncertainty was another mark of his experienced handling of the case; for example, in his complex inductions of the truck driver's position and motives from the map. Feature extraction was mentioned by the earlier magistrate as the complement of pattern recognition in expert judging. This man demonstrated his ability to do that in the more difficult problem.

CONCLUSION

At the beginning I argued that problem-solving in ill-structured domains like judging require representational schemes that can describe procedural operations in combination with pre-existent perspectives. I argued that concepts should reflect the phenomena of the domain, and that first-level reductions of empirical data should be made clear. The simulation and actual case data go some way toward meeting those criteria, especially in attempts to describe and explain links between what the magistrate brings to the case, what he finds in it, and what he does with given and emergent evidence.

In a highly personalized professional role, with individualized ways of defining outcomes and processes, experience provided the experts with patterns for reducing work loads. For these experts, experience also led to similar goals and perspectives on different types of offenses. Experience also brought with it ideas about what to look for, and ways to follow up leads in the data. The simulations of the experts were markedly different from that of the novice in pulling leads out of the files and reports.

Prior perspectives, and procedural selection and use of evidence, could account for inexpertness in experienced magistrates just as well as expertness. In the original metacognitive study some of the subjects mentioned that certain colleagues were known to lawyers for their prejudices. One was known for his hardness on gamblers and prostitutes, another was known as a "hanging judge" in drunk driving cases. By asking for sentencing objectives and views of particular crimes, such prejudices could be empirically identified. Ineffective or inappropriate ways of dealing with data can be revealed in the inferential structures, like one of the expert's incorrect inductions from early file data.

Homel (1981), and Smith and Blumberg (1967) among others have made much of individualized styles of judging and sentencing, but it is important to break down that global concept to take some of the mystification out of the judging profession, and some of the puzzle out of disparate sentencing. Although the once-off solution may not be very illuminating, examining one magistrate's judgments of different but similar cases can help develop empirical identifiers of individualized style, across changing situations. The social significance of outcomes of courtroom processing makes it all the more pertinent to be able to complement archival data with fine-grained specifications of contributing factors.

The *IF–THEN* implication gives a set of concepts and relations that can be tested in further studies, even if the strongest form of the statement does not hold up. We asked students to weight the pieces of information in Henry's case and to simulate the sentencing procedures. While their weightings were influenced by the sentencing objectives we induced, they also reflected students' personal frames of references about drunk driving.

Other factors may emerge, but the general form of the implication statement will cover them. For example, we intuitively attach importance to the defendant's appearance, and there is evidence for the influence of the language and rhetoric of the counsel (Logan, 1982). These features may function as external constraints, or as the information-base of the magistrate, but that distinction must be worked out empirically. The position of the major implication link may shift. But since the q occurs in the magistrate's thinking without discussion, then it would appear that his or her procedural work stays on the consequence side of the implication. At each proposition or node, problem-related features can be specified. For example, I have broken down frames of reference into sentencing objectives, views of crimes, and personal role definitions. Others might be ethical or religious beliefs. Environmental constraints can change, especially with variations in laws. Drug and driving laws, for instance, reflect government policies, and have changed considerably in Australia recently. So magistrates are likely to need to respond to new statutory expectations of appropriate penalties as they become law. Of course it is possible for inferences to presuppose rather than depend upon choice of information. That possibility supports my notion of the essential ill-structuredness of the domain. First-level reductions will show what adjustments are needed to the general implication in particular instances.

One of the limitations of this approach may be the very specificity that makes it relevant to the legal world. But there may be other domains in which problems involve givens that are a mixture of knowns and unknowns, and here all information is not in at the beginning. A problem-solver must find his or her own database; not all information is given. Assessing student performance is another domain in which these factors operate and where the present scheme may be applied. We have no novice data on actual cases, but the categories for description now have been specified. The novice was a genuine, trained aspirant with experience of courtrooms. Even so, the scheme was sensitive enough to show where inexperience was associated with processing deficiencies. Levels of inexpertness can be introduced in further studies. Whereas the representational scheme is still in its early stages of development, it holds promise of ways of identifying expertise at work in professional domains requiring ill-structured problem solving.

ACKNOWLEDGMENTS

This research was supported by the Australian Research Grant Scheme.

REFERENCES

Berger, P. L., Berger, B., & Kellner, H. (1973). *The homeless mind: Modernization and consciousness*. Harmondsworth; Penguin.

Berger, P. L., & Luckman, J. (1966). *The social construction of reality: A treatise in the sociology of knowledge*. New York: Doubleday & Co.

Chi, M. T. H., Glaser, R., & Rees, E. (1982). Expertise in problem solving. In R. Sternberg (Ed.), *Advances in Psychology of Human Intelligence* (pp. 7–75). Hillsdale, NJ: Lawrence Erlbaum Associates.

Diamond, S. S. (1981). Exploring sources of sentence disparity. In B. D. Sales (Ed.), *The trial process: Perspectives in law and psychology* (Vol. 2, pp. 387–412). New York: Plenum.

deGroot, A. D. (1965). *Thought and choice in chess*. The Hague: Mouton.

Gibson, J. L. (1978). Judge's role orientation, attitudes, and decisions: An interactive model. *The American Political Science Review*, 72, 911–924.

Green, E. G. (1961). *Judicial attitudes in sentencing*. London: Macmillan.

Haney, C. (1980). Psychology and legal change: On the limits of a factual jurisprudence. *Law and Human Behavior*, 4(3), 147–199.

Hayes-Roth, B., & Hayes-Roth, F. (1979). A cognitive model of planning. *Cognitive Science*, *3*, 275–310.

Hogarth, J. (1971). *Sentencing as a human process*. Toronto: University of Toronto Press.

Homel, R. (1981). Penalties and the drink-driver: A study of one thousand offenders. *Australian and New Zealand Journal of Criminology*, *14*, 225–241.

Hood, R., & Sparks, R. F. (1972). *Key issues in criminology*. London: World University Library.

Kahneman, D., Slovic, P., & Tversky, A. (Eds.). (1982). *Judgment under uncertainty: Heuristics and biases*. New York: Cambridge University Press.

Kapardis, A., & Farrington, D. P. (1981). An experimental study of sentencing by magistrates. *Law and Human Behavior*, *5*(2–3), 107–121.

Konečni, V. J., & Ebbeson, E. B. (1981). A critique of theory and method in social psychological approaches to legal issues, Chapter 13. In B. D. Sales (Ed.), *The trial process: Perspectives in law and psychology* (Vol. 2, pp. 481–498). New York: Plenum.

Lawrence, J. A. (1984). Magisterial decision-making: Cognitive perspectives and processes used in courtroom information-processing. In D. Blackman, D. Muller, & T. Chapman (Eds.), *Law and psychology*. London: Wiley. pp 319–332.

Lawrence, J. A., & Homel, R. (1987). Sentencing in magistrates' courts: The magistrate as professional decision-maker. In I. Potas (Eds.), *Sentencing in Australia*. Camberra: Australian Institute of Criminology, pp. 151–189.

Lawrence, J. A., & Browne, M. A. (1981). Magisterial decision-making: Cognitive perspectives and information-processing strategies identified by a group of Australian magistrates. In M. Lawson (Ed.), *Inquiry and action in education: Proceedings of the 1981 Annual Conference of the Australian Association for Research in Education* (Vol. 2, pp. 360–365). Adelaide, Australia.

Lawrence, J. A., Dodds, A. E., & Volet, S. (1983). *An afternoon off: A comparative study of adults' and adolescents' planning activities*. Paper presented at Australian Association for Research in Education Meeting, Canberra.

Logan, D. D. (1982, July). *Why you should not kill this man*. Paper presented at Psychology and Law Conference of British Psychological Society, Swansea.

McKnight, C. (1981). Subjectivity in sentencing. *Law and Human Behavior*, *5*(2–3), 141–147.

Revlis, R. (1975). Syllogistic reasoning: Logical decisions from a complex data base. In R. J. Falmagne (Ed.), *Reasoning: Representation and process*. Hillsdale, NJ: Lawrence Erlbaum Associates.

Scribner, S. (1983). Studying working intelligence. In B. Rogoff & J. Lave (Eds.), *Everyday cognition: Its development in social context*. Cambridge, MA: Harvard University Press.

Scribner, S., & Cole, M. (1981). *The psychology of literacy*. Cambridge, MA: Harvard University Press.

Smith, A. B., & Blumberg, A. S. (1967). The problem of objectivity in judicial decision-making. *Social Forces*, *46*, 96–105.

Svenson, I. F., Lawrence, J. A., & Willis, S. G. (1983). Distance university students' processing of mathematics exercises. *Educational Studies in Mathematics*, *14*, 73–85.

Voss, J. F., Greene, T. R., Post, T. A., & Penner, B. C. (1983). Problem-solving skill in the social science. In G. H. Bower (Ed.), *The psychology of learning and motivation: Advances in research theory* (Vol. 17, pp. 165–213). New York: Academic Press.

9 On the Solving of Ill-Structured Problems

James F. Voss
Timothy A. Post
University of Pittsburgh

This paper contains three sections. The first provides a discussion of the seminal papers on the solving of ill-structured problems, those of Reitman (1965) and of Simon (1973). The second consists of comments on the chapters of Johnson and Lawrence (this volume), along with a presentation of some of our own work on the solving of such problems in the social science domain. The final section describes a number of general issues that require consideration if a better understanding of the solving of such problems is to be established.

REITMAN'S AND SIMON'S STRUCTURING OF ILL-STRUCTURED PROBLEM SOLVING

After first commenting that problems have too much variation to have a theoretically meaningful typology, Reitman argued that it nevertheless may be useful to delineate various classes of problems. Reitman then described classes of problems according to whether the initial states and goal states were well-defined or loosely-defined in the problem statement. However, while ill-structured problems may be poorly defined in either or both of these respects, he characterized ill-structured problems in relation to the number of constraints of the problem that required resolution. Specifically, using a broad interpretation of the constraint concept, Reitman used the expression "open" constraint to refer to "one or more parameters the values of which are left unspecified as the problem is given to the problem-solving system from outside or transmitted within the system over time"

(p. 144). To illustrate his point, Reitman considered the composing of a fugue. The problem statement simply consisted of the goal of composing a fugue. The only constraints implied by the problem statement were that the composition was to have the musical structure of a fugue. Implicit of course were the constraints of the rules of tonal structure. The composer must thus, in Reitman's analysis, transform the problem by selecting operators which permit the construction of the composition.

An important point noted by Reitman is that as the composition is being constructed, the composer becomes aware of open constraints that must be closed. This notion has two implications. One is that all constraints cannot be defined when the solving begins. The other is that earlier parts of the solution to some extent constrain what will be subsequently composed. The composer thus faces a number of choice points, and arriving at a solution requires selection of a particular alternative at each point. Reitman's analysis of the solving of ill-structured problems thus was one of constraint resolution, and ill-structured problems were taken to be problems which required resolution of a large number of open constraints.

A second point made by Reitman is that well-structured and ill-structured problems do not constitute a dichotomy but instead represent points on a continuum. Reitman pointed out that a problem may have well-defined constraints at some points in the solution and open constraints at other points, and whether a problem is ill-structured or well-structured is a function of where the solver is in the solution process. Simon (1973) added to Reitman's analysis by arguing that many problems of the world are presented as ill-structured problems, but that they become well-structured in the hands of the problem solver. Thus, Simon emphasized the role of the solver as a provider of organization: "There is merit to the claim that much problem solving effort is directed at structuring problems, and only a fraction of it at solving problems once they are structured" (p. 187). Thus, while Reitman considered problems as relatively well-structured and ill-structured, Simon stressed the idea that initially ill-structured problems become well-structured during the solution process.

Simon used the example of constructing a house to illustrate how order is brought out of near-chaos. While the construction of a house is initially an ill-structured problem, the architect specifies goals, the particular goals taking into account the appropriate constraints, as number of rooms, type of heating, and other factors. Thus, structure is obtained by decomposing the more global problem into a set of well-structured problems which are then solved. Simon also employed an account of battleship construction as a similar illustration. As in the house construction example, the ill-structured problem was decomposed successively into subproblems, with the goals specified in solution to particular constraints.

A third point made by Reitman is of particular interest. Reitman discussed the closing of constraints in relation to members of a problem solving community: "To the extent that a problem situation evokes a high level of agreement over a specified community of problem solvers regarding the referents of the attributes in which it is given, the operations that are permitted, and the consequences of those operations, it may be termed unambiguous or well-defined with respect to that community. On the other hand, to the extent that a problem evokes a highly variable set of responses concerning referents of attributes, permissible operations, and their consequences, it may be considered ill-defined or ambiguous with respect to that community "(p. 151). Reitman further argued that the source of ambiguity is the open constraint set, and that members of a problem-solving community will therefore differ in their solutions when the number of parameter values that may be assigned to the open constraints is relatively large. From this argument Reitman made the additional, quite salient observation that "One unavoidable consequence of the present approach is that no solution to an ill-defined problem can count on universal acceptance" (p. 153).

Reitman's analysis of the role of agreement in constraint satisfaction among the community of solvers is quite related to a point made by Voss, Greene, Post, and Penner (1983) when the latter compared solutions in the domain of political science with solutions obtained in the domain of physics. Although there were differences in the solutions offered in the two domains, Voss et al. argued that the differences were attributable not to fundamental differences in the nature of the solving process itself in the respective domains, but instead (a) to the extent to which the phenomena in the two domains are understood; and (b) to the problems that are studied. Specifically, the problems used in almost all of the investigations of physics problem solving (e.g., Chi, Feltovich, & Glaser, 1981; Larkin, McDermott, Simon, & Simon, 1980), have been problems with known solutions — or, in Reitman's terms, problems which had virtually complete community agreement regarding their respective solutions. However, in the political science domain, and indeed in social sciences in general, for most problems (or some might argue for virtually all problems), the solvers of the community are not in agreement with respect to the appropriate solutions. Or, in Reitman's terms, there is disagreement regarding how to fill the open constraints.

It is possible, of course, as Voss et al. note, to have ill-structured physics problems. Such problems would be expected to occur, for example, in new areas of research; and evidence suggests that the solving of such problems highly resembles the structure of the solutions obtained by Voss et al. in the solving of political science problems (cf. Tweney, 1981). What the Voss et al. results do suggest in the context of Reitman's analysis is that until a generally accepted body of knowledge is developed in the social sciences, one may expect disagreement among the community of solvers of this domain.

An additional issue, in this case raised by Simon, is that a difference of ill-structured and well-structured problems is that the former typically have a relatively large amount of problem-related information stored in long-term and/or external memory, whereas the latter involve a smaller amount of information. The solution of the ill-structured problem thus involves specifying the information especially germane to the solution, thus reducing the ill-structured problem to a well-structured problem (or a set of well-structured problems). Interestingly, Simon points out that solving ill-structured problems requires that the solver has the capability of doing this transformation. Though not developing this point in detail, the statement suggests that the solver of an ill-structured problem must have appropriate conceptual knowledge of the components of the problem as well as the knowledge of how to utilize the appropriate components in the organization of the problem solution.

The discussions of ill-structured problems and their solutions by Reitman and by Simon are thus in considerable agreement. Both writers indicate that the extent to which a problem is well-structured or ill-structured is relative. Also, whereas Reitman speaks of solving ill-structured problems via the filling of open constraints, Simon similarly speaks of reducing the problem space, each notion thus in its own way indicating the need for specification on the part of the solver.

In addition to the above similarities, a comparison of the primary examples of the two writers is of interest. Specifically, a question that could be asked is this: If two composers were given the problem of composing a fugue, and two architects were given the problem of constructing a house (some house specifications being given in each case), which would be more similar, the two fugues or the two houses? Apart from the problem of how similarity would be measured in the two cases, the comparisons would provide an index of the extent to which the two respective problems were ill-structured (as opposed to well-structured). If there was a greater difference in the fugues, then one may assume that there was more variation possible in the closing of constraints in the fugue problem than in the house-construction problem, and vice versa. However, another factor may also be reflected by fugue similarity and house similarity — namely, the extent to which the two composers and the two architects had similar training in their respective fields; or, in Reitman's terms, the extent to which the solvers within the particular community are in agreement with respect to their views. Thus, regardless of which pair of solutions would be more similar, the problems selected as examples provide for variation in the solution offered; this is a characteristic, as Reitman pointed out, of ill-structured problems. In the solving of well-structured problems, which generally have agreed-upon solutions, the solution process would be expected to vary only slightly among solvers experienced in the particular problem area, thereby exposing only relatively small differences in the problem-related memory contents of the respective individuals. However, when individuals are solving ill-structured problems, many more differences in the memory structures of respective solvers are likely to become exposed, regardless of level of expertise.

Neither Reitman nor Simon specifically addressed the issue of expertise in the solving of ill-structured problems. The papers of Reitman and Simon, however, would suggest that experts should excel with respect to two particular aspects of such solving — namely, that they should be better able than novices to decompose an ill-structured problem into appropriate subproblems; and similarly, that they should be better able to select parameter values for open constraints in a manner that leads to a meaningful solution, given the goals at hand.

THREE TYPES OF ILL-STRUCTURED PROBLEMS

Prediction as an Ill-Structured Problem

Chapter 7 by Johnson describes research regarding how readily an expert is able to predict some type of performance occurring in a particular domain of expertise. Among the results presented is the finding that, given a set of data and the task of predicting some type of performance from the data, expert prediction is not as accurate as the prediction provided by a regression model. Commenting upon such results, we shall first consider how the prediction problem may be described as an ill-structured problem.

A diagram is presented in Figure 9.1A which, in a general way, depicts the prediction paradigm as an ill-structured problem. Following a distinction in current use, the problem solution is divided into two components, the representation process and the solution process. The representation phase typically precedes the solution phase, although it may be possible for a solver, in the solution phase, to go "back to Square 1" and develop a new representation. Also, the nature of problem representation development may be such that transition to the solution phase may be difficult to discern. Reitman's example of the composition of a fugue would be such a case. However, in general, the two components are quite discriminable. Finally, results obtained from a variety of problem-solving tasks suggest that the representation phase is extremely important, in the sense that once a specific representation is developed, a particular solution will follow from that representation; that is, the representation largely determines the solution. This is perhaps a way of restating Simon's (1973) comment that most of the problem-solving process involves establishing structure, and once that is established, the solution is a relatively small component.

Given the representation–solution distinction, an important question is how experts represent the prediction problem. As Johnson notes, research

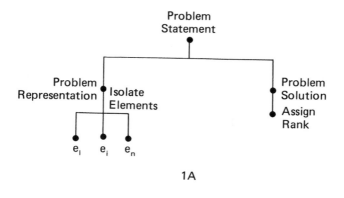

1A

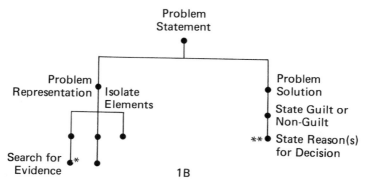

1B

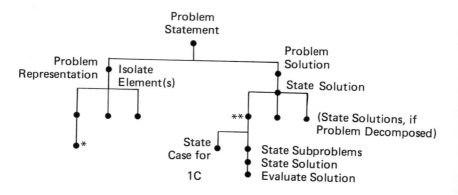

1C

*This process could involve extensive search of evidence (1B) or memory (1C). In both cases domain knowledge is critical.

**For this process domain knowledge is also critical, and extensive argumentation, as described in the text, may be involved.

FIGURE 9.1. Diagrams of the problem-solving process as described in the solvers discussed by Johnson (1A), Lawrence (1B), and Voss, Greene, Post, and Penner, 1983 (1C).

on expert prediction has generally been centered upon the accuracy of the prediction behavior rather than upon the process underlying such behavior. However, assume, as in the house officer assignment example described in that chapter, that the solver is presented with a set of data concerning a group of individuals and is to make a prediction of performance for each individual that is based upon the particular data set. Assume, moreover, that the data set, as shown in Figure 9.1A, contains n elements: e1, e2, ... ei ... en. What apparently happens in establishing a problem representation is that the solver, from his or her experience, selects one or more (most likely more) particular elements as critical to the making of a successful prediction. Moreover, the solver may view one or more of the selected elements as especially critical (i.e., solvers may establish weightings). Finally, the solver may use some type of rule to combine the values of the elements. The rule may simply reflect the weightings, or may involve some type of presumed interaction among the elements (cf. Einhorn, 1972). For example, a conjunctive rule may specify that selected elements may need to have particular values in order for a particular decision to be made, whereas a disjunctive rule may specify that element e1 or e2 or e3 must have some particular value for a decision to be made. Of importance is the observation mentioned by Johnson that although experts may select appropriate elements, they seem to have considerable difficulty in combining the information contained in the elements. Nevertheless, an important point is that the solver's consideration of the dataset information may be quite simple, such as basing a decision on the value of one element, or may be quite complex.

In Johnson's study of house officer ratings the data provided to the physicians consisted of approximately 13 pages per applicant, with the two tested experts taking 7.8 minutes per folder, thus spending less than two minutes per page. Novices spent almost twice that time. But more importantly, Johnson shows that experts read less of the information than did novices and also concentrated upon different information. Finally, Johnson notes that experts employed a top-down, selective search strategy, apparently knowing what they were looking for. Incidentally, Johnson also observes that "experts seem to use their knowledge of medical education to guide their search," a statement which may be overly charitable because (a) no independent data are presented suggesting that this knowledge was employed (although the protocols do suggest that knowledge of particular medical school procedures and awards was used); and (b) the so-called knowledge, in fact, may be folklore. For example, a physician may have had the "knowledge" that key phrases of a dean's letter constitute a critical element, when in fact the element has little to do with house officer performance.

Johnson, supported by four protocol excerpts, advanced the idea that the physicians may have used elements that were unique to each applicant's particular situation, such as whether or not the applicant received a particular award granted by the applicant's medical school. As Johnson points out, this procedure does not involve use of a statistical heuristic but instead reflects attention to critical instances quite similar to broken-leg cues (see Johnson's discussion in chapter 7). Indeed, taking this logic one step further, it could be the case that the solver uses his or her knowledge of the particular medical school setting of the applicant; but given that such idiosyncratic knowledge may not be available for particular applicants, the solver may fall back on default strategies involving selection via more standard elements, such as comments within the letters of recommendation.

In any event, one conclusion that seems warranted concerning physicians' representation of the house officer selection problem is that, despite Johnson's valiant efforts in protocol collection and coding, we cannot determine exactly what elements of the application were selected by the physicians, nor are we able to determine rules of combining that may have been employed. Johnson does suggest, however, that a "noisy linear model" is not applicable, because the physicians apparently tended to use idiosyncratic cues. Nevertheless, as Johnson notes, the search of the application by the physician seems to take place in a top-down manner, guided by a schema that includes a number of parameters and rules, the utilization of which is contingent upon particular application characteristics. Indeed, one could conceive of the schema as a set of productions which, for example, may include, "If this is a Hopkins applicant, then determine whether award was received." Interestingly, if the schema has a relatively large number of such productions, what we find is that expertise, as found in this task situation, may reflect a large amount of specific pieces of knowledge rather than the relatively well-integrated, hierarchical description of knowledge domains that is frequently reported. The most expert expert would then be the individual who knows the most pieces of valid information pertaining to applicant idiosyncracies.

One question worth some speculation is that of the origin of the physician's schema. Does the physician have a casebook of experiences with particular students that is drawn upon in making the decisions? Have there been statistical studies of which the physician is aware that have delineated the best predictor variables for house officer performance? To what extent does the physician's schema include folklore which is presumed to be "medical knowledge"? Are there Harvard, Hopkins, or Stanford "halo" effects operating, or perhaps similar effects related to the physician's own medical school? The fact that we do not have answers to these questions, except for a minimal amount of information provided by the protocols, suggests that (a) we do not have much understanding of the physicians' basis of prediction; and (b) that the physicians may also lack such an understanding or, if not lacking it, have not articulated it in the protocols.

Given the foregoing considerations, the problem representation phase described in Figure 1A evidently involves the selection of elements as noted in the figure, and, when the element search is completed, the problem representation has been established. Two points about this process are especially worth noting. One is that the rapid search shown by the physicians suggests that the physicians have a well-defined routine for searching out critical information. Second, there also are likely clear-cut stop rules such that a search is terminated as soon as a sufficient amount of cogent information is obtained which, in some cases, could even consist of only one item. The finding that the novice search is longer and that more parts of the application are reviewed suggests, of course, that the schema guiding the novice's selection of information is not as well-defined as that of the expert — that is, the novice is not as clear regarding what to look for in the application.

Turning to the solution process, what constitutes a solution in the prediction problem is the assignment of a rating to each of the respective applications. The solution, therefore, in most cases is essentially determined upon the establishment of the representation. In this regard, it is notable that the physicians, in making the judgments, are not required to justify the judgments in any way. Whereas the physician may make a comment to the effect that "I gave him a '3' because his letters seemed good even though his grades could better," there is no reference to this type of statement in Johnson's chapter, and one thus cannot judge whether such evaluation took place. Incidentally, the hypothetical justification just stated would of course suggest the physician was using a combining rule. (On some review panels, individuals are required to provide justification of their ratings, defending their ratings to peers. Such a procedure may, of course, lead to greater individual thought and articulation regarding what criteria he or she is using, as well as perhaps leading the individual to reevaluate and perhaps modify the criteria.)

Related to the fact that the physician apparently does not need to justify the ratings is that, though it appears the ratings made by one physician are independent of those made by other physicians, it is not clear whether a physician is given knowledge of the judgments of the other physicians. Being provided with such information, even without justification, could lead to reevaluation of one's criteria, especially of course if the ratings by others were different than one's own.

Finally, in considering the quality of performance, Johnson reports that a three-variable linear model performed better than all but one expert, with the best expert's prediction accuracy related to nonlinear as well as linear factors. Similarly, the stock market prediction problem described by Johnson yielded results quite similar to the physician prediction problem; once again a regression model fared well, and experts were shown to be sensitive to broken-leg cues.

In one sense, the prediction by experts as described by Johnson is not unreasonable. As pointed out elsewhere (e.g., Crocker, 1981), it would be quite a task for the expert to hold application information in memory and to mentally manipulate different rules for combining the selected elements. Instead, it would require less processing to have in mind a few highly salient criteria, search the applications for information related to those criteria, and make one's judgment accordingly. Using such a heuristic, the Johnson findings suggest that the representation of the problem is established by a quasi pattern-matching procedure in which a schema guides selection of appropriate elements. The problem is then "solved" by transforming the representation into a rating.

The relatively good performance of the novice — that is, when compared to that of the experts — in the Johnson research may at least in part be attributed to the fact that some cues selected by the novices may lead to a level of accuracy above that of chance. This result may be observed in a number of situations. One author is reminded of the first time he saw a rodeo and began to guess the judges' ratings of bronco riding. It was not difficult to be somewhat accurate by making duration judgments — the longer the rider stayed on, the better the rating. While the experts presumably took into account more aspects of the performance, simple judgments of a quite low-level novice could do better than chance. Indeed, any football fan knows that few "expert" sportswriters or coaches are any better in predicting the outcome of football games than are casual fans who have some sense of the game and knowledge of team performance. Thus, as perhaps in the physicians of Johnson's study, what seems to be the case is that the expert does not necessarily have the knowledge base that enables prediction to be better.

Given these observations regarding the Johnson findings, one may ask why the research, interesting as it is, at the same time is so nonanalytic. Basically, the answer is one of paradigm. The Johnson research has emerged from an economic theory orientation that has been developed largely in the context of decision theory. This paradigm is based upon concern, or, perhaps better, upon preoccupation, with whether man makes rational or nonrational decisions in particular task situations. Rationality is, of course, typically defined in terms of some mathematical criterion or optimizing solution. When such is the primary concern, there is apparently little investigator motivation to study the possible bases for decision making. (Indeed, even if a decision is "rational," that is, following the idealized model, it may be possible that the bases of the decision do not involve the factors hypothesized by the model.) It thus would seem incumbent upon the investigators to determine what the bases for the decision are and whether they are those suggested by the model. The Johnson findings as well as others show that compared to a regression equation, experts are not necessarily good predictors — a fact of no surprise to any sports fan, as we have previously noted. Why are predictions not better? Because the phenomena which the expert is being asked to predict are not sufficiently understood in the sense that the variables related to the performance in question have not been isolated. Being an expert does not provide a mystical pathway to accuracy. In sum, Johnson's results are of considerable interest, but it would seem appropriate to study much more intensively the processes underlying such prediction behavior.

Magistrate Judgment as an Ill-Structured Problem

In chapter 8, Lawrence describes the process by which magistrates make judgments of guilt and, if appropriate, of sentencing. Figure 9.1B presents a diagram of the magistrate problem-solving process, when the task is viewed as an ill-structured problem.

One of the interesting aspects of Lawrence's chapter is that evidence is provided, both from the magistrate's comments and from other data, that the experienced magistrate brings into the courtroom a style for determining guilt and for sentencing. In determining guilt, as described in the final two cases of the chapter, the magistrate brought into the situation what Lawrence calls the "frame of reference" which, as it is described, could also be termed a magistrate's courtroom schema. The magistrate approached the case with a well-defined goal, making a guilty or not-guilty decision, and with a set of strategies designed to search out evidence from the information required to reach the goal. As Lawrence notes, the laws of evidence operate as constraints in that situation, with only facts from particular sources and testimony being able to satisfy requirements of evidence. The magistrate's development of a problem representation may thus be considered as a process of obtaining information that is related to the goal, and which hopefully will help to resolve that goal. Finally, it is important to note that in the magistrate's hearing of a case, the development of the representation may be quite an extensive process. Moreover, with the process there typically is a considerable amount of reasoning and decision making, and these factors are what may make the case complicated.

There are interesting similarities and differences in the representation process as found in the accounts of Johnson and of Lawrence. The representation processes, as shown in Figures 1A and 1B, are on the surface quite similar, and the similarity may be shown in a number of ways. One is that the experts in each of the papers have "styles," or particular ways of approaching the problem. But perhaps more importantly, such styles are apparently quite difficult to verbalize. This finding supports the observation of Voss, Greene, Post, and Penner (1983), indicating that the highest level strategies used by the experts as well as other subjects were not verbalized.

Another similarity in the findings of Johnson and Lawrence was that an information search on the part of both sets of experts was conducted with particular goals in mind. One difference, however, is that the search of the magistrates was more "in the open" than that of the physicians; that is, the seeking of evidence by the magistrates followed courtroom procedure while the seeking of information by the physicians was a rapid search. Perhaps a more complete protocol by the physicians would have made the seeking process more observable. At the same time the magistrate search apparently required more "digging" than was necessary for the physicians. As noted by Lawrence, in one case the magistrate had to arrive at a decision despite certain maneuvers of the defense attorney and despite the lack of availability of some cogent information.

Finally, with respect to the elements sought in representation development, both groups of experts apparently stopped when a criterion was met. However, the criterion was a little more discernible in the magistrates' case, although the matter is less than clear. The criterion for a magistrate is apparently met when sufficient evidence is obtained to determine guilt or nonguilt, and the criterion is established by the magistrate's goals and constraints in the particular case. Yet there seems to be a "judgment call" in that the magistrate needs to decide at what point, for example, the evidence needs no further corroboration. On the other hand, when a physician reaches the criterion is more of a mystery because the subgoals of the search — in other words, those elements of an application that are sought — are not well-articulated. Thus, the comparison of the representation process in the situations described by Johnson and by Lawrence suggests that the general process of developing a problem representation is quite similar. However, the processes differ in that the magistrates' development of the representation is more clearly articulated and more easily "tracked" than that of the physicians.

Turning now to the solution process, the magistrate's solution, like that of the physicians, is made once the problem is represented. Thus, when the evidence required to determine guilt or innocence has been amassed, the decision is essentially established. However, a distinct difference exists between the solution process of the physicians and of the magistrates: namely, that the magistrate quite typically justifies his or her decision. The magistrate indicates why, according to law and in the light of the evidence, the particular decision was made.

An additional interesting aspect of the solution process as described in the Lawrence paper is that of how the magistrate arrives at a sentencing decision. The problem representation consists of the given of guilt, with the magistrate deciding among the sentencing options. The representation established by the novice was guided by the strategy of "following the book." On the other hand, the experienced magistrates apparently considered a larger number of options in establishing a representation, options which relate to the conditions of the particular situation and individual. Thus, as Lawrence points out, the experienced magistrate is flexible in that a sentence is not simply stated as a rule of law. In terms of representation such flexibility suggests that an experienced magistrate has a representation which takes into account more factors than does a novice's representation. In the Johnson research, experts may take into account fewer pieces of information. One could therefore suggest that in establishing guilt the experienced magistrate, like the expert physician, may focus upon particular information that is known or thought to be quite germane to the decision. The novice may have considered more information. However, in sentencing, just the opposite may happen.

Political Science Problems
as Ill-Structured Problems

In our laboratory we have been investigating the solving of ill-structured social science problems. While this work is described elsewhere in more detail (Voss, Greene, Post, & Penner, 1983; Voss, Tyler, & Yengo, 1983) a summary is presented here in order to compare this research to that described by Johnson and Lawrence.

Although we have employed a number of different problems, our analysis has focused upon problems related to the Soviet Union, the most frequent being the Soviet agriculture problem. This problem essentially is that, given low crop productivity in the Soviet Union, how would the solver go about improving crop productivity if he or she served as Director of the Ministry of Agriculture in the Soviet Union? We have given the problem to experts, as we have defined political science faculty whose field of specialization is the Soviet Union, and political science faculty with other fields of specialization: also chemists, political science graduate students (some of whom were Soviet specialists), undergraduates who received the problem both before and after a course on Soviet domestic policy, a State Department career officer, and an Eastern-bloc visiting scholar.

The findings of present concern are primarily those of experts. Figure 1C presents a diagram of the problem-solving shown by these experts. The goal of the representation process of all the experts was establishing the factor(s) that are responsible for producing low crop productivity. In developing the representation, the experts used two general problem-solving methods. One was problem *decomposition*, in which case the solver delineated a number of factors, usually no more than three, which were taken to be the primary causes of low crop productivity. The second general strategy was problem *conversion*. In this case the expert converted the problem into one which could then be solved. The conversion also yielded a statement of what was taken to be the primary cause of the problem. For example, the agriculture problem statement could be converted to a problem of lack of capital investment in agriculture.

In addition to utilizing a general problem-solving strategy, experts also stated a history of the problem, and this was also done with the goal of isolating the major factor(s) causing the problem. The problem history statement included such contents as previously attempted solutions to the problem and why they failed, and/or a statement of the history of the problem, showing how it got to its current state.

The problem representation process developed by experts for the Soviet agriculture problem has distinct similarities as well as differences compared to the representation processes of magistrates and physicians. While in all cases the representation was developed via a schema-guided search process, there were differences in how this took place. Both the magistrates and physicians searched externally presented information in order to extract the information that was germane to their respective goals. As previously noted, this process was more obscure in the physicians' case than in the magistrates'. However, the Soviet experts searched internally, seeking from their own knowledge the information which would indicate the major factors contributing to poor productivity. Indeed, their use of problem history could readily be interpreted as the means by which they isolated the factors, not being able to generate them without the account furnished by such an analysis. The representation process across all cases was thus marked by the use of general problem strategies or weak methods (Newell, 1980), with the most frequently employed method being decomposition. In addition, experts used a strategy that involved domain-related problem history search.

With respect to the solution process, Soviet experts departed substantially from the magistrate and physician solutions. The solution was presumed to be stated by the physicians when the representation was established; that is, when the particular information sought from a given application was determined. In the case of the magistrate, a judgment of guilt or nonguilt was made when the representation was established; that is, when the evidence warranted such a judgment. Following the judgment, the magistrate presumably stated why, in terms of the law, the particular verdict was reached. The Soviet experts typically began the solution process by advancing a relatively abstract solution. When a problem was decomposed, the experts would advance a solution for each of the component subproblems, but even then the experts tried to integrate the subproblem solutions into a more general solution encompassing the three components.

Of particular importance is what else the experts did during the solution process. Basically, they built a case for why the proposed solution would work. This part of the solution process consisted not just of telling why the solution would work but, in particular, what specifically could be accomplished if the solution were implemented. The second part consisted of indicating what problems might be encountered if the solution were implemented. Furthermore, solutions to these problems were indicated and, in a number of cases, these further solutions were evaluated. Such evaluation usually took place in relation to a constraint, as the solution would not work because it would violate the ideology.

The solutions proposed by the Soviet experts thus were designed not only to yield a solution but to justify it. In this sense the solution process somewhat resembled that of the magistrates, although the justification provided in relation to the political science problems were much more extensive than that in the court cases.

To this point, the discussion of the Johnson and Lawrence findings as well as those of our laboratory has largely focussed upon similarities and differences in the problem-solving process. The final comparison considered is the nature of the theoretical approaches taken in the three problem-solving situations.

As noted, Johnson's analysis for the most part emerges from the decision model approach largely evolved in the context of economic game theory. Johnson, however, attenuated this approach by protocol collection. Unfortunately, the protocol data were apparently not very effective in providing definitive information about element selection and rating generation. Yet, at the same time, the stock market data as well as the physicians' comments suggest that perhaps the entire judgment process is relatively simple, based to a large extent upon broken-leg cues, when available, and some default strategies or truisms.

Lawrence's theoretical efforts were largely aimed at developing an appropriate framework for the magistrate decision process. Lawrence makes considerable use of the frame of reference notion, which, as previously noted, essentially consists of a schema-guided set of procedures having the goal of ascertaining evidence and judging guilt or innocence. Moreover, the production-like "If–Then" structure used by Lawrence constitutes a reasonable attempt to put complex data in tractable form.

Our primary mode of theory development has been somewhat similar to that of Lawrence, although more detailed. Specifically, we delineated two structures, a problem-solving structure and a reasoning structure, described operators of each, and analyzed the verbatim protocols in relation to the structures and operators. Basically, the problem-solving structure was on a high level whereas the reasoning structure provided for the extensive verbal reasoning developed by the experts in both the representation and solution phases. Moreover, in general, the problem-solving structure consisted of weak methods which initiated the representation and solution phases, but which then gave way to the reasoning structure which was taken to be domain-related.

The final issue considered in this section is that of the computer simulation of the protocols that experts provide in the solving of ill-structured problems. There has been considerable success in the simulation of well-structured problems, and the question is how might the simulation of ill-structured problems be approached.

One of the primary aspects that differentiates ill-structured from well-structured problem solving is conceptual knowledge. As pointed out by Simon (1973) and implied by extensive protocols of Voss, Greene, Post, and Penner (1983), solving ill-structured problems — especially problems in the social sciences — may require extensive knowledge, such as knowledge of politics, history, economics, and technology. Moreover, the experts may differ with respect to interpretative components of such knowledge. Extending problem-solving theory to encompass ill-structured problems and their solutions may thus be facilitated if conceptual representation theory is considered for its potential contribution. Following is a description of a simulation which represents a modest attempt at this endeavor.

The GPS ("General Problem Solver") framework for problem-solving theory outlined by Newell and Simon (1972) provides a basis for the current endeavor. Problem solving, according to this view, is a transversal of possible problem states within a problem space via the application of general operators. The GPS system was intended to be appropriate for a variety of problem-solving situations. Incorporating concept knowledge within the GPS framework may be accomplished in a number of ways. Conceptual knowledge may be represented as operators, or as the "conceptual coat rack" (Woods, 1983) upon which a domain's goal structure is based. The view taken for the current project is that conceptual knowledge may assist in the selection of general operators during problem solution. More specifically, consider a generalized activation network model of conceptual representation (e.g., Anderson, 1983; Collins & Loftus, 1975), in which concepts are represented as nodes in a network, with the links between nodes indicating relationships between pairs of concepts. Each node possesses a degree of activation such that, when the activation is above a certain threshold, the concept is present in working memory. The level of activation is affected by directed attention, and through a spread of activation from active concepts to other nodes in the network. In this manner concepts may be viewed as being brought in and out of working memory for consideration during the solution of a problem. An active conceptual pattern can then be considered as an element of a problem state within a domain's problem space, and as a point at which an operator may be applied. In this manner the selection of operators can in part be guided by the concepts that have become active in working memory.

A test of this model was accomplished using a computer simulation of simple linear reasoning in one expert's protocol of the Soviet agriculture problem. The specific questions asked were threefold: Can a system using simple general operators that act in reaction to concepts in working memory be constructed such that it yields a plausible argument? Would such a system be sensitive to changes in the problem statement it receives? Would the system produce different behavior given a change in the conceptual structure it employs? The system was written in PRISM, a generalized learning production system language (Langley & Neches, 1981).

The model consisted of three components, the first being a network structure of concepts relevant to the Soviet agriculture problem. The concepts were extracted from a protocol used in a previous study (Voss, Greene, Post, & Penner, 1983), and were interconnected with three types of links: positive causal relations, such as "food production *positively relates* to the amount of food"; negative causal relations, such as "buying foreign food *negatively relates* to state finances;" and an instance relation, such as "workers *are an instance of* city people." At the outset, all of the relationships were considered to be of equal weight or strength; that is, no two concepts were viewed as having a stronger relationship than any other pair.

The second component was a set of operators. Five operators were selected from the reasoning and goal structures outlined by Voss, Greene, Post, and Penner (1983): the interpret-problem-statement goal operator, and the state-assertion, state-special-case, qualify, and state-constraint reasoning operators. These were represented with productions. The final component of the system was the executive — that is, the component of the system that spreads activation through the network, maintains the list of active concepts in working memory, and selects the operator to be executive. No other operations were included, or required, by the system.

The results were obtained in a series of computer simulation trials. Inasmuch as the current effort was intended as a test of a qualitative hypothesis, only the germane generalized results are presented here. All three of the previously stated questions were answered in the affirmative. Coherent arguments were constructed. This is not a surprising finding as the network employed was, in a sense, a structure that contained various coherent argument chains. More interesting were the effects that changing the problem statement and the network structure had on the argumentation. When given the objective of increasing food production, an argument chain was produced that "advocated" the increase in acreage of arable land available to farming collectives through technological means, a point made by the expert. When given the task of improving the amount of food available within the Soviet Union, however, the system took a different approach and asserted that private plots could be used, and that this is an instance of capitalism, which would violate the constraint of socialism. In other trials, the network structure was changed by altering the relational strength between two concepts. This changed the nature of the activation pattern that developed within the network, and yielded different arguments. For example, the food production argument changed from asserting the use of private plots to increasing food production on the collectives. The point of this manipulation of the system was to demonstrate the role that a conceptual structure might play during problem solving.

An unforeseen side effect of this project resulted from an examination of the contents of working memory as arguments proceeded. In order to "prime" the concepts in the semantic network at the outset, one of the functions performed by the interpret-problem-statement operator was to spread a (relatively) large amount of activation throughout the network. This had two effects on the concepts that became activated (i.e., appeared in working memory). First, the interpret-problem-statement operator produced an undifferentiated activation of many concepts; in other words, when a large amount of activation is spread throughout a network, items distally-related receive activation. As an argument proceeded, however, the reasoning operators would assert certain concepts, and since the amount of activation that would be spread for an assertion was assumed to be minimal, distally-related concepts would fade from memory. The result was that working memory consisted of an active subgraph (cf. Ortony, 1978) of the initial network structure, the subgraph containing concepts that were related to some central theme, such as agricultural technology. This finding suggests that employing conceptual knowledge within a problem-solving model might provide an account for the consistency or goal-directed nature of problem solving, without directly representing the goal structure.

To summarize this section, a test of a hypothesis regarding the solving of ill-structured problems that employed a computer simulation was described. The position was taken that solving ill-structured problems, as noted by Simon (1973), involves considerable conceptual knowledge which must be organized and reduced in relation to the problem goals.

A few additional comments are now in order regarding the use of computer simulation in solving ill-structured problems. The model just described represents an attempt to integrate a theory of conceptual representation into the information-processing approach to problem solving. It is offered as one of many approaches to the problem. The reader may have already realized that a direct empirical test of some of the positions may be a difficult task. Ideally, one would like to "measure" a subject's conceptual structure at various problem states during a solution. Then changes/differences in the conceptual representation could be compared with changes/differences in the problem solution. Presumably it is possible to "measure" conceptual structure and consistently identify problem states, but it is likely that the act of measurement would change the conceptual structure of the subject. This is strongly predicated by the model's reliance on the notion of spread of activation as a partial account of how operators are selected.

The prevalence of "deep theories" (VanLehn, Brown, & Greeno, 1982) in the solving of ill-structured problems (and cognition in general) has helped to enlarge the role of computer simulation as a means to test theoretical ideas. The advantages and disadvantages of computer simulation have been discussed elsewhere, both pro and con (e.g. Anderson, 1976; Estes 1976). A primary advantage is the ability to develop complex models while allowing a researcher to test hypotheses and receive quick feedback on their thoughts. Research on solving ill-structured problems may also benefit. One advantage would be achieved if a simulation doesn't match behavior at some level. For example, initially the system described above did not include the state-constraint operator because it was felt that this would not be an aspect of reasoning and problem solving necessary for the task at hand (i.e., constructing a simple linear argument). During the programming, the need to post constraints became evident when patterns of reasoning became circular. More specifically, concepts that were from different ideologies were competing for activation (e.g., capitalism and socialism). Upon this realization, the interpret-problem-statement operator was altered to include an explicit posting of a constraint such as "reason from a socialist point of view."

Simulations of solving ill-structured problems may also be used to generate empirical studies. For example, recall the assumption that the interpret-problem-statement operator activates the conceptual network in an undifferentiated manner, and that through the continued application of reasoning operators the active conceptual structure in working memory would be narrowed to a topic. This hypothesis about human behavior may be tested with a semantic priming task (e.g., Foss, 1982; McKoon & Ratcliff, 1981) by comparing the extent and magnitude of priming at different points in a subject's reasoning episode.

The experiment suggested above relies on a relatively specific and quantitative methodology. This raises a final point about the use of simulation in research on the solving of ill-structured problems; namely, the nature of the connection between human behavior and a theory represented as a simulation. Many simulations make loose connections with the protocol data that they are based upon. For example, Hayes-Roth and Hayes-Roth (1979) simulated planning behavior, and compared the computer's output with a subject's protocol at a general level, chosing not to model "all of the subject's idiosyncracies" (p. 298). The simulation constituted a general approximation of the subject's knowledge, and modelling general tendencies of the protocol was desired. Accounting for more details of problem-solving behavior will likely remain problematic until more thorough descriptions of protocol data are made possible through more comprehensive theories. Initially, research within an ill-structured domain employs sketchy models as a matter of necessity, due to the variety of knowledge domains involved, and other things. What simulation provides, at least at this point in time, is an ability to develop complex theories about complicated knowledge material, preferably concurrent with the gathering of experimental data.

SOLVING ILL-STRUCTURED PROBLEMS:
SOME OPEN CONSTRAINTS

In this the final section, a number of issues are considered which are important to the development of a better understanding of the solving of ill-structured problems.

When Is a Problem Solved?

In the type of ill-structured problems considered by Johnson and Lawrence, this question may be readily answered. Essentially, the problem is solved when the house officer rating is assigned or when the magistrate decides guilt or nonguilt. But social science problem solving is another matter, and it is different because of two quite important reasons. First, the Johnson and Lawrence studies involve the actual solution of problems whereas the Soviet agriculture problem as well as many other social science problems basically involve planning. In economics, political science, and sociology, for example, many problems are discussed, a solution is adopted, and then the solution is implemented. But the implementation may take years. This protracted solution process thus means that adopting a solution is basically a planning exercise, and arguments are frequently required that build a case for adopting the particular solution. Second, while the Johnson and Lawrence problems involve selection and judgment, the way in which the Johnson and the Lawrence problems are solved was worked out prior to the solving of these particular problems. Thus, while the physician doing the rating may not be as accurate as possible, the general means by which the rating is calculated is basically established, and the same holds for the magistrate decisions. Furthermore, the illustrations employed by Simon (1973), based on house construction and battleship construction, enjoy the same status. But solving problems such as the Soviet agriculture question is different in the sense that there are no generally accepted modes of solving agricultural productivity problems. There may be examples of solutions to the problem of agricultural productivity that have been established, but taken as a whole, it may be argued that, in Reitman's terms, there is less agreement among the community of solvers in the social sciences than in the community of solvers in the physician's and magistrate's problems discussed by Johnson and Lawrence. That is not to say the latter does not involve disagreement, but it is to say that, in general, the open constraints of social science problems are usually numerous.

Returning now to the question of when a problem is solved, the answer that seems appropriate is that ill-structured problems are regarded as solved via the application of stop rules, with such rules being established for the particular domain, and, quite importantly, often being applied differentially by different individuals. Thus, in hearing a case, the magistrate decides when sufficient evidence has been obtained, and this may be at a different point in the proceedings than would occur for another magistrate. The agriculture problem is solved when a plan is developed that is workable, but when this occurs will vary from one situation to another. Finally, a fugue is completed when the composer regards it as requiring no further revision, but individuals will vary with respect to when they stop. The nature of stop rules and their application thus becomes an important issue (cf. Jeffries, Turner, Polson, & Atwood, 1981).

What is a Good Solution?

Another question quite important for the solving of virtually all ill-structured problems is that of what constitutes a good solution. Reitman pointed out that the solutions to ill-structured problems would not be accepted by the community, but this of course does not mean that all solutions are of equivalent quality. On what basis then should solution quality be judged?

Perhaps the only reasonable answer, albeit not a satisfactory one, is that the solution must be judged pragmatically, the judgment being made by other members of the problem-solving community. There are two important implications of this position, each suggesting why this answer has some merit. First, the pragmatic criterion is what essentially is employed in evaluating solutions. Generally, a solution is regarded as good if other solvers find little wrong with it and think it will work, whereas a solution is regarded as poor if other solvers are able to show why it will not work. Second, the pragmatic criterion puts the burden of evaluation upon solvers with expertise similar to that of the solver proposing the solution. One of the drawbacks of the "peer review," however, is that there always is the risk that the thinking of the peers is structured much like that of the solver; and that, although there may be other, better solutions, members of the problem solving community represent the problem as the solver does, not perceiving other possible representations. The important point to make about "good solutions" to ill-structured problems is that there generally are not "right answers." Thus, whether you arrive at the "right answer" cannot be a criterion. Similarly, there is no set of rules to say that if you "solve by doing these n steps" it will be a good answer. The fact that such criteria do not exist underscores the importance of argumentation as a means to show a solution is "good." Moreover, in a more general sense and perhaps more importantly, it means that solution quality will be based upon the extent to which a solution can be rationalized; and, remembering that the solution is generally a function of how the problem is represented, we find that the particular representation developed is critical to the entire process.

How Consistent Are Solutions Offered by One Individual?

The questions of intraindividual consistency of solution and whether, in solving a number of problems, there is as much variation within a subject as between subjects, are important issues. (There of course has been virtually no empirical work on these issues with respect to the solving of ill-structured problems.) Answering the question of between- versus within-subject variability is important because of what would be required in order to demonstrate a type of within-subject "style" consistency. Given the variability of solutions provided in the solving of ill-structured problems, it would take considerable understanding of the solution process to demonstrate the existence of style in one person, as well as demonstrating style differences among solvers. Moreover, the development of such an understanding would of necessity involve discerning those aspects of the problem-solving process which provide for between-subject differences and within-subject consistency. The potential theoretical contributions which could emerge from such study could be considerable. In addition, the task of determining within-subject consistency across problems would also provide for investigating the extent to which style could be identified across various classes of problems; that is, are there effectively task-related boundary conditions such that an individual solver could be identified for one class of problems but not for another class?

What Generates the Problem Representation and Solution?

Another issue that is in need of investigation involves the relation of the structure and processes of memory to the solutions generated in the solving of ill-structured problems. As previously stated, research on the solving of ill-structured problems has the potential of exposing aspects of memory structure and process to a possibly greater extent than that of well-structured problems, because of the within-solver and between-solver variation found in the former. What is needed at this time is the development and/or utilization of techniques which provide for "teasing out" such information in detail.

CONCLUSIONS

Reitman (1965) and Simon (1973) provided excellent analyses of the nature of ill-structured problems and how they are solved. The research reported in this paper extends the analyses of Reitman and Simon by pointing to a number of the complexities of solving ill-structured problems. The following conclusions seem appropriate:

1. As noted by Reitman and by Simon, the well-structured versus ill-structured distinction is a matter of degree. However, the present findings indicate there is considerable variation in the problems per se. Moreover, in agreement with Reitman, the present work suggests that it is questionable whether any problem typology would be conceptually meaningful. The issue is further compounded by the fact that for an expert a problem may be relatively well-structured but for a novice the same problem may be quite ill-structured. Given these considerations, an important question is whether the solutions provided to ill-structured problems can be described in a manner that will enable investigators to develop legitimate ways of not only scoring, rating, and scaling solutions, but of studying such solving via more traditional experimental methodology.

2. The way in which an investigator studies problem solving is a function of the general theoretical orientation of the investigator. Although this is a truism, the present findings suggest that at least two research paradigms were employed in the work reported in this chapter. One would hope that in the years to come both the information-processing approach to problem solving, and the decision theory model, would undergo a rapprochement, to their mutual benefit.

3. In the solving of ill-structured problems, Reitman's admonitions concerning the role of acceptance or nonacceptance of a solver by a community of solvers cannot be overestimated. This conclusion is especially apparent in social science domains in which solutions to problems often receive relatively little agreement within the community. But the lack of community acceptance also implies that the argument component of the solving process becomes critical.

4. Expertise in solving ill-structured problems is highly domain-specific and, while individuals may use weak methods such as decomposition, the applications of the methods per se will lead to inadequate solutions unless the individual has and employs substantial knowledge of the domain in question.

5. An important factor in producing variation in the problem-solving process is whether the problem has been previously solved and whether the solver has knowledge of that solution or knowledge of the way to solve that class of problems.

6. As a final point, the development of a better understanding of the solving of ill-structured problems will require considerable investigation regarding how memory structure and process is related to solution generation. This is a direct consequence of conclusion number 4. Indeed, developing a theory of problem solving that accounts for the range of problems along the "structuredness" dimension may involve integrating what we know about knowledge and conceptual utilization with current problem-solving theory.

ACKNOWLEDGMENT

This chapter was supported by a grant of the National Institute of Education to the Learning Research and Development Center. The contents of the chapter do not necessarily reflect the opinions held by either organization.

REFERENCES

Anderson, J. R. (1976). *Language, memory, and thought.* Hillsdale, NJ: Lawrence Erlbaum Associates.

Anderson, J. R. (1983). A spreading activation theory of memory. *Journal of Verbal Learning and Verbal Behavior, 22,* 261–295.

Chase, W. G., & Simon, H. A. (1973). Perception in chess. *Cognitive Psychology, 4,* 55–81.

Chi, M. T. H., Feltovich, P., & Glaser, R. (1981). Categorization and representation of physics problems by experts and novices. *Cognitive Science, 5,* 121–152.

Collins, A. M., & Loftus, E. J. (1975). A spreading activation theory of semantic processing. *Psychological Review, 82,* 407–428.

Crocker, J. (1981). Judgement of covariation by social perceivers. *Psychological Bulletin, 90,* 272–292.

Einhorn, H. J. (1972). Expert measurement and mechanical combination. *Organizational Behavior and Human Performance, 7,* 86–106.

Estes, W. K. (1976). Intelligence and cognitive psychology. In L. B. Resnick (Ed.), *The nature of intelligence* (pp. 295–306). Hillsdale, NJ: Lawrence Erlbaum Associates.

Foss, D. J. (1982). A discourse on semantic priming. *Cognitive Psychology, 14,* 590–607.

Hayes-Roth, B., & Hayes-Roth, F. (1979). A cognitive model of planning. *Cognitive Science, 3,* 275–310.

Jeffries, R., Turner, A. A., Polson, P. G., & Atwood, M. E. (1981). The processes in designing software. In J. R. Anderson (Ed.), *Cognitive skills and their acquisition* (pp. 255–283). Hillsdale, NJ: Lawrence Erlbaum Associates.

Langley, P., & Neches, R. (1981). *PRISM User's Manual.* Pittsburgh, PA: Department of Computer Science, Carnegie–Mellon University.

Larkin, J., McDermott, J., Simon, D. P., & Simon, H. A. (1980). Expert and novice performance in solving physics problems. *Science, 208,* 1335–1342.

McKoon, G., & Ratcliff, R. (1981). Priming in item recognition: The organization of propositions in memory for text. *Journal of Verbal Learning and Verbal Behavior, 20,* 269–286.

Newell, A. (1980). One final word. In D. T. Tuma & F. Reif (Eds.), *Problem solving and education: Issues in teaching and research* (pp. 175–189). Hillsdale, NJ: Lawrence Erlbaum Associates.

Newell, A., & Simon, H. A. (1972). *Human problem solving.* New Jersey: Prentice-Hall.

Ortony, A. (1978). Remembering, understanding, and representation. *Cognitive Science, 2,* 53–69.

Reitman, W. (1965). *Cognition and thought.* New York: Wiley.

Simon, H. A. (1973). The structure of ill-structured problems. *Artificial Intelligence, 4,* 181–201.

Tweney, R. D. (1981). Confirmatory and disconfirmatory heuristics in Michael Faraday's scientific research. Paper presented at the twenty-second meeting of the Psychonomic Society.

VanLehn, K., Brown, J. S., & Greeno, J. G. (1984). Competitive argumentation in computational theories of cognition. In W. Kintsch, J. R. Miller, & P. G. Polson (Eds.), *Methods and tactics in cognitive science* (pp. 235–262). Hillsdale, NJ: Lawrence Erlbaum Associates.

Voss, J. F., Greene, T. R., Post, T. A., & Penner, B. C. (1983). Problem-solving skill in the social sciences. In G. H. Bower (Ed.), *The psychology of learning and motivation: Advances in research theory* (Vol. 17, 165–213). New York: Academic Press.

Voss, J. F., Tyler, S., & Yengo, L. (1983). Individual differences in the solving of social science problems. In R. Dillon & R. Schmeck (Eds.), *Individual differences in cognition* (pp. 205–232). New York: Academic Press.

Woods, W. A. (1983). What's important about knowledge representation? *Computer, 16,* 22-27.

10 The Relationship Between Comprehension and Reasoning in Medical Expertise

Guy J. Groen
Vimla L. Patel
McGill University

Most of our knowledge of the nature of expertise has been developed in the context of problem solving rather than comprehension. This is partly due to the fact that there has been, until recently, a general lack of connection between these two domains. Theories of comprehension have been primarily concerned with structural issues, whereas those in the area of problem solving have been concerned with the explication of processes. It seems reasonable to assume that, in verbally complex domains, the issues of general concern in the area of comprehension may play an important role. In fact, many of the studies of problem solving involving verbal tasks (e.g., Hayes & Simon, 1974; Kintsch & Greeno, 1985) have found it necessary to introduce structural notions such as schemata or propositions so that the verbal content of the task could be translated into a symbolic form.

This traditional lack of connection between the two domains may have serious consequences for the study of expertise in verbally complex tasks. Clinical reasoning in medicine is an almost prototypical instance of a realistically messy domain in which verbally complex tasks occur that are dependent on a highly developed knowledge base. In this area, certain results have emerged that are inconsistent with two basic properties of expert performance as found in relatively nonverbal domains:

1. The idea of superior pattern recognition (e.g., Chase & Simon, 1973; de Groot, 1965), on the basis of which it is possible to form more elaborate chunks in short-term memory.
2. The idea of forward reasoning (Larkin, McDermott, Simon, & Simon, 1980a,b; Simon & Simon, 1978), from a given or already

deduced fact about a situation to one that is new in the sense that it is neither given nor previously deduced.

As Greeno and Simon (1984) pointed out, these are intimately connected: The superior pattern recognition results in the ability to do forward reasoning. The problem in extending these notions to a verbally complex domain is that the notion of pattern recognition ceases to make sense. A phenomenon of perception becomes one of comprehension.

Attempts to replicate the Chase–Simon paradigm in the domain of medicine were motivated by the pioneering work of Elstein, Shulman, and Sprafka (1978), which introduced modern cognitive psychology to the field of medical education. This was highly influenced by deGroot (1965), as a result of which there was a strong emphasis on the analogy between a master chess player and an experienced physician. In a variety of tasks involving diagnostic problem solving,[1] they failed to find any differences between experts and novices except for a more highly developed knowledge base. However, they did not use a free recall task, which is the most obvious way of finding differences analogous to those found by Chase and Simon. As a result, a number of investigators attempted to discover differences using this paradigm with clinical cases as stimuli (Claessen & Boshuizen, 1985; Muzzin, Norman, Feightner, Tugwell, & Guyatt, 1982, 1983; Norman, Jacoby, Feightner, & Campbell, 1979). They uniformly found no significant differences in the total number of items recalled.

This raises the issue of whether a theory of expertise developed primarily in the context of tasks in chess and physics, where problem descriptions and solution paths can readily be represented mathematically or pictorially, applies to verbally complex domains such as medicine. It might be claimed, for example, that some kind of imagery is necessary for the stable representation of patterns. If this were the case, one might expect neither enhanced memory for problem situations nor extensive use of forward reasoning in solving routine problems. In fact, Elstein et al. found that both experts and novices used a form of backward reasoning akin to the hypothetico–deductive process often advocated as a paradigm of scientific reasoning. This is consistent with the medical field's widely held belief (e.g., Kassirer, 1984) that the hypothetico–deductive process is an "ideal" method to which students should aspire; it is a process used by medical experts on a routine basis. However, there is little evidence for or against this belief. Elstein et al. used difficult, nonroutine problems which might account for the lack of forward reasoning, especially since they were not looking for

---

[1]The most important source of verbal protocols was a retrospective "method of simulated recall," in which subjects were presented with a tape recording of their performance in diagnosing a clinical case, and were asked to think aloud about their performance.

this phenomenon. Indeed, the tasks appear to have been designed to examine the hypothetico–deductive reasoning process under difficult conditions. While this finding has been criticized for the use of what is essentially a retrospective method of protocol analysis (Kassirer, Kuipers, & Gorry, 1982), similar results were obtained by Rubin (1975) using a direct method. We have argued elsewhere (Groen & Patel, 1985) that, apart from this, support seems to come either from the folklore of clinical practice or interpretations of some of the more traditional approaches to the history and philosophy of science.

On the other hand, it is clear from the chapters on medicine elsewhere in this volume that differences between experts and novices do exist that are quite compatible with the classical results from physics and chess. This then raises the possibility that the inability to replicate the free recall results may be due to methodological inadequacies. The lack of evidence for forward reasoning may be simply due to the fact that it has not been looked for. Moreover, as Clancey argues in this volume, it is possible that the widespread belief regarding hypothetico–deductive thinking in medicine may have resulted in protocols being overinterpreted, so that the data is made to fit the preexisting theory, rather than a theory being created to fit the data.

In this chapter, we explore the possibility that what is needed is a theory of comprehension together with a more precise method of empirically determining the verbal analogue to the perceptual notion of a pattern. This would imply the existence of a unit of analysis that has self-contained properties and also can form the basis of chunking. It has been proposed by a number of authors (e.g., Frederiksen, 1975; Kintsch, 1974) that verbal text or discourse can be decomposed into underlying units of meaning, usually termed *propositions*, which have these properties.

Intuitively, a proposition is an idea underlying the surface structure of a text. More formally, following van Dijk and Kintsch (1983) and also Johnson-Laird (1983), it may be defined as a fact that is true in some possible world. The notion's usefulness arises from the fact that a given piece of discourse may have many related ideas embedded within it. A propositional representation provides a means of representing these ideas, and the relationships between them, in an explicit fashion. In addition, it provides a way of classifying and labelling these ideas. Systems of propositional analysis (e.g., Frederiksen, 1975; Kintsch, 1974) are essentially languages that provide a uniform notation and classification for propositional representations. These all have in common the fact that, as in case grammars, a proposition is denoted as a relation or predicate (usually called the head element) over a set of arguments (frequently referred to as concepts). In this paper we use Frederiksen's system. It is important to bear in mind, however, that the notational details are relatively unimportant. What is critical is the underlying assumption that propositions correspond to the basic units of the representation of the textbase in episodic memory and, more generally, the notion that propositions form manageable units of knowledge representations.

The first of these claims is supported by a considerable amount of empirical evidence. The reader is referred to chapter 2 of van Dijk and Kintsch for a review of the relevant literature. Indirect support for the latter claim comes from the fact that similar representations have recently evolved in those aspects of artificial intelligence concerned with the construction of large databases. The frame representations proposed by Carbonell, Evans, Scott, and Thomason (1986) for medical databases are essentially identical to propositions. Sowa (1984) has recently proposed a knowledge representation system based on "conceptual graphs" that is remarkably similar to the propositional analysis systems of psychology.

We have shown elsewhere (Patel & Frederiksen, 1984; Patel & Groen, 1986; Patel, Groen, & Frederiksen, 1986) that the techniques of propositional analysis yield evidence for both enhanced memory and forward reasoning that would be expected from the studies in chess and physics, and that previous efforts failed because of their inability to define, for complex verbal data, a unit of analysis corresponding to a chunk. However, we did not explicitly relate our results to a theory of comprehension. In the present chapter, we examine these results and extend them in the light of such a theory and its relationship to problem solving.

TEXTBASES AND SITUATION MODELS

Our approach is based on the theoretical framework of van Dijk and Kintsch (1983). The processes of comprehension are viewed as strategies whose use depends on the goals of the individual reader or listener. In combination with prior knowledge and information gleaned from the overall context, they transform text or discourse[2] into two somewhat different kinds of representations in episodic or working memory. In the words of van Dijk and Kintsch, the *textbase* is "the semantic representation of the input discourse." The *situation model* is "the cognitive representation of the events, actions, persons, and in general the situation that the text is about." The difference between the two might best be understood by considering the empirical tasks in which one or the other is dominant. The textbase determines the immediate recall. The situation model determines the nature of problem solving based on the text (e.g. Kintsch & Greeno, 1985). It may

---

[2]Discourse can be either written or spoken. Text is written discourse. Since, in this chapter, we are only concerned with written discourse, we use the two terms interchangeably.

also be more important than the textbase in determining recall of the original text after this problem solving has occurred (Kintsch, 1987). It should be noted that the situation model is not generated after the textbase. Rather, the two are assumed to be constructed simultaneously in an on-line fashion. They also interact. In particular, the situation model may determine the cohesion of the textbase (i.e., the way it represents meaningful connections between successive segments of an input discourse).

The textbase is defined in terms of propositions and relations between propositions. Its structure can be defined at three different levels. The *microstructure* is the structure of the propositions in the input text or discourse. The *macrostructure* consists of the higher level propositions (macropropositions) that are entailed by those in the microstructure. This may be identical to the microstructure, as in the arithmetic word problems studied by Kintsch and Greeno. Finally, the *superstructure* is a schema (an ordered set of labelled slots) that sequentially organizes the macropropositions. Both the input text and the subjects' verbal data may be analyzed in this fashion. Every text has, in principle, a unique microstructure. In practice, however, such representations may vary in level of detail since an extremely fine-grained propositional representation is frequently unnecessary. On the other hand, there may be a variety of possible macrostructures and superstructures. Verbal data is usually analyzed from the point of view of the extent to which its propositional structure corresponds to the structure of the input text. The effect of such an analysis is to determine which of the many possible macrostructures and superstructures in the input text most accurately characterizes the data. These then are presumed to represent the contents of the textbase of the subject.

The notion of a situation model is not as well defined as that of a textbase. van Dijk and Kintsch claim that it is essentially the same as a mental model, but this latter notion has a variety of not entirely compatible definitions.[3] There is, however, an extremely well-worked-out paradigmatic example in the Kintsch–Greeno (1985) model for solving arithmetic word problems, and the series of computer simulation programs that are based upon it (Dellarosa, 1985, 1986). Such problems pose a simple arithmetic problem as a story. The simulation begins with a propositional representation of the story. On this basis, it builds "set frames" that represent each number specified in the story as a set of objects. It then builds a "superschema" that specifies the relational structure between these sets. The presence of a satisfactory superschema triggers an appropriate algorithm that generates the answer. If an incomplete superschema has been created, then the

---

[3]The notion of a situation model may be considerably more general than that of a mental model, which is usually formulated in terms of knowledge of a device or a class of physical phenomena. In contrast, a situation model would seem to be the knowledge required to perform some kind of task.

program produces "intelligent guesses" about the answer. This superschema, together with the set frames that it subsumes, is the situation model.

It may seem that children's arithmetic word problems are a world apart from clinical cases in medicine. However, both involve situations in which the task is to make inferences from narrative discourse. The simulation program, with appropriate parameters, performs like an expert in its domain[4] and has one feature that is extremely important for our purposes: It builds the superschema from the initial frames by means of a simple, well known forward chaining procedure on the basis of a set of production rules. This procedure, which is taken from the first edition of Winston and Horn (1981), iteratively cycles through a given set of facts to produce a new set of facts.

These considerations lead to the possibility that the van Dijk–Kintsch theory of comprehension can be combined with a generalization of the Kintsch––Greeno model and certain aspects of Delarosa's simulation program, to yield a general theory of expert reasoning from narrative text in complex domains. Its important aspects, for our purposes, would be as follows:

- The reading of a text results in the creation of a propositional textbase and a frame-based situation model.
- Reasoning tasks result in an elaboration of the situation model.
- Expertise resides in the rules that develop the situation model. More satisfactory rules result in a more satisfactory situation model.
- An individual will apply these rules by a process of forward reasoning until he or she is aware of an inaccurate or incomplete situation model. This accounts for the phenomenon of forward reasoning by experts, but does not preclude forward reasoning by the less than expert.
- An individual's awareness of an inaccurate or incomplete situation model will result in some form of backward reasoning.
- The situation model (in a preliminary form) will also affect the structure of the textbase by means of the local coherence strategies specified by van Dijk and Kintsch, which would also affect the nature of the macropropositions. An expert situation model would result in higher level macropropositions. This may lead one to expect recall phenomena analogous to the classical results of Chase and Simon (1973).

In the remainder of this chapter, we consider how these notions apply in the domain of clinical reasoning in medicine. We begin by examining the nature of the textbase as revealed by free recall and summarization tasks.

---

[4]The fact that the pioneering paper by Simon and Simon appeared in a book on children's thinking leads one to suspect that a model for children's expertise need not necessarily differ from a model for adult expertise.

We then consider the results of some reasoning tasks and discuss their relevance to the nature of the situation model and the process by which it is generated from the textbase.

THE COMPREHENSION OF CLINICAL CASES

In general, our research in this area has been based on the working hypothesis that the free recall experiments which we described earlier in this chapter failed to yield coherent results because of methodological inadequacies in defining the basic units of recall. We have found in a series of studies that the use of propositional techniques leads to the isolation of systematic differences between experts and novices. All used the same basic paradigm in which the subject was allowed to read a text containing a description of a clinical case for about two minutes, and then was asked to write down what he or she remembered as accurately as possible. Experts were physicians, and novices were students in the first or second year of medical school. The first experiment (Patel & Frederiksen, 1984) consisted of a reanalysis of protocols obtained in one of these previous studies (Norman et al., 1979).[5] This was followed by an experiment of our own which essentially replicated the design of Norman and his colleagues. Some inadequacies in this experimental design were remedied in a master's thesis by L.D.J. Coughlin (1986).

All these studies used the same basic method of analysis. A propositional representation was obtained for each text. Propositions were then classified as to their degree of relevance to the diagnosis of the clinical case, on the basis of a method developed by Johnson (1970) and modified by Patel and Frederiksen (1984), which involves the use of independent experts as judges. The recall protocols were scored by a method of recall–inference analysis developed by Frederiksen (1979, 1981). This distinguishes between propositions in the input text that appear unchanged in the recall protocol, and those that are transformed in such a way as to preserve the basic meaning. Intuitively, if a reposition refers to a fact in a possible world, then the inference refers to the same fact in the same world but in a slightly different way. More technically, an inference is a transformation of a proposition in which the head element remains unchanged. In the terminology of van Dijk and Kintsch that we developed in the preceding section, an inference is essentially a macroproposition.

The results of these studies all show the same basic pattern. An example

---

[5]We would like to thank Geoffrey Norman of McMaster University for providing these protocols.

is shown in Figure 10.1. In routine cases similar to those that a physician frequently encounters, experts make more inferences from highly relevant information than do novices. On the other hand, novices both recall and infer more information of low relevance than do experts. These differences have been highly significant on the basis of multivariate analyses of variance in every set of data analyzed. A summary of these differences, from the various experiments, is shown in Table 10.1. Also included are the results of a task involving summarization rather than recall (Patel & Medley-Mark, 1986).

The data summarized in this table was based only on routine clinical cases. However, the studies on chess compared two conditions: normal game positions and positions randomly generated but in accordance with the rules of the game. The experiments in medicine used atypical (i.e., nonroutine) clinical cases as a second condition, with unclear results. Coughlin's major modification of this previous design was to use, as a third condition, text that had been partially randomized on the basis of its propositional structure, while preserving the basic meaning of the clinical case. He found that,

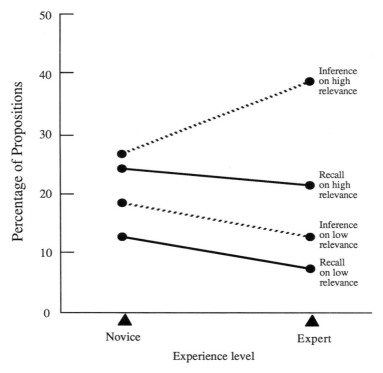

FIGURE 10.1 Mean percentage of propositions recalled and inferred by relevance level and experience level ($F = 20 \cdot 117$, d. f. $= 1,21, p < 0.0003$).

TABLE 10.1
Percent of Highly Relevant Propositions Recalled and Inferred
by Experts and Novices in Various Experiments

| | % Proposition | | | |
| | Recalled | | Inferred | |
	Experts	Novices	Experts	Novices
McMaster University studies reanalyzed (Patel & Frederiksen, 1984)	15	18	26	21
Recall of general cancer and fever tests (Patel, 1984)	15	18	24	21
Summarization of clinical tests on cancer and fever (Patel & Medley-Mark, 1986)	12	15	11	8
Recall of clinical texts on fever and muscular disorder (Coughlin, 1986)	38	46	43	36

with scrambled routine problems, the differences between experts and novices disappeared, thus replicating the results of Chase and Simon. This was not so with atypical cases. In the unscrambled condition, experts recalled as much irrelevant material as did novices, although there was still an overall tendency to make more inferences. The same pattern of results occurred with the scrambled condition.

In general, these results indicate two major kinds of difference from those obtained in chess and other game-like situations. The first is the importance of the distinction between relevant and irrelevant material. The second is the fact that subjects tend to make inferences which retain the meaning or gist of the stimulus text but which would appear incorrect if some scoring scheme were developed on the basis of surface structure properties. This is the basic reason for the anomalous results obtained in the studies previously referred to, which used precisely such kinds of scoring schemes. When one is used that correctly reflects the propositional structure of the input text, a clear-cut picture emerges of experts selectively encoding input information that is consistent both with the free recall research on expert–novice differences, and with related research not directly using this paradigm (e.g., Chi, Feltovich, & Glaser, 1981).

Coughlin's data provides additional information regarding the nature of this encoding. Claessen and Boshuizen (1985) obtained results through the use of a scaling technique that indicated that recall protocols were organized according to a schematic superstructure in which the information regarding the patient was organized into a number of categories, among which were a description of the patient, the patient's complaint, his or her history, the results of the physical examination and of the laboratory tests. A direct test of this notion is possible by examining the fashion in which subjects recalled Coughlin's scrambled texts. A reanalysis of this data yields the surprisingly strong result that *all* experts and almost all novices rearranged the propositions into these categories, with the categories themselves always appearing in the order just indicated. Two examples of such protocols, together with the scrambled texts used as stimuli, are shown in Tables 10.2 and 10.3.

A final issue concerns the relationship between the textbase and the situation model. Intuitively, the textbase represents a story about a patient being examined by a physician, whereas the situation model is some kind of representation of a disease process. For example, in the case studied by Patel and Groen (1986), the story involves a patient and a physician. The patient presents himself in the emergency ward with a set of complaints, including a high fever. The physician then takes a history and performs a physical examination. In the course of this, the patient claims that he was bitten by a cat and the physician discovers wounds on the arm and abnormal heart sounds. This is the textbase. In contrast, the situation model is

TABLE 10.2

Scrambled Text on Infectious Endocarditis

There was no splenomegaly. Physical examination revealed a toxic-looking young man who was having a rigor. A 27-year-old unemployed male was admitted to the Emergency Room. He also complained of some shortness of breath when he tried to climb the two flights of stairs in his apartment.

Funduscopy revealed a flame-shaped hemorrhage in the left eye. Pulse was regular, equal and synchronous. The fever and chills were accompanied by sweating and a feeling of prostration. The apex beat was not displaced. The patient volunteered that he had been bitten by a cat at a friend's house a week before admission.

His temperature was 41° C. Urinalysis showed numerous red cells. He took his own temperature and it was recorded at 40° C on the morning of his admission. He complained of shaking chills and fever of 4 days duration. Pulse was 124/minute. Examination showed no jugular venous distention. There were no red cell casts on microscopic urinalysis.

Functional inquiry revealed a transient loss of vision in his right eye which lasted approximately 45 seconds. This he described the day before admission to the emergency ward. Examination of his limbs showed puncture wounds in his left antecubital fossa. There were no other skin findings. Auscultation of his heart revealed a 2/6 early diastolic murmur in the aortic area. Blood pressure 110/40. Mucous membranes were clear. The pulse was also noted to be collapsing.

Recall of Scrambled Text on Infectious Endocarditis by a Physician (#4B)

Description:	27-year-old man
History:	Presents with shortness of breath after climbing two flights of stairs. He had shaking chills 4 days prior to admission associated with rigors and prostration. He had been bitten by a cat. One day prior to admission he had transient loss of vision in one eye.
Physical Examination:	Physician examination: toxic-looking man, temperature 41° C, needle marks in an antecubital fossa. Skin—? fundi, no hemorrhage—yes hemorrhage but I can't remember kind, cardiovascular exam—diastolic murmur, collapsing pulse rate 120/minute. No splenomegaly. Blood pressure? 120/80, 110/80.
Laboratory Results:	Laboratory urinalysis: Red blood cells. No casts.

whatever enables the physician to deduce from this the fact that the patient is suffering from a case of acute bacterial endocarditis. This involves knowledge of a set of causal mechanisms that imply a quite different kind of "story," involving bacteria transmitted through a wound and attacking the heart valves.

If the situation model were to play a major role in determining immediate recall then we would expect the recall protocols to contain statements related to the disease process. Although we have not performed a thorough quantitative analysis of this aspect of the data, that is clearly not the case

TABLE 10.3

Scrambled Text on Temporal Arteritis

HB-14.0 GM%. There were no localizing neurological signs. Functional inquiry revealed that she had lost two pounds over this three-month period. Examination of her fundi showed no hemorrhages or papilledema.

A 69-year-old housewife presented with a three-month history of extreme fatigue. BUN-20. Physical examination revealed an anxious elderly female looking her stated age. Glucose—120 MGM%. She had a new onset of frontal and temporal headaches. Pulse rate was 82/minute. WBC-5,000. She also complained of difficulty getting out of bed in the morning because of stiffness of her muscles. Her visual acuity was normal.

She ascribed the weight loss to the fact that she had not been able to chew her food properly because of pain in both jaws when she commenced chewing. Her blood pressure was 140/80. CNS examination revealed that she was well-oriented. Chest exam was normal. ESR-80MM/hour. The pulses were regular, equal, and synchronous. One week before admission she also had a transient blurring of vision in her right eye which lasted for about three minutes. All pulses were present and non-tender.

Recall of Scrambled Text on Temporal Arteritis by a Physician (#13b)

Description:	69-year old woman
History:	Three-month history of extreme fatigue, weight loss (2 lbs.), difficulty chewing because of jaw pain, stiff muscles—causes difficulty getting out of bed. Transient blurred vision, temporal H/A.
Physical Examination:	Physical examination: not ill-looking Blood pressure: 140/80 Pulse: 72 reg. Exam unremarkable, particularly no muscle tenderness. Normal eye exam.

Laboratory Results: Lab:
Hgb.	14
BUN	20
Glucose	120
ESR	80

in the protocols given in Tables 10.2 and 10.3, nor in those we have published elsewhere (e.g. Patel & Groen, 1986). Also, as can be seen in these tables, the superstructure is clearly that of a narrative about a patient problem rather than representation of a disease process. This would seem to offer convincing evidence that immediate recall reflects primarily the contents of the textbase, which is consistent with the notion of van Dijk and Kintsch. However, there is also evidence that experts' situation models play a role in determining the textbase that goes beyond that postulated by these authors. This is because the selectivity of experts with respect to relevant information (as indicated in Figure 10.1) can best be explained on the assumption that information in the partial situation model, that is being built up concurrently with the textbase, is being used to filter out irrelevant information. Thus, the superior recall of the expert for relevant information can be explained by the notion that he already knows what is relevant through having developed or accessed at least a partial situation model.

FORWARD REASONING IN DIAGNOSTIC EXPLANATION

In research on cognition and artificial intelligence in medicine, it has been found that pure problem-solving protocols, in which a subject is simply asked to "think aloud" as he or she makes a diagnosis, tend to yield unsatisfactory or excessively sparse information regarding the nature of the knowledge being used. A widely adopted solution has been to use various kinds of probing tasks. This approach is used extensively in the chapter by Clancey in this volume, and, in a more psychological context, in the chapter by Lesgold and his colleagues.

A probe that we have found useful is a task we call diagnostic explanation (Patel & Groen, 1986), in which the subject is asked to "explain the underlying pathophysiology" of a patient's condition. We have found that physicians respond to this question by explaining the patient's symptoms in terms of a diagnosis. A distinction is sometimes made in the literature between a clinical level of explanation and a pathophysiological level, with the latter involving basic pathology and physiology (e.g., Patil, Szolovits, & Schwartz, 1984). However, we find that physicians interpret our question in a much more open-ended fashion. In general, their goal is to explain a diagnosis by indicating its relationship to the clinical symptoms rather than to give a detailed exposition of the underlying mechanisms.

In our investigations of forward and backward reasoning, we embed this question in the following overall paradigm:

1. Present a description of a case.
2. Obtain a free-recall protocol.
3. Obtain a diagnostic explanation protocol.
4. Ask for a diagnosis.

It is important to note that the diagnosis is requested *after* the diagnostic explanation. This is to give the subject the opportunity to provide a diagnosis during the explanation task. When this occurs, it seems reasonable to consider the possibility that the resulting protocol may reflect elements of the solution process. In terms of our adaptation of the Kintsch–Greeno theory, we would expect the subject to have developed a textbase and at least a partial situation model at the time of the free-recall probe. While giving a diagnostic explanation, the subject has the opportunity to develop this partial situation model into a complete one.

Identifying Forward Reasoning

Our basic approach in analyzing this data is to begin by representing the propositional structure of a protocol as a semantic network. In so doing, we make two kinds of distinction. First, we follow Gentner (1983) by distinguishing between propositions that describe attribute information — propositions that form the nodes of the network — and those that describe relational information, that form the links. Second, we distinguish between attributes that appear in the description of the clinical case, or in the subject's summary, and those that do not. We call the former *facts* and the latter *hypotheses*.

Our criteria for distinguishing between forward and backward reasoning were motivated by a resemblance between the causal and conditional relationships that predominated in the semantic networks arising from our data, and the rule system of NEOMYCIN (Clancey & Letsinger, 1981; Clancey, this volume). This incorporates a distinction between hypothesis-directed and data-directed rules that is equivalent to the distinction between forward and backward reasoning. It therefore seemed reasonable to directly transform the semantic network into a set of production rules.[6] A simple test for forward reasoning was to discover whether these rules would correctly execute when implemented in a standard forward-chaining production-system interpreter of the type discussed earlier in this chapter. Backward reasoning could be defined, by default, as any rule that could not be executed.

This rule-based criterion has two disadvantages. The first is that it is somewhat noninformative where backward reasoning is concerned. The second is that it contains a hidden theory. The production system interpreter provides a model of the reasoning process. Hence, it does not provide a neutral means of representing data. This has had the effect of forcing us to treat the diagnostic explanation task as pure problem solving. While this is a plausible hypothesis, and is quite compatible with our version of the Kintsch–Greeno theory (which employs an identical forward chaining interpreter), it renders difficult the consideration of alternative possibilities.

A more satisfactory criterion, which is relational rather than rule-based,

---

[6]On the surface, production rules may seem highly procedural and semantic networks highly declarative. However, they are equivalent for the purpose of our analysis. We are primarily interested in relationships between propositions that appear in a protocol. These can be represented either symbolically as production rules or graphically as links between nodes in a network.

can be formulated in terms of the semantic network representation rather than the rule representation. While complicated to define, it is simple to apply to small networks by straightforward visual inspection without recourse to the formal definition. In order to state this, it is necessary to introduce some elementary concepts from graph theory. The terminology and the definitions are taken from Sowa (1984), to which the reader is referred for an extensive treatment of the relationship between graph theory and semantic networks.

Formally, a *graph* is a nonempty set of *nodes* and a set of *arcs* each leading from a node N to a node N'. A *walk* through a graph is a sequence of nodes such that if a_{i+1} is the immediate successor of a_i in the sequence, then the two nodes are connected by an arc. A *path* is a walk in which all nodes are distinct. In a *directed graph*, an arc connecting N to N' is viewed as distinct from an arc connecting N' to N. To emphasize the distinction, arcs of directed graphs are usually denoted by arrows. If e is an arrow connecting N to N' then N is called the *source* of e, and N' is the *target* of e. A path is said to be *oriented* or *directed* if every node is the source of an arrow connecting it to its immediate successor. In other words, it is a path that follows the direction of the arrows. A *subpath* of an oriented path P is a path that is a subsequence of P. Note that undirected paths are possible in directed graphs simply by ignoring the order of the arrows. A graph is *connected* if there exists a path, whether directed or undirected, between any two nodes. If it is not connected, then it breaks down into *disjoint component*, each of which is connected, but none of which has a path linking it to any other component.

In terms of these notions, a semantic network is a directed graph connecting the facts given in a clinical case with hypotheses, or any subpath.

TABLE 10.4

Summarize the case.
> A 63-year-old woman with gradually increased weight gain and fatigue with tiredness. Hoarseness of voice treated with *high dose of iodine mixture* with progressive increase in constitutional symptomatology.
>
> Admission to hospital based on clinical examination, lab data, and especially blood gasses.

Explain the case in terms of the underlying pathophysiology.
> Classic case of autoimmune thyroid disease supported by history of progressive decrease in thyroid function, and the examination for thyromegaly and vitiligo.
>
> Progressively diminished thyroid function exacerbated by iodine administration resulting in further blockage of thyroxin release. Long-standing nature of disease supported by signs of onset of myxedema, galactoplania, and suggestion of increased TSH with increase prolactin.
>
> The presence of pleural effusion is typical as is the presence of hyponatremia secondary to impaired water excretion related to S.I.A.D.H. The hypometabolic state has resulted in respiratory failure secondary to hypoventilation.

Provide a diagnosis.
> Autoimmune thyroid disease with myxedema and incipient myxedema coma.

Backward reasoning corresponds to an oriented path from a hypothesis to a fact or, once again, any subpath. The presence of subpaths in these definitions is important because it gives criteria for forward or backward reasoning between facts. Pure forward reasoning corresponds to a graph in which every oriented path satisfies the forward reasoning criterion. Pure backward reasoning corresponds to a graph in which every oriented path satisfies the backward reasoning criterion.

The use of these definitions is illustrated in Figure 10.2. This is the network representation of the diagnostic explanation by a cardiologist of a case

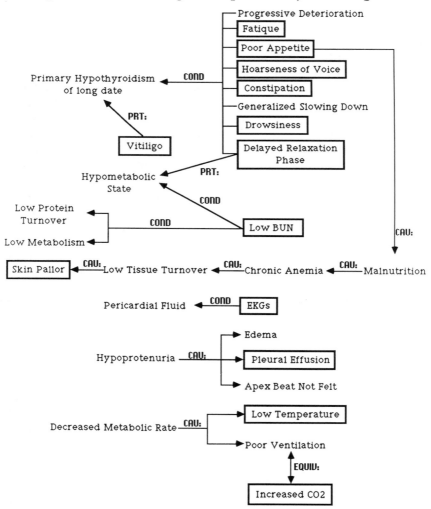

FIGURE 10.2 Structural representation of endocrinology problem by cardiologist practitioner.

in endocrinology (Patel, Arocha, & Groen, 1986). The case and the protocol are given in Table 10.4. The case is not within the subject's domain of specialization, and the diagnosis is complete. Because of this, the representation is far from being the most coherent that we have encountered. However, this makes it useful for illustrative purposes since it contains a rather complex mixture of forward and backward reasoning.

The diagram is clearly a directed graph consisting of nodes linked by arrows. The arrows have labels indicating the relationship between nodes. The two most important are CAU, which means that the source node causes the target (e.g., "poor appetite" causes "malnutrition"), and COND, which means that the source node is an indicator of the target (e.g., the EKG data indicates "pericardial fluid"). The nodes containing facts from the problem text are enclosed in boxes. The diagram also contains four *and* nodes, indicated by forks in the arrows. Two of these are targets (e.g., "progressive deterioration" *and* "fatigue" *and* "poor appetite," and so forth indicate "primary hypothyroidism"). The remaining two are sources (e.g., "decreased metabolic rate" causes "low temperature" *and* "poor ventilation").

The diagram is not a connected graph, and three of the four are disjoint components. One of these consists of pure backward reasoning, and one consists of pure forward reasoning. Another would be pure backward reasoning were it not for a conservative coding procedure ("pleural edema" rather than "edema" appears in the text). As it is, it fails to satisfy the criterion because the path from "hypoprotenuria" to "edema" is not a subpath of one that leads from a hypothesis to a fact.

The remaining component is also the most important because it is the largest and contains the best approximation of a satisfactory diagnosis ("primary hypothyroidism of long date"). This is neither purely forward nor backward for two reasons. The first is again the existence of paths, each of which connects two hypotheses but fails to be a subpath of one beginning or ending with a fact. The second is a path connecting two facts ("poor appetite" and "skin pallor").

Intuitively, this latter path could be seen as representing a different line of reasoning, or a different component of the semantic network. The intuition can be rendered precise by introducing a few more concepts from graph theory. We define a *cutout* of a graph to be a node which, when removed together with all arrows leading to or from it, causes a graph to separate into disjoint components that are themselves graphs. Conversely, if two graphs have a common node, then their *join* is the new graph formed by joining them at that node.[7] This suggests that an algorithm for finding the components can be defined in terms of generating, at each cut-point, two

---

[7]Formally, if a concept c in a graph u is identical to a concept d in a graph v, then the join of u and v is the graph obtained by deleting d from v and linking to c all arcs that had been linked to d (Sowa, p. 94).

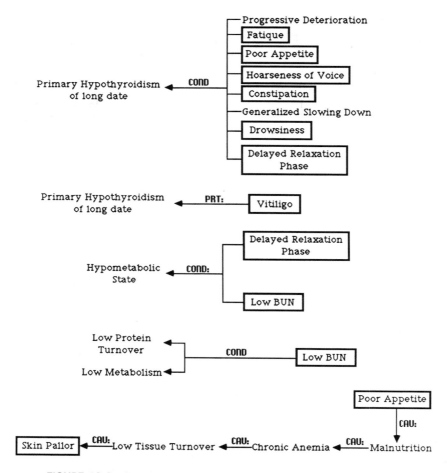

FIGURE 10.3 Components of structural representation of endocrinology problem by cardiologist practitioner.

graphs whose join is the original graph (intuitively, we obtain two graphs by removing the cut-point and then reattaching it into each graph). Unfortunately, every node of Figure 10.2 is a cut-point unless it connects to only one other node. Hence, what results from applying this algorithm is a hierarchy of components, some of which are uninteresting and some of which actually distort the logic of the process we are attempting to represent. Because of this, we prohibit the application of the algorithm in the following two cases: (a) *and*-nodes; and (b) graphs that consist of a single path, without any branches. Carrying out this procedure results in the minimal components shown in Figure 10.3. Although other components exist, they are all joins of these minimal components.

Empirical Results

The clearest results using this approach were obtained with a task involving the diagnosis of a case of acute bacterial endocarditis (Patel & Groen, 1986). The subjects were seven specialists in cardiology. Four of these achieved an accurate diagnosis, whereas the diagnoses of the remaining three were inaccurate or incomplete. Using the production rule criterion described in the preceding section, it was shown that the diagnostic explanations of subjects making an accurate diagnosis consisted of pure forward reasoning. In contrast, subjects with inaccurate diagnoses tended to make use of a mixture of forward and backward reasoning. Two of these resembled the example in the preceding section. The remaining subject used pure back-

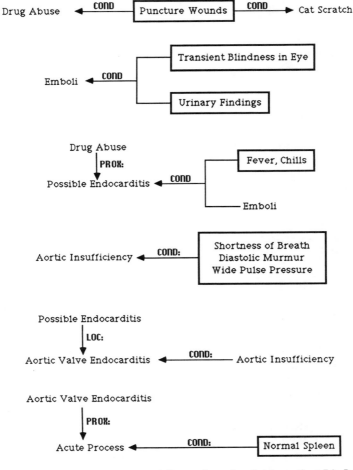

FIGURE 10.4 Components of diagnostic explanation by subject 5 in Patel and Groen (1986).

ward reasoning, beginning with a high-level hypothesis and proceeding in a top-down fashion to the propositions embedded in the stimulus text, or to the generation of irrelevant rules.

The relational criterion gives a slightly different and possibly more revealing characterization of the forward reasoning process. Figure 10.4 shows the minimal components of the diagnostic explanation of the subject for which Patel and Groen (1986) provided a detailed analysis. The components leading to the diagnosis, when joined together, exhibit pure forward reasoning (interestingly enough, each corresponds to one of the production rules used in applying the original criterion). However, one component, linking "puncture wound" to "cat scratch," is indeterminate. This refers to an excuse given by the patient for his puncture wounds, and hence is irrelevant to the diagnosis.

The surprisingly strong results concerning forward reasoning lead to a consideration of the conditions under which this pattern might break down. Patel, Arocha, and Groen (1986) used two considerably less routine clinical cases, one in endocrinology and the other in cardiology, and investigated the diagnostic explanations of subjects in cases both inside and outside their domain of specialization. The subjects were two endocrinologists and two cardiologists. It was found that the subjects made accurate diagnoses of the case in their own specialty, but inaccurate diagnoses of those outside their specialty. In the semantic network representation of the diagnostic explanation for accurate diagnoses, the line of reasoning leading to the diagnosis appeared as a disjoint component consisting of pure forward reasoning. However, these cases contained complicating factors that were not directly related to the main diagnosis, and the subjects felt it necessary, after completing the diagnosis, to explain their causes. These appeared in the semantic network representation as disjoint components consisting of pure backward reasoning. In contrast, the representations of inaccurate diagnoses showed a mixture of forward and backward reasoning similar to that found for subjects with inaccurate diagnoses in the first experiment. The protocol discussed in detail in the preceding section is a typical example.

It is of interest to note that, in these experiments, the recall data was far less informative than the diagnostic explanations, although the recall data was accurate and detailed. In particular, there were very few differences between subjects in the number of propositions recalled. As a result, there was little or no relationship between recall and the accuracy of diagnosis or mode of reasoning. The main usefulness of the recall protocols was in verifying that the contents of the problem text were actually stored in the subjects' episodic memory.

The major weakness of the paradigm used in these two experiments is a certain ambiguity regarding the point in the procedure at which the diagnosis is actually made. An alternative approach is to present a patient's problem in segments and to obtain a diagnostic explanation after the subject has seen each segment. In research conducted for a Master's thesis, G.M. Joseph used this procedure with the same assignment of subjects to cases as in Experiment 2 (i.e., experts inside and outside their domain) (Joseph & Patel, 1986). Clearly, this would not be expected to yield pure forward reasoning, because subjects have far more opportunities to form inaccurate hypotheses on the basis of partial information. However, the results were consistent with the general pattern yielded by the two preceding experiments. Experts in their own domain reached tentative diagnoses by a forward reasoning process on the basis of the patient's history, which was presented in the initial segments. Subsequent information, from the physical examination and laboratory tests, was used only to confirm the diagnosis. In contrast, experts outside their domain generated multiple hypotheses on the basis of the history, and added additional hypotheses as new information was provided.

Theoretical Implications

In general, these results complete the answer to the empirical question with which this chapter began. We showed earlier that the techniques of propositional analysis yields recall data that parallels the classical results of Chase and Simon. We have shown here that, given suitable extensions of these techniques, and problems that suitably match the subjects' expertise, specialists in various domains of medicine do, in fact, exhibit the same kind of forward reasoning that one would expect from the results in other domains such as physics. The results also indicate a possible reason why this phenomenon has not been found in previous research. It may only occur when there is a problem that a physician has already encountered several times and which contains very little extraneous information. Moreover, even slight inaccuracies in a diagnosis would seem to induce backward reasoning. Previous research has concentrated on difficult problems, and investigators have frequently tended to bias their selection toward those that subjects have not previously encountered.

They also lend at least three kinds of support to our claim that a generalization of the Kintsch–Greeno model may provide a basis for a theory of expert problem-solving in domains with a nontrivial verbal component. The first is the use of forward reasoning with accurate diagnoses, which is a necessary condition for any application of the model. The second is the apparent uselessness of the recall data in predicting performance on the diagnostic explanation task. This supports the model's emphasis on the distinction between the textbase and the situation model, and suggests that the latter determines the variability in expert performance. The third is the association between backward reasoning and the formation of inaccurate or incomplete diagnoses. This lends support to our notion, which is absent from the original Kintsch–Greeno formulation of the model, that an individual's awareness of an inaccurate or incomplete situation model will result in some form of backward reasoning.

To make this more specific requires a number of major modifications in the model as originally formulated for arithmetic word problems. One is the replacement of the schemas representing knowledge about sets, by schemas representing knowledge about medicine. One possibility is to consider the schemas to have three slots in which can be inserted symbols corresponding to an abnormality, a consequence of the abnormality, and an indicator of the abnormality. A detailed account of how this can be applied is beyond the scope of this chapter. However, a brief example that at least hints as to how this schema structure might operate with respect to Delarosa's simulation, can be developed in terms of the components in Figure 10.4. A scanning of the textbase, as given in Patel and Groen (1986), obtains the first proposition, which describes a young unemployed male. This triggers a schema in which the abnormality slot is filled by "drug abuse" and the other slots are empty. The next proposition contains the abnormality "fever and chills" which generates a schema in which infection is the abnormality and fever is the consequence. Much later, this schema becomes filled by adding "puncture wounds" as an enabling condition. In the same fashion, a schema for "embolic" is developed. The model can then develop a superschema, or schema set, corresponding to "possible endocarditis." The process is completed by adding schemas for "aortic insufficiency" and "acuteness," to develop a superschema for acute aortic valve endocarditis.

Two other modifications pose a considerably more complex set of issues. The first is to provide a mechanism that explicitly generates background reasoning. The second is to account for the tendency of experts to explain all the remaining facts in a case after they have completed the main diagnosis. One possibility is to bring in certainty factors such are used in many expert systems. Another may be to develop mechanisms based on schemas with unfilled slots. A more drastic possibility is to view diagnostic explanation as more of a true explanation task, with the protocol being generated, at least in part, as a readout of an already existing superschema.

It is important to bear in mind, however, that what forward or backward reasoning consists of in a semantic network representation need not necessarily correspond to forward or backward chaining of production rules in the model, whose primary role is to generate schemas and superschemas rather than propositions in a protocol. These developing schemas are essentially what defines the situation model. A basic assumption of the example in the preceding paragraph is that the minimal components of a semantic network correspond to these developing schemas. Our empirical evidence indicates that it is these components that develop by a process of forward reasoning.

REFERENCES

Carbonell, J. G., Evans, D. A., Scott, D. S., & Thomason, R. H. (1986). *On the design of biomedical knowledge bases.* Paper presented at MEDINFO-86, Washington, DC.

Chase, W. G., & Simon, H. A. (1973). Perception in chess. *Cognitive Psychology, 1,* 55–81.

Chi, M. T. H., Feltovich, P. J., & Glaser, R. (1981). Categorization and representation of physics problems by experts and novices. *Cognitive Science, 5,* 121–152.

Claessen, H. F. A., & Boshuizen, H. P. A. (1985). Recall of medical information by students and doctors. *Medical Education, 19,* 61–67.

Clancey, W. J. (1984). Methodology for building an intelligent tutoring system. In W. Kintsch, H. Miller, & P. Polson (Eds.), *Methods and tactics in cognitive science* (pp. 51–83). Hillsdale, NJ: Lawrence Erlbaum Associates.

Clancey, W. S., & Letsinger, R. (1981). NEOMYCIN: Reconfiguring a rule-based expert system for application to teaching. In Proceedings of the 7th International Joint Conference on Artificial Intelligence (pp. 829–836). Vancouver, British Columbia.

Coughlin, L. D. J. (1986). *The effect of randomization on the free recall of medical information by experts and novices.* M.A. thesis, Department of Educational Psychology, McGill University, Montreal, Canada.

de Groot, A. D. (1965). *Thought and choice in chess.* Netherlands: Mouton Publishers, The Hague.

Dellarosa, D. (1985). Solution: A computer simulation of childrens' arithmetic word-problem solving (Tech. Rep. No. 148). Boulder, CO: University of Colorado.

Dellarosa, D. (1986). A computer simulation of children's arithmetic word-problem solving. *Behavior Research Methods, Instruments, and Computers, 18,* 12–154.

Elstein, A. S., Shulman, L. S., & Sprafka, S. A. (1978). *Medical problem solving: An analysis of clinical reasoning.* Cambridge, MA: Harvard University Press.

Frederiksen, C. H. (1975). Representing logical and semantic structure of knowledge acquired from discourse. *Cognitive Psychology, 7,* 371–458.

Frederiksen, C. H. (1979). Discourse comprehension and early reading. In L. Resnick & P. Weaver (Eds.), *Theory and practice of early reading* (pp. 155–186). Hillsdale, NJ: Lawrence Erlbaum Associates.

Frederiksen, C. H. (1981). Inferences in preschool children's conversations: A cognitive perspective. In J. Green & C. Wallat (Eds.), *Ethnography and language in educational settings* (pp. 303–350). Norwood, NJ: Ablex.

Gentner, D. (1983). Structure mapping: A theoretical framework for analogy. *Cognitive Science, 7,*(2).

Greeno, J. G., & Simon, H. A. (1984). Problem solving and reasoning. In R. C. Atkinson, R. Hernstein, G. Lindzey, & R. D. Luce (Eds.), *Steven's handbook of experimental psychology.* New York: Wiley.

Groen, G. J., & Patel, V. (1985). Medical problem solving: Some questionable assumptions. *Medical Education, 19,* 95–100.

Hayes, J. R., & Simon, H. A. (1974). Understanding written problem instructions. In L. W. Gregg (Ed.), *Knowledge and cognition* (pp. 167–200). Hillsdale, NJ: Lawrence Erlbaum Associates.

Johnson, R. E. (1970). Recall of prose as function of the structural importance of the linguistic unit. *Journal of Verbal Learning and Verbal Behavior, 9,* 12–20.

Johnson-Laird, P. N. (1983). *Mental models.* Cambridge: Cambridge University Press.

Joseph, G. M. & Patel, V. L. (1986). Specificity of expertise in medical reasoning. *Proceedings of the Eighth Annual Conference of the Cognitive Science Society* (pp. 331–343). Hillsdale, NJ: Lawrence Erlbaum Associates.

Kassirer, J. P. (1984). Teaching clinical medicine by literature hypothesis testing: Let's teach what we practice. *New England Journal of Medicine, 309,* 921–923.

Kassirer, J. P. Kuipers, B. J., & Gorry, G. A. (1982). Toward a theory of clinical expertise. *American Journal of Medicine, 73,* 251–259.

Kintsch, W. (1974). *The representation of meaning in memory.* Hillsdale, NJ: Lawrence Erlbaum Associates.

Kintsch, W. (1987). Learning from text. *Cognition and Instruction, 4,* 2, 87–108.

Kintsch, W., & Greeno, J. G. (1985). Understanding and solving word arithmetic problems. *Psychological Review, 92,* 109–129.

Larkin, J., McDermott, J., Simon, D. P., & Simon, H. A. (1980a). Expert and novice performances in solving physics problems. *Science, 208,* 1335–1342.

Larkin, J. H., McDermott, J., Simon, D. P., & Simon, H. A. (1980b). Models of competence in solving physics problems. *Cognitive Science, 4,* 317–345.

Muzzin, L. J. Norman, G. R., Jacoby, L. L., Feightner, J. W., Tugwell, P., & Guyatt, G. H. (1982). Manifestations of expertise in recall of clinical protocols. *Proceedings of the 21st Annual Conference on Research in Medical Education* (pp. 163–168). Washington, DC.

Muzzin, L. J., Norman, G. R., Feightner, J. W., Tugwell, P. & Guyatt, G. (1983). Expertise in recall of protocols in two specialty areas. *Proceedings of the 22nd Annual Conference on Research in Medical Education,* (pp. 122–127). Washington, DC.

Newell, A. & Simon, H. A. (1972). *Human Problem Solving.* Englewood Cliffs, NJ: Prentice-Hall.

Norman, G. R., Jacoby, L. L. Feightner, J. W., & Campbell, G. J. M. (1979). Clinical experience and the structure of memory. *Proceedings of the 18th Annual Conference on Research in Medical Education,* Washington, DC.

Patel, V. L., Arocha, J. F., & Groen, G. J. (1986) Strategy selection and degree of expertise in medical reasoning. *Proceedings of the Eighth Annual Conference of the Cognitive Science Society* (pp. 780–791). Hillsdale, NJ: Lawrence Erlbaum Associates.

Patel, V. L. & Frederiksen, C. H. (1984). Cognitive processes in comprehension and knowledge acquisition by medical students and physicians. In H. G. Schmidt & M. C. DeVolder (Eds.), *Tutorials in problem based learning* (pp. 143–157). Assen, Holland: Van Gorcum.

Patel, V. L. & Groen, G. J. (1986). Knowledge based solution strategies in medical reasoning. *Cognitive Science, 10,* 91–116.

Patel, V. L., Groen, G. J., & Frederiksen, C. H. (1986). Differences between students and physicians in memory for clinical cases. *Medical Education, 20,* 3–9.

Patel, V. L., & Medley-Mark, V. (1986). Relationship between representation of textual information and underlying problem representation in medicine. (CME Report #CME86-CS1).

Patil, R. S., Szolovits, P., & Schwartz, W. (1984). Causal understanding of patient illness in medical diagnostics In W. J. Clancey & E. H. Shortliffe (Eds.). *Readings in medical artificial intelligence.* (pp. 339–360) Reading, MA: Addison-Wesley.

Rubin, A. D. (1975). Hypothesis formation and evaluation in medical diagnosis. (Tech. Rep.No. AI-TR-3116). Cambridge, MA: Artificial Intelligence Laboratory, MIT

Simon, D. P., & Simon, H. A. (1978). Individual differences in solving physics problems. In R. Siegler (Ed.). *Children's thinking: What develops?* (pp. 325–348). Hillsdale, NJ: Lawrence Erlbaum Associates.

Sowa, J. F. (1984). *Conceptual structures.* Reading, MA: Addison-Wesley.

van Dijk, T. A., & Kintsch, W. (1983). *Strategies of discourse comprehension.* New York: Academic Press.

Winston, P., & Horn, B. (1981). *LISP* (1st ed.). Reading, MA: Addison-Wesley.

11 Expertise in a Complex Skill: Diagnosing X-Ray Pictures

Alan Lesgold
University of Pittsburgh

Harriet Rubinson
Albert Einstein College of Medicine

Paul Feltovich
Southern Illinois University School
of Medicine

Robert Glaser
University of Pittsburgh

Dale Klopfer
Bowling Green University

Yen Wang
Thomas Jefferson School of Medicine

For several years, we have been trying to understand what constitutes radiological expertise and how that expertise is acquired. Our goal is to understand the learning of a complex skill and thereby to stretch the limits of existing knowledge about expertise and its acquisition. This chapter is a progress report on that work. Radiological diagnosis is a particularly complex and difficult skill. It has a substantial perceptual component that is different in character from that of other domains, such as chess and physics, that have been previously studied: It involves substantial amounts both of principled knowledge that is already formalized and of knowledge that can be gained only from clinical experience, going far beyond the formal scientific knowledge underlying medicine. It involves the integration of several distinct bodies of knowledge with separate organizing principles, including physiology, anatomy, medical theories of disease, and the projective geometry of radiography. Moreover, formal training in the domain is relatively standardized through residency programs, so that it is possible to trace some aspects of the course of acquisition of the skill as well as the course of instruction.

EXPERT PROBLEM-SOLVING

In essence, this chapter is about the nature of expertise in the domain of radiology. Looking across the body of literature on expert–novice differences in other domains, the following general account emerges:

• The expert spends proportionally more time building up a basic representation of the problem situation before searching for a solution (e.g., Chi, Glaser, & Rees, 1982). This is shown schematically in Figure 11.1, which shows imaginary timelines for expert and novice solutions of a problem. The novice takes much *longer* but devotes a *smaller proportion* of his total processing time to finding/generating an initial problem representation. In some domains, even the absolute time spent on building the right initial representation is *longer* for experts (Chi, Glaser, & Rees, 1982).

• A schema with high probability of being at least in the right problem space is invoked very rapidly by the expert. This schema guides further processing, including the building of a basic representation (Chase & Simon, 1973; Lesgold, 1984).

• Experts are able to tune their schemata to the specifics of the case. This permits them to test more completely whether the schema they have invoked is in fact the right one (Voss, Greene, Post, & Penner, 1983).

As in other areas of expertise, radiologists have spent considerable time learning their profession. One way to think about learning to diagnose x-ray images is to consider each case in which the radiologist participates to be a potential learning experience. Polling our subjects from the studies described in this chapter, we were able to determine that an average resident may see 40 cases per day while a senior staff radiologist may see on the order of 65 to 70. If each case counts as a *trial* in the sense of a classical psychological learning study, then the work described here can be seen as dealing with the 10,000th to 200,000th trials.

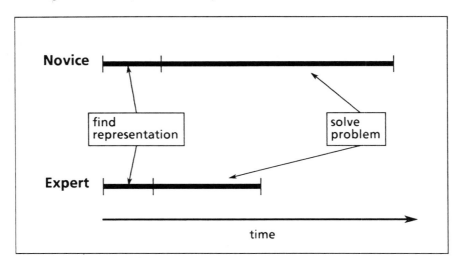

FIGURE 11.1 Imaginary timelines for expert and novice problem solutions.

We can expect then that theories of learning that have been validated in standard one-hour studies in the psychological laboratory may not by themselves provide an adequate account of how radiological expertise is acquired. The smaller number of studies that have dealt with effects of substantial overlearning are also of unclear value, since they mostly measure small changes in speed of performance, while the present work finds improvements in accuracy and even in the qualitative nature of performance extending over long terms of learning. The acquisition time scales and experience scales involved in this sort of learning actually map better onto developmental psychology, which has focused on changes in competence over the course of years rather than minutes. Indeed, certain of our findings, paradoxical from the point of view of some learning theories, are better accommodated by developmental psychology. For that reason, the work reported here builds on both developmental and learning theories.

METHODS

The basic strategy we have taken is to start with naturalistic observation of radiologists doing their work and then move to experiments that intrude minimally into diagnoses. At the beginning of our project, we would sit in a radiologist's office and watch him[1] work. Based on our observations, we fashioned a relatively naturalistic task in which physicians did almost what they do in their offices, examining x-ray films (in our case, of the chest) and then making diagnoses orally (they normally use dictation equipment in making diagnoses). To this, we added some standardized probes as a means of affording a more detailed look at their diagnostic processing. Table 11.1 outlines the approach we followed. It allowed us to ascertain the features that subjects could notice very quickly (within 2 seconds), to separate tentative hypotheses from ultimate diagnoses, and to observe the effects of external input (clinical data) on their decisions.

All radiographs used in our study were standard PA (Posterior-Anterior) thoracic (chest) films. We chose these types of films because plain chest x-ray films are frequently and routinely used, and because the number of organs and range of diseases likely to be found in a selection of such films is reasonably constrained. Further, radiographic interpretation of PA chest films is a frequent requirement of virtually all radiologists, regardless of level of expertise, and one which most of them practice continuously throughout their professional lives. In addition, there already existed a significant body of work in the radiological literature addressing problems of *visual detection* in the interpretation of chest x-rays (e.g. Kundel & La Follette, 1972; Kundel, Nodine, & Carmody, 1978; Revesz & Kundel, 1977;

---

[1]Most but not all of our subjects were male.

TABLE 11.1
Procedure of First Experiment

---

1. Subject sees film for 2 sec.

2. Subject gives free report of what was seen.

3. Subject is prompted with questions such as *Did you see anything else in the lungs? The heart? The skeleton?* and so on.

4. Subject examines film for as long as desired, thinking out loud.

5. Subject dictates formal diagnostic report as he would in his office.

6. Subject given clinical data on the patient (three or four findings).

7. Steps 4 and 5 repeated.

Swensson, Hessel, & Herman, 1980; Tuddenham, 1962) which we could use to guide our endeavors and make meaningful comparisons. Even though our work dealt with the interpretation of abnormality more than with its detection, it was useful to stay close to the stimulus types used in the detection work, since that was the only significant body of work on the psychology of radiological diagnosis that had developed prior to the start of our studies.[2]

In the course of the first experiment, we often had different subjects give us diagnoses and make observations that varied so widely that we wondered if they were seeing the same things. It was apparent that the evolution of a diagnostic choice substantially depended on how an individual *perceived* the features in the x-ray film, and that we had only indirectly measured the interpretation of these ambiguous, albeit critical, areas of the x-ray. This led us to develop a second study in which we specifically asked sub-

---

[2]See Lesgold, Feltovich, Glaser & Wang (1981), for a more complete review of the earlier literature. Since the commencement of our work, interest in the development of radiological skill has continued to grow (e.g., de Valk & Eijkman, 1984; Dijkstra, van der Stelt, & van der Sijde, 1984; Kundel, Nodine, Thickman, Carmody, & Toto, 1985; Kundel & Nodine, 1983; Daffner, 1983; Swensson, Hessel, & Herman, 1985). We must reiterate, however, that our approach to radiological diagnosis is substantially different from those that primarily emphasize the *visual* component of this skill, in that we have attempted to directly study the observer's cognitive evalution of the stimulus, and to characterize expert versus novice behaviors in this domain. Recent claims of Kundel and Nodine (1983) that radiologists perceive radiographs in a "top-down" fashion, driven by a "visual concept," depart from the more "bottom-up" approaches inherent in feature detection studies and thus are closer to our work, though we do not necessarily agree with their conclusions. Whether thought of in terms of the "visual concept" (Arnheim, 1969) or as a "schema," we prefer to think of this complex task as being neither primarily top-down nor bottom-up but as a hybrid of the two, incorporating features of both models in a recursive, interactive decision-making process.

jects to supplement their oral commentary by drawing with marking pens on the film so that we could determine which important contours they were seeing and where they saw these contours. (Not everyone saw the same structure in the same place.)

We did this in two ways. First, we asked them to justify their diagnoses by drawing key borders of organs and other structures that influenced their decisions ("film defense"). Then, based on our experience in the first study, we asked them to trace the outlines of all structures (normal and abnormal) they could see in what we previously knew to be a diagnostically critical region of the film ("target area"). In addition, subjects were asked to draw certain specific anatomical contours in the target area that we suspected were critical to the diagnosis. The steps in the procedure for the second experiment are shown in Table 11.2.

The first experiment involved ten different film diagnoses for each subject while the second involved five. We concentrated our analyses and the present report on three films that were used in both studies and that were relatively difficult. For future reference, we refer to these films as the "lobectomy" film, the "collapse" or "atelectasis" film, and the "multiple tumor" film. Other films included some normal (non diseased) chests and some easier disease cases. The first experiment involved 11 first- and second-year residents, 7 third- and fourth-year residents, and 5 experts each of whom had 10 years or more after residency and was recognized as outstanding by colleagues. The second experiment involved four subjects at each of the three levels.

We emphasize that the cases we report were difficult enough that it would have been imprudent for a physician to diagnose them using only the single frontal thoracic radiograph we provided. Indeed, the cases were difficult enough to produce a substantial amount of variability in diagnoses when

TABLE 11.2
Procedure of Second Experiment

---

1. Subject examines film for as long as desired, thinking out loud.

2. Subject dictates formal diagnostic report as he would in his office.

3. Subject substantiates his diagnosis by drawing relevant anatomy and film features on the x-ray.*

4. Subject draws all anatomy within a specified region of the film (previously known to be critical in diagnostic success). If it does not happen spontaneously, subject is asked to trace anatomical contours predetermined by the experimenters to be crucial.

5. Subject renders another diagnostic report.

---

*Sketches were done with marking pen on an acetate overlay with film in full view.

looking only at the one film for a case. For example, Table 11.3 shows the range of diagnoses made in the first experiment for a film that was an example of collapsed lung (atelectasis). Note the variety of errors made, involving different areas of anatomy as well as different pathologies.

FREQUENCIES OF FINDINGS AND RELATIONSHIPS

Our first approach to analyzing the data was to count protocol events to see if what the subjects said while reaching their diagnoses revealed differences between the groups. We attended first to *findings*, the attribution of specific properties to the film or the patient. Findings exist at many different levels. For example, any of the following would be counted as a finding:

- A triangular density in the right upper lung.
- An abnormally small heart.
- Pneumonia.

We also tallied *relationships*, reasoning paths between findings. For exam-

TABLE 11.3
Diagnoses Offered for Atelectasis Film

1st/2nd Year Residents
Atelectasis (2)
Atelectasis or pneumonia
No interpretation
Tumor (2)
Heart abnormality
Heart abnormality or tumor or hilar abnormality
Calcified lymph node or pulmonary artery abnormality
Right middle lobe lesion or right hilar abnormality
Heart abnormality or pleural thickening

3rd/4th Year Residents
Atelectasis
Tumor
Tumor or esophageal abnormality
Hilar abnormality (2)
Esophageal abnormality
Pulmonary artery abnormality

Experts
Atelectasis (2)
Atelectasis, possibly caused by tumor
No interpretation
Tumor

ple, one might notice spots in the lungs and assert that these were produced by blood pooling. In turn, one might point out that the blood pooling could have been produced as a result of heart failure. Each of these statements of relationship would, in our scoring scheme for our protocols, be called a *reasoning step*, and

Heart Failure → Blood-Pooling → Spots

would be scored as a reasoning *chain* of length 2. A set of findings that had a path from each set member to every other member, ignoring direction, was called a *cluster*. (A disconnected finding was treated as a separate cluster.) The origin of every reasoning step was called a *cause* and the termination was called an *effect*. It should be noted that all findings and relationships produced by the subject were tallied regardless of their relevance to the film diagnosis or their diagnostic accuracy. Therefore, the novice tabulations may be inflated in that they represent the full collection of utterances, rather than merely the appropriate ones. Figure 11.2 illustrates the findings and relationships found in one protocol.

Table 11.4 shows the mean frequencies (per film per subject) from our first study for the three experience groups on each of the measures just described. As can be seen from the table, the experts exceeded the residents on every measure ($a = 0.05$), having more different findings in their protocols, longer reasoning chains, bigger clusters, more clusters, and a greater number of their findings connected to at least one other finding. Put in broader terms, the data support a view of the expert as doing more inferential thinking and ending up with a more coherent model of the patient shown in the film. In contrast, novice representations, as manifested in their protocols, were more superficial, fragmented, and piecemeal.

QUALITATIVE FINDINGS

Qualitative analysis of the protocols allowed us to tease out a general account of the differences between the behavior of the novice and the expert radiologist and to uncover some specific issues that a theory of learning must address. From our data and the expertise literature, we have arrived at the following general account of the behavior of an expert radiologist. First, during the initial phase of building a mental representation, every schema that guides radiological diagnosis seems to have a set of prerequisites or tests that must be satisfied before it can control the viewing and diagnosis. Second, the expert works efficiently to reach the stage where an appropriate general schema is in control. Finally, each schema contains a set of processes that allows the viewer to reach a diagnosis and confirm it. As we

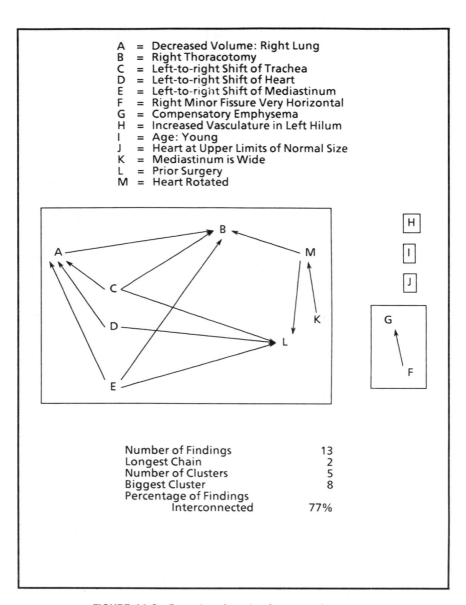

A = Decreased Volume: Right Lung
B = Right Thoracotomy
C = Left-to-right Shift of Trachea
D = Left-to-right Shift of Heart
E = Left-to-right Shift of Mediastinum
F = Right Minor Fissure Very Horizontal
G = Compensatory Emphysema
H = Increased Vasculature in Left Hilum
I = Age: Young
J = Heart at Upper Limits of Normal Size
K = Mediastinum is Wide
L = Prior Surgery
M = Heart Rotated

Number of Findings	13
Longest Chain	2
Number of Clusters	5
Biggest Cluster	8
Percentage of Findings Interconnected	77%

FIGURE 11.2   Examples of scoring for protocol structure.

TABLE 11.4
Quantitative Protocol Measures

Measure	Res 1,2	Res 3,4	Experts
Number of findings	6.58	6.63	**9.09**
Number of causes	2.56	2.58	**3.62**
Number of effects	2.30	2.23	**3.73**
Longest chain	*1.77*	1.90	**2.03**
Biggest cluster	1.60	1.66	**2.47**
Number of different clusters	1.59	1.58	**2.47**
Percentage of findings connected to others	29.7	29.6	**36.5**

For each measure, means in different typefaces were significantly ($\alpha = 0.05$) different.

shall see, many of the faults of the less-expert radiologist involve incompleteness in terms of three aspects: The confirming or refuting tests are not applied to the schema invoked; a generally appropriate schema is not triggered efficiently enough; and/or details of the differential diagnosis process are incomplete.

Beyond the general description, we notice that subsets of the protocols raise interesting issues. On several of the films, more advanced residents actually were less likely to make a correct interpretation than were the less advanced; that is, performance is not a monotonic function of experience. Further, some of the protocols show residents less able to efficiently modify a schema in response to new data, in contrast to the experts, who were flexibly opportunistic, neither too fixated nor uncontrollably labile.

The experts' approach can best be seen in an example. One of the films we used was of a patient who, about a decade earlier, had been operated on to remove a portion of the right upper lung. As a result, there were radiographic signs of a chronic collapsed lung evident in this film, since indeed a once-inflated region was missing. Due to the extent of the ablation and the intervening time, the chest organs had shifted around to fill the void. This meant, among other things, that the heart was both shifted to the right side of the chest and tilted at such an angle that it cast a bigger than normal shadow on the film.

The protocol excerpts in Table 11.5 show what an expert did with this film. After his two-second first look at the film, the expert immediately began searching for a schema to guide his further thinking. Deciding that the film showed a chronic problem, he then tried to find an appropriate schema to match what he had initially seen. One possibility he considered was that the film contained rotational artifacts, that the subject had not been facing directly toward the x-ray plate. Follow-up discussions revealed that there are a variety of tests that must be made to verify a suspected rotational artifact. The rotation schema also contains transforms to be applied to

TABLE 11.5
Protocol Excerpts from an Expert, Showing Early
Schema Invocation, Tuning, and Flexibility

Something is wrong, and it's chronic: "We may be dealing with a chronic process here. . . ."

Trying to get a schema: "I'm trying to work out why the mediastinum and the heart is displaced into the right chest. There is not enough rotation to account for this. I don't see displacement of fissures [lung lobe boundaries].

Experiments with collapse schema: "There may be a collapse of the right lower lobe but the diaphragm on the right side is well visualized and that's a feature against it. . . ."

Does some testing; schema doesn't fit without a lot of tuning: "I come back to the right chest. The ribs are crowded together. . . . The crowding of the ribcage can, on some occasions, be due to previous surgery. In fact,. . . The third and fourth ribs are narrow and irregular so he's probably had previous surgery. . . ."

Cracks the case: "He's probably had one of his lobes resected. It wouldn't be the middle lobe. It may be the upper lobe. It may not necessarily be a lobectomy. It could be a small segment of the lung with pleural thickening at the back."

Checks to be sure "I don't see the right hilum. . . [this] may, in fact, be due to the postsurgery state I'm postulating. . . . Loss of visualization of the right hilum is . . . seen with collapse. . . ."

---

the mental representation of the patient that correct for rotation. However, in this case the test failed, so the schema did not gain control of the subject's processing.

Next, our subject began to let the collapsed lung schema guide his thinking. However, he didn't just accept that schema but he kept trying both to test and to elaborate it. Soon he noticed the irregularities of some ribs that had been broken a decade before when a surgeon needed access to the right lung. He then very quickly changed schemata and cracked the case. Even then, though, he kept testing his new conclusion and seeking a hybrid of the collapse and lobectomy schemata. This was quite reasonable, since a collapse of a lobe has many of the same long-term effects as removal of a lobe.

Experts Build Mental Representations of Patient Anatomy

The center of action for these diagnosis schemata is a representation of the patient's anatomy that is constructed as the schemata are applied. This representation of anatomy serves at least three functions. First, the radiologist's knowledge of anatomical structures themselves is contained in a set of schemata to which many of the film features can be bound. These schemata function heuristically like a prior map of the terrain (Nagao & Matsuyama, 1980). Second, the assignment of x-ray features to normal-anatomy schemata largely determines which features are "left over" and hence show signs of possible abnormality. Third, normal-anatomy schemata may contain attached procedures, or localization rules, for determining where the abnormality resides. Residents are taught to look for a variety of localization cues that allow them to map abnormalities onto anatomic structures.

Our analyses have revealed the involvement of all three forms of anatomical knowledge. The experts and some residents were able to adjust their prior expectations for normal anatomy to the context of a particular chest, and thus were more able to notice abnormality. However, many residents tended to squeeze film features that should have signaled pathology into their schemata for normal anatomical structure, especially when the abnormalities could be subsumed under major structures like the pulmonary artery as normal variations. This occurred for both local film features (e.g., characteristics of the hilar[3] root) and more global characteristics of large regions (e.g., the hyperexpansion of the lungs). See Lesgold (1984) and Lesgold, Feltovich, Glaser, & Wang (1981). Generally, the use of localization cues was more deliberate, more fragmentary, and less appropriate among the least experienced residents.

Experts Evoke a Pertinent Schema Quickly

We turn next to the second of the three aspects of expertise mentioned earlier, that experts evoke a likely schema more quickly. Three bits of data from these studies help support this assertion. First, we have evidence that expertise involves shaping of diagnostic behavior by a preliminary schema. Second, we can see that such schemata are triggered very early, even in the first two seconds of viewing. Third, we have evidence that experts know where in the film to look. Schemata triggered during the first seconds of scanning a film guide their subsequent search of the film.

The first piece of data is in Table 11.6. It deals with the question of whether a general schema guides the observations and conclusions of the radiologist. For a film involving chronic obstructive lung disease, we tabulated the proportion of subjects in each condition who mentioned findings that were either consistent or inconsistent with the chronic lung disease schema. Consistent findings are shown in italics in the table and inconsistent findings in normal typeface. Consistent findings were more frequent in experts' protocols, and findings that are neutral or inconsistent with the chronic lung disease schema were more frequent for residents.

Not only are experts more schema-driven in their diagnoses; the schemata that guide their thinking are triggered earlier, too. Examining protocols from another film in our study that also exhibited chronic lung disease,

---

[3]The *hilum* is the region of the chest where air and blood vessels enter the lung.

TABLE 11.6
Percentage of Subjects who Mentioned Various Findings that are
Consistent or Inconsistent with the Chronic Lung Disease (COPD)
Schema While Examining a COPD/Atelectasis Film

Feature	1, 2 Yr	3, 4 Yr	Expert
Heart			
Consistent			
Small	18	14	40
R-to-L shift	0	14	40
Inconsistent			
Normal	73	71	40
Source of density	36	43	0
Right hilum			
Consistent			
Decreased prominence	0	14	60
Medial displacement	0	0	40
Inconsistent			
Normal	73	57	0
Increased prominence or source of density	45	43	0

we tabulated the frequency with which various schema-consistent features
were mentioned after the film had been seen for only two seconds. As shown
in Table 11.7, experts were more likely to report these features, which we
believe are likely "triggers" for the chronic lung disease schema, after the
two second viewing period. Even after extensive viewing, the residents were
less likely to include chronic lung disease in their final diagnoses.

Schemata also help determine the follow-up film viewing and feature

TABLE 11.7
Percentage of Subjects Who Made Certain
Interpretations of the Heart After Two Seconds
of Viewing Another COPD Film

Observation	1,2 Yr	3,4 Yr	Expert
COPD or Emphysema	18	29	80
Hyperexpanded lung	27	57	100
Low Diaphragms	18	43	100
Small heart or narrow mediastinum	0	29	80
Final decision includes COPD	*36*	*57*	*100*

explaining that is done in reaching a diagnosis. This can be seen in another analysis of the protocols from subjects who viewed our collapsed lung film. This analysis sought to determine the extent to which subjects at different levels of expertise limited their efforts to the lungs — a sensible thing to do if working in the schema context of lung disease. Table 8 shows that for experts, almost all reports of things seen, normal or abnormal, were about the lungs and the lung-surrounding pleurae. In contrast, residents actually talked more about non-lung observations than about the lungs themselves.

Experts Exhibit Flexibility and Tuning of Schemata

We turn again to the collapsed lung (atelectasis) film, referring now to Table 8. Figure 11.3 provides a schematic illustration of that film. The effect of the collapse (at least in the patient shown in our film) is that the middle lobe tissue[4] is pushed toward the center of the chest by the expansion of the lobes above and below. Each lobe may be thought of as a balloon packed into a confined space. The collapse of the middle lobe produces a dense shadow because the collapsed lung tissue is denser than the air-inflated lung would be. The shadow has somewhat concave sides due to the convex upper and lower lobes' pressure on the collapsed tissue. Overall, it looks sail-shaped. The shadow is striking — even nonphysicians usually can see it.

However, such an abnormality can easily be due to a tumor. To diagnose a collapsed lung lobe, the physician must look for other signs, such as displaced lobe boundaries or hyperinflation of the adjacent lobes. This did not always happen. *Tumor* was the most common immediately triggered interpretation for the type of abnormality appearing in our atelectasis film, and *atelectasis* was a more remote interpretation. In our second study, two of four experts but only one of eight novices correctly diagnosed atelectasis; the other nine subjects diagnosed the film as showing a mass or a tumor.

That novices are restricted in some sense to the obvious responses has been a prevalent finding in research on expert–novice differences. We pro-

TABLE 11.8
Regions Mentioned for Collapsed Lung Film

Region	1, 2 Yr	3, 4 Yr	Expert
Lungs and Pleurae	41%	41%	93%
Other Regions	60%	59%	8%
Total	100%	100%	100%

[4]The right lung is divided into three connected lobes; the left lung has two.

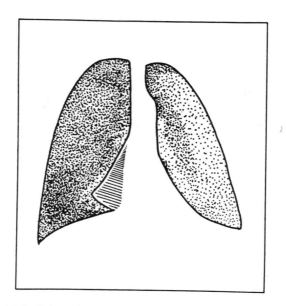

FIGURE 11.3   Schematic of film showing collapsed right middle lung lobe.

pose theoretical explanations for this. One possibility is that when there are a dominant hypothesis and a more remote possibility, consideration of the more remote possibility depends upon availability of mental processing capacity. If any subprocesses of diagnosis are inefficient, they will interfere with the more remote response. Under this explanation the atelectasis schema should be triggered only when both an appropriate target density and certain other features (e.g., a displaced lobe boundary or a hyperexpanded lung) are present. If subprocesses such as localization are not automated and require conscious processing, working-memory interference can prevent the construction of an adequately interconnected representation of the patient. Most subjects did, in fact, detect lung hyperexpansion; they simply did not tie it to atelectasis.

   An alternative explanation is that novices simply do not generate the full range of sensible possibilities in forms that will survive testing and verification. For example, novices have learned the triggering rule for the most salient option, but do not have means for triggering the more subtle special cases or alternatives. As we have seen in this case, there must be a variety of knowledge structures that tune this decision-making. Finally, in some cases, novices may fail because they have not yet developed the fine-tuned visual acuity needed for feature discrimination that is seen in their more experienced colleagues.

   In order to get at the variability in perception of features of the films, we asked the subjects to trace on the film the outlines of the abnormal visual features they had noticed while they were defending the interpretations of their first reports of the film. The novices' failure to tune diagnostic decisions to feature perception was strikingly demonstrated by their tracings in a film which showed a patient with multiple tumors. The film is shown schematically in Figure 11.4. It depicts a patient with multiple densities in the lungs, which represent tumors and other local pathologies. In the acteletasis film, as we have just seen, novices did not perceive global cues that might have keyed the correct diagnosis. In contrast, in this film, the novices merged local features (e.g., tumors) and saw a general lung haziness that is probably not present to the extent that they thought it was.

The general features that the residents thought they saw led them to the incorrect diagnosis of heart failure. There are several features that would, if present, indicate heart failure. These are:

- Enlarged heart.
- Acute cardiac problems.
- Bilateral peripheral lung edema (excess fluid).
- Bilateral hilar edema.
- Bilaterally prominent pulmonary vasculature (the blood vessels more distinct than usual on both sides).

Except for one third-year resident, who gave a clear interpretation of cancer for the film, the residents uniformly proposed interpretations of heart failure supported by bilateral haziness of the hila and at least some of the more peripheral areas of the lungs. In essence, they saw the hazy spots in the

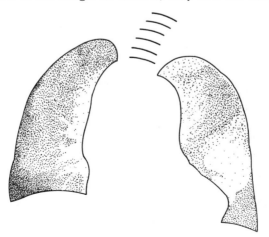

FIGURE 11.4 Schematic of film showing multiple lung tumors.

lungs as being a part of a pattern that indicated fluid in the lungs, or edema. Enlargement of the heart is a standard feature of chronic congestive
heart failure, and half of the residents (split evenly between beginning and
intermediate) interpreted the heart as big or at the upper limits of normal
size. Two beginning residents came up with an interpretation of congestive heart failure even though they correctly saw the heart as normal in
size. They saw signs of heart surgery, which had in fact once been performed, and decided that the other apparent failure-related features were
due to heart failure produced by surgical shock.

In contrast to the residents, experts had more refined schemata that allowed them to make finer discriminations. Experts were more able to distinguish subtle differences in the pattern of haziness in one lung as compared
to the other. They did not see *bilateral* hilar abnormality. Three of the four
experts traced abnormality only in the right hilar region. In contrast, seven
of eight residents traced bilateral hilar abnormality. One hypothesis for these
differences is that residents did not discriminate well the degrees of density
in different parts of the lungs. Rather, they saw a more general and uniform cloudiness or "veiling" which would be highly consistent with interpretations of congestive heart failure.

Figure 11.5 shows the most extreme example of this, from a first-year
resident. A general area of haziness or edema is drawn (indicated by wavy
lines) from the hilar regions far out into the lungs, encompassing regions
which are probably tumors. The insensitivity to differences between the
left and right sides is striking. In fact, there were definite differences in
the level of darkness of the left and right hilar areas. Clearly, at least when

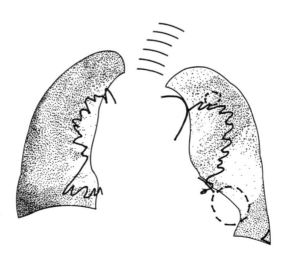

FIGURE 11.5   First-year resident's drawings on multiple tumor film.

their heart failure schemata are triggered by the apparently large heart, some residents cannot make this distinction adequately.

A second-year resident's tracing (Figure 11.6) suggests how the hilar area and nearby tumors may be merged by our novices. Note that these patch areas, which he perceived as edema, are demarcated but that they abut and merge into each other. Our resident partially corrected this mistake, as you can see from these comments:

> OK. Well, something that I didn't really notice before that doesn't really support anything I said are these densities right here (left lung patches). And also, the more I look at it, this density right here (right lung patch). . . . If I go back and put all these together in a better way than I did before, these densities might be metastatic lesions to the lungs. . . .

A contrast to all of these residents' findings is demonstrated by those of an expert, as shown in Figure 11.7. He saw the lung patches as metastatic cancerous masses, reporting no edema anywhere. He saw the left hilar blood vessels as normal and the right hilar region as containing cancer. Unilateral abnormalities are more likely to be cancerous, and are inconsistent, to some extent, with congestive heart failure. In general, the expert evidenced an ability to *tune* his perception of features to the specific case with which he is working.

A second example of the superior ability of experts to tune their perceptions involves more peripheral factors. In the tumor film, the residents tended to see the heart as enlarged, while the experts did not. The shadow cast

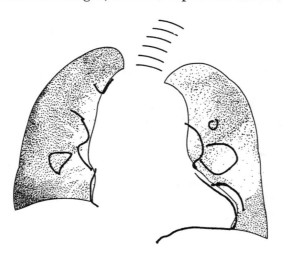

FIGURE 11.6 Second-year resident's drawings on multiple tumor film.

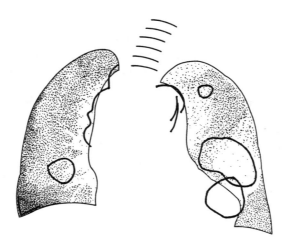

FIGURE 11.7   Expert's drawings on multiple tumor film.

by the heart in this film is 55% to 60% of the chest width, slightly larger than normal. However, experts who made any report of the heart size at all adjusted their evaluation of the heart to technical factors such as poor inspiration (the patient did not breathe deeply), a curvature in the spine, and a generally slumped and twisted posture in the patient. No expert evaluated the heart as actually enlarged. Experts were able to decouple the apparent film features from their models of the patient's anatomy. Samples from two experts' protocols follow:

> *First expert:* It (the trachea) appears to be displaced to the left, but this might be partly due to the position of the chin. It might be partly due to the position of the chin and the effect of rotation of the chest by the scoliosis. . . . There's marked scoliosis of the thoracic spine. And, *taking this into account, the size and shape of the heart are within normal limits.*

> *Second expert:* OK. A frontal projection of the chest shows the patient to be considerably rotated to the left and the film is generally underpenetrated. . . . The *heart is probably normal size, allowing for the projection and rotation of the patient.* . . .

In summary, experts discounted most of the film features which residents thought were evidence of congestive heart failure. They did this by using a mix of technical knowledge about how films are made (such as knowledge about artifacts due to the patient not taking a deep breath) and better developed feature perception. While some experts articulated the adjustment rules they applied, the possibility remains that, in the expert, these adjustments are really automatic aspects of immediate feature perception. Indeed, in our first study, when subjects saw the same film for only two seconds, experts were still able to discount heart failure.

In contrast, residents interpreted their perceptions very literally: a heart *shadow* of large size meant an enlarged heart. There appeared to be little decoupling between the *manifestations* of chest structures and the diagnosticians' internal, mental *representations* of the chest and its structures. This strategy should serve the diagnostician adequately when the film presents an ideal textbook example of a disorder. However, when a more complex case arises, there is need for the representation of the patient's medical condition to be decoupled from film features. This decoupling is what enables immediate perception and the representational process to be tuned somewhat independently.

Experts See Things Differently

The fact that perception is driven by mental representations was strikingly demonstrated in the protocols dealing with the collapsed lung film. What interests us is a phenomenon that complements the one just discussed. Whereas in the previous case the novices' mental representation of the anatomy was coupled to the immediate perception of a feature, in the atelectasis film discussed earlier a salient feature was explained away by many of our novices as part of normal anatomy. We compared the subjects' tracing of the sail-shaped feature (see Figure 11.3) that they perceived as abnormal with a standard template based on our radiologist collaborator's judgments about the nature of the abnormality and on our previous experience with the film. It is clear that not all the subjects saw or interpreted the main abnormality in the same way. Table 11.9 compares the abnormalities identified by the subjects with the abnormality template. For each subject, the middle column represents the size of the region perceived as abnormal as a percentage of the standard template area, independent of the *placement* of the region; the right column represents the placement of the region identified as abnormal by the percentage of the template region overlapped by the subject's tracing.

Each of the experts traced an abnormality that was very similar in size and placement to the template. All the experts delimited abnormalities that were as large as or larger than the template (mean = 109.8 %), and that substantially overlapped the template (mean overlap = 93%). However, only half of the residents identified abnormalities that even approximated the template. Three of the remaining residents traced a smaller triangular density that constituted a subspace of the template triangle, occupying its most medial (spineward) portion (mean size = 41.5% of standard; mean overlap = 38.3%). The last resident, RB4, included the same small triangle within the area of the abnormality. His generally larger abnormality

TABLE 11.9
Dimensions of Subject-Defined Target Areas in
Collpased Lung Film Relative to Standard Template

Subject	Size	Overlap
1st/2nd Year		
RA1	36.1	33.0
RA2	36.7	30.4
RA3	108.9	97.6
RA4	92.8	89.5
3rd/4th Year		
RB1	51.6	51.6
RB2	96.6	95.8
RB3	114.6	99.0
RB4	101.9	45.6
Experts		
E1	127.6	98.5
E2	104.7	97.0
E3	91.1	91.1
E4	115.6	85.5

(size = 101.9%) resulted from extending the small triangle deep into the mediastinum and spinal area, which were outside the template region (overlap = 45.6%). Overall, half of the residents were accounting, in their film interpretations, for a perceived triangular abnormality within the general area of the target space that was roughly half the size of the abnormality perceived by the experts and remaining residents (see Lesgold, 1984, for illustrations of the subjects' drawings.)

If some of our misperceiving novices saw a small abnormality projecting behind the heart while another saw a large abnormality projecting far out into the lung field, we might expect this difference to be reflected in the medical interpretations given for the abnormality. The formal reports in this study do not reflect such a difference, possibly because the diagnoses of "tumor" or" mass" reached by most of the residents do not specify size. The difference in perceptions may, however, explain some interpretations for the same film given in an earlier study (Lesgold, et al. 1981). In that study, which did not call for the subjects to trace the anatomical features, diagnoses of heart and esophageal abnormalities were offered; these would be consistent with abnormalities confined to the smaller triangle. Even in the present study, two residents who traced a small-triangle abnormality raised a cardiac interpretation (cyst in the pericardium) and an esophageal one (esophageal lesions "included within mediastinal lesions") in the course of their thinking aloud; we are inclined to attribute these previously inexplicable diagnoses to misperceptions of the region of abnormality.

In order to determine which anatomical structures subjects thought were involved in producing the region of density, we asked them to identify structures in a rectangular region of the film that included the target abnormality. The results of this analysis are given in Table 11.10. Numbers in the table represent the percentages of the abnormality template region that were attributed to various normal anatomical components. Table 11.10 suggests that the identification of smaller and larger triangular abnormalities can be accounted for by differential attribution of normal anatomy to the target region.

Subjects who traced a small triangle attributed an average of 51.3% of the target space to normal anatomy, principally to the right descending pulmonary artery. Small-triangle subjects traced some or all of the descending pulmonary artery in about its normally expected position, with the perceived area of abnormality (the small triangle) medial to the pulmonary artery near the heart and spine. Experts and large-triangle residents either claimed to see nothing of the descending pulmonary artery in the area of the target space, or, in the case of two experts, traced a small collateral of the pulmonary artery within this area, but not its main descending trunk.

Overall, we can see that some of our residents "used up" the region of abnormal density by seeing it as mostly pulmonary artery. Almost as if they were taking an embedded figures test, they were unable to see collapsed lung tissue as occupying that region because they had already assigned it to normal arterial structure. There are many variations of this problem, some of which affect even the experts. For example, radiologists report that it is not unusual to find disease, such as a tumor, in an x-ray film and then,

TABLE 11.10
Percentage of Normal Anatomy Attributed to the Sail-Shaped Region

Subject	Bronchi	Aorta	Heart	Pulmonary Artery	Total
RA1*	0.5			59.2	59.7
RA2*		2.3	18.5	46.9	67.7
RA3					0
RA4					0
RB1*				26.0	26.0
RB2					0
RB3					0
RB4*				51.8	51.8
E1					0
E2					0
E3				5.2	5.2
E4				10.6	10.6

* indicates a "small triangle" subject.

once having seen it, to become able to see the beginnings of that disease process in an earlier film that was previously judged normal. There is no question that the structural assumptions made in looking at a film determine which features are noticed and how they are accounted for. Subjects who were incorrect in their diagnosis of the film *perceived the film features differently* from their more successful counterparts; similarly, subjects who were wrong in their interpretations of the lobectomy film *did not see* the shift of the chest structures as such, and thus could not initiate the schema for volume-loss dynamics that was necessary for that film. In contrast, the experts test and reject inappropriate schemata (cf. Table 11.5); although they invoke a schema quickly, they appear to hold it tentatively enough to discard it if it does not meet either specific tests or the more global test of supplying an adequate model of the anatomy. Further, the experts are able to appropriate new data: their processing is opportunistic.

Opportunism

Expert problem-solving capability is opportunistic (Hayes-Roth, 1983; Hayes-Roth, 1984; Hayes-Roth & Hayes-Roth, 1979; Hayes-Roth, Hayes-Roth, Rosenschein, & Cammarata, 1979.) That is, it takes account of new possibilities when they arise. With some forms of expertise, opportunism is easily apparent. For example, an expert quarterback, seeing a hole in the defensive line, will run through it even if he had been planning a slightly different play. In the case of diagnosis, opportunism is less obvious. After all, the patient is there, the physician has the data, and it doesn't seem as if any new opportunities will arise. However, there is still room for two types of opportunism. First, it is possible that new data will be obtained, such as lab reports that appear from time to time. Second, the noticing of features takes time, and it is possible that a newly noticed feature may represent an opportunity to view the case from a different perspective. Both forms of opportunity seem to be used to greater advantage by experts.

The use of newly noticed features was apparent in the protocol segment presented in Table 11.5, where, for example, examination of rib abnormalities led to a new schema: previous surgery. To examine the other form of opportunism, we look again at that film.

What initially happened most often in the diagnosis of the lobectomy film is that the subject would see the marked shift of the heart and mediastinal structures toward the right side of the chest. Normally, these structures are expected to be midline in the chest, because the inflation of the lung is homogeneous, and pressure in the chest is equivalent throughout. When a shift of anatomy occurs, this tells a radiologist that a change in the internal pressure of the chest has occurred — that is, that the right and left "halves" of the chest are no longer equally aerated. Most of the time, shift of the mediastinum and heart to one side or the other implies loss of volume due to a collapse in that side of the lung. In this film, our subjects usually saw this shift and deduced a loss of volume in the right chest, which is appropriate; they were at a loss, nevertheless, to specify the locus of the alleged collapse because this phenomenon of differential lung volume is due to the *absence* of lung tissue, not its collapse. Prior to their receiving the clinical information on the patient, which we include below, our subjects could not coherently or confidently explain this phenomenon (except for the expert subject referred to in Table 11.5). The "missing link" for our subjects was the clinical information. The mechanism[5] for different underlying etiologies was the same and the dominant visual cues indicated mechanism, not cause.

The clinical data we provided for this film constrained the set of possible etiologies. New pieces of clinical data influenced experts' diagnostic decisions here, but did not always influence novices'. This can be seen by comparing the final diagnoses rendered by our subjects before and after clinical information was supplied (see Table 11.1). We looked at the direction of change in diagnosis (e.g., wrong diagnosis before clinical history, right diagnosis afterward = W−R) after the following clinical information was supplied:

> This is a 34 year old female, a healthy worker who has no complaints. This is a follow-up employment chest examination. The patient has a history of a right lung operation when she was 15 years of age for a collapsed lung. The patient has had similar chest x-rays in the last ten years during the annual physical examinations and shows no essential changes.

After the presentation of this information, we observed three distinct behaviors by our subjects for this film:[6]

1. **R−R** Subjects who had assessed the correct dynamics in the film (shift due to decreased volume in right lung) prior to the history, and then were able to fit the history in with the x-ray findings to conclude that the patient had no immediate (or worrisome) problems.

2. **W−R** Subjects who were wrong about the diagnosis before the clinical data were supplied, and thought there was something acutely wrong

[5]Compare, if you will, the previously discussed "atelectasis (collapse) film" to that of the present "lobectomy film." In our lobectomy film it is the diagnosis of collapse that is the most salient diagnosis, because radiographic signs that trigger a collapse schema are relatively dramatic. The dynamics are consistent with collapse, but the etiology of this anomaly is iatrogenic.

[6]In this film, subjects never shifted from the right diagnosis to a wrong one, although this direction of change is obviously of interest, as well. It should be noted that the **R−W** category did exist for other films, most notably our atelectasis film (see p. 339).

with this patient, but who were able to incorporate the clinical data when supplied to change their minds to the appropriate diagnosis.

3. **W — W** Subjects who were incorrect before the clinical history was made available, and who continued to err in their diagnoses after the data were supplied. The patient data did not help these individuals and they continued to report that an acute problem existed, requiring medical attention, even though the clinical history clearly says otherwise.

The last category $(W - W)$ is particularly interesting for several reasons. First, these subjects were unable to retreat from the opinion that severe disease existed in this patient, despite a plausible explanation to the contrary. They missed an opportunity to see the film abnormalities in a new context. As an example of this behavior, contrast the following protocol excerpt of a 3rd-year resident in our study with the opportunistic approach that characterizes expertise. Both before and after receiving the clinical information, this resident reported that the patient's heart was enlarged and that the blood vessels, especially in the upper lobes, were ill-defined and congested, suggesting interstitial edema, fluid in the lungs. He originally felt that this patient was in congestive heart failure and he retained this opinion even after receiving clinical information stating that the patient was healthy and had always had an abnormal-appearing x-ray.

> What does it mean that this x-ray shows no changes from the previous. . . I don't know whether this particular x-ray is different because this looks like we're having an acute process going on. . . . Okay, there's no question that we are seeing evidence of heart enlargement, as well as congested vessels and probable pleural effusion. If this patient had this type of chest x-ray in the past, it is possible that she may be having a valvular disease, like mitral stenosis. . . . So I think my diagnosis will still stand as it is — that we're seeing evidence of congested heart failure at this time.

Another interesting observation coming from the data on the effects of supplying clinical information for this film is that the $W - W$ category is seen *exclusively* in the third- and fourth-year residents. Whereas traditional learning theory would predict performance improving steadily with practice, we find that, for certain problems, performance gets temporarily worse.

Nonmonotone Aspects of Skill Acquisition

In previous reports (e.g., Lesgold, 1984), we noted that performance in diagnosing radiographic films is not always a monotone function of experience. That is, third- and fourth-year residents performed less well than either experts or first- and second-year residents on some of our films. While this assertion has sometimes proven controversial when we have made it in various oral reports of our work, it should not be surprising. Indeed, while it was not made particularly salient in their report, a similar finding seems to be present in work on pediatric cardiological diagnosis reported by Paul Johnson and his colleagues (Johnson et al., 1981); and other related phenomena have been reported by colleagues elsewhere (V. Patel, personal communication, June 1984). What has not been offered is an account of why this problem arises.

It is important to note that a similar phenomenon is reported by developmental psychologists[7] (Bowerman, 1982; Karmiloff-Smith, 1979; Karmiloff-Smith & Inhelder, 1974/1975; Klahr, 1982; Richards & Siegler, 1982; Stavy, Strauss, Orpaz, & Carmi, 1982; Strauss & Stavy, 1982). In a variety of developmental studies, a skill is seen to be present at one age, missing a bit later, and then present some time after that. For example, Bowerman (1982; see also Ervin, 1964) reported that children initially produce correct instances of many irregular past-tense verbs and plural nouns (e.g., *went, feet*). Later, they shift to incorrect regularizations of those words (e.g., *goed, foots*). Still later, they gain complete control over the irregularities in their vocabulary and stop making such mistakes. Richards and Siegler (1982) showed similar nonmonotone performance in a task that involved stating which train of a pair of toy trains on parallel tracks ran for more time if the train that ran longer ended up *behind* the other train. Other related phenomena have also been reported by the authors cited above.

Given our findings that performance is not a monotonic function of experience, we consider an account that extends to our acquisition situation. Strauss and Stavy (1982) sorted extant explanations for nonmonotonicities of development into five types, which we list.

- Oscillation between a familiar but inadequate mental representation of the problem situation, and an improved but still new and "untrusted" representation system that is correct.
- The uncoordinated overlaying of one representational system on top of another.
- Using rules that are correct for one representation in another representation system for which they are incorrect.
- Having low-order rules to deal with each of two relevant variables but not having the higher-order rules to coordinate those lower-order rules.
- Temporary problems due to differentiation or specialization of an ini-

---

[7]We thank David Klahr for patiently calling this literature to our attention during a period when we were enthusiastically claiming more novelty for our findings of nonmonotonicity.

tially abstract or general capability, where the specializations may not be as powerful as the initial abstractions.

It is not clear that these different types of accounts are really incompatible. If there is incompatibility, then it lies in whether the changes in knowledge that underlie nonmonotone performance changes are evolutionary or revolutionary; that is, whether old knowledge is supplemented or supplanted. In terms of grain size, the issue is whether the best level of analysis for explaining the phenomenon is in terms of productions (contingent associations between mental states and mental operations) or at a higher, more schematic level. The following preliminary account blends evolutionary and revolutionary components, and is probably best understood for now as a blend of the first two alternatives in the list just presented. That is, we see one aspect of acquiring expertise to be the replacement of simple associations between surface features and diseases, with a deeper recognition-triggered reasoning ability.

From Perceptual to Cognitive Processing

The balance of recognition and inference in diagnosis seems to vary with experience, although both aspects of the task are always present in some form. Viewed as a pattern-recognition task, what a radiologist does might be characterized as detecting some complex of features that can be mapped onto the name of a disease. There are a number of alternative models for this sort of perceptual knowledge, but perhaps the best (Barsalou & Bower, 1984) currently available is the PANDEMONIUM model (Selfridge, 1959).[8] From another point of view, though, radiological diagnosis is largely a matter of qualitative inference. That is, given a set of findings (perceptual features), one has to determine which diseases are consistent with those findings. If more than one disease is consistent, then one either looks further, in hopes of recognizing more features, or suggests additional medical tests to discriminate among the possibilities.

In many perceptual recognition paradigms, there is only one correct response for any given stimulus pattern. In such cases, the output of a PANDEMONIUM processor is simply a pointer to that pattern. However, in the case of radiology, the appropriate classification for many patterns is a set of alternative diseases among which a further differentiation needs to be

---

[8]A PANDEMONIUM model consists of several layers of processors called *demons*. Each demon in the lowest layer watches for a simple perceptual property of the stimulus, and outputs a signal that is modulated by the certainty of the demon that it has seen its target feature. Higher-level demons observe the output levels of the demons below them and respond to specific patternings of those levels. Thus, the system accumulates positive evidence in a hierarchical conjunctive manner.

made. In this case, one can imagine the outcome of the perceptual process as a pointer to a set of diseases with associated probabilities (the strengths of the various suprathreshold disease demons). We use the term *purely perceptual process* to refer to a decision process in which the choice with the highest probability among the differential set indicated by a PANDEMONIUM process is taken as the diagnostic decision, or where the decision is based upon nothing but the magnitudes of the probabilities. Presumably, the substantial practice in diagnosis that interns and resident staff receive has the effect of tuning these probabilities so that they are accurate.

Nevertheless, there is a limit on the overall accuracy one can achieve with such a system. For example, if, given a particular pattern, the probability of Disease A is 0.6, the probability of Disease B is 0.3, and the probability of Disease C is 0.1, the maximum probability of a correct diagnosis based only on the probability information is 0.6, the highest single probability. If a biased decision is merited (e.g., if Disease C produces fatalities unless treated early), then the probability of a correct diagnosis will be even lower. It is conceivable that if one spent a longer period of time looking at the film before making a diagnosis, more features would be noticed and a better set of probabilities might be obtained. However, there is also an efficiency requirement in the role of radiologist.

One could imagine a multistep diagnosis process. First, a perceptual decision is made, the outcome of which is a differential diagnosis set with associated probabilities. Then, cognitive decision-making apparatus is used to resolve ambiguity, either by searching for perceptual features initially missed that might resolve the ambiguity or by taking account of other data sources such as history and tests. It appears that such a process can be evolved from the perceptual process simply by elaborating the reporting part of the decision process, doing extra thinking before acting on the probability information. Note however that such an approach probably cannot ignore the potentially uncertainty-reducing information in the lower layers of recognition responses that are summarized in the overall PANDEMONIUM decision.

Once we assume that cognitive activity will be triggered or driven by intermediate outcomes of the perceptual process, we set the stage for revolutions rather than simply evolutions in processing. That is, cognitive activity occurs in parallel with further summarizing by higher-level perceptual demons. As a result, there are potential conflicts over limited resources for processing and also over which final response will dominate. We hypothesize that purely perceptual learning, the formation and tuning of lower-order demons, can occur earlier in the course of learning than can the cognitive learning that is, after all, dependent on partial products of the perceptual process. Thus, an emerging cognitive capability will have to contend with a stronger perceptual ability already in place. Furthermore, in the development of skill, as control shifts from purely perceptual to cognitive processing, performance may appear to get worse — just as locomotion may become less efficient when a baby whose creeping is secure and automatic begins to toddle.

The points just made can be illustrated with excerpts from the protocols of one of our third-year residents who was diagnosing the film discussed near the beginning of this chapter. In Table 11.5, we presented examples of an expert who invoked a schema, tested it, moved to another schema, tested it, and so on. What is missing in the protocol of our resident is this ability to check the fit of a schema to the case at hand and then either to tune it or, if it doesn't fit, to delete it. After two seconds, the resident has noticed a lot that is important:

> Okay, the big thing I noticed that the heart appeared to be shifted from left to right, more of the heart was in the right thorax than should be. It was not, it was not in the midline. There was abnormal density throughout the right lung field primarily in the mid and lower portions of the right lung field. . . . I wonder whether or not there is a right-sided pleural effusion present, whether there isn't some collapse of part of the right lower lung field.

At this point, the subject is more or less on the right track. He has noticed some shifting of anatomy ("the heart appears to be shifted"). However, he gets stuck as he tries to invoke appropriate schemata — he just doesn't have all the prerequisite tests and tuning rules down, as can be seen in this excerpt from his thinking out loud. What is striking is that he loses the concept of a *shifted* heart and ends up deciding that the heart is too big. Things still don't fit, and he knows he is in trouble:

> As far as the heart is concerned, the right atrium appears to be significantly enlarged and there's possibly, also possibly some enlargement of the left atrium. As of right now, I think this is primarily a right atrial enlargement.[9] I'm wondering about the mediastinum in this area. I'm a little bit stuck on this one. . . .I'm just, you know, wishing that I could — thinking right now I wish I could put this to better — put this all together more quickly. I wouldn't be surprised if this is a child with a cardiac murmur and that this represents what's called a left-to-right cardiac shunt.

In the final report, the heart is no longer thought of as shifted so much as enlarged:

> The heart is increased in transverse diameter with predominantly an enlarged right atrium and also some enlargement of the left atrium.

Overall, the character of the protocol for this subject is that as schemata

---

[9]Each side of the heart consists of two chambers, an *atrium* and a much larger *ventricle*.

are invoked, he reshapes his perceptions to fit each schema. This is in striking contrast both to the situation in experts, in which tentative schemata
are held as tentative until rigorously tested, and to the situation of the true
novice, whose schemata are tightly bound to the purely perceptual. Because
the expert's rigorous testing is not possible at early stages of schema acquisition, the cognitive level of processing shows many signs of being worse,
initially, than the simple recognition response. However, even though less
accurate, it is a step toward higher-quality diagnostic performance.

We end this report with a final example of this phenomenon — a situation in which new data trigger a new schema which then takes hold and
reshapes the perception of the film without first being rigorously tested.
This is exactly what we saw in the protocol of another third year resident
when he attempted to diagnose the right middle lobe collapsed lung (atelectasis) film we have discussed above.

Even after the two-second presentation, he seemed on the right track:

Oh boy! There's a mass in the right, uh, middle mediastinum and it seems
to be obliterating the cardiac border. . . .Uh, so I guess this patient had some
kind of right middle lobe atelectasis — I'm not really certain. . . .I'm not really certain whether or not this is a mass or a middle lobe atelectasis or what it is.

He even does a little testing as he examines the film further:

Okay — now is this — I'm asking myself, is this, uh — what is this? I'm asking — is
this a right middle lobe atelectasis? If so, we should see volume loss in the
right lung and we don't. Of course this is an AP film and the problem with
that being it's not the best way to look for a right middle lobe atelectasis.
A lateral film is much better. I'd love to have a lateral film here. Yeah, this
looks like an anterior mediastinal mass to me. I think I'm going to recom-
mend a lateral film in my report.

However, after receiving clinical data which mentions "unspecified GI
symptoms," this subject totally reshapes his perception to match the clinical data, departing, as it turns out, from a correct view:

I doubt if this patient has a chronic right middle lobe syndrome so I have
to look at that chest x-ray again. Okay, now, is this the esophagus? You know
that might be the esophagus because that's what we're seeing in the superior
mediastinum there. This is . . . probably a patient with achalasia or perhaps
less likely a distal esophagoeal stricture or carcinoma in the distal esophagus.
. . . He's got a dilated esophagus and that's an air fluid level in the esophagus. There's nothing in his lungs at all. In fact, if you look at this more closely you can see the right cardiac border. . . .

No expert can find the right cardiac border. What we have here is the complement of our earlier problem of not responding to the primary indicated meaning of a single newly-presented datum. Here, there is over-responding instead.

We conclude, then, that the acquisition of expertise consists in ever more refined versions of schemata developing through a cognitively deep form of generalization and discrimination. Anywhere along the course of this acquisition, automated responding at a more shallow level may have an advantage over trying to exercise the newly developing deeper level. However, that advantage, if present at all, exists only for specific cases being seen by novices. If the obvious response is incorrect, then deeper processing, which becomes possible only after extended practice, will be necessary. This practice will inevitably involve periods in which deeper processing does not always produce a better outcome. That is the price paid to develop expertise.

There is a strong parallel between the acquisition of this specific complex skill and general cognitive development. Just as children's views of the world change character as their experiences increase, so the ways in which radiologists can see human anatomy in radiographs also change, moving from a superficial, probabilistic approach to a deep ability to reason about film content that is supported by highly refined automatic recognition capability. This learning sometimes reaches points of impasse, where superficial and deep methods conflict. These impasses and reversals mirror the "U-shaped curves" found by developmental psychologists. Designing procedures and job aids to enable learning to take place with minimal losses during these setbacks is an important task, to which further cognitive research on acquisition of expertise in complex skills may be able to contribute.

ACKNOWLEDGMENTS

This research was supported in part by Office of Naval Research Contract No. N00014-79-C-0215 to the University of Pittsburgh's Learning Research and Development Center. ONR does not necessarily endorse or agree with the statements herein. Mark Detweiler contributed important insights that helped us clarify our assertions, and Arlene Weiner contributed substantively and technically in editing this chapter.

REFERENCES

Arnheim, R. (1969). *Visual thinking* (p. 37). Berkeley: University of California Press.
Barsalou, L. W., & Bower, G. H. (1984). Discrimination nets as psychological models. *Cognitive Science, 8,* 1–26.
Bowerman, M. (1982). Starting to talk worse: Clues to language acquisition from children's late speech errors. In S. Strauss (Ed.), *U-Shaped Behavioral Growth* (p. 101–145). New York: Academic Press.

Chase, W. G., & Simon, H. A. (1973). The mind's eye in chess. In W. G. Chase (Ed.), *Visual information processing* (pp. 215–281). New York: Academic Press.

Chi, M. T. H., Glaser, R. & Rees, E. (1982). Expertise in problem solving. In R. J. Sternberg (Ed.), *Advances in the psychology of human intelligence* (pp. 7–75). Hillsdale, NJ: Lawrence Erlbaum Associates.

Daffner, R. H. (1983). Visual Illusions affecting perception of the Roentgen image. *CRC Critical Reviews in Diagnostic Imaging, 20*, 79–119.

de Valk, J. P. J., & Eijkman, E. G. J. (1984). Analysis of eye fixations during the diagnostic interpretation of chest radiographs. *Medical & Biological Engineering & Computing, 22*, 353–360.

Dijkstra, S., van der Stelt, P. F., & van der Sijde, P. C. (1984). *The Effect of Different Levels of Expertise on Interpretation of Dental X-Rays.* Paper presented at AERA annual meeting, New Orleans.

Ervin, S. M. (1964). Imitation and structural change in children's language. In E. H. Lenneberg (Ed.), *New directions in the study of language* (pp. 163–189). Cambridge, MA: MIT Press.

Hayes-Roth, B. (1983, May). *The blackboard architecture: A general framework for problem solving?* (Tech. Rep. No. HPP 83-30). Heuristic Programming Project, Stanford University.

Hayes-Roth, B. (1984, August). *A blackboard model of control* (Tech. Rep. No. HPP 83-38). Heuristic Programming Project, Stanford University.

Hayes-Roth, B., & Hayes-Roth, F. (1979). A cognitive model of planning. *Cognitive Science, 3*, 275–310.

Hayes-Roth, B., Hayes-Roth, F., Rosenschein, S., & Cammarata, S. (1979, August). Modeling planning as an incremental, opportunistic process. *Proceedings of the Sixth International Joint Conference on Artificial Intelligence* (pp. 375–383). International Joint Conferences on Artificial Intelligence.

Johnson, P. E., Duran, A. S., Hassebrock, F., Moller, J., Prietula, M., Feltovich, P. J., & Swanson, D. B. (1981). Expertise and error in diagnostic reasoning. *Cognitive Science, 5*, 235–283.

Karmiloff-Smith, A. (1979). Micro- and macrodevelopmental changes in language acquisition and other representational systems. *Cognitive Science, 3*, 91–118.

Karmiloff-Smith, A., & Inhelder, B. (1974/1975). If you want to get ahead, get a theory. *Cognition, 3*, 195–212.

Klahr, D. (1982). Nonmonotone assessment of monotone development: An information processing analysis. In S. Strauss (Ed.), *U-shaped behavioral growth* (pp. 63–86). New York: Academic Press.

Kundel, H. L. & La Follette, P. S. (1972). Visual search patterns and experience with radiological images. *Radiology, 103*, 523–528.

Kundel, H. L. & Nodine, C. F. (1983). A visual concept shapes image perception. *Radiology, 146*, 363–368.

Kundel, H. L., Nodine, C. F., & Carmody, D. (1978). Visual scanning, pattern recognition and decision-making in pulmonary nodule detection. *Investigative Radiology, 13*, 175–181.

Kundel, H. L., Nodine, C. F., Thickman, D., Carmody, D., & Toto, L. (1985). Nodule detection with and without a chest image. *Investigative Radiology, 20*, 94–99.

Lesgold, A. (1983). Intelligence: The ability to learn, or more? Review of *Handbook of Human Intelligence* by R. S. Sternberg. *Contemporary Education Review, 2*, 111–119.

Lesgold, A. M. (1984). Acquiring expertise. In J. R. Anderson & S. M. Kosslyn (Eds.), *Tutorials in learning and memory: Essays in honor of Gordon Bower* (pp. 31–60). San Francisco: W. H. Freeman.

Lesgold, A. M., Feltovich, P. J., Glaser, R., & Wang, Y. (1981, September). *The acquisition of perceptual diagnostic skill in radiology* (Tech. Rep. No. PDS-1). University of Pittsburgh, Learning Research and Development Center.

Nagao, M. & Matsuyama, T. (1980). *A structural analysis of complex aerial photographs*. New York: Plenum Press.

Revesz, G., & Kundel, H. L. (1977). Psychophysical studies of detection errors in chest radiology. *Radiology*, 123, 559–562.

Richards, D. D., & Siegler, R. S. (1982). U-shaped behavioral curves: It's not whether you're right or wrong, it's why. In S. Strauss (Ed.), *U-shaped behavioral growth* (pp. 37–61). New York: Academic Press.

Selfridge, O. G. (1959). Pandemonium: A paradigm for learning. In *The mechanisation of thought processes*. London: H. M. Stationery Office.

Stavy, R., Strauss, S., Orpaz, N., & Carmi, G. (1982). U-shaped behavioral growth in ratio comparisons. In S. Strauss (Ed.), *U-shaped behavioral growth* (pp. 11–35). New York: Academic Press.

Strauss, S., & Stavy, R. (1982). U-shaped behavioral growth: Implications for theories of development. In W. W. Hartup (Ed.), *Review of child development research* (Vol. 6, pp. 547–599). Chicago: The University of Chicago Press.

Swensson, R. G., Hessel, S. J., & Herman, P. G. (1980). Detection performance and the nature of the radiologist's search task. In J. R. Cameron & A. J. Alter (Eds.), *Optimization of chest radiographs* (pp. 25–32). FDA 80-8124. Washington, DC: U.S. Department of Health and Human Services.

Swensson, R. G., Hessel, S. J., & Herman, P. G. (1985). The value of searching films without specific preconceptions. *Investigative Radiology*, 20, 100–107.

Tuddenham W. J. (1962). Visual search, image organization, and reader error in roentgen diagnosis. *Radiology*, 78, 694–704.

Voss, J. F., Greene, T. R., Post, T. A., & Penner, B. C. (1983). Problem-solving skill in the social sciences. In G. H. Bower (Ed.), *The psychology of learning and motivation: Advances in research and theory* (Vol. 17, pp. 165–213). New York: Academic Press.

12 Acquiring, Representing, and Evaluating a Competence Model of Diagnostic Strategy

William J. Clancey
Stanford Knowledge Systems Laboratory

INTRODUCTION

Over the past decade, a number of Artificial Intelligence programs have been constructed for solving problems in science, mathematics, and medicine. These programs, termed "Expert Systems" (Duda & Shortliffe, 1983; Feigenbaum, 1977) are designed to capture what specialists know, the kind of non-numeric, qualitative reasoning that is often passed on through apprenticeship rather than being written down in books. However, these programs are not generally intended to be *models* of expert problem-solving, neither in their organization of knowledge nor their reasoning process. Consequently, difficulties have been encountered in attempting to use the knowledge formulated in these programs outside of a consultation setting, where getting the right answer is mostly what matters. Their application to explanation and teaching, in particular, (Brown, 1977a; Clancey, 1983a; Swartout, 1981) has necessitated closer adherence to human problem-solving methods and more explicit representation of knowledge. That is, building expert systems whose problem-solving must be comprehensible to people requires a close study of the nature of expertise in people.

NEOMYCIN (Clancey & Letsinger, 1984) is a consultation system whose knowledge base is intended to be used in a tutoring program. While MYCIN (Shortliffe, 1976) is the starting point, we have significantly altered the representation and reasoning procedure of the original program. Unlike MYCIN, NEOMYCIN's knowledge is richly organized in multiple hierarchies; distinction is made between findings and hypotheses; and the reasoning is data- and hypothesis-directed, not an exhaustive, top-down search of the problem

343

space. Most importantly, for purposes of explanation and teaching, the reasoning procedure is abstract, separate from knowledge of the medical domain. The knowledge base is also broadened to take in many disorders that might be confused with the problem of meningitis diagnosis, the central concern of the MYCIN program. Together, the knowledge base and reasoning procedure constitute a model of how human knowledge is organized and how it is used in diagnosis.

In practical terms, we are interested in determining what we can teach students about diagnosis and how this knowledge might be usefully structured in a computer program. In general terms, we want to know what design would enable an expert system to acquire knowledge interactively from human experts, to explain reasoning to people seeking advice, and to teach students. Figure 12.1 shows how a program like NEOMYCIN relates to these three perspectives, providing an idealized overview of our goals.

In teaching, GUIDON2 will use NEOMYCIN's knowledge to model a student's problem solving. A strong parallel occurs in the process of building NEOMYCIN: "Knowledge acquisition" is a process of modeling a human expert's problem-solving, in which the modeler is the learner and the expert is the teacher. Similarly, to provide explanations of advice, a "user model" of the client is required. In all three settings — teaching, knowledge acquisition, and consultation explanation — a model is constructed of the person

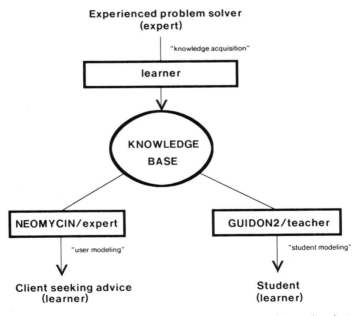

FIGURE 12.1   Three perspectives for acquiring, representing, and evaluating expertise.

interacting with the program, and a common knowledge base (NEOMYCIN) is used. We give different names to the modeling process — student modeling, knowledge acquisition, and user modeling — but the principles are essentially the same. We must determine: What is this person telling me about what he knows? What does he want to know about my knowledge? The purpose of NEOMYCIN research is to determine what kind of knowledge representation facilitates interacting with people in these three settings — as teacher, learner, and expert problem-solver. Indeed, we take the strong stand that a program is not an "expert" system, and certainly not a model of reasoning, unless it is proficient in these multiple, complex settings (see Anderson & Bower, 1980, for a similar discussion).

We don't have such a central program today, and most knowledge acquisition is done between people. But we can still capitalize on the analogies to learn how people organize their knowledge, how they model other people's knowledge, and how they explain what they know in dialogues. For example, we can compare a physician's explanations in knowledge acquisition dialogues to what he tells his students in the classroom. What we learn from this study can be incorporated in a user modeling program. All along we refine our model of diagnostic reasoning.

There are many overlapping perspectives to such a study. For example, in modeling medical diagnosis, we must sort out modeling of disease processes, general search procedures, explanation techniques, pedagogical strategies for interrupting students, and so on. In this paper, we examine NEOMYCIN as it is currently constructed from the perspective of what we might call *the psychology of medicine*. We are interested in issues of model acquisition, representation, content, and evaluation. In particular, we will consider the following questions:

1. Why does NEOMYCIN work? How could a model derived from a problem-solver's explanations about his behavior actually solve problems? That is, what must be true about an *explanation* of reasoning for it to be part of a procedural model?

2. What aspects of the model are *empirical*, based on observations of an expert's behavior and his explanations? What aspects are *rational*, based on mathematical and logical assumptions about the nature of knowledge and the task domain?

3. What capabilities of human reasoning are assumed by the *procedural language* for representing diagnostic strategy? How are considerations of *cognitive economy* incorporated?

4. What constraints imposed by the problem space are implicit in the *content* of the diagnostic procedure? What *correctness* and *efficiency* considerations derive from these task constraints?

5. What must be true about the nature of expertise and task domains for a model of reasoning to be expressed as an *abstract procedure*, wholly separate from the domain knowledge it operates upon?

6. Given that expert knowledge is highly "compiled" into domain-specific form, and that novices do not always know the right procedures, whom does NEOMYCIN model? If NEOMYCIN's abstract procedure of diagnosis is a *grammar*, constituting a model of *competence*, what are the difficulties of extracting such a grammar from expert behavior?

7. What part do multiple settings for using expertise play in evaluating the *sufficiency* of the model? How can knowledge of the underlying cognitive and task constraints be used to evaluate the *plausibility* of the model?

In pursuing these questions, we adopt different perspectives for formalizing and studying the model. We view it as:

- *an opportunistic strategy for remembering "compiled knowledge" of disorders* — emphasizing that diagnosis is an indexing problem. The diagnostic procedure operates upon a network of stereotypic knowledge of disorders, that is, knowledge derived from the experience of diagnosing many cases, not a working model of the human body and how it can be faulted;

- *a set of operators for establishing the space of diagnoses* — emphasizing that diagnosis is at heart a search problem whose bounds must be established and explored systematically;

- *a procedure derived from cognitive, sociological, mathematical, and case-experience constraints* — emphasizing that the determinants of efficiency and correctness are implicit in the procedure, below the level of diagnostic behavior;

- *a grammar for parsing information-gathering behavior* — emphasizing the domain-independent character of the diagnostic procedure, how it selects from a well-structured "lexicon" of medical knowledge and specifies the "discourse structure" of the diagnostic interview.

Building a large, complex program is necessarily iterative, with early versions serving as sketches of the idealized model. Like artists, we start with an idea, represent it, study what we have done, and try again. The state of AI and computational modeling is such that — if it were an artist's body of work — an exhibit of his or her completed paintings would be very small. NEOMYCIN is not a completed program, but a sketch that this chapter studies and critiques. It is reasonable to address the previous questions now to lend some methodological clarity to the enterprise.

Four major sections follow. In the *acquisition* section we illustrate how we collect and parse diagnostic behavior. (A detailed protocol analysis appears in Appendix II.) In the *description* section, we present an overview of our perspective on the search problem of medical diagnosis. (The entire diagnostic procedure appears in Appendix IV.) The *representation* section describes NEOMYCIN's strategy and domain knowledge architecture in detail, along with a summary of constraints implicit in the procedure. Finally, the *evaluation* section considers tests for determining the sufficiency and plausibility of the model. We conclude by considering what NEOMYCIN reveals about the nature of expertise and its implications for teaching.

ACQUIRING THE MODEL:
KNOWLEDGE ENGINEERING AND PROTOCOL ANALYSIS

Related Work and Scope of Effort

In conventional knowledge engineering (Hayes-Roth et al., 1983), an expert system is constructed by an interview process. A program is constructed and critiqued in an iterative manner. In this way, the resident "expert" frequently picks up the jargon and tools of artificial intelligence: He learns how to formalize his knowledge in some structured language, using editing programs and explanation systems to construct a "knowledge base" with the desired problem-solving ability.

NEOMYCIN was constructed in a different way. Our teaching goals required that we improve MYCIN's representation. We found that MYCIN's rule formalism made it necessary to proceduralize all knowledge, combining facts with how they were to be used (Clancey, 1982, Clancey, 1983a). With this experience in mind, we decided not to devise yet another formalism by which an accommodating physician might distort what he knew. Instead, we started (in 1980) by presenting problems to the physician to learn about his knowledge and methods from scratch. Our original objective was just to make explicit a taxonomy of diseases and subtype relations among findings; but the clarity of the approach used by our expert (and its difference from MYCIN's) ultimately encouraged us to construct the model that became NEOMYCIN's diagnostic procedure.

This investigation was influenced in many ways by previous work. For example, Pauker and Szolovits (1977) constructed a model of diagnostic reasoning, called PIP, concurrent with the development of MYCIN. Thus, we knew that a psychological approach, instead of a purely engineering approach, could be used for constructing an expert system without a loss in problem-solving performance. Other studies (such as Elstein, Shulman, & Sprafka, 1978; Kassirer & Gorry, 1978; Miller, 1975; Patil, Szolovits, & Schwartz, 1982; Rubin, 1975), as well as that of Benbassat and Schiffmann, 1976, strongly suggested that diagnostic strategy constitutes a separate, significant body of knowledge that might be interesting to formalize independent of medical facts themselves. Furthermore, previous research in teaching problem-solving strategies with instructional programs using AI techniques (e.g., Brown, Collins, & Haris, 1977; Papert, 1980; Wescourt & Hemphill, 1978), suggested that it would be useful to go beyond MYCIN's purely domain-specific rules and make explicit the underlying general search procedure.

In related psychological research, Feltovich, Johnson, Moller, and Swanson (1984) used fixed-order diagnostic problems to demonstrate the effect of knowledge organization on reasoning. Could we formalize an ideal organization of knowledge for MYCIN's meningitis domain? In AI, Davis (1980) designed a construct he called a "metarule" for controlling reasoning, but he had presented only two examples in MYCIN's domain. Could this representation be generalized for formalizing a complete diagnostic procedure? Concurrent studies at the Learning Research Development Center and CMU (Anderson, Greeno, Kline, & Neves, 1981; Chi, Feltovich, & Glaser, 1981; Feltovich, Johnson, Moller, & Swanson, 1984; Larkin, McDermott, Simon, & Simon, 1980) were concerned with modeling differences between experts and novices in geometry and physics problem-solving. Could we "decompile" MYCIN's knowledge into the components an expert had learned from experience and compiled into specific procedures and rules? Finally, in our previous research (Clancey, 1983a; Clancey, 1984), we had found a convenient epistemologic framework for characterizing the content of an explanation. Could this be used for directing and analyzing a knowledge acquisition dialogue?

In summary, the process of acquiring the NEOMYCIN model from expert interviews is disciplined by three greatly different perspectives:

- *Psychology:* The new program, unlike MYCIN, should embody a model of diagnosis that students can understand and use themselves. Moreover, a program that captures general principles of data- and hypothesis-directed reasoning can be used as the basis for a student model. (See page 385.)

- *Knowledge Engineering:* The new program, unlike MYCIN, should separate control knowledge from the facts it operates upon. The diagnostic procedure should be represented in a well-structured way, just like the medical knowledge, so that it will be accessible for explanation and interpretation in student modeling. See Clancey, 1983a for detailed discussion.

- *Epistemology:* The new program, unlike MYCIN, should distinguish among findings, hypotheses, evidence (finding/hypothesis links), justifications (why a finding/hypothesis link is true), structure (how findings and hypotheses are related), and strategy (why a finding request or hypothesis comes to mind). See Clancey, 1983a for detailed discussion, also see page 364.

Besides not filling in some predetermined representation, we have been wary of incorporating ad hoc features into the model just because the computer allows them. In particular, we are especially wary of all scoring mechanisms: We want every hypothesis and finding request either to be based on explicit principles or to be totally arbitrary. It is essential that NE-OMYCIN avoid numeric calculations that cannot be expressed in terms of facts and procedures known and followed by people. We use MYCIN's evidence-weighing scheme (certainty factors) to signify strength of association; but focus decisions, such as selecting a hypothesis to test and a finding to request, primarily follow from relations among findings and hypotheses (such as "sibling," and "necessary cause").

Furthermore, in proceeding in this principled way, we have avoided making the mechanisms more complex than our empirical observations of physicians' reasoning or the cases to be solved warrant. For this reason, we have not included in the model diagnostic considerations that play an important part in several other programs (Chandrasekdelaran, Gomez, & Mittal, 1979; Pauker & Szolovits, 1977; Pople, 1982). These include: differentiation of the disease on the basis of organ system involvement; a problem-oriented approach (trying to explain the data); consideration of multiple causes; and use of probabilistic information. We have minimized these concerns by focusing on diagnosis of meningitis and diseases that might be confused with it. Of course, some of these considerations may be incorporated as we continue to develop the program.

Our research approach could be characterized as "making a push to the frontier." Some of our results might not stand up because the problems considered are not broad enough. But we will have demonstrated, as a first attempt, that certain epistemologic and knowledge-engineering distinctions are useful for constructing a program that can solve problems and explain what it knows.

As another perspective, we want to determine what good teachers know about their own knowledge and problem-solving methods that students would profit from being taught. In assembling a runnable computational model, we must fill in some details, such as strength of belief and activation of memory. We do this in a minimal way, devising just enough mechanism to get the behavior we want (on our small set of test cases). So, for example, we use the MYCIN certainty factor mechanism because it is convenient and simple enough. We have much to learn about what teachers *know* about their knowledge and problem solving, and much of what we do falls in the realm of the traditional computer science problem of designing an appropriate programming language to encode these structures and procedures. Thus, our first interest is to replicate what people know about what they do; we are only secondarily interested in formalizing models of how the mind works (e.g., activation of knowledge), and not at all in mathematically deriving optimal models that might replace or augment what people do.

With our objective of constructing a tutoring program with useful capabilities, the purpose of NEOMYCIN research is not to make the best medical diagnostic program, but to demonstrate a representation methodology for separating kinds of knowledge and formalizing strategies in domain-independent form. The problem domain is sufficiently complex to be challenging, and we have formalized a sufficient subset of diagnostic strategies to provide an interim report on our approach. We have uncovered a number of cognitive problems of interest that have been little studied, particularly that of how focus of attention changes during diagnosis.

The Hypothesize-and-Test Theory of Diagnosis

In studying diagnostic behavior, we used the epistemologic framework previously mentioned and evolved a set of terms for describing the process of diagnosis. Terms that appear frequently in subsequent sections, such as "task" and "differential," are defined in Appendix I.

In addition, we began with the traditional model of diagnosis, which says that each request for case information, or each finding, directly relates to some hypothesis (Figure 12.2). This model suggests several problems for investigation (points corresponding to numbers in the figure):

1. Where do the initial hypotheses come from?
2. How does the problem-solver choose a finding to confirm or test a hypothesis?
3. What causes attention shift to a new hypothesis?
4. How does the problem-solver know when he or she is done?

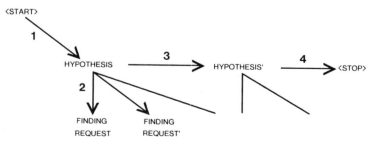

FIGURE 12.2   Hypothesize and test theory of diagnosis.

We define a *diagnostic strategy* to be the control structure that regulates these four decisions. This hypothesize-and-test theory drove our initial investigations, but the NEOMYCIN model eventually became much more complex.

Knowledge Acquisition Technique

With our interest in formalizing the reasoning process of diagnosis, it is particularly important to allow experts to request problem findings in whatever order they desire. Our main concern is to determine what task and domain knowledge leads to each finding request. Contrary to the protocol-collection procedure most often used today (Ericsson & Simon, 1980; Kuipers & Kassier, 1984; Newell & Simon, 1972) with a minimal number of interruptions, we frequently ask the expert specific questions. In retrospect, this is not always done in a consistent way, and is sometimes so late that the expert has clearly moved ahead (see Line 30 in Appendix II). However, the expert appears to be quite tolerant of interruptions, perhaps from his teaching experience, though of course he might not be typical in this respect.

The questioning techniques we use are listed here, in somewhat idealized form.[1]

- Epistemologic distinctions:
  - Be concerned about the specificity of a finding request: Is it a general maneuver or does he have a specific hypothesis in mind?
  - When asking why a finding came to mind, distinguish between strategic and causal explanations.
  - Distinguish between substances and processes; watch out for composed explanations that leave out intermediate processes or refer to substances as if they were processes.
  - Do not delve into explanations of causal mechanisms that go beyond the expert's level of reasoning.
  - Ask for definitions and try to detect synonyms, which might be misunderstood as representing different entities.
- Interactive considerations:
  - Immediately after a finding is requested, and before supplying the information, ask why the finding came to mind (otherwise new hypotheses might be used to rationalize the request).

---

[1]Typical of our attempt to apply expertise in multiple settings, we use such generalizations of our own behavior as expectations of what a student or client watching NEOMYCIN might want to know.

- When the expert indicates that he has formed some hypotheses, ask him to list his differential (this encourages completeness).
- When a specific hypothesis is being tested, ask about ordering of data requests: Are these "routine" questions for the hypothesis, or has the expert been reminded of some particular correlation or causal process?
- When the expert appears to be changing his task and/or focus without commenting, confirm this and find out why.
- Watch for assumptions made by the expert: What is he inferring from the context of his dialogue with you and not explicitly confirming? Ask why certain questions were not asked.

Illustration of Level of Protocol Analysis

We introduce our analysis of an expert's problem-solving and explanation protocol with an excerpt (Figure 12.3) from the end of the case we analyze in Appendix II. Phrases are broken to separate different kinds of statements; MD = the medical expert, KE = the knowledge engineer. (Again, we choose the term "knowledge engineer" to make clear that this is not presented as a formal psychological experiment.) Brief annotations illustrate our terminology. Annotations always *precede* the protocol section they pertain to.

The analysis shows how findings, hypotheses, and tasks are typically related. Lines L5 to L7 are most interesting in this aspect. Here we see plainly the interaction of task knowledge (stating a list of tested hypotheses), focus of attention (hematoma), and application of domain knowledge (what causes hematoma). The hypothesis in focus, hematoma, was tested by considering what could have caused it. (Interestingly, the physician is so caught up in his role as clinician that he addresses the KE as if he were the patient.)

It is also worth noting that the expert states in L2 that he is planning to go back to ask for more information. Again, in L9 he characterizes his own behavior in general terms. This is typical of the abstract statements this expert makes about diagnosis. His "explanations" of what he does abstractly characterize his problem-solving procedure: "Formulate a differential" and "ask more questions." An important aspect of these explanations is that they are not arbitrary "rationalizations," but are abstract descriptions of a procedure that could generate his finding-requests and hypotheses. They do not necessarily correspond to steps of a procedure that he consciously considers, but are rather the "syntax" of his behavior. The expert's statements constitute a set of tasks and goals that can be fleshed out as an executable procedure. This is obviously important if the model we construct from the expert's explanations is to solve problems successfully and to be useful in teaching. We know that our expert was an unusually good teacher, therefore we cannot expect that every expert's explanations would have this property.

A task has been completed . . .

L1 MD: I've gotten a pretty good data base,

A new task is planned . . .

L2   so I am going to go back and just ask a couple more questions.

There is a differential . . .

L3   I have formulated in my own mind what I think some of the possibilities are.

L4 KE: Can you tell me what you think are some of the possibilities?

The differential is stated . . .

L5 MD: I think that there is a very definite possibility that this patient does not have an infectious disease. She could have brain tumor, or a collection of blood (hematoma) in her brain from previous head trauma.

> In reviewing, the expert notices that the task
>
> "PURSUE-HYPOTHESIS (focus = mass lesion)"
>
> was not completed; all of the causes have not been considered. So the problem-solving process shifts task and focus:
>
> > task: TEST-HYPOTHESIS (hematoma)
> > evidence rule: head-trauma -> hematoma
> > task: FINDOUT (head-trauma)

L6   (That is a question I should have asked, by the way . . .)

L7   Have you had any recent head trauma?

L8 KE: Head trauma, no.

L9 MD: You'll find that this happens to physicians. As they formulate their differential diagnosis and then they go back and ask more questions.

L11 KE: What comes after . . . ?

L10 MD: Then I would say a chronic meningitis.

FIGURE 12.3 Example of protocol analysis.

Finally, this excerpt illustrates how during the process of reviewing the differential (a task) the expert realizes that a hypothesis should be tested or refined (broken into subtypes or causes). We do not view this as an error on his part. Rather, as the expert says in L9, reviewing is a deliberate maneuver for being complete; it helps bring other diagnostic tasks to mind. NEOMYCIN does not behave in this way because it is a simplified model that does not precisely model how knowledge of diseases is stored or recalled. This level of modeling may very well be useful for understanding the basis of diagnostic strategies, as well as for considering the space of alternative strategies people are capable of and the causes of errors.[2]

OVERVIEW OF THE DIAGNOSTIC MODEL

Flow of Information

Figure 12.4 provides an overview of the flow of information during diagnosis. The loop begins with a "chief complaint," one or more findings that supposedly indicate that the device is malfunctioning. These findings are supplied by an *informant*, who has made or collected the observations that will be given to the problem solver. By forward reasoning, hypotheses are considered. They are focused upon by a general search procedure, leading to attempts to test hypotheses by requesting further findings.

Keep in mind that this diagram shows the flow of information, not the invocation structure of the tasks. TEST-HYPOTHESIS regains control after each invocation to FINDOUT and FORWARD-REASON. Similarly, the subtask within ESTABLISH-HYPOTHESIS-SPACE that invoked TEST-HYPOTHESIS will regain control after a hypothesis is tested. Tasks can also be prematurely aborted and the "stack popped" in the manner described on page 365.[3]

---

[2]As it becomes clear later, we might link NEOMYCIN's metarules to the domain memory model used by Kolodner in the CYRUS program (Kolodner, 1983). In this paper, we present prosaic summaries of the underlying memory constraints (Appendix IV and p. 371, many of which bear striking resemblance to Kolodner's results, such as the importance we give to disease process features for differentiating among diseases.

[3]An obvious alternative design is to place tasks, particularly PROCESS-FINDING and PURSUE-HYPOTHESIS, on an agenda, so findings to explain and hypotheses to test can be more opportunistically ordered (e.g., see Hayes-Roth & Hayes-Roth, 1979). It is possible that the procedural decomposition of reasoning in NEOMYCIN, which suitably models an expert's deliberate approach on relatively easy cases, will prove to be too awkward for describing a student's reasoning, which might jump back and forth between hypotheses and mix data- and hypothesis-directed reasoning in some complex way.

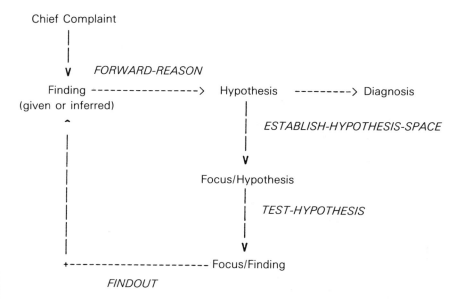

FIGURE 12.4   Flow of information during diagnosis (tasks appear in capitalized italics.)

Tasks for Structuring Working Memory

Figure 12.5 shows the general calling structure of tasks in the diagnostic procedure. An important perspective behind the design of this procedure is that the diagnosis can be described abstractly as a process in which *the problem solver poses tasks for himself in order to have some structuring effect on working memory.* Metarules for doing a task bring appropriate sources of knowledge to mind. Thus, it is very important that the procedure is structured so that the tasks make sense as things that people try to do.

Diagnosis involves repetitively deciding what data to collect next, generally by focusing on some hypothesis in the differential. If we examine the kind of explanations a physician gives for why he is requesting a finding, we find that most refer to a hypothesis he is trying to confirm; this is the conventional view of diagnosis. But we find that a number of requests are *not directed at specific hypotheses* or *relate to a group of hypotheses.* The problem solver describes a more *general effect that knowledge about the finding will have on his thinking.* For example, information about pregnancy would "broaden the spectrum of disorders" that he is considering. He considers fever and trauma, very general findings, in order to "consider the things at the top." Thus, besides being focused on particular hypotheses, finding requests are intended to affect the differential in some way — for

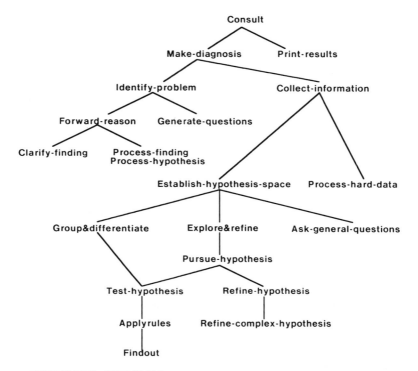

FIGURE 12.5   NEOMYCIN's diagnostic strategy. (All terminal tasks shown here except PRINT-RESULTS invoke FINDOUT directly or through AP-PLYRULES.)

example, to restrict it categorically or to rule out unusual causes. We call the overall task of collecting circumstantial evidence (through a patient's history and physical examination) "establishing the hypothesis space" because it is oriented toward circumscribing the space of diseases that must be considered.

Structurally, we relate this heuristic search to multiple hierarchical organizations of disorders. Figure 12.6 illustrates our model in general terms. The problem solver receives initial information that "places him in the middle" of some hierarchical organization of known diseases. We show here an etiological hierarchy (defined later). In the protocol we analyze in Section II "chronic-meningitis" was first considered, not "infection," something at the top of the hierarchy, or "tb-meningitis" something at the bottom. The process of diagnosis then involves massaging this set of initial guesses by first "looking up" for general evidence that establishes the class, and then "looking down" to be as specific as possible. To establish a diagnosis, the physician must not only attempt to collect direct evidence for it but must establish paths upward through the multiple hierarchies in which the diagnosis is contained.

Put another way, the physician tries to form a set of possibilities that includes the "right answer" and then narrows down the possibilities to a small, treatable number. This is why a premium is placed on questions that would "broaden the spectrum of possibilities that must be considered" or, alternatively, lend confidence that the typical, a priori, most likely diseases under consideration are appropriate.

To repeat the main point, *we explain finding requests in terms of the effect they are intended to have on the differential*. And moreover, at each point, as findings are requested that could have a certain effect, we say that the *task* of the problem solver is to bring about this effect on his thinking, to change what he is considering or to in some respect give him confidence. Each effect provides structure to the problem in some way: characterizing, refining, or confirming the causes that must be considered. Figure 12.7 shows graphically how each of the operators affect the space of hypoth-

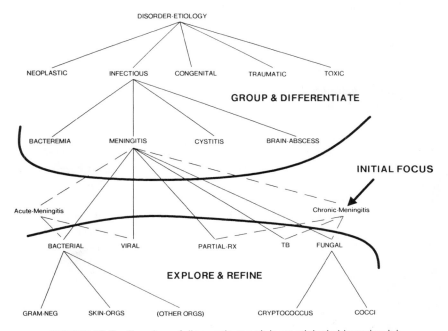

FIGURE 12.6 Overview of diagnostic search in an etiologic hierarchy: Initial information brings problem-solver to an intermediate hypothesis; it must be confirmed by considering classes containing it, and then it must be refined by considering more specific disorders.

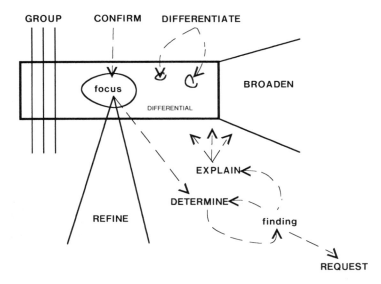

FIGURE 12.7   Graphic interpretation of each task as an operator for affecting working memory. (See text for elaboration.)

eses.[4] This analysis is of course strongly inspired by Simon's study of the role of the problem space and how it pertains to ill-structured problems (Newell & Simon 1972; Simon & Lea, 1979). Pople, in work concurrent to ours, has developed this point very well and appears to adopt the same "task-oriented" terminology for the proposed CADUCEUS follow-on to INTERNIST (Pople, 1982). (Patil, Szolovits, & Schwartz 1981) has defined operators for constructing alternative causal models to explain findings on multiple levels of detail. Returning to Elstein's study of medical problem-solving (Elstein, Shulman, & Sprafka, 1978), we find similar experiments and analyses of how a physician reasons about alternative formulations of the problem he or she is trying to solve. Finally, the idea of an *information-gathering strategy* for classifying objects or phenomena was pioneered by Bruner (Bruner, Goodnow, & Austin, 1956), in experiments that allowed the problem solver to order data requests, so the different strategic motivations could be studied.

Problem Formulation and Other Approaches to Diagnosis

It is worth noting that this model of diagnosis differs from a Bayesian model

---

[4]The objective is to put the "right answer" into the box labeled "differential." Possible answers, hypotheses, are focused on, confirmed, grouped, differentiated, and refined. The box is broadened to include other hypotheses by asking general questions. Determining a finding may involve requesting it or determining another finding. Findings must be explained (accounted for causally) with respect to the differential.

in its emphasis on a structured search. The problem solver is not just working with lists of diseases. There are general maneuvers for contrasting, exploring, and seeking evidence in terms of *relations* among diseases. Nor is this model what medical students are taught in textbooks. Students are commonly given an outline of all data that they might collect, organized by "social history," "previous illness," and so on, suggesting that medical diagnosis is a process of collecting data in a fixed order. The result is that students sometimes collect information by rote, without thinking about hypotheses at all!

The aspect of problem solving that involves forming a set of initially unrelated hypotheses and then finding ways to group, contrast, and refine them is often called "initial problem formulation." The capabilities of NEOMYCIN and systems like PIP (Szolovits & Pauker, 1978) and CADUCEUS (Pople, 1982) should be contrasted with the exhaustive top-down analysis used by programs like MYCIN and CENTAUR (Aikens, 1981). In a sense, the process of "looking up" into categories serves as a "big switch" as conceived in the General Problem Solver (Newell & Simon, 1972). It is the operation of viewing the overall problem in dramatically different ways: Did the patient fall and hit his head? Does he have an emotional problem? Is there a congenital weakness in the vascular system? Is there a tumor? Has the patient been infected by a virus? Did the patient consume something toxic? Diagnosing each of these dramatically different processes requires bringing specialized knowledge into play. So we might imagine constructing specialized subsystems of knowledge to deal with infectious disease diagnosis, psychological analysis, and toxic drug disorders, and integrating them by the GROUP-AND-DIFFERENTIATE procedure of comparing and contrasting likely categories of disease.

A Causal Model of What Happened to the Patient

So far we have described diagnosis in terms of heuristics for carrying on an efficient search of a combinatorially large space. However, it must be remembered that a diagnosis is not just a label, but constitutes *a model of the patient*. This model is a causal story of what has happened to bring the patient to his current state of illness. The general questions of diagnosis regarding travel, job history, medications, and so forth (the categories emphasized to a student) seek to circumscribe the external agents, environments, or internal changes (due to age, pregnancy, or diseases) that may have affected the patient's body. Thus, "establishing the hypothesis space" is more precisely characterized as "establishing the space of causes."

The following protocol excerpt provides a typical causal story, showing how a finding request is intended to establish the space of causes that must be considered:

KE: What about pregnancies? Why is that important?

MD: When I asked about compromised host, that includes a wide spectrum of problems. The pregnant woman is probably the most
common compromised host, in that during the pregnancy period women are more susceptible to dissemination of certain types
of infections, and cocci is a classic of that. Whereas most of us
would localize cocci in the lungs, pregnant women disseminate
cocci to the meninges more commonly. The same thing happens
with TB.

KE: Would it be fair to say that the question about pregnancy is not
necessarily specific to the possibility of a cocci infection, but is
of more general interest?

MD: Yes, I think it is of more general interest. It is pertinent to cocci,
but would also be considered perhaps in other areas, because it
would change your thinking a bit, the pregnant woman having
a little different spectrum of infection than a regular, normal
person.

Here the expert supplies a causal explanation for how pregnancy affects
the body, mentioning the very important concept of "dissemination" —
spread of an infectious agent in the body. In trying to establish a causal
story of an infectious disease, the physician looks for general evidence of
exposure, dissemination, and impaired immunoresponse — all of which are
necessary for an infection to take place, regardless of the specific agent. Importantly, diseases can be ruled in or out on the basis of general evidence
for these *phases* in the causal process, so the physician needn't directly try
to rule in or out all of the specific diseases. Thus, the process of establishing
the space of causes reduces to considering broad categories of evidence (e.g.,
"compromised host" implies impaired immunoresponse), rather than focusing narrowly on every specific causal mechanism and agent that might be
involved. Moreover, this might be generalized even further by characterizing some causal stories as "unusual" and others as "typical." Thus, establishing the space of possibilities reduces to determining whether the patient
is "typical," or whether "unusual processes" might be occurring. In this style
of diagnosis, characteristic of our domain, diagnosis is categorical, with essentially no concern for low-level causal arguments.

In his analysis of the patient, the physician's "process-oriented approach"
is manifested in several ways. The most obvious are the general questions
(ASK-GENERAL-QUESTIONS) for determining whether the patient has
had related problems in the past. This is a key maneuver for circumscribing the problem space. For example, by asking if the patient has been
hospitalized, one learns about all serious illnesses the patient has had. This
is an excellent starting point for determining what causal processes might

be implicated in the current disease. Learning that there have been no previous hospitalizations, illnesses, medications prescribed, and so on, the problem solver can be reasonably sure that he has an accurate database for making decisions: He knows what has affected this patient and can infer that everything else is "typical" or "what one might expect." Thus, the use of general questioning is perhaps the most heuristically powerful technique in medical diagnosis. The anatomically oriented "review of systems" is similar, particularly as a spatial reminder of possible diseases, but it is not used by NEOMYCIN.

Constructing a model of the patient is often described informally as forming a "picture of the patient." The physician establishes the sequence in which findings were manifested and factors this with information about prior problems and therapies, using their time relations to match possible causal connections. For example, a fever might be a precursor to an illness that later manifests itself by abdominal pains. Thus, the physician is not just matching a set of symptoms to a disease; he is matching the order in which the symptoms appeared and how they changed over time to his knowledge of disease processes — a much richer organization than a mere list of symptoms. The physician remembers the sequence, knowing what symptoms to expect or to ask about, based upon his knowledge of the underlying causal process that relates the symptoms to one another.

Another way to understand the importance of process knowledge is to logically consider the importance of differentiating between hypotheses. In a pure sense, this does not mean to confirm them independently, but to gain information that will favor one and disfavor another. This is the sense in which diagnosis is a process of modeling the patient. When the interpretation is ambiguous, it is necessary to gain more information. Discrimination in this way presupposes that there is some *dimension* for comparison. That is, we must have some common way for viewing the competing diseases. In NEOMYCIN, we call this the *disease process frame*. Its *slots* are the features of any disease — where it occurs, when it began, its first symptom, how the symptoms change over time, whether it is a local or "systemic," and so on. This frame applies to more than disease processes, of course. For example, it can be used in the "oil spill problem" (Hayes-Roth et al., 1983) to diagnosis the causes of oil spills by their frequency, amount, change over time, periodicity, and location in the network of drainage ditches.

The following excerpt from a class discussion with our expert illustrates how this kind of process orientation is critical to causal reasoning:

TEACHER: Think of the common anemias that a young person might get, and think of anemia in general. There are two ways to look at it. You start out with an adequate number of red cells and you reach the point of being anemic; there are two ways you can do it. You're losing blood excessively, or you're not making enough to replace your normal losses. These divide anemia into two major categories: production deficits or loss of blood. So you can talk about reasons that a young person might lose blood.

Basically, to lose enough blood to become anemic either you are losing it in your stool, GI bleeding, . . . what's a good question about GI bleeds, or the most common reason for blood loss in the United States is what? What physiologic function causes people to lose blood?

STUDENT: Menstruation. She said that it was normal.

TEACHER: Normal. Normal menstrual periods, okay. So now the question is if you don't get a good history for excessive blood loss then you question, are people producing blood adequately? You can have some serious derangement in production such as sickle cell anemia, or they may not have the basic substrates.

Even here, causal reasoning is categorical, with general consideration of production deficiency, loss of product, or substrate (input) limitation.

Structure of Knowledge

The hypothesis space is structured in many different ways, with different purposes. For example, an etiological taxonomy, based on the *ultimate origins* of disorders, can be contrasted with an "organ system taxonomy," also used in medicine, which is a strict hierarchy by location of the disorder. Siblings of the etiologic taxonomy are alternative causes for a given disease process, which is why the etiological taxonomy is favored over the organ system taxonomy for focusing search during diagnosis.

The task of establishing the hypothesis space blends the good human ability to detect familiar patterns (by data-directed associations) with a critical analysis that considers alternatives and unusual possibilities, with different indexing schemes used for these purposes. Studies indicate that medical experts differ from novices precisely by their ability to call to mind useful categories of disease (Feltovich, et al., 1984). For example, in diagnosis of congenital heart disease, the expert learns the list of causes associated with abnormal noises on the left side of the heart. Feltovich calls this the *logical competitor set*. Significantly, this grouping is often orthogonal to the traditional hierarchies given in textbooks. Similarly, a subset of hypotheses can be remembered by labeling them, as in meningitis we refer to "the unusual causes of bacterial meningitis." Thus, over time the expert evolves a complex organization of hypotheses that is more finely indexed than a simple hierarchy (Feltovich, 1980). The expert efficiently circumscribes the possible causes by relating a familiar interpretation with unlikely but important causes that might be confused with it.

Activation of Knowledge

Modeling human reasoning requires some model of the activation of knowledge. The idea is basic in medical diagnosis: Any given fact about the patient might have many real-world implications, but only those relevant to diagnostic hypotheses should come to mind. As a simple example, consider a physician who is told that the patient has pets. The expert, diagnosing a possible infectious disease, might ask, "Does the patient have turtles?" Some sort of intersection match has occurred that activated salmonella as a diagnosis (because it is a bacterial infectious disease). If the leading hypothesis had been cancer, it is less likely that the salmonella association with turtles would have come to mind when pets were mentioned. If so, we would say that a shift in focus of attention occurred. A model of data- and hypothesis-directed reasoning, such as NEOMYCIN, must specify how data is used and how focus of attention changes.

Most programs use a form of "spreading activation" (Anderson & Bower, 1980; Rumelhart & Norman, 1983; Szolovits & Pauker, 1978) by which knowledge structures are brought into consideration based on their proximity. NEOMYCIN's model incorporates these dimensions:

- *Context:* In simple terms, this concerns when relations between findings and hypotheses are realized. The value of known findings is realized when a new hypothesis is triggered (see PROCESS-HYPOTHESIS). Support for previously considered hypotheses (ancestors and immediate descendents of the differential) is realized when a new finding is received (see PROCESS-FINDING). These are called *focused forward-inferences.*
- *Strength of association:* "Antecedent rules" are applied immediately (discussed on page 371).
- *Level of effort:* Intermediate subgoals are only pursued when applying "trigger rules," interpreting "hard findings," or deliberately attempting to confirm a hypothesis.

Summary of NEOMYCIN'S Reasons for Gathering Information

One measure of complexity of NEOMYCIN's model of diagnosis is the number of reasons for requesting a finding. In MYCIN the only reason for asking a question was to apply a rule that concluded about some "goal." This is analogous to the hypothesis and test, "single-operator" view presented in Figure 12.1 NEOMYCIN's tasks in essence give more structure and meaning to the data-gathering process. Besides testing a hypothesis, the program has the following direct motivations for gathering information (with related tasks in parentheses):

- *follow-up questions that specify previous information* (Given that the patient has a fever, the program will ask what the temperature is.) (CLARIFY-FINDING)
- *process-oriented follow-up questions* (When did a headache begin, how severe is it, where is it located?) (CLARIFY-FINDING)
- *process-oriented discrimination questions* (To discriminate between meningitis and brain-abscess, determine if the disorder is spread throughout the central nervous system or is localized.) (GROUP-AND-DIFFERENTIATE)
- *triggered questions* (Given that the patient has a stiff neck, we might immediately ask whether he has a headache or other neurological symptoms, because of the possibility that this might be meningitis.) (FORWARD-REASON)
- *general questions to determine the availability or presence of findings and tests* (To determine whether the CSF is cloudy, a lumbar puncture must be taken.) (FINDOUT)
- *general questions to establish that the relevant history is complete* (Has the patient been hospitalized recently? Is he taking any medications?) (ASK-GENERAL-QUESTIONS)

The expert-teacher's directives to students are the primary source for formulating the tasks of NEOMYCIN's diagnostic procedure (Appendix III).

REPRESENTING THE MODEL: STRATEGY AND DOMAIN KNOWLEDGE

NEOMYCIN's abstract and explicit diagnostic procedure distinguishes it from other AI programs. The procedure is *abstract* because it is separated from the domain knowledge—a feature common to frame-oriented systems. The procedure is *explicit* because it is represented in a well-structured way, not arbitrary code—a feature common to rule-based systems.[5] (Rumelhart & Norman, 1983, provides a good, up-to-date discussion of the declarative/procedural distinction.) Here we discuss these two knowledge representations.

---

[5]That is, the procedure is expressed in a language for which we can write an interpreter that can reason about how tasks are invoked, as well as their input and output: The notation is *declarative*.

Representing Strategy: Tasks, Metarules, and End Conditions

As already described, the strategy part of the model is represented as sub-procedures we call tasks. Each task has an *ordered* list of rules, sometimes called a "rule set," associated with it.[6] We call them *metarules* because they reason about which domain rules (more generally, "domain relations") should be applied to the problem. The metarules determine which causal, subtype, definition, or disease process relations will be exploited for purposes of adding hypotheses to the differential — contrasting hypotheses, focusing on a hypothesis, refining a hypothesis, confirming a hypothesis, or determining whether a finding is present.

For example, the FORWARD-REASON metarule that says, "If there is a red-flag finding, then do forward reasoning with it," is using the relation "red-flag finding" to index the knowledge base. More specifically, this metarule causes red-flag (or significant, abnormal) findings to be considered first. We say that the relation "red-flag finding" *partitions* set of findings. This is the typical way in which metarules use relations that organize domain knowledge to select findings, hypothesis, and relations to apply to the problem at hand. To the degree that a concept like "red-flag finding" can be given a consistent meaning in several problem domains, the diagnostic procedure is domain-independent. It is plausible that we might construct such a theory of knowledge organization because relations like "red-flag finding" are completely defined by how they are used by the diagnostic procedure.

A task has associated with it a description of how its metarules are to be applied. (To "apply a rule" means to determine whether the "if part" of the rule is satisfied [i.e., the rule "succeeds"]; and, if so, to carry out the action specified in the "then part" of the rule.) There are four possibilities:

1. *simple, try-all:* All of the metarules are applied once in sequence (a simple procedure of multiple steps).

2. *simple, don't-try-all:* The metarules are applied in sequence until one succeeds, then the task is complete (control returns to the calling task) (a "do one" selection).

3. *iterative, try-all:* the metarules are applied in order, repetitively, until no rule succeeds (a simple loop; NEOMYCIN currently has no tasks of this type, probably because "try-all" suggests constantly changing methods or following a breadth-first approach).

4. *iterative, don't-try-all:* The metarules are applied in order, with control returning to the head of the list each time a rule succeeds, until no rule succeeds (a "pure production system").

---

[6]Currently, there are 33 tasks and 80 metarules; thus the procedure is highly structured, with relatively few steps or methods for achieving any one task.

The "if part" of a metarule generally examines the working memory and domain knowledge. The "then part" invokes another task, applies a domain rule, or requests a finding of the informant.

A task generally has an argument, known as the *focus* of the task, or that part of the working memory it is operating upon (a finding, hypothesis, or domain rule). A task can have only one focus, but it might be a list, such as the entire differential.

A history is kept of which tasks have been done, recording the focus, if appropriate. Metarules reference this history, for example to determine if a particular hypothesis has been pursued. Other bookkeeping, such as resetting global registers that characterize the state of the differential, is handled by rules applied before or after the task metarules.

A task may have an *end-condition*, which is evaluated whenever a metarule succeeds. If it is satisfied, the task is aborted. Importantly, end-conditions can be inherited from tasks higher on the stack, and each task along the way will be aborted. End-conditions describe either *preconditions*, which must be true for it to make sense to be doing the task (see the end-condition of EXPLORE-AND-REFINE) or *what the task is trying to achieve* (when it can be halted — see GENERATE-QUESTIONS). NEOMYCIN's end-conditions all refer to the differential: the presence of strong evidence for a "competing" hypothesis; the presence of a hypothesis in a new, unexplored category; an "adequate" differential to begin a diagnosis. Some tasks are always allowed to go to completion (indicated by an end-condition of DONTABORT). We can think of the end-condition mechanism as a means for "backing out of a procedure" when it becomes inappropriate or its goal is no longer of highest priority.

In summary, the knowledge for applying tasks — knowledge for controlling metarules, focussing, bookkeeping, and interrupting — constitutes a knowledge base in its own right.

Figure 12.8 summarizes how the diagnostic procedure interacts with domain knowledge. Figure 12.9 shows a task definition and a metarule ex-

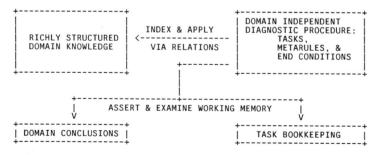

FIGURE 12.8 Interaction of working memory with domain and strategic knowledge: A domain-independent language of relations partitions domain knowledge enabling a domain-independent procedure to index and selectively apply facts.

```
(TASK CONTROL KNOWLEDGE)
        (TASKTYPE PROCESS-FINDING SIMPLE)
        (TASK-TRY-ALL-RULES PROCESS-FINDING)
        (ENDCONDITION PROCESS-FINDING DONTABORT)
        (TASKFOCUS PROCESS-FINDING $FOCUS-FINDING)
        (LOCALVARS PROCESS-FINDING (RULELST SUPERFINDINGS FOCUSQS))
        (ACHIEVED-BY PROCESS-FINDING (METARULE069. . .))
        (DO-AFTER PROCESS-FINDING (RULE381))

(TYPICAL METARULE)
        (IF (AND (SOFT-FINDING $FOCUS-FINDING)
                 (ACTIVE-HYP $HYPOTHESIS)
                 (EVIDENCE-FOR $FOCUS-FINDING $HYPOTHESIS $RULE $CF)
                 (UNAPPLIED $RULE))
            (TASK APPLYRULE $RULE))

(AUXILIARY RULE)
        (IF (OR (DIFFERENTIAL $HYPOTHESIS)
                (AND (DIFFERENTIAL $H1)
                     (CHILD $HYPOTHESIS $H1))
                (AND (DIFFERENTIAL $H2)
                     (TAXONOMIC-ANCESTOR $HYPOTHESIS $H2)))
            (ACTIVE-HYP $HYPOTHESIS))
```

FIGURE 12.9 Internal form of the task PROCESS-FINDING and one of its metarules ("apply rules using the finding to conclude about a hypothesis in focus").

pressed in internal form, using the MRS language, a form of predicate calculus (Genesereth, Greiner, & Smith, 1981). (In MRS notation, $X will match whatever term is in the database and once bound will maintain that value in the rest of the expression.) Note that intermediate relations, such as "active hypothesis," are also defined by rules written in MRS. Further details about the advantages of the MRS notation and NEOMYCIN's procedural language for representing strategy appear in Clancy & Brock (in press).

New strategies are generally expressed by writing new metarules and tasks and defining appropriate new structural relations for indexing domain knowledge. In summary, the control language constructs include: tasks, controlled metarules, problem-solving history, end-conditions, primitive actions (ask, conclude, apply a rule), and a relational language for organizing domain knowledge (referenced by the conditional part of metarules). Domain knowledge and its organization is considered in the next section.

Representing Domain Knowledge: States, Relations, and Strengths

Domain knowledge consists of states, unary and binary relations defined on states and other relations, and information about the strength of relations.

States.   There are two kinds of states: findings and hypotheses. *Findings* are observations describing the problem. There are two kinds of findings: soft (circumstantial or historical) and hard (laboratory or direct measurements). *Soft findings* tend to be categorical, weak, and easily determined. *Hard findings* are specific, strong, and often costly, dangerous, or time-consuming to determine. *Hypotheses* are partial descriptions of the disorder process causing the findings; that is, hypotheses explain the findings and constitute the problem-solver's diagnosis.[7]

Causal and Subtype Relations

Findings and hypotheses can be related by cause and subtype. Various larger structures are built out of these parts:

• *Etiological taxonomy:* a subtype hierarchy of hypotheses. These are the ultimate causes of disorders. For example, in medicine, these hypotheses include poisoning, an injury from falling down, infection by a virus, and psychological problems (refer to Figure 12.6). Associated with each hypothesis are findings or other hypotheses that it causes or that are caused by it. Hypotheses lower in the tree inherit properties of all hypotheses on the path to the root ("ANY-DISORDER"). Thus, bacterial meningitis has manifestations common to all infectious processes, such as fever and inflammation. The leaf-node hypotheses are the most specific causes, usually those that can be treated to alleviate the disorder.

The etiological taxonomy is actually a "tangled hierarchy" based on process relations. Proceeding below INFECTIOUS-PROCESS, the relations of each level are: "location," "chronicity," "class of causal agent," and "causal agent." For example, children of MENINGITIS are ACUTE-MENINGITIS and CHRONIC-MENINGITIS. Thus, each level of the taxonomy further characterizes *the kind of process* in some way. Under this interpretation, the top level of the etiological hierarchy pertains to events in the life process of the device: design, birth, ingestion, growth, injury, and so on. We have found this characterization of the etiological taxonomy to be useful in our initial attempts to apply it to computer software diagnosis.

There may be multiple etiologies requiring treatment. For example, a traumatic injury, such as falling and hitting one's head, can cause certain

---

[7]Technically, distinctions among states, such as "hypothesis," "soft finding" and "red-flag finding" are unary relations, which we express in metarules as (HYPOTHESIS $STATE), (SOFT-FINDING $STATE) and (RED-FLAG-FINDING $STATE). The states themselves are relations (e.g., (HEADACHE $PATIENT)), though as shorthand we write them as atomic propositions (e.g., HEADACHE). Thus, we write (HYPOTHESIS HEADACHE), rather than (HYPOTHESIS (HEADACHE $PATIENT)).

forms of bacterial meningitis. Here the treatable cause is really two etiologies: the bacteria must be treated and, if the patient is elderly, some means must be found to prevent the patient from falling again. (In medicine, this relation is sometimes called a "complication" (Szolovits & Pauker, 1978).)

• *Causal network:* hypotheses that characterize general states, neither findings (directly observed) nor etiologic hypotheses (pertaining to specific processes), which are related by cause. To give them a name, we call these general characterizations of abnormal conditions in the device *state/ categories.* An example in medicine is "unusual space-occupying substance in the brain," a nonobservable condition, which can have many etiologies. We have found it useful to distinguish between *substances* (or structural features) and *processes.* This does not lead to a complete causal model, but it does provide a useful discipline for our level of representation.[8]

• *Hypothesis subtype hierarchies:* hypotheses (either etiologic or state/category) related by subtype. For example, INTRACRANIAL-MASS has subtypes INTRACRANIAL-TUMOR, INTRACRANIAL-HEMATOMA, and INTRACRANIAL-MASS-OF-PUS. Substances are subtypes of substances; processes are subtypes of processes.

• *Finding subsumption hierarchies:* a presupposition hierarchy of findings. For example, HEADACHE subsumes HEADACHE-SEVERITY, HEADACHE-DURATION, and so on, because consideration of headache severity presupposes that the patient has a headache. In NEOMYCIN, a subsumption hierarchy is just a concise way of expressing inference relations among findings. Subsumption can be further characterized by relations such as "component of" and "specialization of" — distinctions we have not yet found to be useful for performance, but that might be useful for teaching.

Source, World-fact, Definitional and Process Relations

Other domain relations are:

• *Source:* a finding can be the source of a set of findings that are collected together. For example, the complete blood analysis is the source of the white cell count.

• *World-fact:* findings can be related by factual relations based on what

---

[8]One potential difficulty is that this representation is more principled than common medical knowledge. For example, in some cases we found that our expert made no distinction among a substance causing a lesion, the lesion itself, and its functional effects. Thus, a tumor is referred to as a type of lesion, a bit like saying that a pair of scissors is a kind of cut. Traversing a more articulated network may require different strategies than those used by the physician. Indeed, to turn the argument around, composition of relations through "compilation," or blurring of cause/subtype distinctions, as we observed in our expert, may be useful for efficient search. See Clancey (1985) for further discussion.

is usually true about the world. For example, males do not become pregnant; we can't determine directly if a 1-year-old has a headache; adults do not frequently suffer from ear infections. Because there tends to be a different underlying relation for each case we have encountered, this knowledge is currently proceduralized in NEOMYCIN in the form of "don't ask" rules. For example, "If the patient is under 2 years old, don't ask if he has a headache."

• *Definitional:* a finding can be defined in terms of other findings. For example, a neonate is a person under five months of age.

• *Process feature:* a finding or hypothesis can characterize in more detail the process partially described by another finding or hypothesis. For example, the patient's temperature characterizes the finding that he has a fever. A pain can be characterized by location and change in severity over time. Every hypothesis in the etiological taxonomy can be characterized by a set of similar process features. Thus, each process feature constitutes a relation upon which a generalization hierarchy can be based. For example, an organ-involvement hierarchy of hypotheses is based on an hierarchy of locations. (While our work has clarified these distinctions, in our limited domain and with our current knowledge base, we use such multiple hierarchies only in the most limited way.)

Figure 12.10 summarizes how findings and hypotheses can be related.

Strength of a Relation

Associated with causal relations is a "certainty factor" (CF), as used in MYCIN. For convenience in associating a CF with a causal relation between states, and to signify that the association is a heuristic that omits de-

FINDING subsumes
        is source of
        is further characterized by (process features are)
        defines
        is usually related to (don't ask when)

FINDING is evidence for (causes or caused by)

        HYPOTHESIS has process subtypes
                is etiologic parent of
                is caused-by

        HYPOTHESIS

FIGURE 12.10 Summary of basic domain relations in NEOMYCIN.

tails, the relation is called a *rule* and given a name. For example, "double vision is caused by increased intracranial pressure" is a rule with CF 0.8. We call the "if part" of the rule the *premise* and the "then part" the *conclusion*.[9] A rule premise is stated as a conjunction and each part involving a finding or hypothesis is called a *conjunct*.

Certainty is dynamically propagated through the network of states by a fairly complicated scheme. Basically, the maximum positive certainty is propagated upward and the minimum negative certainty downward through the multiple hierarchies. Assuming a closed world, a parent will be negative if all of its children are negative. Assuming mutual exclusivity, a sole believed child will inherit all the belief of its believed parent. The "cumulative" CF used in reasoning combines the CF directly inferred from rules with the propagated certainty.

A rule whose strength is very strong might be labeled as being an antecedent or trigger rule. These are defined in terms of activation criteria:

- A causal relation that is *definite,* having a certainty of 1.0, is generally labeled as an *antecedent rule,* so named because the rule will be considered, as part of the program's forward reasoning, when the premise of the rule is known to be true. For example, the double-vision rule is so labeled, so the program will conclude that the patient is experiencing increased intracranial pressure just as soon it learns that the patient has double vision.

- If an antecedent rule is also labeled as a *trigger rule,* then the program will attempt to satisfy the premise of the rule (by gathering additional findings if necessary) as soon as some specified part of the premise (one or more conjuncts) is satisfied.

Implicit Constraints of the Diagnostic Procedure

Metarules for tasks, as well as subtasks in the action of a metarule, are often ordered, and the criteria for this ordering is not explicit in the model. These ordering criteria are *constraints* which the problem solver is trying to satisfy or which are imposed by his or her reasoning ability. From our study of the metarules, we have identified several sources of constraints in diagnosis:

- *Cognitive Economy:* to incur the least costs in terms of mental effort, acting within the constraints of human memory and reasoning capability; specifically,
  - the size or organization constraints of memory for holding the

---

[9]Technically, we should call the "if part" the *antecedent* and the "then part" the *consequent,* but we reserve these terms for characterizing the indexing schemes for applying rules.

current problem description and partial solution ("working memory");

- the organization of domain knowledge ("long-term memory");
- the manner in which knowledge is retrieved ("activation criteria").

- *Computational or mathematical constraints:* properties of combinatorial, categorical, and probabilistic search.
- *Assumptions about the world:* disorder patterns, determined by the frequency of problems previously encountered, in turn determined by device weaknesses and external influences on devices. These assumptions or expectations can be used to constrain search.
- *Sociological economy:* to make the correct diagnosis, with the least expenditure of money and time, with due regard for the value placed on life and equipment, and efficiently communicating information needs and decisions.

In using a categorical search, asking general questions first, requesting hard data sparingly after consideration of soft data, maintaining focus until leads have been exhausted, and so on, etc., the problem solver is satisfying these constraints. We make an attempt in Appendix IV to indicate how the constraints are evidenced by individual metarules and their ordering. The main constraints of concern are correctness, efficiency (speed), and minimizing mental effort. Correctness is best evidenced by the systematic search of ESTABLISH-HYPOTHESIS- SPACE; efficiency, by the categorical reasoning of GROUP-AND-DIFFERENTIATE and the use of general questions by FINDOUT; and minimizing mental effort, by the nature of focus changes in PROCESS-FINDING and EXPLORE-AND-REFINE. The constraints can also be grouped in terms of the problem solver's goals (reflecting cognitive and sociological constraints) and constraints imposed by the task domain (mathematical and statistical).

Each task corresponds to some condition the problem solver is trying to make true; the metarules and task control knowledge constitute a procedure for making the condition true. We say that tasks *proceduralize* constraints (VanLehn & Brown, 1979), that is, they seek to *satisfy constraints by conditional actions.* For example, one of the correctness constraints relevant to EXPLORE-AND-REFINE is that all hypotheses placed on the differential must be pursued eventually. One of the ordered metarules for this task says, "If there is a sibling of the current focus that has not been pursued, then invoke PURSUE-HYPOTHESIS with the sibling as focus." Thus, subtasks with a given focus are invoked to satisfy constraints.

The structural properties of NEOMYCIN's domain knowledge reveal an interesting set of cognitive and task domain constraints. However, these properties are a strong reflection of the cases the model has been developed upon, so they are just a set of unrefuted or convenient (known to be false in general) assumptions:

- Every problem that will be encountered can be uniquely characterized in terms of some single disorder that has been diagnosed before
(an assumption known to be false in general). These "etiologies" can
be organized hierarchically in multiple ways, particularly according
to process relations.
- Evidence for disorders is generally weak, requiring categorical reasoning and inheritance of belief.
  - There are no "deep" causal models that explain the normal functioning of the device's behavior (an assumption known to be false
in general). Therefore, reasoning does not benefit from complete
structural (anatomical) information about the device.
  - There are few "pathognomonic" findings; that is, findings that
clearly identify the disorder.
- Nevertheless, groups of findings strongly "trigger" hypotheses because
of the high frequency with which the disorder exhibits that pattern
of findings, the disorder's relatively high a priori probability over other
hypotheses that explain the findings, and/or the fact that it is a serious
and treatable disorder.
- Patterns in finding/hypothesis relations make it possible to characterize findings as "nonspecific" versus "red-flag," "a good general question," "a good follow-up question."

The tasks and metarules are deliberately formalized at a level of detail
that will be useful for providing explanations to a student in a tutoring system. However, it is becoming apparent that constraint information is essential for deciding what parts of the model should be emphasized during
teaching and what parts might differ with individual abilities and preferences. For example, we might explain student errors by systematically relax-
ing the constraints of the procedure. We are currently extending the model
to include annotations that indicate: what is arbitrary and not part of the
model (e.g., order of GENERATE-QUESTIONS metarules); what may
reasonably vary among individuals (order of PROCESS-FINDING
metarules); what no person could logically expect to do differently (doing
FORWARD-REASON before information is received); what individuals
might do differently, but which would violate the principles of the idealized model (e.g., doing EXPLORE-AND-REFINE before GROUP-AND-
DIFFERENTIATE).

Note that NEOMYCIN's procedure doesn't reflect some of the most important constraints useful for the "present illness interview," namely the
constraints of human interaction that require the problem solver to
paraphrase finding requests in multiple ways and to cross-check information ("interface constraints"). We assume that the informant speaks the

model's language and is always reliable (see FINDOUT). Interactional methods for talking to patients are certainly a key part of what students learn in the classroom diagnosis games. In the six classroom transcripts we have analyzed, one third of the teacher's interruptions (10 of 30) are directed at giving practical advice of this sort.

In summary, at this stage in NEOMYCIN's development we are developing a procedural language that enables the program to articulate its reasoning. By studying the procedures we write down in this language, we may become able to represent them at a more principled level, in terms of the constraints they seek to satisfy. See Clancy, in press, for a significant expansion of this point. Also see page 383 for a discussion of an expert's awareness of constraints on his behavior.

EVALUATING THE MODE: SUFFICIENT PERFORMANCE AND PLAUSIBLE CONSTRAINTS

Having considered how NEOMYCIN's model is acquired and represented, we now turn to its evaluation: A general discussion of what the program really is, what it says about the nature of expertise, and what its limitations are. Evaluation is very difficult. At this time, we can only hope to explicate the issues and discuss how we're handling them, rather than describe formal, completed experiments.

In considering evaluation, we take NEOMYCIN as it exists today as an incomplete artifact, and we ask, "What is it?" What kind of program is it? What is its basis in fact? What does it tell us about human reasoning? About knowledge engineering? About computational modeling? This is an opportunity to take stock of the enterprise, criticize the program, and try to determine what has been accomplished.

Four perspectives are useful for evaluating the program, to be considered in this order:

1. *Performance:* Does the program run? Does its behavior (question asking and diagnosis) suitably match, on some domain of problems, the expert behavior we seek to model?
2. *Articulation:* Is the level of explicitness of the representation appropriate? Do the program's explanations of its behavior correspond to the statements made by an expert teacher explaining the tasks and rationale of diagnosis to students?
3. *Accuracy:* Does the program model human reasoning? Are the constraints of the tasks what experts seek to satisfy in their problem solving? Are the implicit assumptions about correctness, efficiency, and cognitive economy justified?
4. *Completeness:* Is the program a comprehensive model of diagnostic

reasoning? Are the domain knowledge structures and search techniques complete for some domain of problems?

The first two perspectives are concerned with the *sufficiency* of the model for different settings requiring expertise (refer to Figure 12.1). The second two perspectives examine whether this is a *plausible* model of human competence and whether it captures the full range of human diagnostic behavior. We evaluate NEOMYCIN's acquisition and representation from these perspectives in the sections that follow.

Performance of the Model: Problem Solving

Perhaps a nontrivial point, a prerequisite for claiming that NEOMYCIN is a model at all is that it runs: It "computes" behavior that we can match against the behavior of people. This is a property of the representation of the diagnostic procedure; it is structured into recursive subprocedures, with control information for stopping and printing results. Its activities are to gather information and construct a solution. Contrast this with the constraints (given on page 371) which the tasks implicitly satisfy. Such statements might capture what problem solvers try to accomplish and the background in which they work, but they do not specify the *process* by which consideration of specific domain knowledge and actions taken in the world interact. NEOMYCIN's metarules combine considerations of domain knowledge (via indexing relations) and working memory to conditionally invoke the right subtasks (with the right focus) to satisfy the task constraints.

NEOMYCIN solves problems at least as well as MYCIN. In particular, its conclusions are reasonably close to MYCIN's for the ten cases used in a double-blind evaluation of MYCIN (Yu et al., 1979). However, we demand much more of NEOMYCIN. Unlike MYCIN, it should:

- Reason in a focused, hypothesis-directed way. For example, if the infection is chronic, it should not explore acute subtypes of meningitis. In contrast, MYCIN's question-asking is undirected and exhaustive for all types of meningitis.
- Consider meningitis from initial information and decide what tests to request, such as a lumbar puncture. MYCIN is told that the patient has meningitis and that certain laboratory tests are available. NEOMYCIN must begin with more general, nonspecific findings such as "headache" and "malaise," consider meningitis, and decide when a lumbar puncture would be too dangerous to do.
- Consider competitors of meningitis and know when they are more likely. MYCIN has no knowledge of migraines, tension headaches, brain abscesses, etc. NEOMYCIN carries on a "differential diagnosis," know-

ing when to consider these competitors and how to contrast them.
- Reason more generally about findings; for example, determine what lab test to request, based on subtype and definitional information.

There are other differences in performance (e.g., as specified in the task FINDOUT and FORWARD-REASON), but these are the main ones. Our main technique for testing (and developing) the program is to run cases with different correct diagnoses, but having very similar initial findings. This tests the program's ability to elicit relevant additional information and to adopt different lines of reasoning appropriately. Trivially, the program should not always pursue meningitis. The same evaluation technique is essential for measuring completeness of the model as well. Evaluation of the order of questioning pertains most closely to matters of accuracy and is considered on page 379.

A not insignificant question is, "Why does NEOMYCIN work correctly at all?" There are two aspects to this. First, how can abstract explanations given by a physician (e.g., "look for associated symptoms"), coded as tasks and metarules, produce the right answer? Second, what is the nature of reasoning that allows us to completely separate the domain knowledge from the reasoning procedure? The issue of explanation is treated here; the more general characterization of reasoning is treated in the final section of this chapter.

It is plausible that the expert's explanations should constitute at least the outline of an effective procedure. Recall from the first section of this chapter that all behavior is explained in terms of the *effect* it will have on the expert's thinking. He says, "I'm trying to form and test my hypothesis set in some way." Indirectly, we take this to be his general *task* at that point — what he is trying to do — and write rules that will invoke that task and carry it out. A procedure written to have *the same effects on working memory* will generate the same questions as does the expert, with the same final diagnosis, and can be characterized abstractly by the same explanations supplied by the expert.

The question has a deeper side, however. Do NEOMYCIN's metarules really come from the expert? What do we supply from our knowledge of the constraints of diagnosis? All of the major tasks bear some relation to the expert's explanations, visible most clearly in the classroom discussions when he tells students what they should and should not be doing. (Recall the examples on page 364.) Most of the rules for FORWARD-REASON, FINDOUT, and ESTABLISH-HYPOTHESIS-SPACE are *inferred* from conclusions the expert states and the questions he asks. But the nature of the inferences are different. For example, FORWARD-REASON and FINDOUT consist of lists of metarules using straightforward domain relations such as SUBSUMES. That is, we inductively abstract patterns from expert behavior, based on our evolving knowledge of the relations among findings and hypotheses. The simple coappearance of findings in a problem solution is often sufficient to suggest metarules. (For example, the subsumption relation among findings suggests why "travel" would be mentioned at the same time as "lived in Mexico.")

However, ESTABLISH-HYPOTHESIS-SPACE is *a procedure involving search of a taxonomy*. We have to infer both the domain relations and subprocedures from patterns in the expert's questions. Explanations point the way at critical times, and the classroom discussions seem to confirm most of our analysis, as strategies we learn inductively are often stated explicitly in class (particularly the idea of looking up, then down the etiological taxonomy). But most of our confidence in the completeness of the procedure is based on *mathematical considerations of set manipulations*, concepts the expert never mentioned. The idea of getting the right answer into the differential, even at just the highest categorical level, and then winnowing down makes good mathematical sense. In this way, the metarules are designed to work: The constraints of set theory are adhered to at every turn.

In summary, NEOMYCIN's model is not supplied directly by the expert. It is *constructed* by relating his behavior to mathematically logical maneuvers within the data- and hypothesis-driven reasoning scheme. However, our views are strongly guided by the expert's emphasis on what he is trying to do—what he can accomplish, through new evidence, in terms of getting the right answer.

The relation of *empirical* and *rational* approaches for constructing a model has been a subject of much debate (e.g., see Anderson & Bower, 1980). Our methodology is summarized in Figure 12.11.

Given the logical basis for much of the model, we might wonder whether

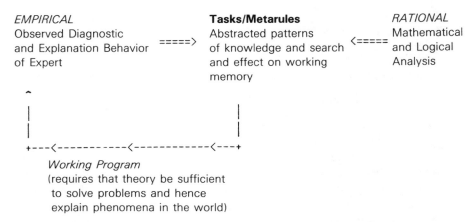

FIGURE 12.11 Combined empirical and rational methodology (After Anderson & Bower, 1980).

we could construct a proof that the program will always output the right diagnosis. One approach is to break the proof into parts:

1. Prove that the hypothesis that explains the findings or some more general hypothesis will be put into the differential.
2. Prove that it and its ancestors will be examined.
3. Prove that it will be refined to its subtypes and causes.

There are many subtle interactions to consider. For example, considering a hypothesis requires inferring evidence for it by some rule. A rule not applied immediately might be considered later. If a rule is not a trigger rule, it still might be invoked by the GENERATE-QUESTIONS task, but this task won't be invoked if the differential is already "adequate." Thus, a hypothesis might not be considered if belief in some alternative explanation is strong enough. Also, the problem is ultimately reduced to proving that the knowledge base's finding/hypothesis relations are complete and correct, a difficult assumption to start with and difficult to prove independently.

However, this analysis can be used to complement the usual test of running cases. Stepping through it, we discovered that NEOMYCIN did not examine ancestors of state/category hypotheses — a GROUP-AND-DIFFERENTIATE metarule was missing. We conclude that this approach is a worthwhile cross-check for developing the model.

Performance of the Model: Articulating Reasoning

Evaluating the explanation capability of NEOMYCIN is perhaps best done in a tutorial setting. Does the program use appropriate terminology? Does the program explain its question-asking with appropriate generalizations? A prototype explanation system demonstrates during problem-solving that the program's level of representation is apparently close to the terminology used by the expert (Hasling, Clancey, & Rennels, 1984). As we begin to use NEOMYCIN for teaching, major explanation issues include: (a) the proper mix of abstract and concrete statements; (b) terminology (e.g., task names like ESTABLISH-HYPOTHESIS-SPACE have to be restated); and (c) use of a model to selectively present and summarize reasoning.

One very interesting test of the program's ability to articulate its reasoning involves use of a "student modeling" program. We have transcripts of the discussions of six cases in a classroom, in which one student interviews (and diagnoses) another student who is pretending to have a particular illness. Can we combine a program that uses NEOMYCIN's model with some (hopefully) simple pedagogical rules, to predict not only when the teacher will interrupt the student/physician but (because of model violation) predict also what he will say? To do this, we either would need more case discussions in NEOMYCIN's domain, or would need to expand the program's domain of expertise.

Accuracy of the Model

By reduction of the metarules to constraint assumptions, and the separating out of accuracy in the *implementation* of the constraints, arguments about accuracy are reduced to showing that the principles upon which the model is based are valid. NEOMYCIN's design, in which the reasoning procedure is stated in a special, well-structured language, completely separate from the domain knowledge, helps makes these principles clear. We start by writing down how knowledge, working memory, and task behavior interact; then we study what we have written down. With the components of the model factored out this way, each can be examined for plausibility: Could human knowledge be structured hierarchically with multiple indices? Could working memory include a list of hypotheses? Does NEOMYCIN allow its differential to get "too long"? Is the recursive, single-argument invocation structure of tasks plausible? Similarly, we might evaluate the end condition mechanism, means for restoring context, and so on. In fact, there are three considerations, though with some common constraints: the *task/metarule control language, the content of the metarules, and the representation of domain knowledge.*

Competitive Argumentation

Our primary technique for constructing the model is a form of "competitive argumentation" described by VanLehn (1983; VanLehn, Brown, & Greeno, 1984). We enumerate alternative designs and choose among them in a principled way. For example, in the extended protocol (Appendix II, line 5), observe that the expert mentions evidence for increased intracranial pressure and goes on to use this information immediately. When NEOMYCIN was first given this case, it gathered additional information because "diplopia" did not make increased intracranial pressure certain. Why didn't the expert do this? We list some alternative "designs":

1. The expert *had* made a definite conclusion; NEOMYCIN's evidence rule is incorrect.
2. The expert knew of nothing that could disconfirm his current belief in increased intracranial pressure, and he believed that the current evidence was fully reliable and not susceptible to retraction. So there was no need to gather additional evidence; the current belief was high enough to be useful in any way.

3. The expert used the information tentatively, planning to try to disconfirm the hypothesis or the single finding upon which it was based, should this conclusion play a pivotal part in the final analysis (e.g., should it suggest that a dangerous, invasive test is necessary). That is, he is capable of retracting his conclusions and reconsidering his decisions.

Having listed these, we can now argue about whether other alternatives should be included, as well as which is most likely. Furthermore, given that most researchers would probably opt for the third ("allow retractions") alternative, and NEOMYCIN now uses the second ("assume reliability"), we can proceed to construct cases in which the program's behavior would fail to be an accurate model of how people reason, thus testing the hypothesis that NEOMYCIN is inaccurate in a particular way.[10]

Difficulties of Extracting Principles from Compiled Knowledge

One effect of experience is that simple domain facts are proceduralized into specific rules for using them, and that rules for controlling reasoning are composed and generalized. This effect is called "knowledge compilation" (Neves & Anderson, 1981). In attempting to formulate a competence model, we want to carefully decompose these rules and state how knowledge is used, separately from the facts themselves. That is, we want to "decompile" expert knowledge, to the extent possible, to get at the primitive knowledge organization and control that lie behind it. Evaluation of accuracy of the model takes place at this lower level.

However, separation of domain facts and abstract control may be difficult if compilation occurs in a principled way. A result of compilation might be systematically mistaken for a new principle, a primitive step of the diagnostic strategy. For example, consider a case in which a finding counts against a hypothesis. Suppose further that the hypothesis has not been considered yet, but is a "child" of some hypothesis that is about to be refined. Now, would the negative evidence be *consciously* noticed by the problem solver at refinement time, when the "children" are logged as hypotheses to pursue (placing them in the differential); or would it not occur until the problem solver focuses on that hypothesis and tries to confirm it? (Similarly, if you are using an agenda, do you note the evidence while putting the

---

[10]Indeed, taking this example, the inability to change conclusions that have been used to form other conclusions is very basic. We should examine the entire model critically from this perspective. For example, we are probably missing FORWARD-REASON metarules that detect that a prior conclusion must be changed or task interruptions (end conditions) that trigger reconsideration of the patient model.

task of pursuing the hypothesis on the agenda [and decide not to schedule it], *or* when you go to do the task?) It appears that there are no simple answers. It all depends on how long ago the finding was revealed, what the problem solver was thinking about at the time, how strongly he is swayed by other hypotheses, and so on.

A similar example suggests that we are dealing with a general problem about attention and focusing. Does the problem solver notice that a task such as testing a hypothesis is trivially done in some context, when he is looking for a new focus (e.g., in EXPLORE-AND-REFINE when examining hypotheses to pursue). Or is this noticed after the operation is scheduled and begun? Put another way, should the metarule predicate do look-up only and require the invoked task to observe and record completion?

In an expert, compilation of knowledge probably combines scheduling and task behavior. In a novice the separation might be more complete, so that although his behavior is methodical it is also clumsy, and inefficient by not being adapted to routine problems. This suggests that NEOMYCIN is a model of *competence* — what the expert is capable of doing (at the task level), rather than the actual operations (*performance*) he does for any given case. He is traveling on familiar roads and takes shortcuts that are compositions of primitive steps.

In building NEOMYCIN, it has been difficult to isolate unambiguous, principled paths by which the expert indexes knowledge. In some cases, more than one inference path is possible. Indeed, when information is useful for more than one inference path, it tends to become one of the "important general questions I always ask" rather than "something I need to confirm a specific hypothesis" (see Figure 12.12). In general, it can be unclear whether the expert is *indexing via findings* (asking things he knows will usefully modify his differential) or *indexing via hypotheses* that he currently cares about. As expert reasoning tends to be more data-directed (Chi et al., 1981), subgoals are set up by "trigger rules" (see PROCESS-FINDING in Appendix IV), rather than arising from a hypothesis-directed line of questioning (TEST-HYPOTHESIS). Rubin's model (Rubin, 1975) and ours differ in this respect. In fact, trigger rules occupy an interesting midway point in our model: They are a form of "compiled" knowledge that beginners need to be taught immediately if they are not to be extremely inefficient. Follow-up questions (CLARIFY-FINDING) are another manifestation of compiled knowledge that must be distinguished from deliberate attempts to confirm a hypothesis.

A model of competence is an idealized, "interpreted" statement of expert reasoning — the conscious steps an expert follows when reasoning in a "careful" mode, rather than routinely solving problems. We claim that the expert's knowledge, full of shortcuts as it is, can be expanded into princi-

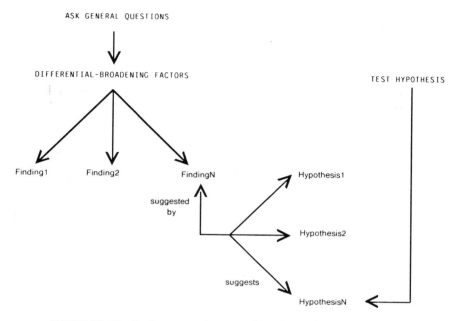

FIGURE 12.12   Finding request interpreted as a ''compiled'' general question or a deliberate attempt to confirm a hypothesis.

pled steps (or alternative principled procedures).[11] A principled procedure is an "interpretive simulation" in which the outward behavior of data requests and conclusions is matched, but many intermediate steps (e.g., decide to EXPLORE-AND-REFINE, choose a focus, REFINE-HYPO-THESIS, TEST-HYPOTHESIS, choose a finding) would only be consciously followed by a novice (knowing the right procedure) or an expert faced with a difficult problem.

---

[11]For example, we disallow a rule of the form, "Headache and fever triggers meningitis," because fever is evidence for an infection and meningitis is a kind of infection. The link between fever and meningitis should be made via propagation of belief from the "parent," infectious process. Otherwise, the evidence of a fever is considered redundantly. However, we allow a specialized rule stating "headache and high fever," or its more correct generalization, "headache and evidence for a fulminating infection," because the information about severity is not factored into the belief that the patient has an infection. In general, when we study a rule of the form "A implies B," we must always ask whether there is some hypothesis X in the knowledge base, where X implies B, meaning that the new rule should state that A implies X. In the example given here, we might also decide to have fever trigger infectious process, and write an ordinary evidence rule of high CF that headache implies meningitis. If the patient has a fever, infectious-process will be triggered; meningitis will then be "active" and noticed should it become known that the patient has a headache (see PROCESS-FINDING in Appendix IV and the metarule stated in Figure 12.9).

Furthermore, we must distinguish composition of procedure and medical knowledge with compilation of the medical knowledge base itself. As a set of schemas characterizing diseases, domain knowledge is knowledge of patterns in the world. The problem solver asks, "Of all the problems I have encountered in the world or am likely to encounter, what are the common causes, the serious findings, the general questions important to ask early on? What are the important causes, and useful follow-up questions?" These patterns all relate to importance in terms of *usefulness* (of a finding, based on the number of evidence links or its ability to discriminate) and *likelihood* (of a hypothesis). Thus, by case experience or general knowledge of the problem population, associations are specialized and abstracted, moving to the level of *heuristic knowledge* as opposed to simple facts about cause and subtype. By some form of structural analysis, it may become possible to derive a theory of when a finding would be a good general, trigger, or follow-up question in a given domain. (See Clancey in press for further discussion.)

In summary, in identifying primitive steps and knowledge relations in the diagnostic model, we need to be clear about:

• *Kinds of knowledge:* Figure 12.13 summarizes the basic elements of NEOMYCIN's diagnostic model. The model consists of domain knowledge relations (kinds of patterns); reasoning tasks for using this knowledge (a classification procedure concerning focus and activation of associations); and constraints that could be used to derive the procedure (the rationale for the procedure).

• *Kinds of "knowing":* We claim that a good teacher knows the domain relations and the general tasks for manipulating the differential. He can talk about this knowledge; it is not just reflected in his behavior. In class-

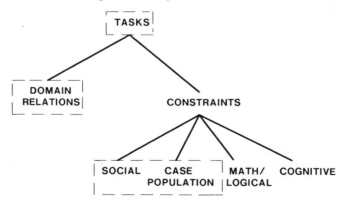

FIGURE 12.13 Types of knowledge relating to diagnostic strategy. Boxes indicate what a physician teacher can articulate.

room explanations, the teacher also mentions many social constraints, as well as some logical constraints (regarding search of trees) and some case experience constraints (such as correlations among findings). This is the substance of what we want to teach students.

However, some of the parts of NEOMYCIN's procedure, particularly FORWARD-REASON, describe what experts do and what is essential to construct a complete, runnable model. We believe that these tasks, corresponding to the "cognitive constraints," are generally not consciously considered by experts and needn't be taught. These tasks are not known in the same sense that "serious causes of sore throat" are known; they are automatic, they are how the mind does diagnostic classification. Perhaps FORWARD-REASON and its metarules are more a description of how the hardware works, rather than of a particular software program or strategy. Does ESTABLISH-HYPOTHESIS-SPACE fall in between, so that grouping and refining categories is automatic, but profits from conscious direction (to be aware of and cope with knowledge gaps)? Thus, given that NEOMYCIN is a model of what experts *do*, we must distinguish between the processor and the program, and then overlay a secondary description of what experts *know about what they do*.

We might conclude that a good teacher knows much more about problem solving than the average practitioner. But it is interesting to conjecture that the mark of an expert is precisely this *metaknowledge* of how he reasons: He knows that there are procedures, that these procedures derive from constraints that problem solving must respect, and that there is a mode of reflective reasoning for checking his behavior for completeness and consistency, both for solving difficult problems and for justifying his conclusions (teaching).

• *Origin and development of knowledge:* As discussed in this section, associations can be learned directly by rote (e.g., trigger rules), composed from primitive associations (e.g., headache and fever suggesting meningitis), generalized from experience (e.g., patterns of serious causes of a disease), or instantiated from more general principles (e.g., testing a given hypothesis might be learned as a specific set of things to do, following the principles for testing any hypothesis in general). Complicating the analysis, what is compiled from experience by one problem solver might be taught by rote to another. Finally, in relating behavior to motivational principles or a plan, we must remember that even a sequence of behavior could be generated by more than one plan. It is even possible that automatic behavior is nondeterministic, in the sense that the problem solver's actions are explained by multiple plans (compiled paths of association) and that no single intention consciously produced his actions (J.S. Brown, personal communication, 1986).

The decomposition of knowledge types in NEOMYCIN has allowed us to make substantial progress toward characterizing what physician teachers know and communicate with their students. However, we have barely begun to properly account for the origin and development of this knowledge.

Using a Competence Model to Explain Variant Behavior

By assumption, the "careful mode" of reasoning is principled. A good way to extract these principles is to give experts difficult problems. In this way we characterize the nature of expertise and how experts and novices might differ. In particular, as already suggested, a principled analysis of mechanisms has real relevance for explaining errors that people make in diagnosis.

A good example of a principled error appears in the classroom excerpt of Figure 12.14. Several students are interviewing the student W1, who is pretending to be a patient. The students' questions about sore throats are not random. The students appear to be looping in the task of CLARIFY-FINDING, following the principle of characterizing a finding in terms of the process (see Figure 12.15, parse 1). The error or misconception is that not every process question you might ask will be useful. If the students know the strategy of characterizing a finding, they are applying it at the right time with the right focus, but their knowledge base is not right: What are the useful follow-up questions to ask about a sore throat? In fact, there might not be any in general; instead a causal analysis should be undertaken (form a hypothesis and test it).

Given that the "useful follow-up questions" are determined by case experience, this analysis suggests that some parts of "compiled knowledge" may normally be taught directly, rather than learned from experience. That is, *experiential knowledge — knowledge about how to efficiently solve problems, given a certain population of cases — may be learned by apprenticeship, rather than individual practice.* Trigger rules and useful general questions, two other forms of "compiled knowledge" in NEOMYCIN, are probably also taught directly to students.

An alternative analysis of the sore throat protocol is that the students might not know what causes a sore throat, so their differential is inadequate. They might be following the strategy of ELABORATE-DATUM, a subtask of GENERATE-QUESTIONS, attempting to elaborate known symptoms until some new clue triggers a hypothesis. This illustrates how we might explain student behavior in a principled way in terms of the expert's diagnostic procedure operating on different domain knowledge. Having stated the procedure separately from the medical knowledge, we have a basis for inferring what students are doing, the state of their working

W2: Have you had a lot of sore throats?

W1: No.

M1: So your throat is getting worse? Is that what you are saying?

W1: Well, it's really bothering me and it just keeps dragging on. And before when I've had a sore throat, I had if for a few . . . a couple days.

M1: I see.

W1: It would be gone, but it just keeps dragging on and I'm just feeling terrible.

M2: Does anything make the sore throat better? Have you tried gargling?

W1: Um, well I haven't really done too much about it. I just thought it would go away, but it hasn't and as they said I'm just . . . I'm feeling really tired and not feeling very good.

M1: Your sore throat is always as painful when you get up in the morning or is it getting worse during a certain time of the day?

W1: Well, I guess I haven't noticed too much difference.

M1: I see.

TEACHER: Let me ask you a question. When you ask these questions about whether gargling makes it better or worse, or whether it's better certain times of the day, are you thinking about how that's going to help you move down different differential diagnoses?

M1: Uh huh.

FIGURE 12.14 Classroom discussion illustrating a diagnostic error.

memory (e.g., an inadequate differential), and hence their knowledge of domain relations. Thus, even if we don't need to teach the diagnostic procedure, it is useful for motivating teaching of domain facts and for detecting deficiencies.

We can of course generate an infinity of interpretations if we relax the assumption that the student's procedures are correct. For example, perhaps stuck with an inadequate differential, the students don't know enough to do GENERATE-QUESTIONS, but are instead attempting to "repair" their

FORWARD-REASON

CLARIFY-FINDING
(SORE THROAT)
any generally useful info

FINDOUT
WORSE?
GARGLING BETTER?
CHANGE DURING DAY?

ALTERNATIVE PARSE #2:
Same strategy, different working memory

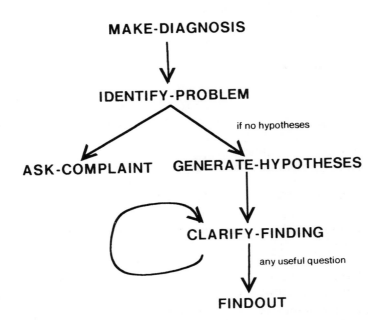

MAKE-DIAGNOSIS

IDENTIFY-PROBLEM

if no hypotheses

ASK-COMPLAINT **GENERATE-HYPOTHESES**

CLARIFY-FINDING

any useful question

FINDOUT

FIGURE 12.15 Alternative parses of student behavior shown in Figure 12.14.

procedure. They can't continue, so they are looping on the last successful operation. In addition, they might not know the useful follow-up questions to ask, but they know the principle that allows them to generate candidates. This kind of analysis could be pursued by competitive argumentation.

As another example of an incorrect procedure, consider the issue of when TEST-HYPOTHESIS can be interrupted. Suppose a finding becomes known that is relevant to some hypothesis that was previously considered, but that is not the current focus. Under what conditions does the problem solver notice the association and when will he actually shift attention to pursue the other hypothesis? Under one scheme, used by NEOMYCIN, "processing a finding" means deliberately widening attention to notice the relevance to any activated hypothesis. Under another scheme, the problem solver might only observe the relevance of findings to his current focus. The narrowly focused problem solver might never realize the significance of data to other hypotheses he cares about.

The very notion of a "task" as something that the problem solver does deliberately, a thinking problem he imposes upon himself, allows us to distinguish among problem solvers according to the tasks they bring upon themselves in various situations, such as when a new finding is revealed. When distinctions in the model have implications for correctness of the diagnosis, it will be important that the model be annotated at this level of detail, so the teaching program can know and point out the important tasks the students are failing to do.

Completeness of the Model

Whereas "accuracy" is concerned with the correctness of the assumptions and constraints of the diagnostic procedure, "completeness" is concerned with coverage of the model: Does a wider population of problems require more problem-solving techniques? Given the association between metarules and constraints, this question approximates asking whether we have identified all of the relevant constraints that the task demands, and taken into account all of the relevant capabilities of human reasoning.[12] As already stated, NEOMYCIN's problem domain does not require all forms of diagnostic reasoning that have been studied elsewhere. Without attempting to examine the underlying issues, we simply list many of the limitations we know about:

- Reasoning about structure and function of the body (Davis, 1983; Genesereth, 1984).

---

[12]Naturally, testing the program for accuracy may suggest ways in which the program is incomplete (e.g., the possibility of retracting conclusions).

- Analogical reasoning using "device models" (Gentner & Stevens, 1983).
- Interview techniques for getting reliable information from laymen (e.g., commonsense ways of detecting weight loss; finding out whether the patient has had rheumatic fever; knowing what the "white pill" is).
- Description of causality and disease processes on multiple levels of abstraction (Patil, et al., 1981).
- Distinguishing among different forms of "subsumption."
- Temporal reasoning: onset and progression of disease.
- Using probabilistic information about findings, such as frequency information, to bias and rule out hypotheses.
- Determining whether there is adequate evidence for a hypothesis should be contextual, taking into account other hypotheses and unexplained findings (Cohen & Grinberg, 1983).
- The problem solver must strive for coherency by explaining the "important" findings and explaining findings inconsistent with each other or which violate expectations formed by his hypotheses. The program's "differential" should be a "case specific model" (Patil, et al., 1982) that merges findings and hypotheses.
- A real-world expert must deal with multiple, interacting, concurrent problems. The problem solver must separate causes from complications (Pople, 1982; Rubin, 1975; Szolovits & Pauker, 1978).
- NEOMYCIN's causal network is too simplistic to determine the completeness of its strategies. For example, when the causal connections between data and the taxonomy are long and complex, it is not feasible to follow each path (possible cause), testing and confirming intermediate states along the way (Pople, 1982). However, as mentioned in the section "The Hypothesize-and-test theory of diagnosis," such an articulated model may even require different strategies than used by people, for it poses different search problems. We speculate that experts are searching a highly composed model of disorders, not based on clear subtype and causal distinctions, but allowing for highly efficient search.
- Urgency, cost, the ability to treat a disease, and human values in general must be factored into the model explicitly.

Demonstrating the difficulty of this problem, the exclusions are more complex than what the model includes. Of course, the aim of the work has been to develop a representation useful for teaching, not the most comprehensive model of diagnosis. It is premature to "flesh out" the model in all possible ways. However, gaps in the model require that we argue for its extensibility, particularly within the task/metarule/end-condition framework, which is the main product of this effort. Here the main considerations are both *psychological*, at the level of interrupting and restoring focus of attention and metalevel reasoning about an agenda of tasks; and *representational*, at the level of belief maintenance, the constructed model of the problem, and intersection-search procedures.

Summary of Evaluation

We have argued that evaluation of the accuracy and completeness of the model should focus on the assumed constraints pertaining to knowledge structure, task requirements, human memory, and reasoning. Evaluation of performance and articulateness requires exercising the program in different, complex settings, including consultation, teaching, and learning. More specifically, we find ways in which the same knowledge must be used in multiple ways. We examine how a particular knowledge organization (e.g., subsumption) is used by different strategies and how a given strategy is applied in different contexts for a single case. Multiple cases enable us to vary the task, preventing us from tailoring strategies to particular cases, and revealing not only where the model falls short but what properties of the task domain made the model appear adequate in other cases. Applying the model to other domains, such as computer software failure diagnosis, further reveals unprincipled or inadequately specified parts of the model (e.g., what is an etiological taxonomy?), and brings out assumptions about the task domain that are implicit in the model (e.g., the nature of the informant).

CONCLUSIONS

The driving force in NEOMYCIN's development has been to design a knowledge representation that can be used to model human diagnostic reasoning and explanation capability. The essential (and novel) aspect of the design is representation of the diagnostic procedure as abstract tasks that capture what structural effect the problem solver is trying to have on his evolving model of the problem. These tasks are invoked in a rule-like way that strongly emphasizes the problem solver's use of relational knowledge about the domain in choosing his or her next move.

What is the nature of reasoning that enables such a model of expertise to work? First, there must be relatively more stereotypical situations (tasks and metarule conditions) than special case rules. It must be possible for problem solving to proceed step-by-step in a principled way (even if this would be unnecessary for the experienced problem solver), without the user encountering combinatorial problems. Second, knowledge about possible solutions and problem features must be richly structured. These relations provide means for multiple, orthogonal hierarchical indexes that greatly facilitate search. Note that these constraints are general; they are what enable us to form *any* abstract model of strategy.

One purpose of NEOMYCIN has been to develop a language for representing abstract strategies. Follow-on work is concerned with using them in explanation (Hasling, et al., 1984) and constructing a student model (London & Clancey, 1982). There are many advantages that can be useful in building any expert system (Clancey, 1983b). In our continuing development we are slowly, but constantly, adding to the strategic model. We are still at the point where a carefully chosen case will reveal one or two important limitations in the model. In short, we are following an "enumeration methodology": Writing what we want to study in some language, organizing the collection to find underlying themes, and further developing the language to express important distinctions.

How applicable is the diagnostic procedure to other domains? The limitations described in section "A Causal Model of What Happened to the Patient" suggest that the model is far from complete. For example, electronic diagnosis often requires low-level causal analysis, working backward from symptoms to component failures (Davis, 1983). However, at a higher and more functional level, particularly for an expert who has debugged a particular device such as a given television or automobile model many times, we can expect that stereotypical matching as in infectious disease diagnosis will occur. In this sense, NEOMYCIN's diagnostic procedure will carry over to other domains. It should be viewed as a subset of a complete procedure, rather than as a specialized or oversimplified model.

What is the relation of NEOMYCIN to what the expert does? The model can be used to explain his or her behavior in the sense that it can generate it; but above the level of finding requests and hypotheses, the procedure is an abstraction, not steps the expert always consciously considers. In this sense, the diagnostic procedure is a *grammar* for parsing a series of information-gathering questions. By analogy with the grammar of natural language, it may reflect the innate nature of human reasoning, specifically how knowledge is remembered. Given that the procedure we have formalized operates entirely upon stereotypic knowledge of disorders, it can be characterized as a *procedure for searching classification knowledge.* Or, since all knowledge may be in some sense compiled (e.g., encoded hierarchically as differences from patterns), the diagnostic procedure is analogous to Kolodner's "executive strategies" for remembering (Kolodner, 1983). However, the NEOMYCIN model pertains to the entire information-gathering procedure of diagnosis, not just a single probe of memory.

As a matter of practice, the diagnostic procedure has some of the same value to an expert that knowledge of grammar provides for a writer. As in grammar, some elements of diagnosis must be taught or at least enforced early on. The orientation toward "things to think about" is directly useful for teaching. Particularly, the idea of thinking in a hypothesis-directed way must be encouraged (but is this because students simply lack the automatic associations?). Perhaps the grammar or logic of diagnosis need not be conveyed explicitly, but certainly it is useful for a teacher of medicine to know it. How often have teachers criticized students, when the latter were just following the procedure used by experts for coping with limited knowledge?

The idea of teaching students strategies or "how to think" has received considerable attention from AI researchers. Papert's work with LOGO (Papert, 1980) is perhaps the most well-known experiment in applying computational ideas to help problem solving in general. Our work raises interesting questions in this regard. For example, could someone familiar with our description of EXPLORE-AND-REFINE in terms of "looking up and looking down," and viewing diagnosis as a set-construction activity, provide *better* explanations than those given by our expert-teacher? That is, having studied the constraints of the task more systematically than has the expert, can we give students a better idea of what they should be trying to do?

A teacher using NEOMYCIN's model could go a step beyond Polya (1957) and others (e.g., Schoenfeld, 1981) who have tried to teach reasoning strategy to students. To contrast this with other research in teaching general strategies, we emphasize the role of domain relations ("structural knowledge") in selecting among different operators that affect the hypothesis space. From our perspective, Polya's heuristics might seem vague and unworkable (Newell, 1983) because:

1. They are not presented as parts of a comprehensive task structure or metastrategy (as pointed out by Schoenfeld).
2. They lack a premise part that refers to working memory, the situation in which the problem solver will find them to be useful for something he is trying to do; that is, they are not stated as conditional operators.
3. The way in which they index particular mathematical solution methods is not clearly worked out; that is, the domain relation vocabulary is missing.

NEOMYCIN's relational vocabulary consists of causal, subtype, and process relations that classify and link findings and hypotheses. Some of the specific terms considered in this chapter are: finding, soft-finding, red-flag finding, substance, and process location. These terms are like parts of speech and syntactic units that classify and organize the problem solver's domain lexicon. This is *knowledge for organizing knowledge*: a means for expressing and using knowledge. A diagnostic strategy says in effect, "To accomplish a certain task, think about some finding (or hypothesis) that is related to your current hypotheses (or known findings) by the X relation." "To refine a hypothesis, consider *common causes*. What are the common causes of a sore throat?" As a self-directive, this is an example of metacognition. Strategies orient the problem solver toward constructing and refining an appropriate problem space. They constitute the *managerial knowledge* by which the problem solver directs his or her attention and so brings his or her expertise to bear on the problem. Having gone beyond MYCIN's single-layer, "quick association" model of thinking (as Schoenfeld has characterized traditional expert systems), we are poised to experiment with teaching strategic reasoning.

Indeed, we have now entered a strange sort of loop in our research. We are teaching the diagnostic strategy to research assistants to make them better computer program debuggers. (The general question, "Has the patient undergone surgery?" becomes "Has this program been edited since it last worked?") This experience suggests ways to generalize the model, helps us to develop ways to teach it, and may enable us to implement the teaching program itself more efficiently. And so again we find ourselves amid the complex web of learning, teaching, and problem solving.

APPENDIX I: BASIC TERMINOLOGY OF DIAGNOSIS

Diagnostic Problem: A situation in which a device exhibits behavior (findings) that suggest that it is malfunctioning. A diagnostic problem has a "cause" that, for our purposes, is one of a set of known processes (hypotheses). Example: A severe headache for a week and double vision in a patient is a diagnostic problem.

Finding: An observable problem feature, generally characterizing the problem in a very narrow, nonexplanatory way. In medicine, these are signs, symptoms and laboratory data. Example: A headache is a finding.

Hypothesis: An interpretation of findings in terms of underlying substances and processes that produce them. A hypothesis can be said to "explain" the findings. Example: "Space-occupying substance in the brain" is a hypothesis.

Differential: The most specific set of hypotheses that the problem solver is considering. By the "single-fault assumption" these hypotheses are mutually exclusive and therefore competing. Example: A typical differential might be brain abscess and chronic meningitis.

Domain Knowledge: Findings, hypotheses, and relations among them that enable inferences to be drawn about their applicability. Example: Medication "subsumes" antibiotics, analgesics, and steroids. Example: An "evidence relation" links a finding to a hypothesis that causes or might be caused by it, as viral meningitis is caused by exposure to the disease.

Task: What the problem-solver is trying to do with respect to findings, hypotheses, and his or her domain knowledge. A task is accomplished by a procedure of ordered conditional actions, called metarules. We say that the metarules "achieve" the task. For example, the metarules of the task PURSUE-HYPOTHESIS test and refine a given hypothesis. Primitive tasks are to request information about a finding and to make an inference about a finding or hypothesis.

Focus: The finding, hypothesis, or differential that is the argument to a task; for example, the hypothesis that the problem solver is trying to test.

Metarule: A conditional statement that partially accomplishes a task by invoking subtasks. For example, "If the task is to establish the space of hypotheses relevant to this problem and the differential has been reduced and refined, then ask general questions." Metarules are either conditional steps in a procedure or ordered alternative methods for accomplishing a task.

Constraint: Some condition that the problem solver must try to satisfy, such as to solve the diagnostic problem in the shortest amount of time; or some limitation or capability of his ability to reason that he must cope with, such as his ability to remember the extent of his knowledge or the differential.

APPENDIX II: DETAILED ANALYSIS OF A PROTOCAL

In the protocol that follows, annotations indicate the NEOMYCIN tasks that would generate the finding requests and hypothesis assertions made by the expert.[13] Numbers in parentheses refer to numbered statements that support the interpretation. *Annotations* precede the expert behavior they are intended to explain. This analysis illustrates the knowledge acquisition technique, the nature of the diagnostic problem, and the model's representation in terms of tasks, focus, and domain relations. Note that the metarules that cause the tasks to be invoked are not indicated here; they are listed in Appendix IV. Figure 12.16 shows a parse tree of the physician's five data requests, which appear *italicized* in the protocol. By comparison with Figure 12.5, this protocol can be seen to illustrate the central part of the diagnostic procedure, but not most of the tasks.

---

[13]Although we have a prototype modeling program that can generate similar annotations, they are still not nearly as good as what we can do by hand. In the interest of making NEO-MYCIN's model as comprehensible as possible, it seems best to show here the best interpretations we can supply.

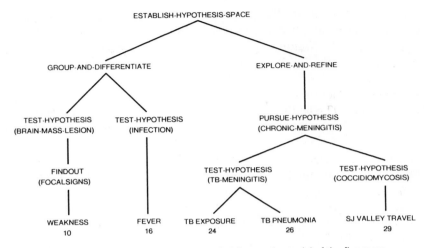

FIGURE 12.16   Parse with respect to the diagnostic model of the five questions asked in the protocol.

1 KE: What I wanted to do different in these cases is to pick cases where I thought you might have to request more information than what I gave originally so we can look at a little bit of that process. In these cases especially, you can be as complete as possible in telling me what you are thinking.

2 MD: So you just want to give me skeleton data?

3 KE: Yes, we'll see how it goes. I am going to try to follow the general principle we had established, which was to tell you why the person was in the hospital and how they got to the point where the lumbar puncture was done.

4   First example: A 15-year-old female. A two-week history of headache, nausea, vomiting; and diplopia one day prior to admission.
    task = IDENTIFY-PROBLEM
    task = FORWARD-REASON (headache, nausea, vomiting,
      diplopia, headache-duration, nausea-duration, vomiting-duration, diplopia-duration)
    structural knowledge: diplopia is a serious (red flag)
      CNS finding
    task = PROCESS-FINDING (diplopia)
    task = APPLY-ANTECEDENT-RULES (causes of diplopia
      evidence rule: diplopia caused-by increased-pressure-in-brain (6)

task = PROCESS-FINDING (diplopia-duration)

task = APPLY-ANTECEDENT-RULES (mentioning diplopia-duration)

definition: max(duration of CNS findings) = CNS-problem-duration (5)

5 MD: (I think this would be a very good case to illustrate whether you should do a lumbar puncture or not.) This is somebody who has evidence of perhaps a pressure buildup in the brain for a two-week period of time.

[Causal explanation: how pressure buildup causes diplopia]

6   The diplopia comes because as the pressure builds up in the brain, you can't focus your eyes properly. It is a very sensitive indicator. One of the nerves that enervates the movement of the eyes together is the first one that is impaired as the pressure builds up,

task: PROCESS-HYPOTHESIS (increased-pressure-in-brain) (7)

7   so that I would be concerned in this situation of increased pressure in the brain

task: APPLY-ANTECEDENT-RULES (causes of increased-pressure-in-brain)

evidence rule: increased-pressure-in-brain -> brain-mass-lesion)

task: PROCESS-HYPOTHESIS (brain-mass-lesion) (8)

add differential: brain-mass-lesion

task: PURSUE-HYPOTHESIS (brain-mass-lesion)

task: REFINE-HYPOTHESIS (brain-mass-lesion)

structural knowledge: brain-mass-lesion subsumes brain-tumor, hematoma, and collection of pus.

8   and worry about tumor—a mass lesion of some type: a collection of blood, a collection of pus.

task: PROCESS-FINDING (serious-CNS-finding)

task: APPLY-ANTECEDENT-RULES (serious-CNS-finding)

evidence rule: serious-CNS-finding -> meningitis (9)

task: PROCESS-HYPOTHESIS (meningitis)

add differential: meningitis

task: APPLY-EVIDENCE-RULES (known findings activated by meningitis)

evidence rule: CNS-problem-duration -> chronic-meningitis (9, 22)

replace differential: meningitis -> chronic-meningitis

9   If it is a meningitis it is clearly a chronic one because we are talking about a two-week history.

         task: GROUP-AND-DIFFERENTIATE (brain-mass-lesion, chronic-meningitis)

         structural knowledge: brain-mass-lesion is a focal process; (12) chronic-meningitis is a systemic process.

         task: FINDOUT (focal-manifestations) (13)

         structural knowledge: focal-manifestations subsume diplopia (13)

         structural knowledge: focal-manifestations subsume weakness (14)

         task: FINDOUT (weakness)

10   The next historical question that I would want to know: *Does she have any weakness anywhere in her body? One side weaker than the other?*

11 KE: Why do you ask that?

12 MD: Since this picture is very suggestive of a focal lesion in the brain,

13   I am wondering if there are any focal manifestations other than double vision,

         [Causal explanation: that brain problem affects body extremity]

         [Structural knowledge: focal neurological findings subsume one-sided hand-weakness and leg-weakness]

14   e.g., "My hand right has been very weak" and I would wonder if there is something happening in the brain which enervates the right hand. Or, has she been having trouble walking, with one leg being weaker than the other, or is her balance off. Those are what are called focal neurological findings.

15 KE: Okay. Focal signs in general . . . unknown.

         task: GROUP-AND-DIFFERENTIATE (brain-mass-lesion, chronic-meningitis) (18)

         structural knowledge: chronic-meningitis is an infection

         task: TEST-HYPOTHESIS (infection) (18)

         evidence rule: fever - > infection (21)

         task: FINDOUT (fever)

16 MD: *Has she had fevers?*

17 KE: Unknown.

18   I think that is an important question to help distinguish between an infectious cause versus a noninfectious cause.

    [Structural knowledge: blood clot = hematoma and
    brain tumor are not infectious causes]

19   A noninfectious cause being a blood clot or brain tumor.

20 KE: So the fact that if there weren't a fever, that would suggest
    . . . ?

21 MD: Not having a fever does not necessarily rule out an infection.
    But if she had a fever, it would be more suggestive of it.

22   The situation we are dealing with is a chronic process.
     task: TEST-HYPOTHESIS (chronic-infection)
     evidence rule: low grade fever -> chronic-infection (23)

23   Sometimes with chronic infections fever can be low or none
    at all.
     task: PURSUE-HYPOTHESIS (chronic-meningitis)
     task: REFINE-HYPOTHESIS (chronic-meningitis)
     structural knowledge: chronic-meningitis subsumes
      TB-meningitis, fungal-meningitis, and partially-
      rx-bacterial-meningitis (33)
     add differential: TB-meningitis, fungal-meningitis,
      and partially-rx-bacterial-meningitis
     task: EXPLORE-AND-REFINE (TB-meningitis, fungal-
      meningitis, and partially-rx-bacterial-meningitis)
     task: PURSUE-HYPOTHESIS (TB-meningitis)
     task: TEST-HYPOTHESIS (TB-meningitis)
     evidence rule: tuberculosis-exposure -> TB-meningitis
     task: FINDOUT (tuberculosis-exposure)

24   *Has she had any exposure to tuberculosis?*

25 KE: No. No TB risk.
     task: PROCESS-FINDING (negative TB-risk)
     task: FINDOUT (TB-risk)
     structural knowledge: TB-risk subsumes tuberculosis-
      pneumonia
     task: FINDOUT (tuberculosis-pneumonia)
     structural knowledge: pneumonia subsumes tuberculosis-
      pneumonia (26)
     task: FINDOUT (pneumonia)

26 MD: *No recent pneumonia that she knows of? Tuberculosis-*
    pneumonia?

27 KE: Let me see how complete "TB risks" is. According to MYCIN,
    they include one or more of the following: Positive intermedi-
    ate trans-PPD; history of close contact with person with ac-
    tive TB; household member with past history of active TB;

atypical scarring on chest x-ray; history of granulomas on bi-
opsy of liver, lymph nodes, or other organs.
> task: FORWARD-REASON
> > (+PPD, contact-TB, family-TB, x-ray-TB,
> > granulomas)
> structural knowledge: TB-risk subsumes
> > +PPD, contact-TB, family-TB, x-ray-TB,
> > granulomas

28 MD: That's pretty solid evidence against a history of TB.
> task: EXPLORE-AND-REFINE (fungal-meningitis and
> partially-rx-bacterial-meningitis)
> task: PURSUE-HYPOTHESIS (fungal-meningitis)
> task: REFINE-HYPOTHESIS (fungal-meningitis)
> structural knowledge: likely fungal-meningitis causes
> are coccidiomycosis and histoplasmosis (33)
> add differential: coccidiomycosis and histoplasmosis
> task: PURSUE-HYPOTHESIS (Coccidiomycosis)
> task: TEST-HYPOTHESIS (Coccidiomycosis)
> evidence rule: San-Joaquin-Valley-travel -> Coccidi-
> omycosis
> task: FINDOUT (San-Joaquin-Valley-travel)
> structural knowledge: travel subsumes San-Joaquin-Valley-
> travel (29)
> task: FINDOUT (travel)

29   *Has she traveled anywhere? Has she been through the Cen-*
        tral Valley of California?

30 KE: You asked TB risks because?

31 MD: I asked TB risks because we are dealing here with an indo-
        lent (chronic) infection since we have a two-week history.

32   I am thinking, even before I have any laboratory data,

33   of infections, chronic infections are most likely. So I'll ask a
        few questions about TB, cocci, histo and other fungal in-
        fections.

34 KE: Histo is a fungal infection?
        [structural knowledge: histo location is Midwest]
        [structural knowledge: cocci location is Arizona and
        California]

35   Histoplasmosis is a fungus infection of the Midwest. Cocci is
        the infection of Arizona and California.

36 KE: So you are focussing now on chronic infections. Why would
        you look at the history now before doing anything else?

37 MD: I am trying to approach it as a clinician would. Which would be mostly to get a lot of the historical information and do a physical exam, then do a laboratory.

38   A lot of times, people think *from* the laboratory, whereas I think you should think *for* the laboratory. People are talking more about that now, especially because the cost of tests are an issue. You can get a lot from just talking with the patient. I could ask for the LP results, then go back and ask questions. But without knowing the LP results, which would bias me in the way I am going to ask the questions.

39 KE: This helps you. . . .

40 MD: This is the way you approach a patient.

APPENDIX III:
EXPERT-TEACHER STATEMENTS OF DIAGNOSTIC STRATEGY

We summarize here the general principles of the model, with excerpts from expert problem-solving and classroom protocols. The tasks of the model are a set of directives for changing focus, testing hypotheses, and gathering information. Note the expert-teacher's method of combining abstract and concrete explanations.

- ESTABLISH-HYPOTHESIS-SPACE — Establish the breadth of possibilities, then focus.

TEACHER: . . . All the cases we have had have fit pretty nicely into trying to establish a breadth of possibilities and then focussing down on the differential within one of the categories.

- GROUP-AND-DIFFERENTIATE — Ask yourself, "What are the general processes that could be causing this?"

TEACHER: Do you have in mind certain types of sore throats that . . . ? Because the types of questions that you ask early on, once you have a sense of the problem, would be to ask a couple of general questions maybe that could lead you into other areas to follow up on, rather than zeroing in.

STUDENT: Ok.

TEACHER: I was asking that because I think it's important to try to be as economical as possible with the questions so that each question helps you to decide one way or the other. At least with sore throat and my conception of sore throat, I have a hard time thinking of how different types of pain and different types of relief pattern are going to mean different etiologies to the sore throat. . . .

TEACHER
(later):   Ok, so we think about infectious, but what other things might be running through your mind in terms of broadening out again? We've got a new set offindings now, besides fever and sore throat, we have. . .

- EXPLORE-AND-REFINE — Scan the possibilities and choose one to explore in more detail.

TEACHER: Anything else? Well there are probably a couple of other areas to think about, . . . you know, like autoimmune diseases, inflammation of the throat . . . Why don't we get back to infections now, because we have a story of fever and sore throat, that is a common problem with infectious diseases. So we're talking about strep throat, we're talking about upper-respiratory, viral . . . Any other type of infectious problem . . . ?

STUDENT: . . . Pneumococcus would give you sore throat too, right?

TEACHER: Pretty rarely.

TEACHER (different case):   Well, how about some questions about mononucleosis now. I'd have you zero in on that.

- FORWARD-REASON — Ask yourself, "What could cause that?" Look for associated symptoms.

TEACHER: Well, what's another possibility to think about in terms of weakness? What do a lot of older people think of when they just think of being weak, a common American complaint. Or a common American understanding of weakness. How about tired blood?

STUDENT: Iron deficiency.

TEACHER: I think of anemias.

TEACHER (different case):   Most important is to develop a sense of being reasonably organized in approaching the information base and trying to keep a complete sense of not homing in too quickly. Look for things to grab onto, especially if you have a nonspecific symptom like headache, weakness. Ten million people in the country probably have a headache at this given point in time. What are the serious ones, and what are the benign ones? Look for associated symptoms. Some associated symptoms definitely point to something severe, while others might not.

- REFINE-HYPOTHESIS — Ask yourself, "What are the common causes and the serious, but treatable causes?"

TEACHER: What anemias do young people get?

TEACHER (different case):   What diseases can wind up in congestive heart failure? Congestive heart failure is not a diagnosis, it's kind of an end-stage physiology and there are lots
of diseases that lead into congestive heart failure; lots of
processes, one is hypertension. What's the other most common one? There are two that are common in this country.
One is hypertension, what's the other most common one?

STUDENT: Atherosclerosis?

• TEST-HYPOTHESIS — Ask yourself, "How can I check this hypothesis?"

TEACHER: How can you check whether someone is anemic? What
question might you ask?

• ASK-GENERAL-QUESTIONS — Ask general questions that might
change your thinking.

TEACHER: Well, that's an important question I think. Sometimes you
can ask it very generally, like, "Is there anything . . . have
you had any major medical problems or are you on any
medications?" Then people will come back and tell you.
And that's an important issue to establish, whether somebody is a compromised host or a normal host because a normal host. . . . Then you have a sense of what the
epidemiology of diseases is in a normal host . . . When you
talk about compromised host, you're talking about everything changing around, and you have to consider a much
broader spectrum, different diagnoses. So, you might ask
that question more specifically, you know, "Are you taking any medications or do you have any other medical
problems, like asthma," or sometimes they're taking steroids.
Those types of general questions are important to ask early
on, because they really tell you how soon you can focus
down.

STUDENT: Are you on any medication right now?

• GENERATE-QUESTIONS — Try to get some information that suggests hypotheses.

TEACHER: You're jumping around general questions and I think that's
useful. I don't know where to go at this point. So this is
the appropriate time for a kind of a "buckshot" approach
. . . every direction till we latch onto something that we
can follow up, because right now we just have a very nonspecific symptom.

APPENDIX IV: THE DIAGNOSTIC PROCEDURE

This section describes in detail the content of NEOMYCIN's metarules. The tasks are listed in depth-first calling order, assuming that they are always applicable (refer to Figure 12.5). For each substantial task (FORWARD-REASON, FINDOUT, ESTABLISH-HYPOTHESIS-SPACE and its subtasks), we attempt to list exhaustively all of the implicit assumptions about task and cognitive constraints proceduralized by the metarules. These are an essential part of the model. The model is constantly changing; this is a snapshot as of July 1985. To give an idea of how the program is evolving, metarules now on paper are listed as "< <proposed> >."

CONSULT

This is the top-level task. A single metarule unconditionally invokes MAKE-DIAGNOSIS and then prints the results of the consultation. (We have disabled MYCIN's therapy routine because the antibiotic information was out of date; it would be invoked here.)

MAKE-DIAGNOSIS

A single unconditional metarule invokes the following tasks: IDENTIFY-PROBLEM, REVIEW-DIFFERENTIAL, and COLLECT-INFORMA-TION. REVIEW-DIFFERENTIAL simply prints out the differential, modeling a physician's periodic restatement of the possibilities he or she is considering. (In a teaching system, this would be an opportunity to question the student.) Hypothesis-directed reasoning is done by COLLECT-INFORMATION.

IDENTIFY-PROBLEM

The purpose of this task is to gather initial information about the case from the informant, particularly to come up with a set of initial hypotheses.

1. The first metarule unconditionally requests "identifying information" (in medicine, the name, age, and sex of the patient) and the "chief complaint" (what abnormal behavior suggests that there is an underlying problem requiring therapy). The task FORWARD-REASON is then invoked.

2. If no diagnoses have been triggered (the differential is empty), the task GENERATE-QUESTIONS is invoked.

FORWARD-REASON

The metarules for FORWARD-REASON iterate over the list of new conclusions, first invoking CLARIFY-FINDING for each finding and then PROCESS-FINDING for each serious or "red-flag" finding. PROCESS-FINDING is then invoked for nonspecific findings and PROCESS-HYPOTHESIS for each hypothesis. These tasks perform all of the program's forward reasoning.

It is important to "clarify" findings, that is, to make sure that they are well specified, before doing any forward reasoning. Thus, before considering that the patient has a fever, we first ask what his temperature is. "Red-flag" in contrast with "nonspecific" findings often trigger hypotheses; they are serious, indicative of a real problem to be treated and not just a "functional" imperfection in the device;[14] nonspecific findings may very well be explained by the hypotheses that red-flag findings quickly suggest. These considerations are all matters of cognitive economy, means to avoid back-tracking and to make a diagnosis with the least search.

CLARIFY-FINDING

Using subsumption and process relations among findings, these metarules seek more specific information about a finding, asking two types of questions:

1. Specification questions (e.g., if the finding is "medications," program will ask what drugs the patient is receiving).
2. Process questions (e.g., if the finding is "headache," the program will ask when the headache began).

PROCESS-FINDING

The metarules for this task apply the following kinds of domain rules and relations in a forward-directed way:

---

[14]In medicine, a headache usually indicates a functional, as opposed to an "organic," disorder. By analogy, a high load-average in a time-sharing computer often indicates a functional disorder, just a problem of ordinary "life" — though, like a headache, it may signify a serious underlying disorder.

1. Antecedent rules (causal and definitional rules that use the finding and can be applied now).
2. Generalization (subsumption) relations (e.g., if the finding is "neurosurgery," the program will conclude that "the patient has undergone surgery").
3. Trigger rules (rules that suggest hypotheses; the program will pursue subgoals if necessary to apply these rules). If a nonspecific finding is explained by hypotheses already in the differential, it does not trigger new hypotheses.
4. Ordinary consequent rules that use soft findings to conclude about activated hypotheses (those hypotheses on the differential, plus any ancestor or immediate descendent); no subgoaling is allowed.[15]
5. Ordinary consequent rules that use hard findings, as above, but subgoaling is allowed.
6. (< <Proposed> > Rule out considered hypotheses that do not account for a new red-flag finding.)
7. (< <Proposed> > Refine current hypotheses that can be discriminated into subtypes on the basis of the new finding.[16]

These metarules (and their ordering) conform to the following implicit constraints:

- The associations that will be considered first are those requiring the least additional effort to realize them.

  Effort in forward reasoning, an aspect of what has also been called *cognitive economy*, can be characterized in terms of:

  - *immediacy* (the conclusion need only be stated vs. subgoals must

---

[15]Should the concept of a trigger rule be generalized to allow specification of any arbitrary context? In particular, is the idea of applying rules relevant to children of active hypotheses just a weak form of trigger rule? Perhaps the "strength" of an association corresponds to the *extent of the context* in which it will come to mind. Trigger rules are simply rules which apply to the entire domain of medical diagnosis. We might associate rules with intermediate contexts as well, for example, the context of "infectious disease diagnosis."

Resolving this issue may make moot the issue of whether trigger rules should be placed before ordinary consequent rules. Their relevance is more directly ascertained; applying consequent rules in a focussed, forward way requires intersection of the new finding with specific hypotheses on the differential and their descendents. Trigger rules also have the payoff of indicating new hypotheses. However, if applying a trigger rule requires gathering new findings and then changing the differential, some cost is incurred in returning to consider the ordinary consequent rules afterward.

[16]This would again promote refocussing, and thus the cost of losing the current context. An agenda model could explain the ability to realize these new associations and come back to them later.

be pursued or the problem solver must perform many intersections of the differential, related hypotheses, and known findings)
- *relevance* (make conclusions focused with respect to current findings and hypotheses vs. take actions that might broaden the possibilities, require "unrelated" findings, and change thefocus).
- The metarules are directed at efficiency by:
  - Drawing inferences in a data-directed way, rather than doing a search when the conclusions are needed. The primary assumption here is that the structure of the problem space makes forward reasoning more efficient.
  - Drawing all possible focused inferences (each metarule is tried once, but executes all inferences of its type) and refining findings to a useful level of detail by asking more questions (not hypothesis-directed).

In summary, the order of forward reasoning is based on cognitive issues, not correctness.

PROCESS-HYPOTHESIS

These rules maintain the differential and do forward reasoning:

1. If the belief in the hypothesis is now less than .2, and it is in the differential, it is removed.
2. If the hypothesis is not in the differential and the belief is now greater than or equal to .2, it is added to the differential. The task APPLY-EVIDENCE-RULES is invoked. This task applies rules that support the hypothesis, using previously given findings (the hypothesis might not have been active when the data was processed). Only rules that succeed without setting up new subgoals are considered.
3. (< <Proposed> > If the belief is very high (greater than .8) and the program knows of no evidence that could lower its belief, then the hypothesis is marked as explored, equivalent to completing TEST-HYPOTHESIS.)
4. (< <Proposed> > Apply ordinary consequent rules that use soft findings to conclude about new activated hypotheses.)
5. If the hypothesis has been explored (either because of the previous rule or the task TEST-HYPOTHESIS is complete), then generalization (subsumption) relations and antecedent rules are applied.

Adding a hypothesis to the differential is bookkeeping performed by a

LISP function. While NEOMYCIN'S differential is a list, it cannot really be separated conceptually from the hierarchical and causal structures that relate hypotheses. The hypothesis is not added if a descendent (causal or subtype) is already in the list. If an ancestor is in the list, it is deleted. If there is no previous ancestor or descendent, the program records that the differential is now "wider" — an event that will effect aborting and triggering of tasks. Thus, the differential is a memory-jogging "cut" through causal and subtype hierarchies.

The ordering of PROCESS-HYPOTHESIS metarules is cognitively based, as for PROCESS-FINDING, but follows a more logical procedural ordering: bookkeeping of the differential, recognition of more evidence, completion of consideration, and drawing more conclusions. The orderliness of this procedure again reflects the cognitive (and computational) efficiency of locally realizing and recording known information before drawing more conclusions (i.e., returning to the more general search problem).

FINDOUT

This task models how the problem solver makes a conclusion about a finding that he wants to know about. (This is a greatly expanded and now explicit version of the original MYCIN routine by the same name (Shortliffe, 1976). The rules are applied in order until one succeeds:

1. If the finding concerns complex objects (such as cultures, organisms, or drugs) then a special Lisp routine is invoked to provide a convenient interface for gathering this information.
2. If the finding is a laboratory test whose source is not available or whose availability is unknown, then the finding is marked as unavailable. (E.g., if it is not known whether the patient had a chest x-ray, nothing can be concluded about what was seen on the chest x-ray.)
3. If the finding is subsumed by any more general finding that is ruled out for this case, then the finding is ruled out also. (E.g., if the patient has not received medications, then he has not received antibiotics.)
4. As a variant of the above rule, if any more general finding can be ruled out that has not been considered before, then the finding can be ruled out.[17]
5. If any more general finding is unknown, then this specific finding is marked as unavailable.

---

[17]That is, the premise of this metarule invokes FINDOUT recursively. To do this cleanly, we should allow tasks to return "success" or "fail."

6. If some more specific finding is known to be present, then this finding can be concluded to be present, too. (E.g., if the patient is receiving steroids, then the patient is receiving medications.)

7. If the finding is normally requested from the informant, but shouldn't be asked for this kind of problem, then try to infer the finding from other information.[18]

8. If the "finding" is really a disorder hypothesis (we are applying a rule that requires this information), then invoke TEST-HYPOTHESIS (rather than backward chaining through the domain rules in a blind way).

9. If the informant typically expects to be asked about this finding, then request the information, and then try to infer it, if necessary.

10. Otherwise, try to infer the finding, then request it.

The constraints that lie behind these rules are:

- Economy: use available information rather than drawing intermediate inference or gathering more information. Keep the number of inferences and requests for data to a minimum. Solve the problem as quickly as possible.

- First requesting more general information attempts to satisfy the economy constraint, but assumes that more than one specific finding in the class will eventually be considered and that the general finding is often negative. Otherwise, the general question would be unnecessary.

- It is assumed that the informant knows and consistently uses the subsumption relations used by the problem solver, so the problem solver is entitled to rule out specific findings on the basis of general categories. For example, knowing that the patient is pregnant, the informant will not say that she is not a compromised host. General questions help ensure completeness. When a more general question is asked, a different specific finding than the one originally of interest could be volunteered. Later forward reasoning could then bring about refocussing.

- Typical of the possible interactions of domain knowledge that must be considered, a finding with a source must not be subsumed by ruled-out findings; otherwise, considering the source would be unnecessary, and doing it first would lead to an extra question. Obviously, if there are too many interactions of this sort, the strategic "principles" will be very complex and slow to apply in interpreted form.

---

[18]"Inferring" means to use backward chaining. Given that source and subsumption relations have already been considered at this point, only definitional rules remain to be considered. That a finding should not be asked is determined by the "don't ask when" relation, requiring the task APPLYRULES to be invoked in the premise of this metarule.)

Note that we could have added another metarule to rule out a general class if all of its more specific findings have been ruled out, but the "closed-world assumption" does not make sense with NEOMYCIN'S small knowledge base.

APPLYRULES

NEOMYCIN has "internal" tasks that control how domain rules are applied: "only if immediate" (antecedent), "with previewing" (looking for a conjunct known to be false), and "with subgoaling." An important aspect of NEOMYCIN as a cognitive model is that new findings, coming from rule invocation, are considered in a depth-first way. That is, the conclusions from new findings are considered before returning to information gathered earlier in the consultation. Implementing this requires "rebinding" the list of new findings (so a "stack" is associated with rule invocations) and marking new findings as "known" if no further reasoning could change what is known about them, thus adding them to the list of findings to be considered in forward reasoning. The basic assumptions are that the informant does not retract findings, that the problem solver does not retract conclusions, and that FORWARD-REASON is done for each new finding.

GENERATE-QUESTIONS

This task models the problem solver's attempt to milk the informant for information that will suggest some hypotheses. The program generates one question at a time, stopping when the differential is "adequate" (the end condition of the task). The differential is adequate in the early stage of the consultation if it is not empty; otherwise the belief in some considered hypothesis must be "moderate" (defined as a cumulative CF of .3 or greater, the measure used consistently in domain rules to signify "reasonable evidence").

The metarules generate questions from several sources, invoking auxiliary tasks to pursue different lines of questioning:

1. General questions (ASK-GENERAL-QUESTIONS).
2. Elaboration of previously received data (ELABORATE-DATUM). (The subtask ELABORATE-DATUM asks about subsumed data. For example, if it is known that the patient is immunosuppressed, the program will ask whether the patient is receiving cytotoxic drugs, is an alcoholic, and so on. The subtask also requests more "process information." For example, it will ask how a headache has changed over time, its severity, etc.)

3. Any rule using previous data that was not applied before because it required new subgoals to be pursued is now applied.
4. The informant is simply asked to supply more information, if possible.

This task illustrates the importance of record-keeping during the consultation. These metarules refer to which tasks have been previously completed, which findings have been fully specified and elaborated, and hypothesis relations that have been considered.

ASK-GENERAL-QUESTIONS

These questions are the most general indications of abnormal behavior or previously diagnosed disorders, useful for determining whether the case is a "typical" one that is what it appears to be, or an "unusual" problem, as described at the beginning of this chapter. These are of course domain-specific questions. They generalize to: Has this problem ever occurred before? What previous diagnoses and treatments have been applied to this device? When was the device last working properly? Are there similar findings manifested in another part of the device? Are there associated findings (occurring at the same time)? These questions are asked in a fixed order, consistent with the case-independent, "something you do every time" nature of this task.

COLLECT-INFORMATION

These rules carry out the main portion of data collection for diagnosis; they are applied iteratively, in sequence, until no rule succeeds:

1. If there are hypotheses appearing on the differential that the program has not yet considered actively, then the differential is reconsidered (ESTABLISH-HYPOTHESIS-SPACE) and reviewed (REVIEW-DIFFERENTIAL).[19] If the differential is not "adequate" (maximum

---

[19]To avoid recomputation, the function for modifying the differential sets a flag when new hypotheses are added. It is reset each time the task ESTABLISH-HYPOTHESIS-SPACE completes. Generally, the goal of each task (e.g., GENERAL-QUESTIONS-ASKED) is used for history-keeping; but tasks like ESTABLISH-HYPOTHESIS-SPACE are invoked conditionally, multiple times during a consultation, as the program loops through the COLLECT-INFORMATION metarules. The use of flags brings up questions about the mind's "register" or "stack" capabilities, whether NEOMYCIN should use an agenda, and so on. In our breadth-first approach to constructing a model, we hold questions like this aside until they become relevant to our performance goals.

CF below .3), an attempt is made to generate more hypotheses (GENERATE-QUESTIONS).

2. If the hypotheses on the differential have all been actively explored (ESTABLISH-HYPOTHESIS-SPACE completed), then laboratory data is requested (PROCESS-HARD-DATA).

ESTABLISH-HYPOTHESIS-SPACE

This task iterates among three ordered metarules:

1. If there are ancestors of hypotheses on the differential that haven't been *explored* by TEST-HYPOTHESIS, then these are considered (GROUP-AND-DIFFERENTIATE). (For computational efficiency, the records *parents-explored* and *descendents-explored* are maintained for each hypothesis.)
2. If there are hypotheses on the differential that haven't been *pursued* by PURSUE-HYPOTHESIS, then these are considered (EXPLORE-AND-REFINE).
3. If all general questions have not been asked, invoke ASK-GENERAL-QUESTIONS.

The constraints satisfied by this task are:

- All hypotheses that are placed on the differential are tested and re-fined (based on correctness).
- Causal and subtype ancestors are considered before more specific hypotheses (based on efficiency and assuming that the best model for explaining findings is a known stereotype disorder, and that these stereotypes can be taxonomically organized).

Group-and-Differentiate

This task attempts to establish the disorder categories that should be explored:

1. If all hypotheses on the differential belong to a single top-level category of disease (appear in one subtree whose root is at the first level of the taxonomy), then this category is tested. Such a differential is called "compact"; the concept and strategy come from Rubin (1975).
2. If two hypotheses on the differential differ according to some process feature (location, time course, spread), then ask a question that dis-

criminates on that basis. (This is the metarule that uses orthogonal indexing to group and then discriminate disorders.)

3. If there is some hypothesis whose top-level category has not been tested, then test that category. (E.g., consider infectious-process when there is evidence for chronic-meningitis.)

The first metarule is not strictly needed since its operation is covered by the third metarule. However, we observed that physicians remarked on the presence of an overlap and pursued the single category first, so we included this metarule in the model.

The second metarule uses process knowledge to compare diseases, as described early in this chapter.

To summarize the constraints behind the metarules:

- When examining hypotheses, intersection at the highest level is noticed first. The etiological taxonomy is assumed to be a strict tree.
- Use of process knowledge requires two levels of reasoning: mapping over all descriptors, and intersecting disorders based on each descriptor. This is more complicated than a subtype intersection, requiring more effort, so it is done after testing the differential for compactness. For this maneuver to be useful, disorders must share a set of process descriptors.
- Because a stereotype disorder inherits features of all etiological ancestors, these ancestors must be considered as part of the process of confirming the disorder (a matter of correctness). This assumes that knowledge of disorders has been generalized and "moved up" the tree (perhaps an inherent property of learning, the effect is beneficial for search efficiency). Furthermore, circumstantial evidence that specifically confirms a disorder can only be applied if ancestors are confirmed or not ruled out. That is, circumstantial associations are context-sensitive.

TEST-HYPOTHESIS

This is the task for directly confirming a hypothesis. The following methods are applied in a pure-production system manner:

1. Preference is first given to findings that trigger the hypothesis.
2. Next, causal precursors to the disease are considered. (For infectious diseases, causal precursors include exposure to the disease and immunosuppression.)
3. Finally, all other evidence is considered.

Each metarule selects the domain rules that mention the selected finding in their premise, and conclude about the hypothesis being tested. The MYCIN domain rule interpreter is then invoked to apply these rules (in the task APPLYRULES). (So applying the rule will indirectly cause the program to request the datum.) After the rules are applied, forward reasoning using the findings and new hypothesis conclusions is performed (FORWARD-REASON).

< <Proposed> >: The task aborts if belief is high (CF greater than .8), and if no further questioning can make the belief negative. The task also aborts if there is no belief in the hypothesis, and if only weak evidence (CF less than .3) remains to be considered after several questions have been asked.

Relevant constraints are:

- Findings bearing a strong relation with the hypothesis are considered first because they will contribute the most weight (a matter of efficiency).
- Disconfirming a hypothesis involves discovering that required or highly probable findings — causal precursors or effects — are missing. NEOMYCIN's domain lacks this kind of certainty. Therefore, the program does not use a "rule-out" strategy.
- The end conditions attempt to minimize the number of questions and shift attention when belief is not likely to change (a matter of efficiency).

EXPLORE-AND-REFINE

This is the central task for choosing a focus hypothesis from the differential. The following metarules are applied in the manner of a pure production system:

1. If the current focus (perhaps from GROUP-AND-DIFFERENTIATE) is now less likely than another hypothesis on the differential, then the program pursues the stronger candidate (PURSUE-HYPOTHESIS).
2. If there is a child of the current focus that has not been pursued, then it is pursued (this can only be true after the current focus has just been refined and removed from the differential).
3. If there is a sibling of the current focus that has not been pursued, then it is pursued.
4. If there is any other hypothesis on the differential that has not been pursued, then it is pursued.

This task is aborted if the differential becomes wider (see PROCESS-

HYPOTHESIS), a precondition that requires doing the task GROUP-AND-DIFFERENTIATE.

Relevant constraints are:

- All selection of hypotheses is biased by the current belief (a matter of efficiency).
- Focus should change as soon as the focus is no longer the most strongly believed hypothesis (a matter of correctness; perhaps at odds with minimizing effort, due to the cost of returning to this focus).
- Siblings are preferred before other hypotheses (a matter of cognitive effort to remain focused within a class; also a matter of efficiency, insofar as siblings are mutually exclusive diagnoses).

PURSUE-HYPOTHESIS

Pursuing a hypothesis has two components: testing it (TEST-HYPO-THESIS), followed by refining it (REFINE-HYPOTHESIS). After these two metarules are tried (in order, once), the hypothesis is marked as *pursued*.

Pursuing self followed by children brings about depth-first search. (Specifically, PURSUE-HYPOTHESIS puts the children in the differential and EXPLORE-AND-REFINE focuses on them.) This plan is based on the need to specialize a diagnosis (correctness), to remain focused (minimizing cognitive effort), and to consider more general disorders first (efficiency).

REFINE-HYPOTHESIS

The effect of this task is to put taxonomic children or the causes of a state/category into the differential. If the hypothesis being refined has more than four descendents, a subset of possibilities is considered (REFINE-COMPLEXHYPOTHESIS). For each child considered, the task APPLY-EVIDENCE-RULES is invoked (see PROCESS-HYPOTHESIS).

In order to reach a diagnosis in the etiologic taxonomy, this task requires that there be causal or subtype links from state/category hypotheses into the taxonomy, allowing them to be "refined" as etiologic hypotheses.

REFINE-COMPLEX-HYPOTHESIS

Two metarules are used to select the common and unusual causes of the hypothesis. Ordinary domain rules, marked accordingly, are used to define these sets. The assumption is that, if only a few specializations can be considered (for economy), one should consider the common as well as the serious, unusual causes (for correctness). The less important hypotheses will be covered by the strategies of asking general questions and focused forward reasoning.

PROCESS-HARD-DATA

Briefly, special functions are used to assemble a set of "hard findings" that support hypotheses on the differential, reduce them to a set of "sources" (a lumbar puncture is the source for the CSF findings), and request the sources from the informant. Subsumption and definition relations are used to infer the sources. Contraindications (dangerous side effects) of gathering certain information is also considered. As described in PROCESS-FINDING, rules used by these findings are applied with subgoaling enabled. The program will return to GROUP-AND-DIFFERENTIATE and EXPLORE-AND-REFINE new hypotheses as necessary.

ACKNOWLEDGMENTS

We are especially grateful to the late Timothy Beckett, M.D., for serving as the expert-teacher in this research. Reed Letsinger participated in early discussions and helped implement the program. Bob London, Diane Hasling, Curt Kapsner, M.D., David Wilkins, and Mark Richer have also contributed to the development of NEOMYCIN. I would like to thank Lewis Johnson for his careful reading and helpful suggestions. This chapter was prepared in September 1983, then revised in February 1984 and August 1985.

This research has been supported in part by joint funding from ONR and ARI, Contract N00014-79C-0302, and more recently by ONR Contract N00014-85K-0305 and a grant from the Josiah Macy, Jr. Foundation. Computational resources are provided by the SUMEX-AIM facility (NIH grant RR 00785). NEOMYCIN is implemented in INTERLISP-D.

REFERENCES

Aikins, J. S. (1981). Representation of control knowledge in expert systems. *In Proceedings of the First AAAI* (pp. 121–123).Stanford, CA.

Anderson, J. R., & Bower, G. H. (1980). *Human associative memory: A brief edition.* Hillsdale, NJ: Lawrence Erlbaum Associates.

Anderson, J. R., Greeno, J. G., Kline, P. J., & Neves, D. M. (1981). Acquisition of problem-solving skill. In J. R. Anderson (Ed.), *Cognitive skills and their acquisition* (pp. 191–230). Hillsdale, NJ: Lawrence Erlbaum Associates.

Benbassat, J., & Schiffmann, A. (1976). An approach to teaching the introduction to clinical medicine. *Annals of Internal Medicine, 84,* 477–481.

Brown, J. S., Collins, A., & Harris, G. (1977). Artificial intelligence and learning strategies. In A. O'Neill (Ed.), *Learning Strategies.* New York: Academic Press.

Bruner, J. S., Goodnow, J. J., & Austin, A. A. (1956). *A study of thinking.* New York: Wiley.

Chandrasekaran, B., Gomez, F., Mittal, S. (1979). An approach to medical diagnosis based on conceptual schemes. *Proceedings of the Sixth International Joint Conference on Artificial Intelligence* (pp. 134–142), Tokyo.

Chi, M. T. H., Feltovich, P. J., & Glaser, R. (1981). Categorization and representation of physics problems by experts and novices. *Cognitive Science, 5,* 121–152.

Clancey, W. J., (1982). Applications-oriented AI research: Education.   In A. Barr and E. Feigenbaum (Eds.), *The handbook of artificial intelligence .* Los Altos: Morgan Kaufmann.

Clancey, W. J. (1983a). The epistemology of a rule-based expert system: A framework for explanation. *Artificial Intelligence, 20,* 215–251.

Clancey, W. J. (1983b). The advantages of abstract control knowledge in expert system design. *Proceedings of the National Conference on AI* (pp. 74–78). Washington, DC.

Clancey, W. J. (1984). Methodology for building an intelligent tutoring system. In W. Kintsch, J. R. Miller, & P. G. Polson (Eds.), *Method and tactics in cognitive science* (pp. 51–83). Hillsdale, NJ: Lawrence Erlbaum Associates.

Clancey, W. J. (1985), Heuristic classification. *Artificial Intelligence, 27,* 289–350.

Clancey, W. J. (in press). Representing control knowledge as abstract tasks and metarules. In M. J. Coombs & L. Bolc (Eds.), *Computer expert systems.* New York: Springer-Verlag.

Clancey, W. J., & Letsinger, R. (1984). NEOMYCIN: Reconfiguring a rule-based expert system for application to teaching. In W. J. Clancey & E. H. Shortliffe (Eds.), *Readings in medical artificial intelligence: The first decade* (pp. 361–381). Reading: Addison-Wesley.

Cohen, P. R., & Grinberg, M. R. (1983). A framework for heuristic reasoning about uncertainty. *Proceedings of the Eighth International Joint Conference on Artificial Intelligence* (pp. 355–357). Karlsruhe, West Germany.

Davis, R. (1980). Meta-rules: Reasoning about control. *Artificial Intelligence, 15,* 179–222.

Davis, R. (1983). Diagnosis via causal reasoning: Paths of interaction and the locality principle. *Proceedings of the National Conference on AI* (pp. 88–94). Washington, DC.

Davis, R., & Lenat, D. (1982). *Knowledge-based systems in artificial intelligence.* New York: McGraw-Hill.

Duda, R. O., & Shortliffe, E. H. (1983). Expert systems research. *Science, 220,* 261–268.

Elstein, A. S., Shulman, L. S., & Sprafka, S. A. (1978). *Medical problem solving: An analysis of clinical reasoning.* Cambridge, MA: Harvard University Press.

Ericsson, K. A., & Simon, H. A. (1980). Verbal reports as data. *Psychological Review, 87,* 215–251.

Feigenbaum, E. A. (1977). The art of artificial intelligence: I. Themes and case studies of knowledge engineering. *Proceedings of the Fifth International Joint Conference on Artificial Intelligence* (pp. 1014–1029). MIT, Cambridge, MA.

Feltovich, P. J., Johnson, P. E., Moller, J. H. &, Swanson, D. B. (1984). *The role and development of medical knowledge in diagnostic expertise.* Presented at the 1980 Annual meeting of the American Educational Research Association. In W. Clancey & E. H. Shortliffe (Eds.), *Readings in medical artificial intelligence: The first decade.* New York: Addison-Wesley.

Genesereth, M. R. (1984). The use of design descriptions in automated diagnosis. *Artificial Intelligence, 24,* 411–436.

Genesereth, M. R., Greiner, R., & Smith, D. E. (1981). *MRS Manual.* (Heuristic Programming Project Memo HPP-80-24). Stanford, CA: Stanford University.

Gentner, D., & Stevens, A. (Eds.). (1983). *Mental Models.* Hillsdale, NJ: Lawrence Erlbaum Associates.

Hasling, D. W., Clancey, W. J., Rennels, G. R. (1984). Strategic explanations for a diagnostic consultation system. *The International Journal of Man–Machine Studies, 20*, 3–19.

Hayes-Roth, B., & Hayes-Roth, F. (1979). A cognitive model of planning. *Cognitive Science, 3*, 275–310.

Hayes-Roth, F., Waterman, D., & Lenat, D. (Eds.). (1983). *Building expert systems.* New York: Wesley.

Kassirer, J. P., & Gorry, G. A. (1978). Clinical problem solving: A behavioral analysis. *Annals of Internal Medicine, 89*, 245–255.

Kolodner, J. (1983). Maintaining organization in a dynamic long-term memory. *Cognitive Science, 7*, 243–280.

Kuipers, B., & Kassirer, J. P. (1984). Causal reasoning in medicine: Analysis of a protocol. *Cognitive Science, 4*, 363–385.

Larkin, J. H., McDermott, J., Simon, D. P., & Simon, H. A. (1980). Models of competence in solving physics problems. *Cognitive Science, 4*, 317–348.

London, B., & Clancey, W. J. (1982). Plan recognition strategies in student modeling: Prediction and description. *Proceedings of the Second AAAI* (pp. 335–338), Pittsburgh, PA.

Miller, P. B. (1975). *Strategy selection in medical diagnosis.* (Tech. Rep. AI-TR-153). Cambridge, MA: MIT, Artificial Intelligence Laboratory.

Neves, D. M., & Anderson, J. Jr. (1981). Knowledge compilation: Mechanisms for the automization of cognitive skills. In J. R. Anderson (Ed.), *Cognitive skills and their acquisition* (pp. 57–84). Hillsdale, NJ: Lawrence Erlbaum Associates.

Newell, A. (1983). The heuristic of George Polya and its relation to artificial intelligence. In R. Groner, M. Groner, & W. F. Bischof (Eds.), *Methods of heuristics.* Hillsdale, NJ: Lawrence Erlbaum Associates.

Newell, A., & Simon, H. A. (1972). *Human problem solving.* Englewood Cliffs: Prentice-Hall.

Papert, S. (1980). *Mindstorms: Children, computers, and powerful ideas.* New York: Basic Books.

Patil, R. S., Szolovits, P., & Schwartz, W. B. (1981). Causal understanding of patient illness in medical diagnosis. *Proceedings of the Seventh International Joint Conference on Artificial Intelligence* (pp. 893–899). Vancouver, Canada.

Patil, R. S., Szolovits, P., & Schwartz, W. B. (1982). Information acquisition in diagnosis. *Proceedings of the National Conference on AI* (pp. 893–899). Pittsburgh, PA.

Pauker, S. G., & Szolovits, P. (1977). Analyzing and simulating taking the history of the present illness: Context formation. In Schneider & Sagvall-Hein (Eds.), *Computational linguistics in medicine* (pp. 109–118). Amsterdam, North-Holland.

Pauker, S. G., Gorry, G. A., Kassirer, J. P., & Schwartz, W. B. (1976). Toward the simulation of clinical cognition: Taking a present illness by computer. *American Journal of Medicine, 60*, 981–995.

Polya, G. (1957). *How to solve it: An aspect of mathematical method.* Princeton, NJ: Princeton University Press.

Pople, H. (1982). Heuristic methods for imposing structure on ill-structured problems: The structuring of medical diagnostics. In P. Szolovits (Ed.), *Artificial Intelligence in Medicine* (pp. 119–190). Boulder, Westview Press.

Rubin, A. D. (1975). *Hypothesis formation and evaluation in medical diagnosis.* (Technical Rep. AI-TR-316). Cambridge, MA: MIT, Artificial Intelligence Laboratory.

Rumelhart, D. E., & Norman, D. A. (1983). *Representation in memory.* (Tech. Rep. CHIP-116). San Diego: University of California, Center for Human Information Processing.

Schoenfeld, A. H. (1981). *Episodes and executive decisions in mathematical problem solving.* (Tech. Rep. unnumbered). Presented at the 1981 AERA Annual meeting. Los Angeles: Hamilton College, Mathematics Department.

Shortliffe, E. H. (1976). *Computer-based medical consultations: MYCIN.* New York: Elsevier.

Simon, H. A., & Lea, G. (1979). Problem solving and rule induction. In H. A. Simon (Ed.), *Models of thought.* New Haven: Yale University Press.

Swartout, W. R. (1981). Explaining and justifying in expert consulting programs. *Proceedings of the Seventh International Joint Conference on Artificial Intelligence* (pp. 815–823). Vancouver, Canada.

Szolovits, P., & Pauker, S. G. (1978). Categorical and probabilistic reasoning in medical diagnosis. *Artificial Intelligence, 11,* 115–144.

VanLehn, K. (1983). Human procedural skill acquisition: Theory, model and psychological validation. *Proceedings of the National Conference on Artificial Intelligence* (pp. 420–423). Washington, DC.

VanLehn, K., Brown, J. S., & Greeno, J. (1984). Competitive argumentation in computational theories of cognition. In W. Kintsch, J. R. Miller, & P. G. Polson (Eds.), *Method and tactics in cognitive science* (pp. 235–262). Hillsdale, NJ: Lawrence Erlbaum Associates.

VanLehn, K., & Brown, J. S. (1980). Planning nets: A representation for formalizing analogies and semantic models of procedural skills. In R. E. Snow, P. A. Frederico, & W. E. Montague (Eds.), *Aptitude learning and instruction: Cognitive process and analysis.* Hillsdale, NJ: Lawrence Erlbaum Associates.

Wescourt, K. T., & Hemphill, L. (1978). *Representing and teaching knowledge for troubleshooting/debugging* (Tech. Rept. 292). Stanford: Stanford University, Institute for Mathematical Studies in the Social Sciences.

Yu, V. L., Fagan, L. M., Wraith, S. M., Clancey, W. J., Scott, A. C., Hannigan, J. F., Blum, R. L., Buchanan, B. G., & Cohen, S. N. (1979). Antimicrobial selection by a computer: A blinded evaluation by infectious disease experts. *Journal of the American Medical Association, 242,* 1279–1282.

Author Index

Ervin, S. M., 335, *341*
Estes, W. K., 279, *284*
Evans, D. A., 290, *308*

F

Fagan, L. M., 375, *418*
Faloon, S., 24, *70*, 76, *127*
Farrell, R., xxiii, 153, 154, 155, 164, 170, *183*
Farrington, D. P., 234, *259*
Feigenbaum, E. A., 72, 95, *127*, 343, *416*
Feightner, J. W., 288, 293, *309, 310*
Feltovich, P. J., xix, xxvi, *xxvii*, 210, 227, 263, *284*, 296, 299, *308*, 314, 321, 330, 335, *341*, 348, 362, 363, 381, *416*
Feltovich, R. J., 225, 227
Femberger, S. W., *127*
Fendrick, P., 13, *21*
Fitts, P. M., 88, 114, 123, *127*
Foss, D. J., 279, *284*
Frederiksen, C. H., 289, 290 , 293, 295, *309, 310*
Fuchs, A. F., 97, *127*

G

Galanter, E., 68, *70*
Genesereth, M. R., 367, 388, *416*
Gentner, D., 300, *309*, 389, *416*
Gentner, D. R., xviii, xxii, 8, 10, 16, *21*, 203, *204*
Gibson, J. L., 234, *258*
Glanzer, M., 104, *127*
Glaser, R., xvii, xix, xx, xxvi, *xxvii*, 210, 227, 232, *258*, 263, *284*, 296, 299, *308*, 312, 314, 321, 330, *341*, 348, 381, *416*
Goldberg, L. R., 209, 210, 211, 227
Gomez, F., 349, *416*
Goodnow, J. J., 358, *416*
Gorry, G. A., 289, *309*, 347, *417*
Graesser, A. C., 130, *150*
Green, E. G., 232, *258*

Greenblatt, R. D., xv, *xxviii*
Greene, T. R., 230, 231, 232, *259*, 263, 266, 271, 273, 276, 277, *285*, 312, *342*
Greeno, J. G., 279, *285*, 287, 288, 290, 291, *309*, 348, 379, *415, 418*
Greenspan, J., 129, *151*
Griener, R., 367, *416*
Grinberg, M. R., 389, *416*
Groen, G. J., xxvi, 289, 290, 296, 298, 299, 301, 304, 305, 306, 307, *309, 310*
Grudin, J. T., 8, 13, *21*
Guyatt, G. H., 288, *309*

H

Halstead, M. M., 134, *150*
Hanney, C., 231, *258*
Hannigan, J. F., 375, *418*
Harcum, E. R., 68, *70*
Harris, G., 348, *416*
Harter, N., 75, 109, *126*
Hasling, D. W., 378, 391, *417*
Hassebrock, F., xvii, *xxxviii*, 225, 227, 335, *341*
Hatano, G., 97, *127*
Hayes, J. R., 287, *309*
Hayes-Roth, B., 231, *259*, 279, *284*, 332, *341*, 354, *417*
Hayes-Roth, F., xvi, *xxviii*, 231, *259*, 279, *284*, 332, *341*, 347, 354, 361, *417*
Hemphill, L., 348, *418*
Herman, P. G., 314, *342*
Hessel, S. J., 314, *342*
Hill, L. B., 2, *21*
Hirtle, S. C., xvii, *xxviii*, 76, 97, *127*, 130, 132, *151*
Hitch, G. J., 85, *126*
Hogarth, J., 234, *259*
Homel, R., 229, 234, 257, *259*
Hood, R., 229, 231, 234, *259*
Hooper, J., *203*
Horn, B., 292, *310*
Hornstein, N., 160, *183*

Subject Index

A

ACT*, 154

Accuracy, *see* Errors

Analogy,
  learning by analogy, xxiv, 164
  recursive functions, xxiv, 168–171
  structured mapping, 168

Attention,
  memory load, 84–85
  role in semantic network, 276
  see also Cognitive Resources, Encoding, Perception

Automatization, xxii, 14–15
  clinical diagnosis, 324
  encoding, xxii, 328
  feature perception, 328
  mental calculations, 123–124
  practice, xviii
  see also Cognitive resources

B

Backward reasoning, *see* Reasoning

C

CADUCEUS, 358–359

CENTAUR, 359

Capacity, *see* Attention, Automatization, Chunking, Cognitive resources, Memory span, STM, Working memory

Causal modeling
  clinical diagnosis, 225, 359–361, 368–369, 371–372, 391
  ill-structured problems, 279
  program comprehension, 137–145
  see also Expert novice differences, Representation, Situation model

Children,
  arithmetic problems, 113
  developmental curve, 335–340
  memory Span, xxx

Chunking, xv–xvi, xxii, xxiii, xxxi–xxxii, 130
  internal structure, 107
  skilled memory, 24–25, 33–35, 51–53, 56, 76, 85
  see also Cognitive resources, Memory span

Clinical diagnosis, xxvi–xxvii
  automatization, 324
  certainty factor, 370–371
  compiled knowledge, 346

427